D1083534

ROYAL BOUNTY

ROYAL BOUNTY

The Making of
a Welfare Monarchy

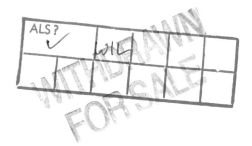

Frank Prochaska

Yale University Press
New Haven & London   1995

Set in Bembo by Best-set Typesetter Ltd, Hong Kong
Printed and bound in Great Britain by The Bath Press

Library of Congress Cataloging-in-Publication Data

Prochaska, F. K.
    Royal Bounty: The making of a welfare monarchy/by Frank Prochaska.
    Includes bibliographical references and index.
    ISBN 0–300–06453–5 (hardback)
    1. Charities—Great Britain—History. 2. Monarchy—Great Britain—
History. 3. Public welfare—Great Britain—History. 4. Welfare state—
History. I. Title.
HV245.P87   1995
361.6′5′0941—dc20   95–12271
                                                        CIP

A catalogue record for this book is available from the British Library.

for
Elizabeth and William Prochaska

A man never rises so high as when he does not know where he is going.

Oliver Cromwell

Contents

Illustrations

Illustrations

Acknowledgements

Associated Press: 57, 58, 67, 68, 69, 71, 72; British Library: 1, 8; Sir Richard R. Holmes, *Edward VII: His Life and Times* (1910): 15, 17, 18, 20, 24, 31; Hulton Deutsch Collection

Preface

W hen I mentioned to a friend that I was writing a book about 'The Making of a Welfare Monarchy', he replied, 'Yes, of course, the monarchy has always been a recipient of welfare'. This was not my point, though it is an interesting one, and it plays a part in this history. My essential interest is in the welfare role of the monarchy, or what may be called its social policy, which is a neglected, yet vital, aspect of royal activity. The book should add to our knowledge of social reform, but it may also contribute to the contemporary debate on the role of the crown in modern society. Whatever one's views, the place of the monarchy in Britain cannot be addressed constructively except on the basis of research into what members of the royal family actually contribute. In this debate their voluntary activities may well turn out to be more significant than previously imagined.

There are a great many books on the monarchy and members of the royal family. Publishers relax their critical faculties when an author appears with a manuscript on a royal subject. Many of the recent works, apart from a few distinguished biographies, are devoted to gossip or to polemic. Often they portray the royal family as a symbolic sideshow or a perennial soap opera. Academic historians, with some notable exceptions, appear not to take the modern British monarchy very seriously. Transfixed by high politics or royal ritual, they have emphasized the decline of the crown's political authority. Ensnared in a conventional view of the constitution, they ignore the monarchy's substantive role in civil society, its promotion of voluntary activity outside the state. Whether they praise or ridicule the plumage, they forget the living bird.

It is impossible to give a precise definition of voluntarism. As it encompasses a range of institutions from the Mothers' Union to the Transport and General Workers' Union, it has to do with the question of independence rather than the type of activity pursued. Many of the voluntary bodies supported by the royal family, polo clubs and the Royal Opera House for example, are not agencies of benevolence, though they often have a charitable dimension that the monarchy enlivens. (The hundreds of service associations on the monarchy's patronage list are a subject in themselves.) My special interest has been in philanthropic or welfare causes, that is health, education and what are now called the 'personal' social services. But we should keep in mind that before the twentieth century the word 'welfare' was not identified with state action to anything like the extent it is today and that much benevolence took place in areas which fit ill with our contemporary perceptions. For example, philanthropists in the past, including royal ones, did not usually make distinctions between religious and social welfare.

In recent years, the issue of what constitutes voluntarism has been confused by the increased government funding of charities and by statutory bodies taking on what amounts to charitable status. When the Prince and Princess of Wales assisted the Wishing Well Appeal, which raised £54 million for the Great Ormond Street Children's Hospital in the 1980s, they contributed to the rebuilding of a state institution, though formerly a voluntary one. In the past, royal benevolence was characteristically antithetical to statutory provision. Today, having imbibed the social gospel of 'partnership', the 'Welfare Monarchy' crosses the arbitrary boundaries between voluntary and state provision.

In February 1992, to mark the 40th anniversary of her accession, Queen Elizabeth II visited a hospice. Amid the celebrations surrounding the anniversary, this symbolic and beneficent act passed largely unnoticed, though it was unforgettable to those directly involved. Accustomed to the charitable routine of the monarchy, the public had come to expect such events to characterize royal occasions. Indeed, charitable work takes up a vast amount of the time of the royal family and Palace officials, as a glance at the daily court calendar will attest. In 1993, members of the royal family, including the Queen Mother and Princess Margaret, the Kents and the Gloucesters, carried out about 3,000 engagements in Britain, most of which were of a philanthropic nature. The Princess Royal alone attended over 500 charitable functions.

Why do they do it? Who benefits? When did the crown's charitable patronage begin? What has been the individual contribution of particular members of the royal family? How much have they given away and how successful have they been in raising funds generally? What part has charity played in the transformation of the idea of nobility and the royal family's changing social role? Why did the monarchy become a voice for middle-class opinion and what part did it play in the rise of respectable society? Has the promotion of welfare causes been a calculated defence of the monarchy, a strategy for its survival, in a rapidly changing world? How have the relationships between the crown, civil society and the central state shifted over the last 250 years and what have been the effects of these shifts? What, in the end, is the underlying meaning of royal philanthropy for the nation? These are among the questions addressed in this book.

I would like to thank the many institutions and individuals who have helped with the writing of this book. The Department of History, Royal Holloway College, supported the project with a small grant from its Research Fund. The staff of the British Library, the Bodleian Library, Oxford, the Greater London Record Office, the Institute of Historical Research, the King's Fund, the Public Record Office, the Royal National Life-boat Institution, St Bartholomew's Hospital, the Wellcome Institute for the History of Medicine, and a host of other institutions, have given me painstaking assistance. Miss E.M. Gwyer kindly loaned to me papers in her possession from her grandfather Sir Henry Burdett. By gracious permission of Her Majesty the Queen, I have been able to make use of material from the Royal Archives at Windsor and to reproduce pictures from the Royal Archives and the Royal Collection. I am indebted to Sheila de Bellaigue and her colleagues at Windsor for making me welcome, for their scrupulous attention to my many inquiries and for guiding me through the sources.

Among those individuals who will permit me to mention them, I would especially like to thank José Harris, John Sainty, Bernard Semmel and Michael Thompson for their helpful remarks on the manuscript. On detailed points to do with the research or publication I am grateful to Ivon Asquith, Monica Charlot, Bronwyn Fysh, Andrew Griffin, Brian Harrison, Matthew Kilburn, Christopher Maggs, David McKitterick, Peter Marshall, Colin Matthew, Robert Maxwell, Victor Morrison, William Rathbone and Lesley Rees. My old friend and now editor, Robert Baldock, has been unwavering in his support for this project since its inception, and he and his colleagues have made a great difference to the final result. Finally, I would like to thank my wife and fellow-historian Alice Prochaska, who, despite a career that makes unremitting demands, has cheerfully put up with my preoccupations and has read, and read again, the manuscript with charity and understanding. I have dedicated the book to our children, one of whom has become a monarchist, the other a republican, as a result of our many discussions.

Frank Prochaska
London

King George V and a boy, Sunderland, June 1917.

1

Royalty and Philanthropy in the Reign of George III

No people on earth can lay claim to a greater philanthropic tradition than the British. Generation after generation prided itself on its benevolence, and that of the late eighteenth century, described by contemporaries as the 'age of almsgiving' or the 'age of charity', was no exception.[1] When George III died in 1820, an evangelical divine proclaimed that under the King's benevolent auspices more voluntary societies had united for the expansion of religious, educational and moral culture among the poor 'than had been formed during the whole period from the commencement of the era of redemption'.[2] He was probably right, for in the years 1760–1820 charitable organizations expanded at a phenomenal rate. The memoirist Charles Greville, noting the development, remarked: 'we are just now overrun with philanthropy, and God knows where it will stop, or whither it will lead us'.[3]

To a degree unimaginable today, voluntary organizations performed those services thought necessary for the running of an ordered society. In the reign of George III, most people assumed that central government simply provided the basic conditions of life which enabled the citizenry to carry out self-imposed duties. (Until the 1880s the only officials of the central state who were widely seen outside the capital were postmen.)[4] Social ills were of great immediacy, but few expected central government to address them. People lived, worked and died in a little administered world where the pressures were largely local and individual. With few alternatives to charity and self-help, the care and benefits they received in time of trouble centred on the family and the parish. A sense of duty to civil society, that commonwealth of voluntary associations outside the state, outstripped the assertion of rights to social assistance by the deprived.

The Poor Law assisted the sick, the aged, and the unemployed, but in the reign of George III it was administered at parish level, with the workhouse, that 'mill to grind rogues honest', as a deterrent. Misused and badly managed by parish officials, poor relief came under fierce attack. Workhouses did keep many of the 'undeserving' out of sight, but they had little success in teaching them the habits of honest industry. In turn, the practice of paying cash allowances in lieu of or supplementary to wages, instituted in the 1790s, often had ruinous effects and aroused the ire of liberal political economists. If poor relief was a dismal failure as a remedy for poverty, it was also an expensive failure. By the 1760s, it cost ratepayers over £1 million a year, a figure which had soared to over £4 million by the early nineteenth century.[5] Such spending was not only profligate, said the critics, but created a culture of dependency.

The failings of the Poor Law were a further inducement to self-help and voluntary initiative. Estimates of charitable expenditure in the reign of George III are rare. But Frederick Morton Eden, in his *State of the Poor*, published in 1797, put the figure at over £6 million a year for the whole country.[6] A decade later, Anthony Highmore, an authority on London charity, put the figure for the metropolis alone at £850,000 annually, excluding private relief to individuals.[7] Until the twentieth century the amount of money contributed to philanthropic causes each year far exceeded the gross expenditure on poor relief. The charitable receipts for the country at large represented a massive redistribution of wealth.

Georgian philanthropists echoed Edmund Burke in believing that it was largely beyond the power of the state to do good. They were extremely reluctant to seek state assistance and were apt to think that government intervention in charitable causes led to corrupt adminis-tration.[8] Inclined to attribute the source of social problems to individual failings, they concluded that the remedy must be found in personal reformation, assisted by discretionary charity. Steeped in an individualist and familial ethic, they believed that state action in the social sphere obstructed the free development of home and community life. These sentiments were music to the ears of Treasury officials, whose passion for retrenchment was in harmony with a belief in individual accountability. In the social economy, much was to be left, in Eden's words, 'to the faithful trusts of the sentiments of our minds, the feelings of our hearts, the compunctions of our consciences'.[9] A distinctive advantage of charity, he might have added, was that it produced benefits for the givers; for in choosing between the objects of benevolence, they received a moral training and lessons in self-discipline.

Such views were particularly marked among Christians. To the Chris-tian mind, the philanthropic disposition was inseparable from religion. To evangelicals or Bible Christians, who set the pace and tone of phil-anthropy from the late eighteenth century onwards, the word charity itself was synonymous with the conduct of Christ. Unlike secularists in a later age, they believed human suffering to be ineradicable. And unlike later collectivists, they did not exaggerate the moral potential of politics, or the state's capacity to eliminate distress. Inspired by that central doctrine of the Atonement, they recoiled from Caesar. Nonconformists had good historical reasons for distrusting the state, and their emphasis on the freedom of religious sects evolved naturally in the direction of voluntary associations, jealous of their independence. To the Christian mind generally, the state was an artificial contrivance, useful in punishing sinners, but incapable of redemptive action. The individual, not as ratepayer but as fellow-sufferer, was responsible for the cares of the world.[10]

'Take free will away from man,' said St Bernard, 'and there is nothing to save.' By the end of the eighteenth century, many Bible Christians, including the founder of Methodism, John Wesley, agreed with the Catholic saint on this point at least. They had rejected Calvinist predestination in favour of the view that salvation was provisional and conditional on 'good works'. The psychical turmoil which resulted from Christian self-examination predisposed the faithful to charitable conduct and animated piety. Increasingly, British Protestants assumed that individual behaviour determined spiritual progress, a view very much in tune with the *laissez-faire* ethos of the secular world in which material success corresponded to salvation. In the communion of Christianity and commerce, religious virtues resembled those of successful businessmen, with an echo of the Calvinist's suspicion of wealth, which encouraged giving some of it away. Philanthropy may be seen as the human face of capitalism, addressing the social and individual ills which capitalism often created or exacerbated.

In keeping with evangelical imperatives, much benevolence of the period was missionary in character. Georgian philanthropists commonly held a holistic view of human life. They did not usually make distinctions, which to them were arbitrary, between religious and social welfare. In a time when medicine could do so little for the body, the needs of the soul demanded more attention. Institutions whose objectives were educational or recreational had underlying moral and spiritual purposes and were part of a pattern of benevolence often seen as having a welfare element. When the propertied classes turned their minds to social conditions it was not simply to maintain social order, though that was often part of it. The dictates of religion compelled them. Evangelicalism harnessed social conscience to liberal doctrine. It carried forward the Puritan ethic, while adapting it to changing circumstances. At the end of the eighteenth century, a time of political and social uncertainty, it allied faith, hope and charity to national purpose.

Philanthropy, of course, had long-established traditions in Britain, as elsewhere; and while it is risky to attempt to measure its level between one period and another, the peculiar configuration of events taking place in the reign of George III heightened and redirected philanthropic impulses. Apart from the shift in theology which encouraged religious activism, the pressures of industrial development and a rapidly growing population enlivened charitable enterprise and required its more judicious organization. The French Revolution and the suffering caused by the prolonged war with France, which coloured the lives of a generation, had similar effects. War and revolution not only invigorated piety and paternalism, it also deepened the conservative hue of British philanthropy. Against the background of war abroad, and a level of deprivation at home that triggered unrest, the British government, the monarchy, and the philanthropic establishment found common cause.

Whatever the reasons for charitable activity in the reign of George III—among them national interest, humanitarianism, piety, self-regard, or the subordination of the poor—the practice of benevolence was customary. But the structure of philanthropy was changing. As society was becoming more urban and industrial, poverty and distress were becoming more concentrated. In the rapidly growing towns and cities knowledge of hardship was not so easy to come by, and it was more difficult to distinguish between real and feigned distress. Consequently, traditional forms of philanthropy, such as casual almsgiving and charitable trusts, were coming under attack and were thought to be inadequate. Gradually, the benefactions of wealthy individuals were giving way to what that early theorist of civil society, Alexis de Tocqueville, called 'the habit of association'. Older forms of benevolence persisted, but by the end of the eighteenth century the hallmark of philanthropy was collective effort, the patronage of worthy societies, each with an array of patrons, elected officials and subscribers.[11]

Charities proliferated in a society unsettled by social change and splintered by religious, class and local allegiances. A veritable pharmacopoeia, they supplied balms and palliatives for the nation's ills, whether individual or social, physical or spiritual. They defined the relationship between the benevolent and the needy, laid down and administered policy, encouraged new methods of fund-raising, and in many cases created a system of auxiliaries which extended their influence through the country. Entrepreneurial, they competed for converts and custom. Acquisitive, they had an insatiable appetite for funds and put the public under relentless pressure to contribute. Thriving on advertisement and favourable notices, they merged philanthropy and fashion. In a society deeply imbued with hierarchical views and social snobberies, they made every effort to find prominent backers.

Enterprising institutions invited public figures to be patrons and patronesses, though what constituted a public figure in a Devon village would have counted for little in London or Liverpool. The patrons they enlisted were usually sincere in their support, but they did not need to be reminded that philanthropic attachments offered respectability and opportunities for display, perhaps even a knighthood. The innumerable small, parish-based charities, often centred on church or chapel, could not recruit a bishop or an actress, much less George III or a royal duke. They would be content with a magistrate or the vicar's wife. Ambitious, well-connected societies in London and elsewhere required more glamorous officials. Bishops and bankers, even MPs, could be made to do, especially if they had a title. Increasingly, such institutions aspired to the highest accolade—royal patronage.

Before the reign of George III, there was a long, if limited, tradition of charity associated with the monarchy. Sovereigns distributed money and clothing to the poor at the 'Royal Maundy' ceremony, which harked back to the Last Supper and the example of Jesus washing the feet of his disciples. St Bartholomew's and St Thomas's, the Royal Hospital of St Katharine and the Royal Hospital, Chelsea were institutional expressions of crown patronage, even though the royal family did not always take a personal interest in their development. The reign of Queen Anne had seen some remarkable displays of royal bounty, including the establishment of a leper hospital near Bodmin and the touching of subjects for 'the King's Evil', a practice abolished by George I as 'inappropriate to the enlightened House of Hanover'.[12]

George II, like monarchs before and after him, made donations to needy widows, pensioners and other claimants. In 1731, he ordered £30 a year to be distributed to the poor of St Mary-le-Strand.[13] During the severe winter of 1739–40, Frederick, Prince of Wales (1707–51), the father of George III, in disguise to avoid a disturbance, travelled from St Paul's to the Tower, distributing 'large Sums of Money' to 'distressed watermen'.[14] On a visit to Bath he cleared all the debtors in a manner more readily associated with the despotic style of his wretched nephew Christian VII of Denmark, who on his travels in England distributed largesse so lavishly that it aroused comment in London's court circles.[15] Not all the British royal family wished to curry favour with the mob. George III's mother, the Princess Dowager of Wales, was the soul of discretion; she gave away vast sums, said to be more than £10,000 a year, to indigent families.[16]

In search of cash and respectability, the emerging charitable institutions turned naturally to the monarchy, and as they acquired royal patronage the royal family's good works became more widely advertised. In the 1730s, George II aroused the expectations of hospital voluntarists when he granted a royal charter to the Edinburgh Infirmary and contributed £200 to the County Hospital in Winchester.[17] He also became the first patron of that great monument to eighteenth-century charity, the Foundling Hospital in London, the brainchild of Thomas Coram. Frederick, Prince of Wales, was likewise conspicuous among hospital patrons. He accepted the Presidency of St George's Hospital, Hyde Park Corner, where a ward was named in his honour.[18] But supplicants of royal favour did not always succeed. When Coram approached George II's

1. Charles II touching for scrofula, the 'King's Evil'.

daughter Princess Amelia with his petition for the Foundling Hospital, he was told to 'be gone' in no uncertain words by a Lady of the Bedchamber.[19]

Charitable motives are rarely pure, and the patronage of the monarchy cannot be explained simply by reference to compassion for the sick or love of the poor. The royal hospitals and the other institutions associated with the monarchy served useful social purposes, but they were also expressions of the sovereign's authority in bricks and mortar. Charles II and Queen Anne did not touch the scrofulous in their tens of thousands because they enjoyed proximity to disease. It was part of a pattern of royal ceremonial, which implied sacerdotal, if not divine, curative powers.[20] William III once reluctantly performed the ceremony, but is reported to have remarked to the patient, 'God give you better health, and more sense'.[21] No monarch after James II washed the feet of the poor; the practice was delegated to the Lord Almoner by the early eighteenth

2. The Henry VIII Gate at St Bartholomew's Hospital, built in 1702.

century. Still, the Maundy service, with its potent symbolism, intimated the monarch's lineage to Christ and divine powers.

'Nobility', wrote Bacon, 'is but the act of power.'[22] Whatever the intellectual context of royal patronage, from medieval spiritualism to enlightenment humanism, princely charity was characteristically ostentatious. Members of the royal family displayed a sensitivity to matters spiritual in their good works; and they displayed discretion too, in part to ward off endless appeals. One loyalist criticized George III and Queen Charlotte for not giving greater publicity to their gifts to the poor.[23] Yet royal patronage had an underlying meaning, which was propagandistic: to create a Christian image of spiritual elevation which enhanced the monarchy's political authority. Charity created dependent clients, while making power *visible*.

The rise of royal philanthropy has complex origins, but it should be seen in the light of the transformation of the idea of nobility. To put it

7

in human terms, compare the respective views of Henry VIII and Queen Victoria on social duty and the royal prerogative. The former imbibed a warrior tradition of nobility, characterized by self-glorification and an obsession with wealth and influence. The idea of *noblesse oblige*, which Queen Victoria had drummed into her, was alien to Renaissance princes. With a despot's instinctive sense of rank, Henry VIII assumed that his essential duty was to himself and to his equals. One does not picture him taking pity on the lower orders or popping out to visit a Sunday school in Windsor. He gave weekly alms because he believed that in doing so he would ensure his own salvation; he gave gifts to palace beggars and surrounded himself with pensioners to enrich his reputation, impress his rivals and express his authority.[24] His charity had little to do with social pity, but was a sign of self-esteem and superabundant wealth and power.

Over the years, social, political and religious changes emasculated this atavistic conception of nobility, and out of it emerged the idea that moral values applied to actions, that privilege entailed responsibility to the less fortunate. By George III's reign, conceptions of the royal prerogative and princely duty, though still deeply attuned to display and social hierarchy, bore little resemblance to the assumptions of Henry VIII. As the monarchy's power waned, its political and social views became more benign and inclusive. Regicide in 1649, the Revolution of 1688 and other restraints on royal authority had taken their toll. Eighteenth-century writings on the duty of kings did not draw their inspiration from the political philosophy of Hobbes; theories of mixed government had replaced those of divine right and absolutism.

Increasingly, political theorists saw the king as the servant of his people, and they sought to establish the basis of royal authority on a popular paternalism that showed itself sensitive to social needs. Although kings and princes did not always live up to expectations, the British monarch was becoming idealized as the benevolent head of a united people, above the political fray. As the statesman Henry St John, first Viscount Bolingbroke, argued: 'to govern like the common father of his people, is so essential to the character of a Patriot King, that he who does otherwise forfeits the title'. 'Popularity', he added, was the sole foundation of royal authority in a mixed government, and popularity depended on 'appearances'.[25]

'Appearances', however useful to the monarchy with the populace, were not enough for those well-connected leaders of society who sought to use the royal family for their own purposes. Most notably, the evangelicals wanted substantive royal support in their campaign to reform the nation's manners and morals. Hannah More despised Bolingbroke's doubting theology, but she elaborated his constitutional views in her advice to the monarchy to practise the 'arts of popularity' through benevolence and religious example. Her ideal sovereign was a high-minded Christian, widely seen reading the New Testament, uplifting the poor and bestowing favours on the righteous. The king was to be the focus of national morality, leading the campaign for an extension of charity throughout society.[26] As early as 1782, she exclaimed:

> A Crown! What is it?
> It is to bear the miseries of a people!
> To hear their murmurs, feel their discontents,
> And sink beneath a load of splendid care![27]

It was an article of faith among the evangelicals, who were in the ascendancy both inside and outside the Church of England, that where the higher classes led, the lower orders would follow. 'High rank is not a property but a trust,' declared Wilberforce.[28] Evangelicals were nothing if not inclusive: everyone, high or low, rich or poor, could be saved. They were eager to increase the contact between rich and poor, but they believed the privileged classes, having become effete, undervalued their own influence. They tapped a rich vein of opinion, for there was growing unease that Britain's problems stemmed, as the scientist and philanthropist Count Romford put it, from 'the alarming progress of luxury and the corruption of taste and morals' among the upper classes.[29] The campaign to awaken the aristocratic social conscience had effects both great and small. Queen Charlotte, after reading Hannah More's *Thoughts on the Importance of the Manners of the Great to General Society*, gave up her Sunday hairdresser.[30]

Astute propagandists like More and Wilberforce, who prepared the royal ground by obsequious flattery, shamelessly exploited the monarchy's good offices in their moral crusade. In 1787, they scored a signal triumph when George III issued his 'Proclamation against Vice and Immorality', though it seems to have done little to reform the behaviour of some of the nobility who signed the prospectus. While it is difficult to measure the success of the Proclamation, it fuelled the growing exaltation of the monarchy, in More's words, as 'the fountain from whence the vulgar draw their habits, actions and characters'.[31] The moral philosopher Thomas Gisborne, a friend of Wilberforce, put the case of the philanthropic king: 'streams of happiness flow from a sovereign who regards his subjects as his children and watches over them with charity.'[32] He and a growing body of authors encouraged the public to idealize George III as the nation's premier gentleman; and like other gentlemen he should display those qualities of morality, compassion and social responsibility.

Political events in the late eighteenth century encouraged the concrete and visible expression of the ideals espoused by moral philosophers and charity organizers. Over the century, the growth in ministerial authority had circumscribed the king's room for political manoeuvre. The trend had been accelerated by protracted warfare, population growth and prosperity, which vastly increased the volume of public business. The irreversible decline in the king's power, as Linda Colley explains, 'made it much easier for the public to distinguish between monarch and minister and to celebrate the former without owing allegiance to the latter'. What amounted to a royal 'face lift' had its origins in 'that mood of introspection which followed the defeat in the American war'.[33] The British defeat in America and the Revolution in France helped to give George III a more popular, paternal image, part national icon and part touching, if sometimes pathetic, domestic figure.[34]

The political difficulties and setbacks which enlivened the charitable establishment also enlivened royal paternalism. The fall of the Bastille and the execution of Louis XVI stunned the British ruling class and so horrified the royal family that even the Prince of Wales rallied to his father's defence. Remembering the behaviour of the London mob in the Gordon Riots in 1780, there was widespread fear that a bloodthirsty republicanism might take hold in England. As the armies of France swept across Europe, many former enemies closed ranks to preserve Britain's *ancien régime*. It is said, somewhat misleadingly, that when the French became republican, the English became religious. Cynics might argue that French principles did more to arouse the religious sensibilities and charitable inclinations of the House of Hanover than all the moral reformers combined. The moral reformers themselves were acutely aware of the dangers. In Hannah More's words, the poor should be instructed 'with a view to check the spirit of insubordination'.[35]

Robespierre and Napoleon pricked the religious and social conscience's of Britain's wealthier classes, but this is not to say that late Georgian charity can be reduced to a reactionary strategy for national survival or the survival of the monarchy. Many societies, including those set up by the poor themselves, fit uneasily with theories of punitive benevolence or 'social control'. Moreover, British traditions of *richesse oblige* and *noblesse oblige* had merged before Napoleon was born. Both George III and Queen Charlotte had shown a penchant for philanthropy well before the great troubles of the reign began. Over a long reign, the vicissitudes of politics and family life brought out the King's utilitarian character and deepened his association with a philosophy of social betterment. He headed an expansive philanthropic movement which patriotic Britons readily linked to national purpose in an era of foreign wars and domestic unrest.

Patriots and moral reformers found George III a reliable, and willing, tool for their designs. He was conservative in politics and, unlike the Bourbons, prudent in financial matters. Sound in religion, he was regular in the observance of public worship. His behaviour, if sometimes eccentric, was moral and decorous. He was well and truly married to Queen

Charlotte, a woman of charitable disposition whose upbringing in Germany, with its pronounced charitable traditions, left her with a marked sense of social duty. John Wesley, a staunch defender of Church and King, summed up George III's virtues: 'He believes the Bible . . . he fears God . . . he loves the Queen.'[36] Not only was the King endowed with a greater sense of *noblesse oblige* than his forebears, but the society in which he found himself encouraged him to demonstrate it at every opportunity. As his biographer John Brooke noted, he was the 'first of the Victorians'.[37]

George III does not compare with most later British monarchs in the time he devoted to philanthropic work, but in his own day he was portrayed as immensely charitable by charitable promoters. Taking their cue from constitutional writers, they saw him, as the influential philanthropist Sir Thomas Bernard put it, as a 'kindly parent' promoting 'the happiness of his subjects' through his benefactions.[38] Gillray took a less charitable view, and in his *Temperance Enjoying a Frugal Meal* he included a framed picture with the title *The Triumph of Benevolence* hanging on the wall above the head of a miserly George III. The picture was blank. Both promoters and debunkers of the monarchy had their agendas, but in

3.   'Temperance enjoying a Frugal Meal', by James Gillray.

regard to the King's largesse, Gillray's contorted portrait is in need of correction.

Just how much George III personally gave to charity is not entirely clear. On the evidence available, his giving as a proportion of the national whole was small, yet no British monarch since has given away a greater proportion of his or her private income. Lady Charlotte Finch, royal governess and confidante of Queen Charlotte, said the King's largesse was 'prodigious'.[39] John Brooke looked at the royal finances in detail, but found the archival record patchy for charitable contributions. (The patronage books no longer exist.) The King's private income, the Privy Purse, had been set at £48,000 per annum at the beginning of the reign. Among the many charges on the Privy Purse were salaries, retirement pensions, pensions to poor dependants of former royal servants and the traditional gifts to staff at Christmas and New Year. After all his expenses were paid, the King had an average balance of £27,500 a year between 1763 and 1772 (a period for which the records survive). According to Brooke, he spent most, if not all, of this money each year on private charity.[40] Most of it went on casual donations to needy individuals rather than to institutions.

George III had various sources of personal income, including money from the Duchy of Lancaster, worth about £5,000 a year in the 1770s, and the profits from his privately owned properties, many of them around Windsor, but he depended on his Privy Purse for charitable donations. In 1782, he protested against any reduction of his Privy Purse income on the grounds that it was 'the only fund from whence I pay every act of private benevolence'. Charitable distributions, as he lamented, 'alone make the station bearable'.[41] When he was incapacitated by illness in 1789, a committee which investigated the Privy Purse accounts concluded that the King never gave away less than £14,000 per annum to charitable objects.[42] This figure, not cited by Brooke, was about one quarter of George III's private income from the Privy Purse, which had risen to £60,000 per annum in 1777. Fourteen thousand pounds a year was charity on a grand scale, but it still made up only a fraction, well under 1 per cent, of Britain's total annual philanthropic revenue.

Figures alone, however, do not represent the full impact of the King's beneficence. Every charitable fundraiser knows the importance of recruiting prominent patrons who can extract contributions from others. In the deferential world of British philanthropy, success depends not so much on the cause but on whom you can get to support it. The excitement generated by the news that an application by a Georgian charity for royal patronage had been granted is difficult to recreate today, when so many institutions already possess it. In the reign of George III, royal patronage was not only less common, but the monarchy's standing in the nation was far more potent, inspiring awe and reverence in enormous measure. The condescension of the King, accompanied by even a small donation from his Privy Purse, was precious beyond rubies.

As the founder of the Royal Academy and the Observatory at Kew, George III is well known for his interest in the arts and sciences; his interest in charitable causes has attracted less attention. He would typically allow his name to head a patronage list without appearing in person at annual meetings. Furthermore, illness restricted his movements in later years and discouraged institutions from applying to him for support. Still, he was formally attached to nine charities, including the Foundling Hospital, St George's Hospital, the Society for Bettering the Condition and Increasing the Comforts of the Poor, the Royal Jennerian Society, and the Hospital for Small Pox Inoculation.[43] Apart from the fundraising potential of the King's annual subscription, the effects of royal patronage could be crucial to a charity's objectives.

The example of George III's interest in small pox, no doubt aroused by the death of his son Octavius from inoculation in 1783, is but one example of how the public can be converted to a cause by royal intervention, and of how royal patronage can turn an experiment into an institution. The royal family had shown an interest in the treatment of small pox since the 1720s, when Caroline, Princess of Wales, had her daughters Amelia and Elizabeth Caroline inoculated. When Edward Jenner, the discoverer of vaccination, asked for permission to dedicate the second edition of his *Inquiry* into small pox to the King in 1800, it was granted. It was a crack in the door of the Palace, and like others who wished to promote a cause by way of the royal sanctum, Jenner offered tribute: 'To a monarch no less justly than emphatically styled the Father of his People, this Treatise is inscribed with perfect propriety; for conspicuous as your Majesty's patronage has been of arts, or sciences, and of commerce, yet the most distinguished feature of your character is your paternal care for the dearest interests of humanity.'[44]

In early 1803, Admiral George Berkeley, MP for Gloucester, asked the Duke of Clarence (later William IV) to entreat the King to become the patron of a charity dedicated to extending Jenner's work. As Berkeley wrote: 'It would greatly promote its important object, that of rescuing a very large proportion of his Majesty's subjects from an untimely grave.'[45] The Duke of Clarence, who had had his servants and two of his children inoculated several years earlier, found the King a willing recruit. In an extraordinary gesture of support, the entire royal family added their names to the patronage list of the newly formed Royal Jennerian Society. Amidst the rejoicing, Jenner and the officials of the institution attended a levee to return thanks to the King for his goodness. The excitement in the Society was such that medical men turned to poetry: 'The gen'rous friends in social league combin'ed/And Bless the ROYAL BREAST that feels for all mankind.'[46]

George III's support for education was no less effective than his support for vaccination, and it led a Victorian biographer to call it 'the brightest passage in the history of his long and eventful reign'.[47] The King visited schools, attended services at St Paul's for charity children, and invited the educational philanthropists Robert Raikes and Sarah Trimmer to Windsor. Unlike conservative churchmen, he was not unhappy at the prospect of poor children being able to read. Such views aroused expectations among educational reformers, including the Quaker Joseph Lancaster. An ingenious teacher, Lancaster had devised a 'monitorial system', in which the pupils themselves, coached by a master, taught other pupils and carried out routine administration.[48] Whatever its qualitative failings, the method promoted a rapid expansion of cheap education for the poor. George III's patronage of Lancaster's schools, which began in 1805, and the active support given to them by several of the royal dukes, transformed a local initiative into a national institution.

Lancaster told a friend of his crucial interview with George III, and it was later recorded. The schoolmaster had been brought to the attention of the King by Lord Somerville, a Lord of the Bedchamber, and by the philanthropic Countess Harcourt, who had herself founded a charity school near Windsor. The King was staying at Weymouth and sent for Lancaster. After questioning him about his methods, George III said that 'every poor child in my dominions should be taught to read the Bible'. He promised Lancaster royal subscriptions amounting to over £200, which he offered immediately, to which Lancaster replied: 'Please, your Majesty, that will be setting thy nobles a good example.'[49] Reportedly, this remark amused the King, who was well aware of the opposition to Lancaster from Anglican churchmen but also aware that where royalty led the aristocracy would follow. As we shall see, others down the social ladder also followed, including middle-class radicals and republicans.

George III took a keen interest in the schools and local charities around Windsor Castle, his principal country residence. He sometimes showed a quality of mercy that is at odds with Gillray's caricature in which he is seen walking about Windsor terrifying a farm-worker. One eyewitness remembered the King as a popular figure in the neighbourhood: 'his beneficence to the poor . . . was accompanied with a certain originality of manner which extended the reputation of his good deeds.'[50] On one of his solitary walks in the winter of 1785, George III happened upon two starving children, who told him that their mother had been dead for three days and that their father lay sick and helpless by her side. Appalled by what he witnessed at their hovel, he gave them money and rushed back to Windsor Castle to organize relief. Though the father recovered, the King continued to support the children.[51]

Such experiences aroused George III's compassion, but they would also have stimulated his interest in the local economy, estate management and

4. 'Affability'. George III terrifying a farm-worker on a royal walkabout at Windsor, by James Gillray.

education. Like all British sovereigns since, he was well informed about the condition of his tenants and the population living near his residences. His reign saw a dramatic rise in the availability of amenities to the citizens of the royal borough of Windsor. In addition to his patronage of local shops and schools, the King gave £1,000 towards street paving, presented the parish church with an organ, helped to establish a theatre in the town, and built a hospital for soldiers.[52] Such displays of royal benevolence resulted in an exceptional level of deference in Windsor, but it was also practical and profitable in the management of the King's estates.

The opportunity for royal charitable display reached its zenith on the King's tours, and his condescension and example were long remembered. George III was not a great traveller, but on his occasional forays into the provinces his generosity left a memorable impression. On a visit to Salisbury in 1778, he contributed £1,000 to a cathedral appeal and £200 for the discharge of debtors, a gesture noticed by the prison reformer John

Howard.[53] (Ten years later, George III received Howard at Windsor and headed a subscription to put up a statue to him.)[54] In 1788, the King, the Queen and the Princesses, Charlotte, Augusta and Elizabeth made a visit to Worcester. Amidst the usual round of dinners, music-making and granting of honours, the royal family distributed £550 to the city's needy.[55] On a visit to Saltram the next year, George III gave £1,950 to the dockyard labourers and the poor of Plymouth.[56] When five onlookers fell out of a sloop and drowned, the King offered assistance to the orphans.[57]

In 1809, the fiftieth anniversary of the reign, the links between the monarchy and charity grew apace as civic dignitaries exploited the auspicious occasion and more and more institutions took advantage of even the vaguest identification with the monarchy. The arch-royal Society of Friends of Foreigners in Distress exclaimed that 'the best mode of commemorating the 50th year of the reign of our gracious Sovereign is by acts of beneficence'.[58] The association of jubilees with mass celebrations and charitable appeals expanded into a great tradition in 1887 and 1897. The celebrations in 1809, like those in later jubilee years, largely bubbled up from below, created by public demand.

As Linda Colley has shown, urban authorities seized upon the royal anniversary in 1809 'as a means to advertise their town's particular affluence, identity and culture, as an outlet for civic pride as well as British patriotism'.[59] The results ranged in character from balls and public monuments to new gas lights and hospitals. In York, the authorities feasted 9,000 of the city's poor; in Oxford, the university distributed money to 7,000 people.[60] If many institutions used the Jubilee as an excuse to raise money or to give it away, others threw a party. The Royal Military Asylum in Chelsea gave its 1,200 children a special meal of roast beef and plum pudding, with the added attraction of two pence placed by the side of each plate. The children sang 'God save the King' before and after dinner, words which resounded in charities across Britain.[61]

In a different setting, the Prime Minister, Spencer Perceval, wrote to George III that the 'universal sympathy' for an example of royal charity might be used to set up a fund for the relief of poor prisoners, or debtors, or for more general charity. The King replied that £6,000 from the Privy Purse could be made available, and it was distributed equally between England, Ireland and Scotland.[62] As part of the celebrations, he also pardoned army and navy deserters and released prisoners of war. Such calculated acts of benevolence were advertisements for monarchy itself, being at once expressions of royal kindness and Christian forgiveness in keeping with the New Testament sovereign of the evangelical imagination.

As the examples of Jenner and Lancaster suggest, those who sought or received royal favour were quick to lavish praise on the King. Highmore, who dedicated his first survey of metropolitan charity to George III, called the King 'unrivalled' in his beneficence.[63] Hannah More, who was given to obsequious effusion on the subject of royalty, congratulated George III on the 'numberless' charities of his reign.[64] Mrs Trimmer, whose fear of French principles warped her philanthropy and drove her to excessive moralizing, declared that 'a general joy' prevailed among educational reformers after a visit by the King to her school for industry at Brentford.[65] Those who applauded the benefits of royal philanthropy made it a rule to avoid the slightest criticism of the monarchy in public, whatever the provocation. This rule, which applies to any important benefactor, has been followed by charitable campaigners with royal connections ever since. In return for royal favour, the monarchy received a steady stream of perfected praise.

Queen Charlotte's charities endeared her to a public well prepared for news of royal benevolence. Loyalist writers knew that displays of royal patronage encouraged attachment to the throne, and they played an important part in shaping the royal image to suit the moral and deferential temper of their time. The contemporary biographer John Watkins, whose reverence for monarchy was unbounded, revelled in stories of the Queen's benevolence. Drawing on an eye-witness account, he related that at the naval levee at Saltram, an elderly woman pushed though the crowds and thrust an application for admittance to an asylum for decayed widows through the window where her Majesty stood. The Queen, in an act of 'extraordinary condescension', picked the petition from the floor and granted it.[66]

Such stories suggest the complex psychology that surrounded monarchical sentiment in the reign of George III (and ever after). Percy Black, a Canadian psychologist interested in the 'mystique of monarchy', once argued that the presence of members of the royal family at public events could be 'translated by the believing and unwary into a false connection: good deeds are, *ipso facto*, caused by royalty'. In this analysis, the 'monarchy becomes it own best press agent. Every time it appears in public, reads a few prepared words, or smiles upon a crowd of children, it chalks up for itself another notch in the unbounded sentiment.'[67] There is some truth in this insight. Certainly, members of the royal family reaped advantages by simply turning up at public events. They received few favourable notices, however, from their private benevolence. What Black fails to appreciate is that members of the royal family often *did* cause good deeds to be done.

Through charitable associations, George III and his family kindled an acceptance of social hierarchy and a reverence for monarchy bordering on delusion. But members of the royal family did not simply stamp their seal on the status quo by their philanthropic work, as Black's analysis would lead us to conclude. An acceptance of social hierarchy showed itself to be compatible with social improvement. The belief that reform works best within a hierarchical framework was, and remains, implicit in the monarchy's philanthropic work. Through its voluntary public service, the royal family encouraged the spread of traditional values and a sense of social unity. It offered British society, as Black concedes, 'integration and a bulwark against disorganisation'.[68] The monarchy expected loyalty in return.

Such ideas seem not to have occurred to Queen Charlotte, who had little inclination to analyse her charitable actions. Characteristically, her philanthropy was a pragmatic response to immediate and individual problems and flowed from her sense of social obligation. One of her habits was to disguise her benevolence by using intermediaries, who would hand money over to families in need.[69] Still, the Queen certainly gave the public opportunities to rejoice in her charitable deeds, as for instance at Saltram. On another festive occasion, to mark the defeat of Napoleon in the spring of 1814, she gave a dinner to 2,000 poor people at Windsor.[70] It is difficult to judge whether she and her advisors consciously calculated the advantages to the monarchy of such events, or whether they were simply falling into line with public expectations of royal bounty.

According to a recent biographer, 'an untiring interest in charities . . . was Queen Charlotte's contribution to social history and a substitute for the political influence which . . . she never wished to exercise.'[71] Despite a reputation for parsimony and domestic economies, the Queen supported a large number of institutions, some of which owed their existence to her intervention. Apart from unrecorded alms, she gave away over £5,000 a year, including pensions to needy widows and sums to schools and the Bible Society. A charity for distressed needlewomen in Bedfordshire, which was largely financed by her donations, received £25,000 from her over a period of fifty years.[72]

Queen Charlotte's benevolence was unsystematic, but she showed some discrimination in her social work and a preference for causes relating to women and children. Typically, she worked behind the scenes, the embodiment of those female virtues of modesty, compassion and morality which respectable society encouraged in women of all social ranks. In addition to innumerable casual donations, she regularly gave away coals, clothing and food to the poor in winter, and oversaw the manufacture of necessary articles to be sent to the troops fighting Napoleon's armies. In Windsor she and her daughters made inquiries into deserving local families and prepared clothing for them. In one of the more curious royal charitable traditions, she dispensed money to deserving women who gave birth to girl triplets (the King paid for boy triplets), a custom which the monarchy retained in a somewhat altered form until 1957.[73] In such ways the monarchy tied itself to familial values and made its beneficence felt throughout the kingdom, albeit in a highly arbitrary fashion.

Along with her daughters, Queen Charlotte worked on behalf of the Ladies' Society at Kensington for the Education and Employment of the Female Poor. She was also a frequent visitor to Bailbrook Lodge in Bath, which assisted genteel widows, and she sometimes dropped in on the orphanage at Oatlands, an institution founded by the childless Duchess of York. Her patronages included the Westminster Hospital, the Friendly Female Society, and the Lying-In Hospital, later Queen Charlotte's Hospital. On her marriage, she inherited the patronage of the Hospital of St Katharine's, an ecclesiastical foundation belonging to the queens of England. Her attachment to the Magdalen Hospital, a refuge for prostitutes, turned out to be especially beneficial, because the royal seal of approval enabled the institution 'to triumph over the prejudices raised against it in the public mind'.[74] One is reminded today of the Princess of Wales and her role in altering perceptions of Aids.

As an educationalist, Queen Charlotte was portrayed as a guardian of morals, an apostle among the young. She established a school for poor children in Windsor and founded another to celebrate the recovery of George III from his first illness, an example of commemoration tied to a royal recuperation. Mrs Trimmer dedicated her book *The Economy of Charity* to Queen Charlotte, and paid lavish tribute to the importance of royal patronage to the Sunday school movement. Having secured the Queen's blessing for her own schools, she wrote: 'Her example will cause them to be universal: they will soon be extended over the whole kingdom.'[75] In missionary work and religious education, the monarchy's impulses were latitudinarian. As George III stood patron to the Royal Lancasterian Association (later the British and Foreign School Society), with its Nonconformist overtones, it was thought 'just' that Queen Charlotte should become attached to its Anglican rival, the National Society for Promoting the Education of the Poor in the Principles of the Established Church.[76]

Queen Charlotte's last public act was a visit to the National Society at the Egyptian Hall in 1818, a grand occasion attended by leading churchmen and Elizabeth Fry. To mark the event, she contributed the sum of £500. The level of the Queen's generosity had for years alarmed her financial advisors, who cautioned her against 'profuse liberality'.[77] After George III fell ill she found it more difficult to control her spending, for she inherited his pension list. At her death she was said to be £9,000 in debt, with personal property valued at under £140,000. According to her treasurer and later executor, her charities were so extensive that there was 'never a pecuniary balance in her favour'.[78] Perhaps he was including in her extended charities the £50,000 she provided from her private purse for the construction of that great drain on royal finance, the Brighton Pavilion.[79]

Publicized through newspapers, sermons and public meetings, the Queen's charities fuelled the crusade to reform the nation's manners and morals, while they served the associated conservative propaganda campaign, aroused by the French Revolution and nourished by the Napoleonic wars. Mrs Trimmer approached the Queen, and dedicated her writings to her out of sincere royalist sentiment; but at the back of her mind was how the monarchy might be used to inoculate the lower orders against immorality and sedition.[80] Though Queen Charlotte's charities were extensive, by the time of her death in 1818 loyalists had embellished them in the interests of public safety. The evangelicals, who assumed that women were distinctive moral agents, also turned her into a model of female propriety palatable to middle-class culture and suitable for the education of young ladies.

Queen Charlotte's obituaries said little about the realities of her daily life, the luxurious surroundings, the seemingly endless round of parties and concerts.[81] Rather, they emphasized the Queen's familial virtue, domestic religion and charitable conduct. The words of one churchman sum up this trend:

> We needed during the late eventful years (when all other thrones in Europe were thrown down with their monarchs) such lofty examples of conjugal affection, domestic religion, economy, and virtue. And not withstanding all the calamities which convulsed the world, and the dangers which threatened these kingdoms, God preserved them. . . . [Queen Charlotte] was spared to foster all the charities which her prudence and benevolence had planned or preserved and to exercise her maternal regards for her own numerous family and her solicitude for the British people.[82]

★ ★ ★

As parents and grandparents, King George and Queen Charlotte wished to point their offspring in the direction of the straight and narrow, into what Hannah More called 'the right channel of Christian Benevolence'. Charitable behaviour was inculcated systematically through formal lessons and not left to casual exercise. They had rather more success, it should be said, with their daughters than with some of the royal dukes. The daughters' lives, according to John Brooke, 'were like that of novices in a well-regulated convent'. Queen Charlotte, who ruled over them like a drill sergeant, favoured devotional literature in their education, and she was eager to bring them into contact with her many charities.

The Queen also kept in close touch with the education of her granddaughter, Princess Charlotte, the daughter of the Prince and Princess of

Wales. In keeping with the prevailing views about female education, which stressed practical religion, the Princess was taught 'generosity by degree'. At the age of six, her account books show that she spent small sums from her pocket money on the poor and the sick.[83] Though pliable, the young Princess sometimes felt defeated by the rigours of evangelical enthusiasm. Compelled to read for two hours a day from Hannah More's *Hints Towards Forming the Education of a Young Princess*, she wrote to a friend: 'This I believe is what makes me finde the hours so long. I am not quite good enough for that yet.'[84]

With the years, Princess Charlotte's interest in the sick and the poor had to compete with her growing interest in dresses, cardplaying, and life. Despite an eye to propriety, her spending on her wardrobe much exceeded her spending on charities. Still, her charitable donations, to institutions such as the Friendly Female Society for Decayed Widows, came from the £800 allotted for her wardrobe.[85] With a strong parochial sense, she distributed £50 to the local poor on her birthday and passed out Bibles to aged cottagers. In a happy conjunction, she slipped pound notes between the scriptures.[86]

The 'best charity of all', the Princess wrote to her friend Miss Mercer Elphinstone, flowed from the improvements taking place on her estate, Claremont, for they employed a vast number of labourers who might otherwise starve.[87] As with other members of the royal family, self-interest and an ingrained sense of the monarchy's ancient privileges, which were under siege during the Napoleonic wars, informed her philanthropy. Attuned to politics as a teenager, she was well aware of events taking place on the continent, grieved 'excessively' for the Bourbons and feared for the British state.

In the summer of 1816, the Princess recoiled, as she put it, from the 'horrid speeches in the City' which breathed 'a true spirit of revolution'.[88] This was a reference to a meeting at the Guildhall on the calamitous economic conditions at the end of the Napoleonic wars. The government took little interest in the matter; philanthropists had launched an appeal. At the Guildhall, the firebrand Henry Hunt had attacked Princess Charlotte and her husband, Prince Leopold of Saxe-Coburg, for their paltry contribution to the campaign. 'The Prince and the Princess of Coburg', he railed, 'had given £400, but they had received £120,000. This was the comparative rate at which the great paupers thought it their duty to contribute to the support of the little paupers.'[89] What was needed, argued Hunt, was the abolition of sinecures and the return of the British army from France.

Unlike the supporters of Church and King, alienated English radicals tended to see charity as a lubricant of 'Old Corruption' or as a 'sinecure-soup project', as Hunt once called an appeal supported by the Duke of York.[90] Shelley, in his *Address to the People on the Death of the Princess*

Charlotte, published under a pseudonym, remained unmoved by Charlotte's public charities. His Princess was not a construct of Hannah More, bent over her needlework or busy on her visiting rounds: 'For the public she had done nothing either good or evil.' And he added: 'Such is the impotence of royalty—princes are prevented from the cradle becoming anything which may deserve that greatest of all rewards next to a good conscience, public admiration and regret.'[91]

For the more strident reformers like Shelley and Hunt, philanthropic aims were sometimes difficult to square with the rights of man. In an age of revolutionary politics, much royal philanthropy had taken on a counter-revolutionary character, despite the radical associations of the Dukes of Kent and Sussex. Indeed, the monarchy's ever-increasing contribution to charitable institutions alienated some radicals from philanthropic remedies, which they were prone to see as inadequate in any case. The fact that charities traditionally worked within the existing social structure made them anathema to many radicals (and later socialists), who took the view that everyone who accepts the reality of social divisions approves of them.

One of the repercussions of the French Revolution in Britain was that it tended, with many individual exceptions, to widen the differences between philanthropists and political radicals. The crown was a focus of dispute. In the second part of the *Rights of Man*, published in 1792, an uncharitable Thomas Paine branded the royal family as a 'band of parasites', living off the public taxes. The monarchy was the 'master fraud', he added, 'which shelters all others. By admitting a participation of the spoil, it makes itself friends; and when it ceases to do this, it will cease to be the idol of courtiers.'[92] Such incendiary views did not endear Paine to the authorities, and he fled to France. Nor did Paine endear himself to the charitable establishment by his tirades against the crown.

One should not underestimate the importance of radicals and republicans during the turbulent years of the French Revolution and the Napoleonic wars. As we shall see, some of them advanced their causes through warming to the royal embrace. But for every caricature or criticism of the royal family, there were scores of favourable notices from the standard-bearers of Church and monarchy. On the occasion of Princess Charlotte's death in 1817, one finds little criticism of the sort voiced by Shelley, or even much in the way of acknowledgement that she was a victim of parental neglect and miscalculation. Few wished to impugn a girl so high born but so ill-starred—better to point a moral with her tragic tale. Judging from the hundreds of addresses delivered, she was a woman of the most refined accomplishment and a blessed model of melting charity. As one preacher intoned: 'Goodness and charity were wafted into her soul as by the airs of heaven.'[93]

Churchmen and loyalist writers transformed Princess Charlotte into a creation worthy of Hannah More, just as Hannah More intended when she published her *Hints Towards Forming the Education of a Young Princess* in 1805. They did the same for George III's daughters. When the invalid Princess Amelia died in 1810, the memoirists embellished her reputation in their sermons and the ladies' magazines. 'To "Heaven-born charity" this amiable Princess united a spirit worthy royalty,' remarked one of their number, adding: 'Isolated from sad realities by their station, children of Kings can rarely understand poverty. The Princess sought poverty; her attendants brought to her bed the blessings of the poor, as the only balm that could gladden her heart.'[94]

It is perhaps an exaggeration to say that members of the royal family were unknowable in the reign of George III, a *tabula rasa* on which the public imprinted its own desires, but with so little reliable information available, biographers and royal commentators dressed them up to suit themselves. With the advent of cheap print and a growing middle-class readership, newspapers and magazines, deeply imbued with a sense of social hierarchy, required a steady stream of stories to supply the expanding market for royal news. Whenever there was a birth or death in the royal family, aspiring biographers and churchmen reached for their pens and pulpits with uplifting sentiments and improving words. Paradoxically, the more they said, the more obscure the personalities of members of the royal family became.

In the religious climate of the late eighteenth and early nineteenth centuries, royal commentators drew attention to those qualities which were in tune with prevailing opinion. Philanthropic behaviour, an outward sign of respectability, was at a premium. Some members of the royal family needed no touching up to look pious and benevolent. The daughter of George III, Princess Mary, Duchess of Gloucester, was a model evangelical and served at least fourteen charities.[95] The public demand for royal paragons was so insatiable that even that tragic vapour Lady Jane Grey (1537–54) was resurrected in the early nineteenth century as an evangelical girl of the period.[96]

Queen Caroline, George IV's wife, was rather more intractable, though even she did the charitable rounds on occasion. As Princess of Wales her name appeared on the patronage lists of the Royal Jennerian Society, the Friendly Female Society and the Blackheath branch of the Bible Society. And though she was said to fall asleep at meetings, she made public appearances on behalf of the Royal Lancasterian Association. In a display of female solidarity, she once turned up to hear Joseph Lancaster's wife lecture on female education to an assembly of ladies. The ladies approved, but the event proved a great embarrassment to Lancaster, for he was informed that the meeting had 'much displeased' the Prince

Regent, who threatened to withdraw his patronage from the Association.[97]

The Prince Regent doubtless had good reason for taking offence at his estranged wife appearing on behalf of one of his charities, yet her presence at a philanthropic function was a tremendous boost to female philanthropy. In the early nineteenth century, public lectures by women were highly unusual, and much frowned upon, especially by churchmen. As late as 1820, the prejudice against women simply attending charitable meetings was so strong that they sometimes had to be hidden behind an organ screen.[98] When the Princess of Wales appeared to hear Mrs Lancaster, it was said that she was 'the only Princess who could probably have felt herself at liberty to attend a public lecture on female education and to encourage a worthy but long afflicted woman in commencing a career of public benevolence'.[99]

If Queen Caroline was an unconvincing lady bountiful, George III's motley collection of sons also cut rather curious figures in the charitable world. Scores of charitable societies were eager to recruit them as patrons or presidents. Although pretty impenetrable as personalities, the Dukes of Cambridge, Kent and Sussex appear to have had charitable impulses. They certainly put in long hours on behalf of benevolent causes, though in the Duke of Kent's case it is difficult to tell whether he personally or the charities he promoted received the greater benefit. What philanthropy meant, if very much at all, in the lives of their brothers is uncertain. If one believes the officials in the societies to which they were attached, they were charity incarnate. If one believes later historians and biographers, who have been influenced by Victorian obfuscation, one gets a very different impression. But whatever their attitudes and motives, all of the sons of George III carried out charitable duties, if for no other reason than that their position in society required them to do so.

In the reign of George III, at least three institutions could claim the distinction of having secured the entire royal family on their patronage lists: the Royal Jennerian Society, the Royal Infirmary for Diseases of the Eye, and the Society of Friends of Foreigners in Distress. The latter charity enrolled virtually every prince in Europe and the President of the United States. A number of institutions, including schools, hospitals, and societies for the ruptured poor, recruited more than one of the royal dukes. (It was estimated in 1818 that about one in five of the entire male population in ports and manufacturing districts had a hernia.)[100] The patronage lists of leading charities were among the few places where the sons of George III could be seen together in agreement.

Despite his waywardness, Augustus Frederick, the Duke of Sussex (1773–1843), was remarkable, as one of his early biographers noted, 'for the zeal with which he promoted the cause of charity'.[101] Even many who disliked his Whig politics respected him for his benevolence. Known as the 'best beggar in Europe', he was a persuasive fundraiser and an active supporter of over thirty London charities, and was often seen in the chair at their annual meetings.[102] Among his charitable enthusiasms were the Lying-In Hospital, which became Queen Charlotte's Maternity Hospital, and a variety of societies in aid of Catholics and Jews. Many of his liberal associations would have been thought inappropriate for the King or the Queen and would have disturbed his conservative relations; but they created bonds between royalty and religious groups and minorities which were cut off from the mainstream of British life. The Duke of Sussex, like his brother the Duke of Kent, widened the monarchy's charitable net and encouraged allegiance to the throne beyond the establishment.

Francis Place, the radical tailor and lifelong republican, attended meetings of the Royal Lancasterian Association, a charity identified with Nonconformity, when Sussex was in the chair. Like many others who have mixed with royalty, he was attracted by the glamour yet found the courage to be dismissive. He described the Duke of Sussex as a 'foolish fellow' with 'a most miserably shallow understanding'. Yet he thought the Duke 'a remarkable man', so affable and good humoured that he could put an audience at its ease. The Duke certainly put Place at his ease. At meetings of the Association at Kensington Palace, others were prone to introduce their words with 'Your Royal Highness', whereas Place kept his republican purity. If we are to believe him, the Duke respected him for it.[103]

For a member of the royal family, the ability to charm republicans was charm indeed, and the Duke of Sussex seems to have possessed it, along with considerable forbearance. At his death Whigs and freemasons grieved, schoolgirls put on mourning dress, and even the Duke of Wellington, who disliked his politics, said something positive about his charities. The Marquis of Northampton paid him fulsome tribute in the House of Lords, with the hope that future historians would note that the Duke's name was associated 'in common with all the members of the royal family, with all the charitable institutions in the country.'[104] That he fulfilled his charitable role is clear, but why he gave so much time to it is less easy to fathom. As we shall see, he was sensitive to the issues of public order and social stability; but he was a man of liberal sympathies, and his motives cannot be explained simply by self-interest or the needs of the monarchy.

The eccentric Adolphus Frederick, Duke of Cambridge (1774–1850), though pleasing in manner, had rather less tact than Sussex. In his charitable work, he carried earnestness to the point of meddling interference. The number of his patronages increased when he returned to England from Hanover, where he had served as Viceroy. In later life he was president or patron of about thirty institutions, including fifteen hospitals and the Royal Society for the Prevention of Cruelty to Animals, which did not extend its protection to grouse. A frequent visitor to the Military School at Chelsea, he was an especial friend to the widows and orphans of soldiers; and while he 'unhinged' more than a few clergymen with his loud running commentaries on their sermons, he was also a friend to the Bible Society.[105]

Interested in the minutiae of charitable administration, the Duke of Cambridge did not simply 'preside over turtle and venison', though, as one wit remarked, his mouth was 'always open to the call of charity'.[106] Whenever disputes or professional rivalries broke out in one of his charities, he would suddenly appear in the midst of the battle. As an admirer put it: 'He did not seek solely to dignify that which was harmonious or to give grace and solemnity to the administrative skill of others.'[107] In other words, he knocked a few heads together. He was in a strong position to do so, for few dared to oppose a member of the royal family. But whether the officials at the Middlesex Hospital and the German Hospital at Dalston, two charities in which he 'rushed into the breach', were happy with the results is uncertain. One supporter, eager to glorify His Royal Highness, made the interesting remark that through his charitable work the Duke 'was emphatically the connecting link between the throne and the people'.[108]

George III's fifth son, the arch-reactionary Ernest Augustus, Duke of Cumberland (1771–1851), did not arouse such encomiums, and certainly not from the radical press, which vilified him as a rake, a martinet and a deranged political partisan. Dubbed the 'King of Ogres', even his friends found him surly. He may seem an unlikely advocate of the Bible Society and the Royal Jennerian Society, or a friend of distressed foreigners and the blind. But judging from the way in which he was treated by some charitable institutions he might be mistaken for St Francis. However, at his death, *The Times* could find little positive to say about him, but it did point to the £2,000 he gave to the Irish Famine Fund, a 'noble deed which may atone for some of his faults'.[109] There was no mention of the person from whom he might have borrowed the money.

The charities of the Duke of Cumberland, arguably the most unpopular prince of modern times, suggest a general truth about philanthropic administration: however tiresome or unpalatable a member of the royal family may be, it will not put off a charity in search of his or her patronage. Has there ever been a charity which has asked a member of the royal family to withdraw his or her patronage because of moral turpitude or any other failing? When George III was struck down by what the public perceived to be madness, the charitable societies to which he was attached did not quietly drop his name from their patronage lists; they continued to refer to him as if nothing had happened.

It is not clear what qualities of character charitable officials were looking for in George III's second son, Frederick Augustus, Duke of York (1763–1827); yet he was the president or patron of more than a dozen reputable institutions, including the Lock Hospital, the Refuge for the Destitute in Lambeth, and the London Ophthalmic Infirmary, Moorfields. (He inherited several more from his wife after her death.) He was an active participant in the Royal Jennerian Society, which he helped to survive some difficulties, and the school at the Chelsea Barracks, which he had established for the orphans of soldiers.[110] Anthony Highmore, who dedicated his second volume on London charities to the Duke of York, paid lavish tribute to his 'munificence and condescending affability' on behalf of the Small Pox Hospital.[111] As the Duke had an interview with Jenner in 1800, and introduced inoculation for smallpox into the army in 1804, the disease may be seen as one of his genuine concerns.[112]

Contemporaries tended to generosity when writing about the Duke of York. Charles Greville believed that he had the feelings of an English gentleman.[113] And while Sir Walter Scott admitted that the Duke had 'an imprudent passion for the turf and deep play', he nonetheless claimed that he was 'humane and kindly . . . accessible to the claims of compassion.'[114] How do we square these contemporary remarks with the Duke of York's unhappy reputation in the twentieth-century as 'an idler, a voluptuary, and a knave'?[115] A student of philanthropy assures us that he had 'no recorded moral inclinations' and that his charitable associations were 'mere decoration'.[116] Contemporaries, of course, were far more deferential and inclined to play up any sign of virtue in the behaviour of a member of the royal family, whether justified or not. As suggested, this was especially true of charitable promoters. Highmore was not only a compiler of philanthropic information; he was an official of the Small Pox Hospital patronised by the Duke of York. No one was better placed to recognize the advantages of royal patronage or the perennial need to cultivate benefactors.

Suspicious of philanthropic motives, modern historians are prone to see the Duke of York's charities as simply part of a campaign to tranquillize or to discipline the poor. As suggested, war and revolution, trade depression and high unemployment aroused many would-be philanthropists from their slumbers; and the Duke of York, whose claim to fame as Commander-in-Chief of the army had been to improve discipline, was probably one of them. Against a background of Luddism and domestic unrest, he chaired meetings of associations and funds in 1812 and 1816 to relieve the labouring classes.[117] And he also joined the Mendicity Society, a quasi-police agency which sought to reduce beggary by a mixture of relief and the prosecution of vagrants.[118] Undoubtedly, such projects defended the interests of the propertied classes; but many of those who contributed to them, perhaps even the Duke of York himself, were more sympathetic and less calculating than such a one-dimensional analysis suggests.

The twentieth-century view of the Duke of York and his brothers as heartless and boorish misfits is not out of tune with interpretations encouraged by Queen Victoria's court. The 'wicked uncles' have never recovered from the inclination of Victoria's defenders, especially her advisor Baron Stockmar, to vilify them. Stockmar's policy was to represent the young Queen as a model of *Englishness* and respectability, and he believed, rightly or wrongly, that the background and behaviour of the sons of George III had diminished respect for the monarchy and weakened loyalty to the throne.[119] In the end, Queen Victoria herself referred to her uncles as 'disreputable'.[120] The monarchy jettisoned the royal dukes as unworthy of the great family tradition.

Whatever the failings or the motives of the sons of George III, they made a significant contribution to the expansion of charitable enterprise. Their very number provided a wide choice of potential royal patrons. With the emergence of ever-greater numbers of institutions, it was just as well that George III's family was as large as it was. As more and more societies enlisted the monarchy's support, the reciprocal benefits of royal patronage became increasingly apparent. It offered prestige and financial rewards to charities; it also offered respectability to members of the royal family, not least to the less reputable ones, who were most in need of favourable publicity. Into the bargain, it could be a pretty painless process for all concerned.

To apply for royal patronage, all that a *bona fide* charity needed to do was to draft a letter or petition, preferably backed by someone with a position in the royal household or connections at court. Ladies-in-waiting were very useful allies.[121] Such intermediaries were often instrumental, but during most of George III's reign the King and his family also gave private audiences to supplicants and petitioners. Before the King's loss of eyesight in 1805 and the appointment of a private secretary, there appears to have been greater informality at court, which gave charitable campaigners relatively easy access to the Palace. No documents have survived from the reign of George III, if there ever were any, which lay down the monarchy's policy on royal patronage. During the Regency, the Home Secretary vetted charitable petitions and advised the Prince Regent.[122] In later years the sheer number of applications and weight of correspondence resulted in the implementation of guidelines and more formal procedures.

From the eighteenth century onwards, it was understood that if a charity wanted a royal patron, the duties would be nominal. Charities might expect duties to be performed by royal presidents or vice-presidents. But these were usually light, often enjoyable, and easily acquitted, even by the dimmest of royalty. William Frederick, the Duke of Gloucester (1776–1834), who married his cousin Mary, George III's fourth daughter, was a familiar figure on the charitable circuit. His stupidity, which earned him the nickname 'Silly Billy', proved no great handicap. When asked why he supported the abolition of corporal punishment in the army, he remarked, famously, that 'he had always thought it hard military flogging should be made to fall only on the corporals.' Though pilloried by radicals and royalists alike—Charles Greville pictured him at breakfast and quoted Dryden's 'And lambent dullness plays around his face'—he was rescued for the evangelical cause by Wilberforce, despite his love of the theatre.[123]

A royal evangelical, the Duke of Gloucester found himself attached to over thirty charities, including the London Hospital, the African Institution and the Society for Bettering the Condition and Increasing the Comforts of the Poor.[124] Despite his deficiencies, his contemporaries respected, and perhaps feared, his authority. It is difficult to recapture the expectancy and alarm which the royal dukes excited in their day. After a meeting of the Anti-Slavery Society, Zachary Macaulay chided his son Thomas Babington for folding his arms in the presence of the Duke, who was in the chair.[125] On such occasions, well-wishers briefed and fortified the Duke of Gloucester. At receptions, he honed his conversational skills by repeating stock phrases as each fresh face approached: 'how long have you been here', 'charming weather', or 'very pretty breakfast'.[126] This technique has come in handy to many charitable officials, and not only royal ones.

If the Duke of Gloucester did good work because he could do nothing else, Edward, Duke of Kent (1767–1820), did good work because he had exhausted the alternatives. Stranded in England, his military career frustrated, his political views unpopular, he found little outlet for his talents save charitable work. He devoted his time to charities, as one writer remarked, 'as an anodyne for his disappointment'.[127] Well-spoken, he could make an effective public address; affable, he was good at chairing meetings; sober, he could make a royal toast without sinking under the table. The public generally approved of his charitable rounds, and the radical press, which found his unorthodox opinions agreeable, began to present him 'as a victim of a Palace plot'.[128]

The Duke of Kent was in great demand when a meeting needed chairing or a school needed opening. By the time of his death, he was an active patron, chairman or president of no fewer than fifty-three charities, including the British School of Industry, the Literary Fund for the Relief of Indigent Authors, and, rather ironically, the Loan Society, which assisted gentlemen in financial distress.[129] With more than a hint of Hanoverian thoroughness, he inspected schools, hospitals and orphanages

5. A page from the account book of Edward Duke of Kent, 1814.

in such detail that Thomas Creevey, the political gossip, called him 'tiresome'. Wellington, who despised the Duke of Kent's radicalism, said: 'whenever you start out with any of the royal family in the morning, and particularly *the corporal*, always to breakfast first'.[130]

In 1816, the Duke of Kent attended seventy-two charity meetings.[131] Few men could have had more free dinners. Few men were more in need of them. A man of monumental imprudence, the Duke's finances were in a state of perennial crisis, which his charitable contributions exacerbated. (His wife, the Duchess of Kent, and his daughter, Queen Victoria, eventually paid off his debts.) His account books show a steady stream of subscriptions: thirteen guineas to the City of London Truss Society; ten guineas to the Lock Hospital; fifty guineas to the North London Auxiliary Bible Society.[132] By 1815 he was giving away more than £1,000 a year to charity, nearly a tenth of his income, after he put his finances in the hands of trustees. Still, in 1806 he spent £11,000 on furniture to decorate his Kensington Palace apartments.[133]

The Duke of Kent was well aware of the reciprocal benefits of charity, and what he gave with one hand he borrowed with the other. His philanthropic associations provided him with ample opportunities to pass around his own begging bowl. He chaired meetings of a society to ameliorate the poor set up by his philanthropic friend Robert Owen. Perhaps softened up by royal flattery, Owen proved a ready source of cash and loaned the Duke over £1,000. The Duke of Kent promised to honour his debt, but in the end the utopian socialist lost it all to his 'best disciple'.[134] It is not known whether the Duke of Kent borrowed money from the Quaker philanthropist William Allen, whom he knew through the Royal Lancasterian Association. But he asked him to become his trustee and financial advisor.

Most intriguingly, the wealthy jeweller turned prison reformer, James Neild, loaned the Duke of Kent many thousands of pounds. Neild was the leading light of the Society for the Discharge and Relief of Persons Imprisoned for Small Debts, and, after Howard, the country's foremost expert on prison conditions. The Duke would have been aware of his reputation as a philanthropist, and it is likely that the two men would have come into contact at one charitable venue or another. In any case, the Duke of Kent borrowed heavily from Neild from the 1790s on, as his large interest payments to him show.[135] Perhaps it was this history of royal indebtedness that prompted Neild's son, the recluse and miser John Camden Neild, to leave his fortune to the Duke's daughter, Queen Victoria, in 1852.[136]

As the King's fourth son, and therefore unlikely to ascend the throne, the Duke of Kent was relatively free to express progressive opinions and to join unorthodox societies. Whether he took up radical causes as a revenge on his more dissembling brothers is unclear. At all events, many in his family thought him a tedious crank, and worse, a middle-class crank. Probably better acquainted with social problems than his brothers or most politicians, the Duke of Kent did not believe that charity alone was able to solve the nation's ills; and he flirted with Robert Owen's utopian social schemes. In 1819, he supported a plan, devised by the Manchester philanthropist David Holt, to parcel out crown and waste land to the unemployed. What the government and his family thought of the notion can only be imagined. But they must have known that his radical enthusiasms rarely got beyond the talking stage.[137]

Despite the historical interest in the Duke of Kent because he was the father of Queen Victoria, he remains a shadowy figure, a man whose motives and behaviour are difficult to judge. Princess Lieven, wife of the Russian ambassador, described him as 'false, hard and greedy. His so-called good qualities were only for show'.[138] Others, like Owen, admired him for the 'power and goodness' of his mind.[139] How can such views be reconciled? Perhaps it is fair to say that when the Duke of Kent escaped into the realm of utopian social schemes, as with Owen, he was full of lofty ideas and compassion. But when he had to deal with the realm of everyday existence, as in the army, he inclined to caution and suspicion. There was more than a hint of public safety about his participation in the work for the Royal Lancasterian Association, which he carried off with considerable aplomb.

The Duke of Kent's initial experiments in education had to do with regimental schools. During his army career he had a reputation as a martinet, happy to see his soldiers flogged for leaving their buttons undone.[140] It is probable that his primary aim in setting up schools for the children of soldiers was to inculcate habits of obedience. As Governor of Gibraltar, he had been given the express command to improve discipline in the ranks. He and the Duke of Sussex, introduced to Lancaster by the King, joined the Royal Lancasterian Association, in their words, 'to contribute all in their power by example and influence to the propagation of a system, which could not fail to promote the morals of the people, and also to insure the safety of the nation'.[141]

To judge from their comments and those of contemporaries, their efforts bore fruit. After a visit by the Dukes of Kent and Cambridge to Lancaster's Borough Road School in Southwark, it was reported that their conduct had a powerful effect on the children, 'exciting them to renewed diligence, and tend[ing] to create a bond of affection and loyalty in those of inferior stations, which in future time may render them proof against all seditious influence'.[142] At an outing of Lancasterian schoolchildren in 1818 to commemorate the King's birthday, attended by 4,000 pupils, Sussex remarked that the charity had 'improved discipline and morals of the lower orders'.[143]

Such objectives were not altogether compatible with the views of many of their colleagues in the Royal Lancasterian Association (British and Foreign School Society). Of course, the incongruous collection of royalty, radicals, dissenters and freethinkers who made up the institution had various motives and priorities. At times, they were probably at cross purposes. Francis Place saw the education of poor children as the foundation of working-class dignity and independence. Like him, James Mill, another member of the Committee of the Association, also linked the cause of parliamentary reform with the need for popular education. So did Joseph Hume, a radical MP influenced by Bentham's utilitarianism. Perhaps their views were not incompatible with instilling that 'great lesson' in the minds of the young, 'Fear God and honour the King', which was used as a toast of the Association. But freethinking republicans like Place, who admired the French Revolution for subverting established order, must have found such remarks unsettling.[144]

The importance of royal patronage to the success of the Lancasterian schools and the importance of the schools to the social and political agenda of the radicals were such that Francis Place and others simply had to swallow their criticisms. The institution's promoters proclaimed on more than one occasion that it owed its existence and momentum to royal assistance.[145] Undoubtedly, the King's patronage made an enormous difference; so did the 'Royal Fund', the unpublicized contributions of the royal family which defrayed the cost of training teachers.[146] Lancaster himself told the Prince Regent that 'whatever good I have been doing, thy name, thy Father's name, and the names of all the royal family have been my passports to usefulness—my plans would have been cried down but for your support'.[147]

When a scandal broke out in the Association in 1813, precipitated by Lancaster's bankruptcy and accusations that he was homosexual, the royal family remained loyal to the institution. The Duke of Kent played a crucial role in the proceedings to relaunch the charity under a new name, the British and Foreign School Society.[148] Lancaster himself, his reputation shattered, eventually took up a nomadic life in the Americas. Arguably, royal patronage was fatal to him. It incited him to 'reckless speculation' and excited his enemies, who had previously regarded him only with 'passive disapproval'.[149] He died in 1838, after an accident in a New York street.

Charity, like politics, makes strange bedfellows. One might ask whether the royal presence distorted Joseph Lancaster's objectives. One must ask why so many leading figures from the world of Nonconformity and reform politics supported a 'royal' organization. Francis Place, who took 'more pleasure than was consonant with his republican principles' from rubbing shoulders with royalty, was in little doubt.[150] He thought it 'remarkable' that whenever a meeting of the committee was held in Kensington Palace, a large number of men appeared, even Quakers, who were usually 'so averse to public forms and titles'. The whole scene of 'bustle and parade' as the Dukes arrived, the bowing and scraping, was 'enough to make a dog sick'.[151] Place was not the only one to comment on the social snobbery that permeated philanthropic societies. A French visitor to London in 1816 noted 'l'ostentation et la vanité . . . dans tous ces actes de bienfaisance'.[152]

The Quaker William Allen, who recruited the Duke of Kent to the Association, would have waved away such remarks. He had his own reason for cultivating the monarchy, and he put his finger on it when he admitted that if he were to be a successful philanthropist he needed royal patronage.[153] The scramble for the favour of George III and members of his family was not all social climbing and empty glitter, though that was often part of it. By the end of the eighteenth century, the message radiated: the royal touch could nurture a new charity or revive a flagging one as if by magic. There were few philanthropists unwilling to bow and scrape in order to advance their own programmes, which they believed to be of unquestionable and overriding social worth.

Links between the monarchy and charitable institutions were not invariably popular, especially among rival agencies which did not have them. In the early nineteenth century, high-church Anglicans took umbrage at royal support for Nonconformist and evangelical societies. Windsor churchmen reacted with alarm when Lancaster turned up in their town with a scheme to establish a school locally. The Dean, appalled by the idea, told him to mind his own business. Undaunted, Lancaster went to the castle and asked for an audience with the King. As it transpired, George III supported Lancaster against the local Anglicans, but advised him not to 'tease' them.[154] It should be remembered that George III's belief that poor children in his dominions should be able to read the Bible was thought dangerous and 'levelling' by many churchmen.

The battle between Protestant factions in the reign of George III, each believing it had a special historic mission, was as bitter as the infighting associated with sectarian socialism in later years. Members of the royal family had to tread warily or risk being caught in the crossfire. The high-church party was particularly hostile to the dissenting connections of the Dukes of Kent and Sussex. The editor of the *Anti-Jacobin Review* once warned them that they should 'never forget the principles which seated their family on the throne of these realms'.[155] Unhappy with the monarchy's attachment to Joseph Lancaster's schools, the Archbishop of Canterbury took the Duke of Kent aside and told him so. He also disapproved of the Duke's enthusiasm for the Bible Society, an institution which was 'antagonistic' to the older Society for Promoting Christian Knowledge. 'He that is not with us is against us,' pronounced the Archbishop.[156]

There was an element of sour grapes in the reaction of the high-church party to the monarchy's association with evangelical missionary work and Nonconformist education. Assiduous promoters like Lancaster and Wilberforce had scooped the royal field for their charitable causes. Their rivals had to catch up. In the history of charity it is not uncommon for one royal society to trigger the creation of another. By such means the monarchy maintains a balanced portfolio of benevolent causes. Ultimately, the royal family's support for the Lancasterian schools encouraged the promotion of a rival Anglican charity, which appeared in 1811 as the National Society for Promoting the Education of the Poor in the Principles of the Established Church.

The monarchy quickly granted the National Society royal patronage, in the form of the Prince Regent, who had previously been an advocate of Joseph Lancaster.[157] In a gesture of consummate diplomacy, several members of the royal family, including the Prince Regent and the Dukes of York, Cumberland and Cambridge, donated thousands of pounds to the institution.[158] Meanwhile, the King and the Dukes of Kent and Sussex maintained their links with the British and Foreign School Society. In 1813, Kent and the Archbishop of Canterbury attempted to unite dissenters, Catholics and Church of England children in a single school, but the scheme was aborted.[159] Whichever of the two charities could claim greater royal favour, the monarchy's patronage of education produced what was probably the most beneficial charitable work of the reign. Between them, the National Society and the British and Foreign School Society had over 145,000 pupils in their schools by 1820.[160] In later years, they provided the seedbed for government interest in education.

★   ★   ★

If the monarchy was a priceless, highly polished tool for philanthropists, the charitable agencies were becoming a more and more useful implement for the monarchy as well. Apart from the respectability and visibility which charitable associations provided, they put members of the royal family in touch with contemporary issues and opinion. In some fields, such as in education, philanthropic activity gave the monarchy real influence in reform movements. In the anti-slavery campaign, members of the royal family earned favourable notices for simple expressions of support, though the Duke of Clarence once defended slavery in the House of Lords as 'congenial to the manners, laws, and customs of Africa'.[161] In 1814, the Prince Regent, in a reply to an address of the House of Commons, announced that the country could rely on his 'unremitting exertions to give effect to your views for the abolition of the slave trade'. Thomas Clarkson, the anti-slavery agitator, extracted what propaganda value he could from the remark: 'in this great question of humanity, justice, and religion, the whole nation, including its rulers, may be found to be but one people.'[162]

By publicly identifying the monarchy with popular causes such as education and anti-slavery, charitable patronage reaffirmed the royal family's importance. This was of no small significance at a time when the monarchy's capacity to influence politics through money, contracts and favours was under attack as costly and corrupt. Unlike the patronage of placemen, the patronage of worthy causes did not much foster republicanism, rather the reverse. On the social front, the monarchy retained its traditional allegiances to aristocratic society, and in the wake of royal patronage many an aristocrat discovered charity's allure. But through its support of worthy causes the monarchy was becoming a mouthpiece for middle-class values, and it served as a resplendent focus for respectable opinion across a wide social spectrum.

With its more popular members, the Dukes of Kent and Sussex, in the spotlight, the monarchy was even able to claim a progressive middle-class constituency. Royal support for Lancaster's experimental schools, for example, forged links with advanced opinion, while promoting wider loyalty to the throne. The publicity and public adulation which the monarchy received in return for patronage was often out of all proportion to the energy expended. One is reminded of the public dinner when an MP pronounced that in England, unlike abroad, 'you see Princes of the Blood Royal, dining in public, and seating by their side, and treating with all condescension, a poor man [Lancaster], an individual of obscure origin, who had merely rendered himself conspicuous by his attentions to the poorest children of the land'.[163] One is then reminded of the 4,000 charity children, pupils of Lancasterian schools, who gathered on Highbury Tavern lawn some years later and cried 'Hear! Hear!' when the Duke of Sussex returned the toast 'Fear God and Honour the King'.[164] We shall never know how many of these children carried royalist sentiments into the Empire in later years.

The monarchy reaped considerable advantage from its growing charitable role. And those philanthropists who had so assiduously recruited members of the royal family to their causes were eager to elaborate the point. Some of them hailed the crown as a cornerstone of a new moral constitution. Recalling the charities of the Duke of Kent, Wilberforce pronounced that they 'softened' the glare of royalty, 'confirmed' attachment to the throne, and 'manifested' new benefits to the British constitution. 'Princes strike out for themselves a road', he concluded, 'which has now become well worn with many tracks on it, all in the same direction, and all leading alike to esteem, public benefit, and individual comfort.'[165] He might have added that through philanthropy princes promoted the general good without attaching themselves to political factions. The Duke of Kent declared at a festival dinner that 'true charity is of no particular party, but is the cause of all parties'.[166]

Anthony Highmore, in the rhetorical style favoured by royalists, argued that 'the munificence and liberality of princes . . . forms the chief lustre that irradiates their Crown, and transmits their names with honour to posterity. The numerous channels by which they may diffuse the sources of public good, afford them incalculable returns for the just estimate of their glory; and the proudest blazonry upon their banners does not more expand their fame than the exercise of their beneficence for the welfare of their people.'[167] The Manchester radical David Holt, whose own Lancasterian school received royal patronage, wrote to the Duke of Kent in 1819: 'I never see a public charity advertized when the names of thyself and any other Branches of the Royal Family appear but I feel the name of Briton dignified and exalted, and I cannot but exclaim, truly these deserve the people's love.'[168] Philanthropists not only believed that royal patronage afforded 'incalculable returns' to the monarchy, but they were beginning to identify it with British greatness.

We should not assume that members of the royal family themselves believed that their charities were so vital to the standing of the monarchy and the nation. They were little attuned to such sentiments in the early nineteenth century, despite their extensive philanthropic contacts. For their part, George III and Queen Charlotte were well aware that good works made a favourable impression on the public, but they did not dwell on the benefits that accrued to the monarchy from charitable attachments. Nor did their circle of aristocratic allies and advisors, whose thoughts centred on the whirl of society, high politics and foreign affairs. As Lord Esher, the influential royal advisor, commented a century later: 'the attitude of faith towards the beneficent influence of the sovereign power was a new thing, unregarded by the statesmen of the House of Hanover.'[169] Still, the accumulation of royal patronages in the reign of George III had transformed the monarchy's traditional charitable role out of all recognition. The royal family, with little forethought, had become allied with ascendant middle England—respectable and patriotic.

2

George IV and William IV: The Bonds of Civil Society

T he reign of George IV is widely seen as something of an aberration in the history of the monarchy, a blip in the popularity of kingship in Britain. Whether the King was the 'selfish, unfeeling dog' of Greville's imagination, or simply a misguided profligate redeemed by charm and taste is a matter of opinion.[1] No one doubts that, compared to George III or Queen Victoria, George IV was foolish. The neglect of his duty gave him more time to adorn his person, but it did little to protect the crown's prerogatives, which diminished over his reign. His personal failings and political vagaries, along with reckless spending, not only weakened the reputation of the crown, but promoted the growth of cabinet government. As conventional wisdom has it, the reign thus marked another step in the development of a constitutional monarchy. With hindsight, George IV's very deficiencies may be seen as a perverse defence of the constitution.

George IV was a *poseur* who looked back to the heroic age of kingship and longed for glory. But the political and military ground had been cut from under his feet. Like monarchs elsewhere, he put on fancy dress and full regalia and had the painters in to convince himself that he was part of a great tradition. His enemies found his wardrobe empty. Certainly he sported few of those sober fashions that suited the measurements of royalty by the 1820s. But as the monarchy had aligned itself with respectable opinion in the reign of George III, George IV covered his nakedness with a fig leaf of charity. For all his princely *hauteur*, the dissolute King did not have the audacity to ignore the suffering of others. Like the rest of his family, he had contracted a chronic case of *noblesse oblige*.

The King's relations with civil society, that array of voluntary institutions outside government control, were, unlike his relations with ministers, untroubled. And they were much more congenial than might be expected, given his reputation as a libertine untouched by religious impulses. The reformation in manners and morals taking place in the country made his errant behaviour look all the more reprehensible. But religious reformers and charitable campaigners drew on the deep well of Christian forgiveness where the monarchy was concerned. Just as those with an eye to what the court could do for their causes were reluctant to criticize the behaviour of the Duke of Cumberland, they overlooked George IV's indiscretions, while praising him to the heavens for small favours. William Wilberforce, who typified their attitude, combined 'an unexpressed condemnation' of George IV's vices with 'perfect respect for his office'.[2] Hannah More was well aware of the King's immorality but at his accession preferred to write of his 'unimpeachable honour', 'royal liberality' and devotion to 'the helpless and homeless'.[3]

Contrary to Greville's opinion that George IV had no 'good feeling', the King often showed consideration for others and was given to spontaneous acts of charity. He dutifully fulfilled what he saw as his financial obligations to Palace servants in reduced circumstances, many of them former employees of George III.[4] The Keeper of the Privy Purse, Sir William Knighton, once remarked that George IV's private benevolence was unrivalled, but perhaps he was thinking of the King's generosity to his family. Given the capacity of his brothers to run up debts, George IV's charity had to begin at home, and he directed much of his largesse to his relations.[5]

But the King was also merciful to prisoners, a patron of artists, including Beethoven, and a friend to widows, orphans, and Mrs Arbuthnot's family.[6] In 1825, he contributed £3,000 to the poor of Spitalfields, who had earlier received royal donations of £5,000.[7] Given his love of the theatre, the King also had a soft spot for thespians. On one occasion, a characteristic 'charitable impulse', to use his words, induced him to offer a pension to the impoverished actor John O'Keeffe.[8] Writers too received special favour, for he gave the Literary Fund for Indigent Authors £5,000 over twenty-five years.[9] Arguably, George IV's greatest act of beneficence was the gift of George III's library to the British Museum, although it was said that he had originally intended to sell it to the highest bidder.[10] As his republican critics might have said, the King was good at giving things away that he had not paid for.

The documentary records of George IV's charitable payments are patchy. Given the unpredictable nature of his benevolence his annual financial contribution to philanthropic causes is difficult to estimate. As Prince of Wales, he had subscribed £1,261 to twenty-three charities in one year in the 1790s.[11] By the end of his reign, the number of his patronages had doubled to nearly fifty.[12] Like the rest of his family, he was generous to educational charities. In 1822, the royal family contributed over half the income of the National Society for Promoting the Education of the Poor.[13] Most of the King's donations, however, were modest, usually between £20 and £105 annually. (His hairdresser received £150.)[14] As King, his annual contribution to *institutions* was

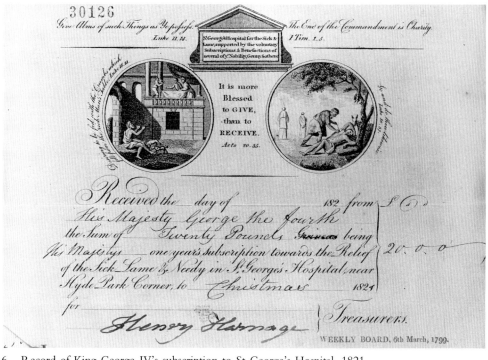

30126

Give Alms of such Things as Ye possess.
Luke 11.41.

St George's Hospital for the Sick &
Lame, supported by the voluntary
Subscriptions & Benefactions of
several of ye Nobility, Gentry & others

The End of the Commandment is Charity.
1 Tim. 1.5.

It is more
Blessed
to GIVE,
than to
RECEIVE.
Acts 20.35.

Received the   day of   182 from £
His Majesty George the fourth
the Sum of   *Twenty Pounds* being
His Majesty's   one year's subscription towards the Relief   20   0   0
of the Sick, Lame & Needy in St George's Hospital near
Hyde Park Corner, to   Christmas   1821
for
        Henry Harnage   } *Treasurers.*

WEEKLY BOARD, 6th March, 1799.

6. Record of King George IV's subscription to St George's Hospital, 1821.

probably between £3,000 and £4,000, though royal tours and exceptional payments added considerably to the figure in some years.

One writer put the cost of the King's 'charities', including donations to individuals, at £17,000 in 1829. This sum was comparable to the annual charitable contributions of George III, although it seems a modest outlay when we consider that George IV spent £326,000 on furnishings and repairs and £40,000 on horses and stabling in the same year.[15] But his subscriptions, though less than the amount he spent on curtains, 'were like the china eggs planted in a nest to encourage the hen to lay'.[16] The societies assisted had every reason to be grateful to the King, however small his donations. He would not have agreed with his father's remark that charitable distributions 'alone make the station bearable', but he was conscious of the benefits they bestowed on the recipients, whose lives or societies were often transformed by royal favour.[17]

As the pinnacle of the charitable establishment, the King accepted the associated duties, though it must be said that they were largely nominal, which made them all the more agreeable to him. Still, he befriended leading philanthropists like Joseph Lancaster, the educational reformer, and Richard 'Humanity' Martin, a founder of the Society for the Prevention of Cruelty to Animals. In 1823, he issued the first in a series of

7. The head of George IV, engraved by William Wyon, on the Royal National Life-boat Institution's medal for gallantry, 1824.

'Royal Letters' in aid of the National Society for Promoting the Education of the Poor. Read out in churches and chapels throughout England and Wales, it brought in £28,000.[18] As patron of the Royal National Life-boat Institution, established in 1824, he encouraged life-boat design and permitted his head to be engraved on the society's silver medal.[19] (In a hierarchical society, the humble subject looked on a royal medal with the same respect as a magnate looked on a peerage.) The King also condescended to support less well-established agencies and supplicants. Some represented mutual aid or trade societies rather than charities; the bucklemakers of Birmingham, for example, once asked for his help in combating the 'dangerous innovation of shoe-strings'.[20]

Applications for royal favour bombarded the Palace from all sides. They arrived on behalf of blind clerks and chimney sweeps; on behalf of cottagers in need of coals; and on behalf of institutions, from the London Episcopal Floating Church Society to the Marine School, Mounts Bay, Cornwall, which educated the orphans of sailors, 'to keep them in some order on the Sabbath'.[21] The Secretary of the King's Free School in Kew, which received a 'kind intercession' of £300, wrote a telling note to Sir William Knighton in 1826: 'The present times are full of those excellent fruits of the most noble and generous charity which have sprung from the throne; and if any thing were wanting to excite the loyalty of the subject, the unprecedented benevolence and munificence of our most gracious monarch, could not fail to make us "love, honor, and obey the King, and all that are put in authority under him".'[22]

George IV was well aware that the 'sunshine' of royal charity, as one petitioner put it, illuminated the giver as well as warmed the recipient, and he carried forward most of the charitable associations that had been built up in George III's reign. Although he took over his father's patronage list, most of the charities he accumulated were his own, including several in Brighton.[23] None of them did more to highlight the monarchy's benevolent offices than the patriotic Royal National Life-boat Institution. The charity might never have been initiated by its founder, Sir William Hillary, had he not had an entrée at court as Equerry of the Duke of Sussex.[24] Hillary obtained permission to dedicate the pamphlet which launched the institution to George IV. With the King in tow, others came on board, including five royal dukes and Prince Leopold.[25]

Apart from his support for life-boats, schools, chimney sweeps, orphanages, and Masonic institutions, George IV expanded the royal family's tradition of hospital patronage. At least seventeen hospitals appeared on his books by 1830, all but two of them in London. He took over the Foundling Hospital and St George's from his father, Westminster Hospital from his mother, and added, among others, the Seamen's Hospital in Greenwich and the Royal Metropolitan Dispensary for Children. The latter must have had an especial appeal, for it was consecrated to the memory of his daughter, Princess Charlotte. Not every hospital which applied to him for patronage succeeded. In 1830 he turned down a request from an 'Institution for the Cure of Cataract' because he was already a patron of the Eye Infirmary in Cork Street.[26]

One type of institution favoured by George IV was the benefit society, which represented one of the fastest growing forms of voluntary activity in the early nineteenth century. Philanthropy operates within classes as well as between them, and scores of pension and benefit societies were emerging in Britain, which catered to a wide range of applicants, from tradesmen to old Etonians. As institutions, they merged with traditions of self-help and mutual aid. Most of them provided annual grants to those in reduced circumstances who had fallen from familial grace. Typically, they specialized in particular employments and localities, such as the widows of medical men in the metropolis or distressed tradesmen and manufacturers in Leeds. A few, like the National Benevolent Institution (1812), later patronized by Queen Adelaide, provided pensions to a wider range of applicant, from superannuated governesses to decayed gentry.[27]

In a new departure for a British monarch, George IV added at least eight such institutions to his patronage list, including the Artists' Benevolent Fund, the Masonic Benefit Society, and the Benefit Society of St Patrick. Eventually, the extension of royal patronage to these bodies helped to offset the loss of royal influence brought about by the reduction in the number of crown pensioners. Benefit societies were an example of the capacity of citizens to protect their own interests in response to changes in the social economy. Many of them saw the advantage of inviting the monarchy to help them along. Here, as elsewhere in the voluntary world, the royal family found common cause with the middle classes and was drawn ever more deeply into their worries and aspirations.

Like his father before him, George IV supplemented his formal patronages by public displays of benevolence on his tours. Horse-drawn transport circumscribed the number of royal trips possible, but in 1789, a few days after the outbreak of the French Revolution, he had visited York as Prince of Wales. There he distributed £200 for the relief of debtors and £50 among several charities.[28] (The sons of George III had an understandable weakness for debtors.) As King he visited Dublin in 1821, the first visit by a sovereign of the House of Hanover to Ireland. As part of the royal ritual, he dispensed £1,400 to a host of the city's charities, an act of royal condescension which attracted, and was meant to attract, the attention of the press and the public.[29]

On the King's departure from Dublin, champagne and sovereigns showered on spectators. When he entered the royal barge, one reporter marvelled that 'to those on land he appeared to be walking on water'. A deranged woman, whose son had been convicted of robbery and sentenced to death, followed His Majesty into the water, but was unable to walk. After her rescue, the King enquired into her case and on hearing the particulars, 'with a well timed humanity, was pleased to extend his mercy to the culprit'.[30] Arguably, George IV was more mawkish than humane. But in an age when a man could be hanged for stealing a sheep or picking a pocket, the scope for mercy was inexhaustible. The King exploited his capacity to forgive.

In 1822, George IV made a successful tour of Scotland. When it comes to the monarchy, it seems that seeing is believing. One eye-witness commented on the 'line of pale faces, with expectation wound up to actual pain, and a sort of bewildered smile on their first glimpse of that being called a king—Britain's king—Scotland's king—their own king'![31] In between visits to the theatre, the King played the philanthropist. When he entered the Church of St Giles he handed over a sealed packet containing £100, with the words that it should be used for the benefit of the poor.[32] Such public demonstrations of benevolence, at relatively little cost, added to the magical effect of the monarchy on the public. One account of the tour ended with the tribute: 'We do not profess to have obtained information of all the charitable acts of His Majesty during his residence in Scotland; and it is probable that many of these will never become known to the public; but his munificent donations to the different charitable institutions of the city, will long endear him to the citizens of Edinburgh.'[33] Like other monarchs, George IV was able to inspire a belief in his philanthropy without providing much evidence for it.

By means of royal tours the monarchy embraced provincial Britain and extended its reputation for benevolence into communities distant from the capital. After George IV's visit to Edinburgh, the local Society for the Relief of the Destitute Sick wrote to thank him for his patronage, and children from the city's Asylum for the Deaf and Dumb praised his acts of charity in letters to the Palace.[34] Such contacts were more significant than they might appear, for in the 1820s royal societies remained concentrated in the capital. Outside London, philanthropic links with the monarchy were on the rise, but they depended largely on royal tours and great institutions like the Bible Society and the National Society for Promoting the Education of the Poor, which had local associations and affiliated churches and chapels dotted across the country.

Dislike of London rule was intense in provincial Britain, not least among the independent citizenry who gave philanthropy its impetus. The King's patronage was much sought after and taken to be a testimonial of the highest quality. His support for local causes did not suggest political interference from London, but simply the goodwill of the sovereign. This was all the more apparent as the monarchy was becoming less and less identified with party faction and political power. Provincial citizens could admire the King and link the fortunes of their communities to his own while continuing to be chary of central government. And like their counterparts in the capital, they could admire the monarchy without admiring the monarch.

If philanthropists treasured the King, or said they did, many of those outside the patronage system abhorred his politics and extravagance. Some of them did not separate the throne from its inhabitant and turned their venom on the monarchy itself. In their view, royal philanthropy was a deceit played on a gullible public by an anachronistic institution. They could draw on a tradition of radical dissent, which, as we have seen in the case of Thomas Paine and Orator Hunt, associated monarchical charity with self-interest and the subordination of the poor. If Paine thought George III a 'parasite' living in 'luxurious indolence', one can imagine the fury that George IV aroused in the radical camp.[35]

The propagandist John Wade, a scourge of aristocratic privilege and royal patronage, took up the banner in the reign of George IV. A disciple of Jeremy Bentham, Wade believed that the object of government was the greatest happiness at the least expense. Instead, Britain had a bloated monarchy which had created a 'beggarly greatness, an absurd system in an impoverished population'.[36] Contemptuous of the charitable enthusiasms of the establishment, Wade denounced the philanthropy of George IV as mere 'ostentation' under the pretext of mitigating the sufferings of the poor.[37] More pointedly, he saw the crown as the premier beneficiary of the nation's charity, a view which had much to recommend it, although he did not fathom its complexities. He was in his element when he got wind of a controversial case in the Court of Chancery. In his will, a Mr Troutback had left nearly £100,000 for the purpose of building an orphan hospital and a charity school in London, but the court found legal difficulties, and as the testator had no next of kin, it set aside the will and awarded the money to the crown, which, according to Wade, used it to defray debts on the Brighton Pavilion.[38]

By retailing such information Wade and his radical allies hoped to isolate the monarchy from respectable opinion and foment a desire for reform. But their attacks on the crown probably did more to isolate radical opinion from the charitable establishment. In denouncing privilege, they wrapped themselves in utilitarian virtue and moralized in a manner worthy of Hannah More. By seeing only the trappings and the abuses, they little appreciated how entrenched the monarchy had become in civil society, for reasons other than handouts to placemen. Rarely seeing beneath the surface, they innocently believed that the absurdity of the monarchy would be revealed once and for all by the compilation of a few embarrassing facts. They cursed the 'titled mendicants' in the Palace, but without any understanding of royal philanthropy and its reciprocal benefits. It might have been wiser for them to have introduced George IV to Bentham's ideas on the diminishing marginal utility of money: that is, the better off one is, the less one derives additional happiness from additional income.[39]

Where radicals saw abuses, the beneficiaries of royal philanthropy saw possibilities; consequently they forgave George IV's profligacy and forgot his marriage. The Coronation in the summer of 1821 was a test case. Not every town showed enthusiasm for the event, but as in the celebrations surrounding the fiftieth anniversary of George III's reign, a wave of philanthropic sentiment and civic pride rose up. It lifted the King's reputation upwards like a lifeboat. In communities across the kingdom, children were fêted, hospital and workhouse inmates feasted, charities founded, and subscriptions raised for a host of causes. (George IV opened his reign with the gift of a piece of land on Dartmoor for the protection of the homeless.)[40] Existing charitable institutions sought to cash in on the occasion. Perhaps the grandest event was a music festival in Westminster Abbey under the 'special patronage of His Majesty', which boasted a galaxy of the nobility and a host of distinguished performers. The proceeds went to re-building Westminster Hospital.[41]

The festivities and acts of charity organized by civic leaders often consisted of lighting bonfires and plying citizens with free food and drink, in the hope of inducing loyalty to King, country and themselves. Not all the celebrations were smooth sailing. At Carlisle, for instance, 'Sir John Barleycorn and successive libations to his and His Majesty's honour were promised to all who were desirous of pouring them down; and not a few, it was expected, would rapturously rush to the feast, their minds swelling with loyalty as their bodies were distended with beer'. But on the day, a body of radicals 'refused to taste a drop of the beer or a crumb of the bread that were so generously provided for them'. Instead, the more violent among them 'crowned an ass'. Taking Queen Caroline's side in that great royal showdown, the Coronation, they cried 'The Queen—the Queen'. The military, half-intoxicated, did little to calm the proceedings, which deteriorated into a riot.[42]

Readers of royal biography may be forgiven for assuming that there were more celebrations at George IV's death than at his Coronation. Few have seen the reign as glorious, despite the King's charm, taste and love of pageantry. He was too idle or too bored by politics to defend the crown's prerogatives and was consequently unable to take the measure of his ministers. The most significant political reform in the 1820s, Catholic Emancipation, was carried out against his opposition. Many of his subjects had imbibed the anti-royal doggerel of 'Peter Pindar' or the caricatures of Gillray, which described him as the fatuous Prince playing with a yo-yo or 'a voluptuary under the horrors of digestion'. Perhaps most damaging to his reputation, and the reputation of the monarchy, was his calamitous marriage, and the abortive attempt to divorce Queen Caroline after his accession.

Out of touch politically, and sensitive about his bulk, the King spent his final years in retirement, having rid himself, as Elizabeth Longford put it, 'of all his better qualities except good taste'.[43] One of the last images of the King was of his mistress, the rapacious Lady Conyngham, crawling out of the King's cottage by the back stairs with her 'ill-gotten gains'.[44] At his death, George IV received notices that would have killed a production in the West End. The Duke of Wellington, who despised him, laid a transparent wash of hypocrisy over his 'tribute' in the House of Lords. The article published in *The Times* after the funeral suggests a monarch unregretted by his subjects, who had to pick up the bill for his extravagance: 'Nothing more remains to be said about George IV but to pay, as pay we must, for his profusion.'[45]

Perhaps something more may be said, for the notices from charitable campaigners and clerics were rather more generous than those of *The Times*. They illustrate that George IV had supporters outside conventional politics, who, if they did not grieve excessively over his death, had reason to lament his passing. Philanthropists with connections at court, uncritical to the last, eulogized the King for his generosity and 'characteristic benevolence'.[46] The officials of the Society for the Promotion of Christian Knowledge, who once received a small subscription from George IV, sent a public message of condolence to the new King 'on the death of our late Most Gracious Sovereign, whose paternal attention of the welfare of his people will be remembered to the latest generations with gratitude and affection'.[47]

In their sermons on the death of George IV, clerics tended to drift into biblical exegesis for want of qualities to praise, but they did find the King's charities a subject worthy of encomium. The Reverend Robert Crawford Dillon, a preacher at the Asylum for Female Orphans, an institution with a long royal pedigree, chided the King for his choice of friends, but warmed to his humanity: 'Everything . . . that tended to the welfare of the people whom he governed received his prompt and permanent approval.'[48] Another churchman found the King wanting in religious character, but applauded his 'tender humanity', for which 'he deserved the unqualified admiration of all his subjects'.[49]

The philanthropists and the divines were speaking on behalf of the many citizens who had some personal experience or nodding acquaintance with the benevolence of George IV. We should not forget the many activists in royal institutions, whose work the King made possible or extended. Nor should we underestimate the number of direct recipients of his charity. In the National Society for Promoting the Education of the Poor alone there were 3,678 schools by 1830, with 346,000 scholars in attendance. Without the financial and promotional contribution of George IV and his family, the rapid expansion of charity schools would have been inconceivable, as the National Society's officials were happy to admit.[50] The pupils themselves were reminded of the monarchy's role in their education at church services and Sunday schools, annual festivals and royal birthdays.

Royal charities rarely let their supporters or charges forget their debt to the monarchy. One has only to look at the reception given to the mention of George IV's name at annual charity meetings. The officials of the Royal Humane Society 'for the Recovery of Persons who are supposed Dead of Drowning', which saved 100 people a year through artificial respiration, toasted his health with hearty enthusiasm only a few weeks before his death.[51] If royal institutions took a decidedly uncritical view of George IV, so did innumerable subscribers, who took pride in seeing their contributions publicly displayed on a list headed by the King. Few innovations taking hold over George IV's lifetime returned such dividends to the monarchy as the patronage list.

Charitable citizens committed to voluntary principles were forming a new and expanding constituency for the crown, which would prove of immense value to the monarchy in the wake of political reform in the 1830s. In return, the crown was giving the growing voluntary sector a sense of identity and pride, for even the most tenuous royal association was a sign of respectability and status to philanthropic campaigners. Not surprisingly, they refused to bite the hand that fed them, even one as unsteady as George IV's. They took what advantage they could from the

8. Patrons of the Society of Friends of Foreigners in Distress, 1825.

King's death, briefly draped themselves in mourning, and moved on to William IV, who received a spate of begging letters.

★　★　★

'Look at that Idiot!', George IV once said about his brother, the Duke of Clarence, 'they will remember me, if ever he is in my place.'[52] The prediction proved inexact, for, as King, William enjoyed a better reputation than his predecessor, despite his boorishness and lack of education. Philip Ziegler, the King's finest biographer, argues rather too neatly that 'he inherited a monarchy in tatters, he bequeathed to his heir the securest throne in Europe'.[53] Such praise would seem to fit uneasily with the image of a King without subtlety or vision, and who, in Wellington's opinion, did not even have any serious interests or opinions.[54] But

48

William IV's admirers are not put off by such criticism. Indeed, they celebrate his very deficiencies. One early biographer remarked that the King was 'peculiarly fitted to supply the British Empire with a monarch', for he had 'no capacity for public business, and little inclination to interfere in it'.[55] Such a comment tells us something about Anglo-Saxon attitudes as well as the state of the crown by the 1830s.

Perhaps it is because so little was expected of him that the King's defenders have amplified his role in the legislation that reshaped the constitution during the early years of his reign. In their view, nothing did more to alter William IV's reputation as a loose cannon than his 'negative virtues' in dealing with the passage of the Reform Bill. The King, haunted by the spectre of the French Revolution, found any idea of political reform alarming. He opposed the reduction in his pension list because he saw it as a move towards democracy.[56] But in the agitation for reform he had little room for manoeuvre; and being less obstructive than George IV, he took refuge in delay, in the hope of encouraging reaction. In the end, he reluctantly did his duty by promising to create enough peers to carry the Reform Bill through Parliament. As every student of British history knows, the act made more rational what had been a corrupt political system and extended the franchise to the middle classes, though partly 'as a prophylactic against demand from the people below them'.[57]

Whatever plaudits may be due to William IV for giving way to reform, the establishment survived the crisis and turned to building a new constituency. It is often said that in politics after 1832, 'things were really not so different after all'.[58] To many constitutional experts, including Queen Victoria, the monarch's role as head of state in a parliamentary system remained ill-defined. But after the Reform Act things would never be quite the same for the monarchy. The power of the crown had been in decline for decades because of the failings of successive monarchs and because of administrative reforms which had gradually reduced the sinecures and favours it had at its disposal to sway parliamentary affairs. But the widening of the franchise and the elimination of rotten and nomination boroughs by the Reform Act virtually ended its political influence through traditional forms of patronage and honours.[59]

The crown's inability to play a decisive part in choosing ministers after 1832 set the seal on cabinet government. But just as importantly, the act brought a new element into the political equation by its recognition of the power of the middle classes. The extension of the franchise meant that public opinion would have to be taken much more seriously. Politicians had to work harder for votes, for placating new middle-class electors was now imperative. Die-hard Tories predicted the rule of shopkeepers, the collapse of ancient institutions, and the disintegration of deference to the crown. But the monarchy still had much to play for, despite the erosion of its political authority. It stood to benefit as never before from an alliance with the middle classes.

One effect of the Reform Act was to encourage middle- and upper-class alliances in support of British institutions. The monarchy's capacity to influence parliamentary politics through political patronage was negligible after 1832, but its longstanding institutional patronages were money in the bank. It had lost in the high-political struggle, but it had everything to gain in social esteem and influence through further investment in the nation's civil institutions. As far as one can tell, the monarchy did not explicitly make the connection between the Reform Act and its patronage of middle-class voluntary bodies. But after 1832, the royal family's support for popular causes and reputable societies became much more important. It was the most uncontentious way for the monarchy to develop in the changing political and social atmosphere.

Fortunately for the monarchy, William IV had a deserved reputation for generosity, albeit of an erratic character. As a young naval officer, he was given to spasms of compassion and sometimes picked penniless waifs off the streets and set them up for life. On one occasion he put two poor boys into service at the Captain's table.[60] On another, he found an orphan, Albert Doyer, in Plymouth, paid for his clothes and education, and sent him into the Navy as a midshipman. Years later, he signed his commission as a rear admiral.[61] Many such examples of William IV's spontaneous benevolence have been recounted by his biographers, and the retelling suggests that nothing adds greater glamour to royal philanthropy than its unpredictability.[62]

Though he did not have the extensive charitable contacts of his brothers, the Dukes of Cambridge, Kent and Sussex, William IV nevertheless accumulated an impressive list of institutional associations. As early as 1801, when Duke of Clarence, he became a joint-president, with the Prince of Wales, of the Royal Naval Asylum.[63] Soon after, he added the Royal Jennerian Society, the Choral Fund, the Westminster General Dispensary and the Rupture Society. In the 1820s, he began to appear more often in the chair at annual meetings and took on several more patronages, including the Royal National Life-boat Institution. As a 'subscribing member' of the Society for the Promotion of Christian Knowledge, he presided at a meeting of the institution in 1827. He later said that he had hoodwinked the bishops about his views on Catholic Emancipation; for their part, the bishops took what advantage they could from his address, celebrated his visit in the Society's reports and made an appeal for his continued support.[64]

William IV's willingness to become identified with philanthropic causes can be explained partly by his marriage, in 1818, to the dutiful Princess Amelia Adelaide of Saxe-Meiningen. (What would George IV's reputation be had he had such a wife?) It can also be explained by the number of deaths in the royal family—Queen Charlotte in 1818, George III and the Duke of Kent in 1820—which put pressure on the survivors. Between them, the deceased had been associated with nearly a hundred institutions, all of which were eager to find royal replacements. The 1820s may be seen as the first decade in which the possibility of running out of royalty became a source of anxiety in the charitable sector.

Apart from his routine patronage work, William IV performed charitable duties and distributed sums of money on his tours. As Duke of Clarence he was the first member of the royal family to go down a coal pit, but whether it was out of sympathy for the miners or the owners is unclear.[65] On a trip to Portsmouth in 1827, as Lord High Admiral, he took time off from the usual round of inspections to visit the local hospital. It was on this occasion that he addressed the corporation of the borough and made the intriguing remark that 'as an Englishman, he was most warmly a friend to the institutions of the country, and amongst the most respectable and interesting of which were Corporations like the present—the guardians of the People's civil rights'.[66] The speeches of William IV were often inept, but here he was quite acute, celebrating the rights of citizens and suggesting that they depended on institutions which prided themselves on their independence from central government.

In keeping with the orthodoxies of political economy, the monarchy, like its allies in the voluntary sector, did not pressure the government to expand its responsibility in the social sphere. When the New Poor Law of 1834 swept away the former system of poor relief in favour of centralized administration and the workhouse test, its intention was to discipline the pauper and spare the ratepayer. Behind the act of 1834 was an assumption that public assistance was incompatible with market economics and consequently must be kept within narrowly defined limits. In private remarks to a minister from Paisley, William IV showed himself to be in general sympathy with the act.[67] Yet it had an ambiguous meaning for the monarchy and philanthropists. By abolishing outdoor relief in favour of the workhouse it helped to clarify the boundaries between charity and state assistance; and by reducing the rates it stimulated charitable activity. But it weakened the powers of the localities and undermined the role of religion in social policy, which was a blow to paternalists.[68]

Historians, perhaps taking their cue from early nineteenth-century radicals, have been critical of the monarchy's apparent lack of understanding of the nation's social problems and its failure to promote a more active role for government in tackling the causes of distress.[69] The apparent social myopia of George IV and William IV make them easy targets. But such criticism ignores the prevailing assumptions about the proper limits of government responsibility in the first half of the nineteenth century, which the New Poor Law of 1834 typified. Moreover, it underestimates just how valued organized charity had become in the public mind. Philanthropists pioneered innovative social schemes when government had neither the capacity nor the will to do so. And they did so without threatening the monarchy's power.

In the early nineteenth century, the voluntary sector, not the government, was the cutting edge of social action, and the members of the royal family were increasingly part of that cutting edge, even if they did not often think about it. Most of the social schemes of the day, apart from those initiated by the poor themselves, had a paternalistic flavour, which flowed from age-old beliefs in hierarchy and the rights of property. If the propertied classes needed more immediate evidence of the superiority of a paternalist society they had only to look at the anarchy of the French Revolution, so eloquently dissected by Edmund Burke. Sovereignty was taken to be synonymous with paternalism, and paternalists assumed that a strong monarchy was both socially beneficial and a counterweight to the power of central government.[70]

Paternalists admired voluntary work not because they thought it would *eliminate* the ills of society, but because they thought it would *reduce* them in a way that was compatible with the maintenance of social order. As a form of pluralism in practice, voluntarism was ideally suited to their rather special definition of democracy. In the early nineteenth century, democracy did not necessarily mean majority government. To many conservatives, including the political thinker and poet Samuel Taylor Coleridge, it meant participation in local spheres: corporations, parishes and the expanding array of charities. Charity was an expression of democracy in the sphere of social and moral reform; it gave a civic voice to individuals while regenerating the governing classes and mitigating distress.

To religious thinkers philanthropy was essentially redemptive in character and consequently the antithesis of collective action.[71] Like private property, charity promoted the autonomy of the individual, whereas the administrative state threatened it. As suggested earlier, Christians, and particularly Nonconformists, saw the state as an artificial contrivance, useful in defending the nation and policing the wicked, but incapable of promoting social good. The voluntary principle, on the other hand, opened up visions of individual salvation as well as social reform based on 'subscriber democracy' and active citizenship. It made a special appeal to clerics, merchants and professional people, not least in the provinces, where suspicion of central government was entrenched. In the reign of William IV more and more of these citizens began to look to the monarchy as an ally in their voluntary causes, as the number of petitions to the Palace attests.

Voluntary principles, or political ideas more generally, did not preoccupy William IV, although he was not oblivious to them. Like royalty elsewhere, he rarely moved in academic circles and never confused the intellectual aristocracy with the real thing. While he could hold forth on the Poor Law, he was more at home thinking about his turnips. In politics he was a conservative and a conciliator, whose first purpose was to ensure the stability of the kingdom. Like Bolingbroke in *The Idea of a Patriot King*, a formative book in his development, he saw the kingdom in terms of a family with a benevolent sovereign at its head.[72] It was not by accident that he was referred to by contemporaries as 'the Patriot King', a tag that stuck.[73]

The image of the king as the 'common father of his people', to use Bolingbroke's words, was a staple of conservative propaganda, which for popular consumption reduced royal paternalism to a simile. Members of the royal family were among the first to be captivated by the image, and they found it a useful substitute for more sophisticated thinking about the monarchy and the constitution. William IV once said that the English and the Scots, unlike the French, had no predisposition to riot.[74] Such assumptions about the social order were wholly in keeping with the simple messages that radiated from the pages of Hannah More's *Cheap Repository Tracts*, written in the 1790s to wean the lower orders from the poisonous writings of Thomas Paine. The solutions to the nation's economic and social problems revolved, rather nebulously, around a harmonious vision of 'King and Country'. The King's charitable 'patronages' were conceived to illustrate the sovereign's role as 'father' of the people's institutions. They were a demonstration of paternalism in practice, binding together 'King and Country' in mutual causes.

As the nation's pre-eminent paternalist, it was natural for William IV to take over the charitable patronages of George IV at his accession, just as George IV had taken over most of those of George III. To these he added a number of his own, including several in aid of sailors, fishermen and the orphans of seamen. Most of his papers dealing with charitable payments are lost, but one surviving document shows he contributed at least £2,500 altogether to fifty institutions in 1832.[75] In addition he made substantial donations to a host of individuals, including £6,000 a year to George IV's discarded morganatic wife, Mrs Fitzherbert.[76] (Paying for the casualties of former reigns has always been a royal burden.) If the annual total cost of his spending on individuals and institutions is impossible to judge, it is clear that William IV worried about the charitable demands made on his Privy Purse. In 1831, Sir Herbert Taylor, his Private Secretary, complained to the Prime Minister that every week 'some claim' was preferred, 'either for a subscription, donation or annual provision, which it is difficult for His Majesty to resist. The demands continually made . . . are a heavy charge.'[77]

The long list of William IV's annual donations to societies and payments to individuals would have been a greater burden to his Privy Purse had he not put his finances in better order, Gradually, he was able to reduce his indebtedness as a result of increased income, more careful attention to his accounts, and the good offices of Queen Adelaide. By one notable philanthropic act he saved himself some money—the gift of George IV's collection of animals to the Zoological Society's garden in Regent's Park.[78] Whatever his financial position, as king he was the head of the nation's charitable establishment. It was a position thrust upon him by his office, and it may be seen as something of a departure for a man so long at sea, untouched by the evangelical revival on the upper deck, and, compared with others in his family, not much identified with charitable causes. Still, the combined influences of personal kindliness, inherited duties, and Queen Adelaide turned the erstwhile buffoon and defender of slavery into a philanthropist.

By the 1830s, the public expected public displays of benevolence from their monarchs. As George IV lay dying, the Marquess of Anglesey, a veteran of Waterloo and former cabinet minister, rushed to Bushy with some honest advice for the Duke of Clarence. Anglesey insisted that a king must be seen among his subjects, maintain a 'splendid court' and perform 'creditable acts of liberality', but 'without preying upon the pockets of the people'.[79] As king, William IV warmed to such advice. Like George IV, he developed a taste for the rituals of kingship, but he tempered the spectacle with economy. He certainly showed flair in fulfilling his philanthropic duties. One contemporary argued that 'no king, perhaps, felt less inconvenience, or more sincere pleasure, at giving his personal attendance, and example, to great public meetings for humane and charitable purposes'.[80]

On his birthday in 1830 William IV feasted 3,000 poor people at Windsor, an event much noted by the press. With great fanfare, he toured hospitals and attended charitable festivals. In 1833, accompanied by Queen Adelaide, the Duchess of Kent and Princess Victoria, he attended four concerts in Westminster Abbey in aid of several music funds. Largely owing to royal patronage, the festival raised £7,600.[81] Such events, along with tours and excursions, had a meaning beyond their immediate and declared purposes. They suggested, as Colley puts it, 'ritual splendour, an appearance of domesticity, and ubiquity: this was the formula that George III taught and bequeathed to his royal successors. That it made them captives after a fashion, at the same time as it captivated large numbers of Britons, was the price of its success.'[82]

With the rapid growth of charitable agencies throughout the country in the early decades of the nineteenth century, the pressure on the monarchy to extend its support to institutions outside London increased. As mentioned, George III and Queen Charlotte had founded or supported institutions in Windsor, Bath and elsewhere. George IV, when Prince Regent, had granted favour to charities in his beloved Brighton and was

Patron of the Royal Sea-Bathing Infirmary at Margate. As Duke of Clarence, William IV had extended his patronage to the Naval Charitable Society and the Royal Navy Annuitant Society in Plymouth.[83] But, in general, provincial charities were the poor relations of their London cousins and often had to make do with royal tours. Several were denied patronage on the somewhat dubious grounds that they were 'local', while those in the capital were deemed 'national'.

Envious of what royal patronage had delivered to London institutions, more and more provincial charities wanted to reap the same benefits. A typical application from outside the capital arrived at Buckingham Palace from the Manchester Infirmary a few weeks after the accession of William IV. It had been drawn up by the Infirmary's board and was presented to the King by the Earl of Stamford. It was a model of its kind, providing details of the charity's financial stability, its longstanding services to the sick poor, the number of patients treated, and the eminence of its medical officers. The Infirmary's expectations were explicit: 'It is the opinion of the Board of Trustees that should the Institution be so fortunate, as to meet with His Majesty's Patronage, its reputation, and consequent utility, would be thereby greatly enhanced.'[84]

Robert Peel, the Home Secretary, replied to the Earl of Stamford, saying that the King had so many applications from local institutions that he had to limit them, but he had consented to the Manchester Infirmary's request because of the quality of its services and its importance to Manchester. Thus the Manchester Infirmary became the Manchester Royal Infirmary, a change of status celebrated in the local press and noted by other provincial institutions.[85] It might be argued that the charity wished to add 'royal' to its name simply to upstage rival hospitals; no doubt the institution's enhanced status triggered a degree of social snobbery among the staff and local supporters. But we should not ignore the calculation on the part of the Infirmary's governing body that royal patronage would bring with it more tangible benefits.

★ ★ ★

The gradual rise in the number of provincial charities admitted to the list of royal patronages had more than a little to do with Queen Adelaide, who did so much to expand royal philanthropy generally. Sober but amiable, she softened her husband's rough edges and made him 'presentable', as Philip Ziegler points out. But she also enlivened his charitable impulses and steered him into channels of benevolence in keeping with her exceptional sense of Christian mission. As King and Queen they appeared jointly on the patronage lists of over a dozen institutions.[86] William IV headed an appeal to relieve Protestant clergymen in Ireland, contributed £1,000 to provide church accommodation in London, and gave £3,000 to enlarge the parish church at Kew, all causes which suggested Queen Adelaide's influence.[87] There was even a donation for churches in Barbados, an early example of royal philanthropy overseas, an act that also had the Queen's stamp on it.[88]

Like Queen Charlotte before her, Adelaide came from a society with strong charitable traditions. (The German influence on British philanthropy is a subject in itself.) Her 'chief delight' as a girl at the court of Meiningen had been overseeing parish relief and supervising schools for the poor.[89] Once in England, she performed her official duties rather stiffly, as if she were acting a part. In contrast, her philanthropy, first at Bushy and then more widely, was natural and heartfelt. Like her maternity dress, it was ever spotless and ready to be worn at a moment's notice. Charitable preferences are stamped with family experiences, and many of Queen Adelaide's subscriptions to orphanages and lying-in charities flowed from the loss of her own children. At the Clergy Orphan School she once picked out a little girl who reminded her of a niece, a German princess, who had just died. She took the child under her own charge.[90]

During Adelaide's prime, few schools or churches were built without her support, and suppliants from children's charities and hospitals rarely left her company empty-handed. As William Carus Wilson, founder of the Clergy Daughters' School in Westmorland remarked, 'never did I apply to her in vain'.[91] When another cleric approached her on behalf of the Westminster Spiritual Aid Fund, she sent £1,000 by return of post.[92] Popular with churchmen, she was also the target of many impostors who could tell a moving but fictitious tale of woe. It was estimated that in the 1830s impostors wrote a thousand begging letters each day in London alone.[93] On one list of people 'most likely to be touched for a fiver', the Queen's name appeared alongside that of Charles Dickens.[94]

Quite a few invented tales arrived in Adelaide's post each year, but she was less often deceived than might be expected. Deluged with claims for relief, she had mendicity reports carried out in doubtful cases. With those categories of deserving and undeserving in mind, she rejected nearly half of all applicants. The successful petitioner typically had a good character and showed promise of becoming independent. Former respectability was no guarantee of success. Despite 'great distress', Edwin Caplen, the creator of the gold pen, was among those rejected.[95] The shortest route into the Queen's purse was to have some connection at court. A word from a housekeeper or her infatuated Lord Chamberlain, Earl Howe, could make all the difference. The successful applicant could expect up to £10, but had little hope of a repeat performance.

Among her more notable benefactions, Queen Adelaide founded the King William Naval Asylum at Penge for the widows of naval officers and gave generously to new cathedrals in Adelaide, Australia and Valetta, Malta. Her very presence aroused others to open appeals and purses. Her

	Annual Donations to Charitable Institutions				
194	——— Orphan School	10			
195	——— Society for Dist.d Widows	5			
196	——— Suffex County Hospital	20			
197	Dublin Deaf & Dumb Institution	10			
198	——— Female Orphan House	10			
199	——— Mendicity Society	10			
200	——— Sick & Indig.t room keepers	10			
201	Edgeworth Town Schools	10			
202	Edinburgh Dean Bank Asylum	10			
203	——— House of Industry	10			
204	——— House of Refuge	10			
205	Episcopal Floating Church	10			
206	Gaelic Schools	10			
207	German Poor, at Christmas	30			
208	Hanwell Lunatic Asylum	25			
209	Lewes Deanery Orphan fund	10			
210	Merchant Seamens Orph.s Asylum	5.5			
211	Paris Infant School	8			
212	Southampton Adelaide Institution	20			
213	Spine Society for the Diseases of the	10.10			
214	Staines Infant School	5.5			
215	Totemany Infant School	10			
216	Welch Charity School	25			
217	West London Coal Association	25			
218	Windsor General Dispensary	10			
219	——— Infant School	10			
220	——— Lying-in Charity	10			
221	——— National School	10			
222	——— Poor	50			
223	Winkfield National School	5			
	Carr.d over	474		1,371	7

9. A sample of Queen Adelaide's annual donations to charitable institutions.

friend Colonel Clitherow founded a lunatic asylum at Hanwell from the proceeds of an appeal he called 'The Queen Adelaide Fund', to which the Queen herself contributed.[96] Her donations to philanthropic causes often received a level of praise which seems out of all proportion to the gift. When she gave the modest sum of £100 to the Worcester Infirmary in 1843, the governors exclaimed that it exceeded 'anything that human imagination can suggest, surpassing even the "Change and Tower of London"'.[97]

The Queen's spending on charity rose over the years. In the first nine months of 1837, she contributed £1,120 in annual donations to eighty-five institutions, twelve of them in Brighton, and over £6,000 in casual donations to individuals in distress.[98] As Queen Dowager, her charities increased dramatically, and it was said that she gave away £20,000 a year to institutions and about the same amount to needy individuals out of an annual income of £100,000.[99] Donations of £40,000 a year would make her one the biggest charitable spenders, if not the biggest, in the history of the modern British royal family. That was certainly her reputation in her day. As Queen Dowager, her philanthropy became legendary. Her death was a loss to mendicants across the country and drove the obituarists to maudlin verse:

> Left by her consort with abundant means,
> She liv'd the most benevolent of Queens.[100]

Benevolence, it seems, is not enough to sustain the posthumous reputation of a queen, and Adelaide's reputation, like the embroidery with which she whiled away her evenings, faded. Twentieth-century historians have ignored her altogether or have treated her with disdain. It is not only the working classes that suffer 'the enormous condescension of posterity'. To those who see history through the lens of class conflict, her good works will be seen as counter-revolutionary, a thinly disguised form of self-interest. Certainly, her political views, shaped by the French Revolution, were reactionary, and during the campaign over the Reform Bill they made her unpopular. She was aware that royal charity was not only an antidote to social unrest but also raised the monarchy in public esteem. From the perspective of the crown, she did her duty.

Whether her charity was politically motivated or simply the result of evangelical enthusiasm, Queen Adelaide played a significant part in identifying the monarchy with rectitude and respectability. Few members of the royal family were so finely tuned to the pieties of the day. To parents, her sober and righteous behaviour was an example of the godly life to their children. But Adelaide had a message for the monarchy as well, for through religious and charitable work she redeemed herself in the public mind and overturned her unhappy reputation for political meddling. To other members of the royal family, not least Queen Victoria and her daughters, she was both a warning and a model of 'the virtuous female in her rightful position'.[101]

One of Queen Adelaide's important, though uncelebrated, contributions to the charitable world was her patronage of bazaars. The bazaar, or ladies' sale, emerged in the early nineteenth century as a response to the charitable world's insatiable appetite for new sources of revenue. Pre-eminently a female affair, it was both cause and effect of the expanding influence of women in philanthropy. No other charitable innovation was more successful in extracting funds from the public. By the end of the century, bazaars had raised tens of millions of pounds for innumerable purposes, from the building of schools and hospitals to the extension of parsonages and working men's clubs. A secret of their success and continuing popularity was that they were so admirably suited to human behaviour, providing a pleasure dear to the human heart—shopping.[102]

Queen Adelaide was the first in a long line of British royalty swept up by the bazaar. She often turned up or contributed goods to be sold, including personal cards on which she had written scriptural texts.[103] In 1833, she took a stall at a 'Grand Fancy Fair and Bazaar' in London, which raised £5,000 for the Society of Friends of Foreigners in Distress.[104] Charles Greville, who sauntered through the sale admiring the ladies, wrote that 'it was like a masquerade without masks. . . . They sold all sorts of trash at enormous prices'.[105] The Queen's blessing was the final accolade and put the ladies' sale firmly on the social calendar. Around the country more humble women imitated the royal example. Could they resist the opportunity to play at shopkeeping when the Queen had taken a stall?

Queen Adelaide's attendance at a bazaar in aid of the Hospital Ship on the Thames in 1831 was particularly telling, not for the amount of money raised, but for illuminating the relationship between aspiring philanthropists and royalty. The Quaker prison reformer Elizabeth Fry and her sister Catherine decided to attend the sale only on discovering that the Queen was to be present. The gaiety of the scene unnerved them, but persevering they met the Duchess of Gloucester, an old ally, who introduced them to several other members of the royal family. When the Duke of Sussex arrived, he presented Mrs Fry to the Queen in 'the handsomest manner'. Their conversation, as reported by Mrs Fry, turned 'almost entirely' on charitable work: 'I expressed my pleasure in seeing the royal family so much interested in these things; my belief that it did much good, and that being engaged in them brought peace and blessing.'[106]

Mrs Fry admitted in her *Memoir* that she had been hoping to meet the Queen, 'and by night and day had weighed it, lest my motives should not be right; but when I remembered, that from not having been presented to her, I could never on any point communicate with her in person, I felt that if there should be an opportunity to put myself in her way, I had better do it'. The bazaar offered her a 'singular' opportunity. 'It was striking how the whole thing was opened for me, I may say providentially; for already I believe some good has been done by seeing one of the party.' In retrospect, she looked upon the audience with the Queen 'as a very important event in my public objects for the good of others'.[107]

But in dealing with royalty there was always a potential for embarrassment, which terrified a woman of Mrs Fry's sensibilities. During her conversation with the Queen, she kept to a simple mode of speech, showed 'every respect and polite attention' and studiously avoided religious subjects. Still, she felt anxious afterwards; for 'how far it was for me thus to be cast among the great of this world; how far it was even right to put myself in the way of it'.[108] As with so many other importunate philanthropists, her nervousness in the company of royalty gave way to expectation, which turned to joy on discovering that the monarchy took notice of her work and was willing to assist her cause. Deference had its rewards for the humble petitioner, despite the potential damage it might do to self-esteem.

Elizabeth Fry was no stranger to royalty before her presentation to Queen Adelaide, for she had been present when Queen Charlotte attended the National Society in 1818 and had been introduced to the Prince and Princess Royal of Denmark by the Duchess of Gloucester.[109] (Fry corresponded with the Danish Princess on philanthropic matters for years.) Only a month before she met Queen Adelaide, she and her fellow Quaker William Allen, formerly the Duke of Kent's financial advisor, visited the Duchess of Kent and Princess Victoria armed with a selection of books on slavery, with which they hoped to influence the young Princess.[110]

Allen was, if anything, a better example than Fry of the usefulness of royal patronage. His work with the British and Foreign School Society mentioned earlier suggests that few philanthropists cultivated the monarchy with greater tenacity or effect. Having received introductions to foreign royalty from the British royal family, he travelled widely and forged charitable links between the European courts.[111] He was a precursor of that next generation of campaigners, including Moses Montefiore and Mary Carpenter, who carried their philanthropic bags, full of improving schemes, around the palaces of Europe. As such contacts suggest, charitable activity was a feature of all nineteenth-century monarchies but more specific research on its variety and extent is needed before comparisons between courts can be made.

★　★　★

Although its roots were in London, the royal family was extending its charitable tendrils into parts of the country, indeed parts of the world, previously uncultivated. Health and education remained at the top of the royal agenda in the 1830s, but there were advances into virtually every other need or affliction, from distressed animals to decayed gentry. Given the phenomenal growth in the number of new institutions, most of them small parish charities, it was impossible for the royal family to keep pace. But if the percentage of societies with royal connections was smaller in 1830 than in 1800, the monarchy had endeared itself to many of the larger, better established institutions. Partly owing to the number of aspiring doctors with connections at court, the voluntary hospitals were particularly well represented on royal patronage lists. In gratitude, the hospitals put pictures and statues of their patrons on display and named their wards King's, Queen's, Princess, Kent, York, and Cambridge, which were marvellous advertisements for royal beneficence among the sick poor.[112]

King William and Queen Adelaide extended their patronage to at least 125 institutions, about a quarter of them medical charities, and they made innumerable casual donations. But campaigners did not overlook the other members of the royal family. As we have seen, the Dukes of Cambridge, Sussex and Cumberland were attached to about eighty institutions between them by the 1820s. Augusta Sophia (1768–1840), the unmarried daughter of George III, who was distinguished by little other than a 'benevolence of disposition and general goodness of heart', contributed to many others, among them six hospitals and the Society for the Promotion of Christian Knowledge.[113] The Duke and Duchess of Gloucester patronized fifty or so charities, and the King of Belgium, Prince Leopold, retained a large number of British institutions on his patronage list, including ten London hospitals.[114] Altogether, the number of charities with royal connections, taking into account the many joint patronages, exceeded 250 in the reign of William IV.

Few members of the royal family contributed to more charitable causes than Victoria Mary Louisa, the Duchess of Kent, Queen Victoria's mother. Within weeks of her marriage in 1818, the Duke of Kent had introduced her to his charitable rounds. On their first official outing together, when they were joined by Prince Leopold, they inspected the Borough Road School of the British and Foreign School Society in south London. At a meeting later the same day at a school on the City Road, at which medals were presented to the boys, the Society announced the formation of a Committee of Ladies, to be headed by the Duchess. As she was not yet fully conversant in English, the Duke of Kent returned thanks on her behalf, and he announced that she would make a subscription of £50, her first to any charitable society in Britain.[115]

Crossing the river to the Borough Road School was the beginning of the unique, albeit brief, charitable partnership of the Kents; and it heralded a long-term commitment to benevolent causes on the part of the Duchess. Hector Bolitho, one of the only historians to note the subtle changes taking place in the monarchy's role through its patronage of charity, saw the visit to south London as symbolic of the royal family's new spirit of responsibility for the lives of ordinary people. As he put it, 'the age of princely aloofness was almost over and the day of princely service was beginning. As they drove about London, presenting prizes and interesting themselves in "charity", the Duke and Duchess of Kent were heralding the new monarchy of which their daughter was to be the real founder.'[116] Bolitho's comments were discerning, but his belief that Queen Victoria was the 'real founder' of royal public service undervalues the foundations laid by George III and Queen Charlotte, not to mention their children.

Whoever 'founded' the tradition of royal philanthropy, there is no doubt that the Duchess of Kent brought her daughter Princess Victoria into the charitable arena and impressed on her the need to be seen to be benevolent. In so doing, she was following the prescription of leading churchmen, who argued that 'the sovereign has it in his power to contribute most effectually to the true welfare of his subjects'.[117] The Duchess had taken over some patronages, including St George's German and English School.[118] But when her husband died in 1820, she inherited about fifty more. The family's charitable affiliations, along with visits to schools, gypsy encampments and the neighbouring poor, inculcated *noblesse oblige* in the young Princess. In 1836, for example, she visited the Victoria Asylum in Chiswick, which taught domestic skills to vagrant girls before sending them to South Africa as servants. It was a 'delightful establishment', she noted somewhat innocently in her diary.[119]

The education of royalty was always a serious affair, but in Princess Victoria's case it was arranged against the background of rising middle-class influences and the crown's diminished political power. The object was to give her a well-rounded training, which would encourage a tolerant religious outlook, decent manners and morals, and a predis-position to social pity. Religious texts, in which the improving works of Sarah Trimmer loomed large, were a staple. Though brought up in the Church of England and familiar with its doctrines, she did not delve deeply into theology. She preferred the simple piety described in the scriptures, and, anticipating the advice of her future mentor Lord Mel-bourne, she showed little sign of letting religion invade the sphere of her private life. As the Duchess of Kent wrote to the Bishops of London and Lincoln in 1830, the Princess was 'morally impressed' with religion and aware 'that a Sovereign should live for others'.[120] The Bishops examined the Princess and expressed themselves 'completely satisfied'.[121]

To acquaint Princess Victoria with her future subjects, the Duchess of Kent took her on an extensive tour of the provinces in 1832, a 'royal progress' carried out in such style that it irritated William IV. Amid the celebrations, salutes and visits to great houses, the royal party travelled through the Midlands, where the Princess, appalled by conditions in the coalmining districts, noted the wretchedness of blackened huts and ragged children.[122] The cities on the royal itinerary, Chester and Shrewsbury among them, expected expressions of royal benevolence. The Princess encouraged useful improvements and made donations of £100 each to the infirmaries. In her reply to the Bishop and the clergy in Chester Cathedral, the Duchess developed the charitable theme: 'I cannot better allude to your good feeling towards the Princess, than by joining fervently in the wish, that she may set an example in her conduct of that piety towards God, and charity towards man, which is the only sure foundation either of individual happiness or national prosperity.'[123]

The Duchess of Kent and Princess Victoria included a visit to Shrewsbury School in their tour, an event which illustrates the feverish preparations for, and the unpredictable consequences of, a royal appearance. The Duchess saw the occasion as an opportunity to see the habits of 'sacred learning and religious education' which shaped the pupils 'to be loyal subjects and valuable members of society'.[124] The visit had other meanings for the Master, Dr Samuel Butler, who was highly sensitive to the honour accorded to his school, yet anxious about the potential for embarrassment to his station. He had the school bedecked in green cloth and fresh carpets. Detailed instructions went out to the boys, who were to stand like soldiers, cheering their royal highnesses until the Master signalled them to stop by raising his cap. Further, they were warned not to make a 'hideous squeal' when cheering, as some of them were prone to do.[125]

When the cheering was over and the royal party had departed, the visit was deemed a success, at least by all but one concerned. The Duchess had made a pretty speech, and Princess Victoria, who noted in her Journal that Dr Butler had taken them aside to explain his teaching practices, appeared duly impressed.[126] One pupil, however, suffered the consequences of an episode left unexplained to his visitors. The boy had missed the event, with the excuse that it had been raining, and he felt it best not to turn up in wet clothes with royalty in attendance. Dr Butler, however, saw the boy's absence as an insult to the dignity of the school on such an important occasion, and wrote a blistering letter to the mother in which he recommended that she withdraw her idle and worthless son from the institution.[127] What happened to the pupil is a mystery (Dr Butler became Bishop of Lichfield), but his treatment by the school illustrates the sometimes unhappy fallout of a royal visit once the carpets are rolled up.

In 1833, the Duchess of Kent encouraged her daughter to accept her first formal patronage, the Kent Dispensary, a charity formerly associated with her father.[128] Over the next three years, the Duchess added her daughter's name to the patronage lists of several other institutions, including the Infant Orphan Asylum, the Children's Friend Society, and the London Ophthalmic Hospital, Moorfields, which became the Royal London Ophthalmic Hospital.[129] Such events loom large in the collective memories of these charities. It was proudly announced in a history of the Society for the Prevention of Cruelty to Animals, which was granted the 'Royal' prefix in 1840, that Princess Victoria's patronage in 1835 'relieved its supporters from all anxiety about its future'.[130]

By the last years of William IV's reign, Princess Victoria was well acquainted with the charitable sector and several of its leading lights, and she was fully aware that further patronage would be expected of her as Queen. Given her upbringing, it is unlikely that she believed that these inherited duties would be a dismal burden. They had been, after all, an important part of her father's life and continued to be in her mother's. They formed a seemingly natural inheritance, another aspect of a sovereign's responsibility, not unlike looking after aged retainers or bankrupt relations. Just how much she knew about the history of royal patronage is unclear, but she is unlikely to have been aware of the extent to which the monarchy's popularity at her accession depended on the long-standing charitable associations of her extended family.

Princess Victoria's inheritance of 'the securest throne in Europe' was not simply the result of the amiable William IV steering the monarchy through the turbulent politics of the 1830s without calamity.[131] It owed something to the Princess herself, and also to the Duchess of Kent, who had worked so assiduously to promote her daughter's cause and causes. Altogether, it owed much more to the philanthropy of Victoria's predecessors than has ever been allowed by historians of the monarchy. Concentrating on personalities and parliamentary affairs, they have emphasized discontinuity, while failing to notice the royal family's longstanding, and endearing, associations in the wider society. Sir Sidney Lee's oft-quoted remark that the Queen succeeded 'an imbecile, a profligate and a buffoon', though nicely turned, is misleading, for it suggests a dramatic change in the monarchy in 1837.[132]

The public noted the obvious differences between the Queen and her predecessors—in sex, age and temperament—but in other respects the monarchy had reaped advantage from changes that had already taken place in the political and social economy. Queen Victoria was inclined to inflate the powers of the crown, for like other sovereigns she could not accept 'how small, of all that human hearts endure, that part which laws or kings can cause or cure!'[133] But the running down of the monarchy's political patronage and power may now be seen as a blessing to Victoria, for it placed her above politics. It sheltered her from party infighting and relieved her of responsibility for unpopular policies and reverses. On the other hand, the shift in the monarchy's attention from high political to civil society, which was well under way before her accession, identified the Queen and members of her family with moral reform and social good. And no one publicly criticized the crown when things went wrong in a voluntary society.

Edward VII's advisor Lord Esher once said that the crown exchanged 'authority' for 'influence' in the nineteenth century.[134] Having lost most of its political authority before the accession of Queen Victoria, the monarchy was well placed to embrace moral leadership and social welfare through its longstanding charitable associations. In one of the many funeral orations which paid tribute to William IV's benevolence, Edward Copleston, Bishop of Landaff, touched on the defining role of the monarchy in the nation's welfare. In the Bishop's view, love and veneration of the monarchy were as natural 'as anything that is called an instinct in the species'.[135] But what bound the nation together and formed 'a moral link' between the subject and the sovereign was not simply an instinctive reverence for high station, but the communion of interest between the royal family and the country's civil institutions.

The extended royal family's associations with the growing array of institutions in civil society had enlisted a great army of supporters, seemingly invisible to historians, behind the monarchy's banner. Charities supported by the royal family had hundreds of thousands of members across the country by the 1830s. The Bible Society alone, whose patronage lists boasted Queen Caroline, the Duchess of Kent, and the Dukes of York, Cumberland, Sussex and Cambridge in 1820, had a vast nationwide membership though its 630 or so branches.[136] Even the smaller royal institutions such as orphanages and asylums often had a thousand or more subscribers. Not all of them can be counted as monarchists, but in a society obsessed by social hierarchy and riddled with snobbery, it can be assumed that a decision to have one's name published on a list headed by the king or a royal duke did not suggest rabid republicanism.

By the time Queen Victoria ascended the throne, philanthropy had become, if not crucial to the monarchy's survival, extremely useful. Members of the royal family had entered the wide open doors of charitable institutions and found it warm inside. No other role offered such rich returns in publicity and deference for so little effort. George IV, for example, heightened his reputation for advancing the cause of mass education simply by issuing those public letters on behalf of the National Society's campaign to establish schools for the poor. Between 1823 and 1852, seven 'Royal Letters' raised £185,000 for the Society.[137] The reigns of George IV and William IV bequeathed to Queen Victoria a distinguished list of patronages on which to build in the burgeoning world of moral reform and voluntary social action. In philanthropy at least, Victoria's 'wicked' uncles had encouraged growth and continuity; and their popular associations in civil society compensated for their losses in high politics.

Set aside for a moment the perspectives of sex and politics in the lives of George IV and William IV. From the perspective of voluntary activity, that great engine of social change in nineteenth-century Britain, they look rather less sordid and ineffectual. In philanthropic matters, unlike politics, there were few barriers to royal attainment or renown. Anchored in charitable institutions, these two brothers salvaged something from the whirlpool of kingship and worked out a better goodness than their own.

If they did not appreciate where their good works and patronages would take the monarchy, none of their courtiers, consumed by high politics or the bedchamber, was much wiser. But then, as Cromwell put it, 'a man never rises so high as when he does not know where he is going'.

3

Queen Victoria and Prince Albert: Civic Pride and Respectability

If philanthropy was ascendant in Georgian Britain, it was triumphant in the reign of Victoria. The Victorians' apparent confidence that charity could cope with the dimensions of distress baffles us today. But in their hazardous and uncertain world, benevolence was a necessity, if not a moral obligation or a test of faith. It found expression in the best of times as well as in the worst, which helps to explain why the prosperous mid-Victorian years were a charitable golden age. Philanthropy made a massive contribution to reducing human misery in the nineteenth century, but in practice it meant much more than a simple wish to relieve the suffering or to uplift the benighted. Humanitarian impulses were certainly a characteristic of charitable activists, but in a culture so profoundly voluntarist, philanthropy was an essential sphere of politics and social relations, an expression of local democracy and civic pride, of individual hope and aspiration.

The British have always been most interested in what happens around their homes and streets, despite the sporadic outpouring of public sympathy for national causes or foreigners in distress. And the Victorians did not need to read Samuel Smiles to know that propping up the family and the parish with good works and a little self-help was often the only way of preventing the deterioration of those vital social institutions. Alarmed by social conditions and aroused by religion, Victorians looked to a philosophy of personal service and civic duty for solutions. Perhaps the desire to reinvigorate the bonds of parish life was inevitable in a time of religious revival and increasing urban decay. It has continued to make an appeal in a world that has lost its religious moorings but which has not solved the crisis of the cities. The ideal of a Christian commonwealth of stable communities grew in proportion to the pains of an industrial society.

In an era when the government had little interest in social policy beyond the Poor Law and 'sanitary reform', the needs of the community bound the citizenry together in a web of kindness, obligation and expectation. A central aim of philanthropy was to reunite 'the severed sympathies' of the nation's classes.[1] The sick and the outcast, it was argued, could only be integrated into society through discretionary charity and the personal intervention of another human being who cared enough about them to be interested in their future. But the achievements of charity could not be measured by a simple calculus of tracts distributed and cases relieved, for the beneficiaries as often as not included the givers, even those whose altruism was little tainted by personal aspiration. Philanthropists recognized the ambiguity in that well-worn phrase, 'to help the poor to help themselves'. If their labours were disproportionate to the needs of the recipients, they were proportionate to their own.

In the day-to-day life of the community, a variety of philanthropic motives can be detected which were as compelling as religion and not irreconcilable with it. The pressures to contribute were certainly considerable and not easily dismissed in surroundings both stark and familiar. Yet the pleasures and advantages of charitable work were what made it irresistible to many volunteers. It represented basic human impulses: to be useful, to be seen to be useful, to be respectable, to be informed, to be amused, to 'keep up with the Joneses', to gossip, to wield power, to love and be loved. Social guilt, a feature of our more egalitarian age, was a less prominent motive in a time of accepted social hierarchy. However high or low in station, philanthropic associations signalled that a person was getting on the world. And for all those who valued social stability, it promised social amelioration without revolutionary upheaval.

Charity failed to conquer poverty in the nineteenth century, but that did not make it less compelling to the giver, for combating distress was only one of its purposes. To those of a philanthropic disposition, charitable motives may be independent of social and economic conditions, though they often accommodate them. Much philanthropy had to do with saving souls and the inculcation of religion, which was understandable in a time when medicine dealt not with cures but with prognosis and therapy of symptoms. In any case, expectations of life *on earth* were less visionary in the nineteenth century than in the secular twentieth century. Christian traditions did not create expectations of the redemption of mankind through politics. Indeed, the religious belief of charitable activists, which put such a premium on individual reformation, insulated society from collectivist utopias or worship of the state.

Philanthropy, like Christianity itself, was a great treasure chamber of hope and consolation that bound the social classes together in mutual dependence. It suggested a moral relationship and in the face-to-face setting promoted deferential behaviour. Active benevolence justified the social standing and increased the authority of the propertied, but it did not create a subservient class of Mr Pooters. (There are many ways around a philanthropist.) The organization of charity turned privilege into virtue and sometimes propelled people into good works who had little goodness in them. But selfish motives are no less pure than selfless ones. As so much unpleasantness resulted from the best of motives, it was only just that social betterment sometimes issued from the worst.

Philanthropy was not the preserve of the propertied and, whatever the background or social station of the giver, it heightened status and self-esteem. Working-class philanthropy rarely gets a mention from historians, especially Marxist ones, for it fits uncomfortably with the conception that charity is a piece of middle-class deceit to keep the poor in their place. Yet the kindness 'of the poor to the poor' was so extensive that Friedrich Engels declared that workers were 'more charitable' than the rich.[2] A survey of working-class and artisan families in the 1890s showed that half of them subscribed each week to charity.[3] One cleric said that the assistance provided by the poor to one another stood between 'civilization and revolution'.[4] Working-class charity was often carried out in cooperation with wealthier neighbours. But whatever its character, it suggested decency and propriety and distinguished the giver from the 'rough' or 'dangerous' poor. It acted as a springboard into the existing social and economic system, which was no small matter at a time when most of the working classes remained outside the political nation.

Middle-class women were also excluded from politics, and for them philanthropy was a form of self-expression, a readily available way of breaking out of the domestic routine and of wielding social influence.[5] Charitable work both broadened their horizons and pointed out their limitations. By the end of the nineteenth century, their charitable experience was a lever which they used to prise open the doors closed to them in other spheres, for in its variety it was experience applicable to just about every profession in Britain. If women valued and exploited their philanthropic associations, so did members of religious minorities, for charitable organizations gave them a voice in the community and protected their distinctive cultures within the prevailing culture. Dissenters, Catholics and Jews, among others, founded innumerable charities that mirrored Anglican ones. Such institutions were necessary, if only as safeguards against proselytizing evangelicals.

Recreating the world of Victorian charity is difficult because so many of the societies, once so familiar, are part of a lost, little remembered culture. The array of voluntary institutions, often interrelated and mutually supportive, varied with the needs of the community. Increasingly, they were local auxiliaries of national institutions, though many remained wholly autonomous. By the 1860s, most large towns and cities could boast of voluntary hospitals, infirmaries or dispensaries, asylums, benefit societies, lying-in and maternity charities, ragged schools, national schools, domestic missions, temperance societies and district visiting charities. There also would have been a range of smaller bodies, which were common in villages too: among them, clothing clubs, boot clubs, coal

10.   Queen Victoria visiting a cottage home.

clubs, mothers' meetings, working parties, Dorcas meetings, Sunday schools, and missionary associations attached to one or other of the great national institutions. Such charitable vitality was not simply a response to the *problems* associated with industrial change. It was a response to the *opportunities* that greater prosperity afforded.

Enterprising philanthropists realized the truth in that cliché that charity begins at home, while assuming that the home was the school which taught the sympathies and skills necessary to perform good works in a wider sphere. The benevolent took it for granted that the family was the fundamental social unit of British society, its protection the cornerstone of social policy. The philosopher of parochial idealism, Thomas Chalmers, provided an elaborate rationale for charity in his *Christian and Civic Economy of Large Towns* (1821–26). In it he argued that the best way to sanctify the home was to work through it, a view shared by virtually all philanthropists, from the ragged-trousered to Queen Victoria. The managers of institutions such as orphanages, asylums and 'homes' saw them in terms of the family and sought to return their charges whenever possible to the domestic fold. Abroad, missionaries held up to those they saw as benighted heathens the model of the free and happy British family, ennobled by Christianity's domestic qualities. The home, the very wellspring of the nation's life, was the most invigorating image in the philanthropic world and was commonly raised to metaphor.

The image of home and family was all the more potent because so often charitable needs and motives had domestic origins. The great diversity of family experience and opinion created the specialized character of much philanthropy. Many an orphanage or lying-in charity owed its existence to the death of an infant or the desire of the childless to find a surrogate family. Medical charities, great and small, benefited substantially from familial loss due to illness. Domestic education and religious upbringing could be vital in determining philanthropic predilections— children followed in the charitable footpaths travelled by their parents. Class and occupation also influenced philanthropic choices. Ownership of estates brought with it certain charitable responsibilities, sometimes taken with political purposes in mind. Family life among the respectable poor imposed its own distinctive obligations. Diversity and specialization were then hallmarks of philanthropy stamped by family circumstances.

As a focus of communal values, voluntary societies attracted individuals from differing backgrounds to cooperative ventures. While bringing people together with little in common beyond an interest in a cause often created friction, it helped to break down personal barriers and reduce social fragmentation. Indeed, voluntary bodies were unique institutions precisely because they could overcome social divisions. Open to the general public, they had sufficient flexibility to permit people to join or to resign at will. As 'subscriber democracies' with public meetings and elected committees, they were run with a minimum of interference or contractual obligation.[6] They were a most promising way for diverse social groups, which were often culturally vulnerable or politically isolated, to forge a relationship with the wider society. And they could achieve their *ad hoc* purposes without being stifled by ritualized conventions or enmeshed and consequently immobilized by politics. Indeed, the fluid, instrumental traditions of civil society made a rigid, monopolistic political system less likely to develop in Britain.

The proliferation of voluntary institutions reflected values which have come to be seen, somewhat misleadingly, as the preserve of the middle classes. Indeed, some historians define the middle class by reference to these values, having first defined the values as 'middle-class'.[7] But while the majority of organized charities were driven by the middle classes, the desire to protect one's community or to express one's aspirations through local institutions appealed right across the social divide, from the aristocracy to the labouring classes. As a glance at working-class memoirs will attest, the poor knew the difference between 'deserving' and 'undeserving' behaviour, and they did not need to be reminded that fitness, decency and self-help were wholesome. The historian of respectable society remarks: 'independence, self reliance, and self respect, pursued through companionship, co-operation, and voluntary collectivism, were hallmarks of the Victorian working classes.'[8] Respectability was elastic, more an attitude of mind than a set of rules, and charitable institutions of all descriptions, whatever their size or social makeup, spoke its language.

The belief in material and spiritual advancement acted as a powerful incentive in bringing together supporters from different social backgrounds. The hospitals, for example, attracted large numbers of working-class subscribers and not a few aristocrats. In some general hospitals outside London, workmen's contributions provided over half the income, although the working men themselves rarely turned up on management committees.[9] In the more affluent charities of the nineteenth century, the local middle-class elite, professional men and merchants, were usually in charge. Many societies in London, though elsewhere too, had aristocrats and royalty on their governing bodies. Whoever ran them, charitable institutions were both cause and effect of pride in the community.

Richly endowed with distinguished individuals and societies, London took the lead in the development of civic life. The royal family's support for the capital's institutions was both a cause of its leading role and a tribute to it. The annual reports of London's great societies and the guides which listed the patrons and chronicled the workings of charities in the capital were themselves expressions of civic pride. All of them, it should be said, from Highmore's *Philanthropia Metropolitana* (1822) and Sampson Low's *The Charities of London* (1850) to Herbert Fry's *The Shilling Guide* to the London Charities (1863) and W.F. Howe's *Classified Directory to the Metropolitan Charities* (from 1875) paid scrupulous attention to royalty.

Civil society had the great merit of encouraging men and women in obscure places to feel part of the moral and social economy, and to meet their local needs free from the constraints of a centralized state. One should keep in mind that Britain was administratively less uniform and centralized than continental countries, at least those conquered by Napoleon. In the mid-Victorian years, local authorities provided a multiplicity of goods and services that would astound many of today's local government officials, whose powers have been reduced so drastically by Parliament. Cities and towns in the four distinctive nations were jealous of their autonomy and proud of their local customs.[10] Their leading municipal and voluntary institutions were pre-eminent symbols of civic virtue, often products of the new wealth created by manufacturing and industry. In the 1840s, a general hospital or a philosophical society, especially one with royal patronage, was the equivalent of an orchestra or football team today in the local support it attracted.

In the expansive provincial cities, envious of the capital's affluence, a search for status was in full swing by the reign of Victoria. Outside London, aspiring philanthropists sought to put their own schemes on the map, and royal patronage was the most excellent fillip. In Birmingham the local elite asked the Queen for her recognition when they founded the Queen's Hospital in 1840. The older hospital in the city, the Birmingham General, established in 1766 without royal patronage, could only look on with envy as the new institution went from strength to strength. (The Birmingham General later sought royal patronage and received it.) At the Queen's Hospital, Queen Victoria served as Patron, the Prince Consort as President. The Duke of Cambridge was a Vice-Patron and Earl Howe, Queen Adelaide's Lord Chamberlain, was a Vice-President. Queen Adelaide made a donation. The governors named the two principal wings 'Victoria' and 'Adelaide'.[11]

At the ceremony to launch the hospital, the Vicar of Stoneleigh, Vaughan Thomas, thanked 'their Majesties for the health of a largely increased and increasing population of manufacturers, miners, and labourers in trade and agriculture'; and in passing, he made the connection between royal benevolence and loyalty to the throne.[12] When the hospital expanded in later years, an exposition of local arts and manufactures sanctioned by the Queen and the Prince Consort paid for it, along with penny-a-week subscriptions from working men. The success of the Queen's Hospital was a tribute to the acumen of local doctors, businessmen and manufacturers, who recognized the great utility of royal patronage in rallying local support from disparate groups of citizens. The new institution sent out the signal that Birmingham was not falling

behind Manchester, whose Infirmary had received a royal charter ten
years earlier.

In honour of the royal wedding in 1840, the Bristol Infirmary named
its new wards 'The Victoria' and 'The Albert', and ten years later it
received permission to change its name to the Bristol 'Royal' Infirmary.
At the time, Bristol was a deeply divided city politically. Its Hospital,
supported chiefly by Liberals, did not apply for royal assistance. The
Infirmary, which had a Tory reputation, did so with success. As one
insider remarked: 'The patients who want a *sovereign* remedy will now go
to the Royal Infirmary; but those who want a *radical* cure will go to the
Hospital!'[13] Most charities were not as politicized as those of Bristol,
although many had detectable political leanings. In London, St
Bartholomew's Hospital was a Tory stronghold, St Thomas's a Whig
institution. Both received royal support.

Societies richly endowed with well-connected Tories were predisposed
to seek royal patronage, but voluntarists of virtually every political persuasion exploited the crown's charitable offices. For its part, the monarchy
did not wish to be seen to favour one political party over another. In
years of social stability, it tended to be reactive in its dealings with
charities. Given the weight of applications it did not need to seek them
out. The decision to grant royal patronage depended largely on whether
the charity in question was useful and solvent and whether it was likely
to remain so. If an institution were identified with narrow beliefs,
especially of a religious nature, the monarchy tended to be circumspect.
When the Bible Society appealed to the Privy Purse for support in
1853, its Jubilee year, Queen Victoria made a donation but declined
to make a 'public answer', because it might arouse factions in the
Church of England.[14] The great hospitals of Birmingham, Manchester,
Bristol, London, and elsewhere, whatever their politics, were less
contentious.

Typically, the 'royal' hospitals, like many other charities, were managed
by the middle classes, even though they attracted aristocratic and working-class subscribers. As suggested, a distinctive feature of voluntary bodies
was their capacity to forge effective but flexible alliances for specific
purposes. They brought the diverse and fragmented middle classes
together and give them a greater degree of unity and common identity.
It has even been suggested that the 'dignified and independent classes'
became a recognizable 'middle class' through their voluntary organizations.[15] Whatever one thinks of this thesis, there is no doubt that
middle-class voluntarism was a tremendous social force in the mid-
nineteenth century. As Robert Morris put it:

> The aristocracy retained their titles and often their seats in Parliament
> and cabinet, but, increasingly they danced to the tune of an organized,

hierarchical, responsible, family based, property-owning middle class. The middle class was well on its way to changing its name to 'respectable' or even 'the British people' and inviting everyone, aristocrats and working class to join, providing of course they obeyed the rules and paid their subscriptions.[16]

The middle classes were especially eager to invite members of the royal family to assist them in their great cause, so eager that they risked making fools of themselves in the process. But the contribution of the monarchy to the rise of middle- and working-class respectability has not been explored.[17] Nothing else gave greater momentum to charitable work, which signified respectability, than royal associations. Nothing else so convincingly persuaded diverse parties in a charity to set aside their differences for the common good. Nothing else made members of the public reach for their chequebooks with greater alacrity. The grant of royal approval to the parvenu often had the effect of increasing his subscription. To cap it all, the monarchy held out the prospect of audiences, annual charity dinners, balls and banquets, garden parties (from the 1860s), and honours for services to philanthropy. The monarchy's capacity to transform duty into pleasure was enough to make many an aspiring citizen feverish.

When the middle classes came to the ball, the royal family danced to their tunes. By the reign of Victoria, the communion of interest between the middle classes and the monarchy had taken hold. In an age in which the word 'duty' resounded like a drumbeat, they discovered that they had a duty to one another. As decades of administrative reform and the 1832 Reform Bill had curtailed the monarchy's political role, the crown needed to widen its social appeal. The middle classes found the monarchy both an enabling institution and a theatre of loyalty, which gave its disparate elements a sense of belonging, unity and purpose. The reverence for monarchy, which bordered on religious faith, and was conditioned by it, encouraged people at all social levels to feel they were part of some great, unfolding historical narrative, and not simply dedicating their lives to Mammon.

★   ★   ★

By precept and training, Queen Victoria was well suited to represent and extend the prevailing values of her subjects. Her religious upbringing accommodated the pieties of her day, and she was sympathetic to the evangelicals when they spoke of good works and not damnation.[18] Her cast of mind was hierarchical, moral and down-to-earth. This was in keeping with those paternalistic and practical philanthropic campaigns which offered inducements to individual reformation rather than laboured analyses of social deprivation. Social movements and 'social science' had little charm for Queen Victoria. She was not a person to be reasoned out of her humanity by the dismal scientists of the *Westminster Review*. Like other female members of her family she had absorbed the charitable culture as it applied to women. It showed itself in a well-developed sense of social obligation, which came to the fore in times of personal crisis or national emergency.

Schooled in charitable matters by her mother, Queen Victoria also came under the influence of her German advisor, Baron Stockmar, who had concluded that the new court must be identified with the highest standards of moral conduct. In his view, a reputation for 'practical morality' was 'the indispensable necessity' to the welfare of both sovereign and the people.[19] Stockmar detested George IV and William IV for their immorality, and he wished to ensure that in future the public associated the royal family with rectitude and benevolence.[20] As such, he has been seen as a principal architect of 'Victorian values'. But there was nothing new about the latter. They were essentially Georgian values in Victorian dress.

The religious lobby wasted no time in advising the Queen of her obligations. A sermon on the Coronation delivered at the Scottish Church in Covent Garden, penned by a clergyman familiar with works of Hannah More, suggested the general tone. Entitled *Our Queen's Responsibilities and Rewards*, it encouraged the Queen to seek advice from the wise and just. Such luminaries would remind her of her sacred duties and 'will be aids to schemes of philanthropy and breathe, in faithfulness and reverence, into your ear—"Be thou faithful unto death, and Christ will give thee a crown of life"'. Whether Queen Victoria saw herself as 'the nursing-mother of a Christian population' is uncertain, but she would have seconded the preacher's opinion that 'all influence, for good or evil, descends from the higher to the lower. The moral influence of a Queen, in a nation where the female character is revered, and the royal looked up to, must necessarily be vast.'[21]

While churchmen reminded the Queen of her public duty, the public itself used the auspicious moment of the Coronation for their own ends. The monarchy's well-wishers launched into benevolent schemes with seeming abandon. At workhouses and prisons, labour ceased for the day and inmates received extra rations of beef and porter. At voluntary hospitals, patients drank the Queen's health with donated wine. At innumerable charity schools, pupils devoured their coronation puddings to cries of 'Long live Victoria' and the national anthem. Societies advertised, recruited, and expanded, and to offset the costs female philanthropists launched a thousand fêtes. In London, the Royal Lying-in Hospital and the Royal Dispensary for Diseases of the Ear recruited the Queen Dowager and Duchess of Kent for their bazaars. At Dundee, the festivities got out of hand and a playhouse burned down in a riot. But this was not allowed to spoil the occasion, for it was said that the theatre had been a danger to public morals in any case.[22]

As Queen, Victoria was quick to take up the additional charitable duties expected of her. She hardly had time to recover from the Coronation itself before the appeals for patronage began to appear. Needy friends of the family and the well-connected tended to get in first. Among charitable institutions, few were as quick off the mark as the Kent Dispensary, which provided free medical assistance to the sick poor of Deptford, Greenwich and Lewisham. The Duke of Wellington spoke to the Queen on behalf of the charity within a few days of her accession, and he was able to announce at the Dispensary's annual dinner, to the cheers of assembled supporters, that he had obtained Her Majesty's patronage. A few weeks later the institution received the Queen's permission, through the Home Secretary, to use 'royal' in its title. At this happy moment, Wellington assented to the request to add his name to the list of vice-presidents. The institution's finances picked up.[23]

As with earlier monarchs, the Queen inherited her predecessor's patronages and added to them her own. Eventually she was the patron of, as opposed to simply a contributor to, about 150 institutions, three times as many as George IV. She gave more of her money to institutions than individual applicants, which was a significant departure from earlier reigns. By 1851, her patronage books show that she contributed to more than 210 charities, including fifty schools, thirty-seven hospitals, twenty-one churches, and eighteen asylums.[24] There were also donations for the relief of victims of earthquakes and storms, fires and shipwrecks, famines and colliery disasters.[25] Temperance interestingly hardly figured. Between 1837 and 1871, her donations to individuals and institutions came to a total of £277,439, or £8,160 a year.[26] This represented nearly 15 per cent of her Privy Purse income, set at £60,000 annually. (The percentage drops if we add the other sources of her private income.)

With the years, Queen Victoria's contributions increased. In 1882, for example, she gave away £10,964 to 216 charities in annual donations. In addition, she made fourteen one-off payments to other causes, at a cost of £1,571. She thus spent a total of £12,535 on 230 charities in 1882.[27] This was 20 per cent of her annual Privy Purse income, not counting the other sources of her private fortune. All told, her patronage books show that she gave away something in the order of £650,000 to charitable purposes during her reign, excluding cash handouts to the poor and pensions to retired servants.[28] But she was not only a dispenser of charity. The biblical saying 'Unto every one that hath shall be given' might have been written with monarchs in mind. In 1852 the Queen received about £250,000 in a bequest from the recluse John Camden Neild, the son of James Neild, who had loaned her father, the Duke of Kent, large sums of money fifty years earlier.[29]

Donations given by Her Majesty and the late Prince Consorts towards the relief of Sufferers from Fires and other causes.

			£	
Sufferers by Fire				
At Southampton	Dec. 1837		100	
Surat	July 1838		200	
Hamburg	May 1842	The Queen	200	
"		Pce Consort	100	
Quebec	July 1845	The Queen	200	
"		Pce Cons	100	
Newcastle	Oct. 1854		100	
Sufferers by Explosions				
At Ardsley Main Colliery	Apr. 1847		30	
Darley Main "	Feb. 1849		25	
Jarrow Coal Pit	Sep. 1845		20	
Of Fireworks	Oct. 1850		10	
Isle of Man	Jan. 1853		50	
Leipzig	Oct. 1856		200	
Hartley Colliery	Jan. 1862		200	
Lundhill	Mar. 1857		200	
Sufferers by Shipwreck				
Of the Fairy	1837		100	
from Shipwreck	Feb. 1843		10	10
Forced Shipwreck ANY.	1867		10	
Adelaide	1856		25	
The Birkenhead	Sep. 1852		200	
The Amazon	Jan. 1853		150	
The Dalhousie	Nov. 1853		50	

11. Donations from Queen Victoria and Prince Albert towards the relief of disaster victims.

Queen Victoria's spending on charity was considerable, but was she generous by the standards of her day? The money she paid out in charities drops to under 10 per cent of her private fortune if we add to her Privy Purse income the money that she saved from other classes of her Civil List and the revenues paid to her from the Duchy of Lancaster, and, before the birth of the Prince of Wales, the Duchy of Cornwall.[30] Still, the level of her spending on philanthropic causes compares favourably with those great landed aristocrats whose records have been studied for charitable donations. Typically, they gave away between 4 and 7 per cent of their incomes to charity by the middle of the nineteenth century. The gentry, it seems, were considerably less charitable.[31] But a study of middle-class families in the 1890s puts their spending on philanthropy at over 10 per cent of annual income, more than on any item in the budget except food.[32] On the evidence available, the Queen was more munificent than the landed magnates in her economy of charity, but she was not quite keeping up with the Joneses.

★ ★ ★

Queen Victoria's marriage to Prince Albert in 1840 resulted in a further expansion of royal patronage and a shift in charitable emphases. Indeed, with her husband's arrival the monarchy discovered causes that it had previously little appreciated. Albert was that rarity among princes, an intellectual, whose adaptive mind, free of burdensome originality, penetrated what members of the royal family often ignored—the obvious. As Baron Stockmar, his 'second parent', noted, he also had a moral seriousness about him, which 'sacrifices mere pleasure to that which is useful'.[33] As Walter Bagehot said of him: 'His circumstances, and perhaps his character, forbade him to attempt the visible achievements and the showy displays which attract momentary popularity. . . . It was discretion which Prince Albert eminently possessed.'[34] Discretion was a welcome attribute in the monarchy's social administration, especially when so many rival interests were competing for patronage.

Within a year of the royal marriage, the Prince, anxious to find a purpose at court, became the Queen's principal advisor, and he effectively replaced Lord Melbourne as her Private Secretary. The contrast was striking. In politics, Prince Albert steered the monarchy towards neutrality. In manners and morals, he steered it towards respectable opinion. Like Stockmar, he believed the monarchy had to be identified with the values of a gentleman to avoid unpopularity. In an unfanatical way the Prince was religious, and he had little time for Melbourne's laxity, summed up in his motto 'you had better try to do no good, and then you'll get into no scrapes'.[35] The desire to be of service, combined with an industrious, progressive temperament, disposed the Prince to look favourably on worthy causes and the entreaties of philanthropists. As a foreigner, free from British conventions, he wished to make his mark on his adopted country. He was in a unique position to be of service, for as the philanthropist Lord Shaftesbury once said to him: 'You can speak as a king, represent a king, without the necessary and inevitable restrictions of a king.'[36]

A man of comprehensive interests and wide sympathies, Prince Albert had an acute sense of the British monarchy's uneasy historic role and its need to develop along lines suited to the post-1832 political settlement. In constitutional matters, he took the view that if the crown shed party political associations it would have the independence to see Britain's problems in the round and develop an impartial view of the public good.[37] By avoiding party ties, which so often produced little more than embarrassment to the monarchy, he hoped that the crown would become more influential, not less. The purpose of royal influence, as Stockmar's biographer put it, was 'to act as a balance-wheel on the movement of the social body'.[38] G.M. Young, that most perceptive historian of Victorian England, put the monarchy's position neatly: 'as its power pursued its inevitable downward curve, its influence rose in equipoise'.[39]

It did not take great insight to recognize that a most fruitful way of ensuring social equilibrium was to consolidate and to expand the royal family's partnership with respectable society. Lord Shaftesbury wrote to Prince Albert in June 1842 that 'the people of this country, who are sincerely attached to Monarchy as a principle, will love it still more in the person of a Queen, who feels and expresses a real interest in their welfare'.[40] Through its patronages and active benevolence, the monarchy would emerge as a centre of loyalty to citizens with traditional allegiances. By developing popular links with the voluntary institutions of middle England, it would not only promote the betterment of the working classes, but it would be seen to be doing so. Charity added lustre to the monarchy in an era of social dislocation and democratic ferment: 'A virtuous and domestic sovereign,' as Young observed, 'interested in docks and railways, hospitals and tenements, self-help and mutual improvement, was impregnable.'[41]

Prince Albert believed the purpose of royalty to be the 'headship of philanthropy, a guidance and encouragement of the manifold efforts which our age is making towards a higher and purer life'.[42] His own philanthropic career was in addition to his many other duties, but it grew like Topsy and often required him to speak on behalf of benevolent causes. At an anti-slavery meeting in June 1840, he regretted that 'so holy a cause' had not yet succeeded, and allied the monarchy with the righteous in their crusade.[43] On such occasions, he reminded his audiences of their sovereign's admiration and support for their charitable exertions. At a meeting to celebrate the work of the Golden Lane Schools, accompanied by the young Prince of Wales, Albert spoke of 'the deep interest which the Queen takes in the well-being of the poorest of her subjects; and that gratification will be greatly enhanced if by this public expression of the sympathy of the queen and of her family . . . this noble cause shall be still further advanced'.[44]

Prince Albert began to subscribe to British charities immediately after his marriage and within a decade had contributed many thousands of pounds to over 160 causes.[45] Along with staff salaries and the demands for money from Coburg, his donations depleted his allowance, which Parliament had set at £30,000 a year. Despite his recurring financial worries in the 1840s, the Prince continued to expand his patronages. It is impossible to give a very precise account of his spending on charities before the reorganization of the Privy Purse by Colonel (later Sir Charles) Phipps in

1855	Donations to Institutions		£ s d			£ s d
Sept 29	Brought forward					970 2 8
Oct 5	Female Servants' Home	210	20			
	Wraysbury Agricultural Soc. per Col Wood	211	5			
	Huddersfield Mechanics' Institute		25			
Nov 19	Staatsrath Seebech, Subs. to Statue of John Frost the Magnanimous	212	143 10 5			
Dec 31	St. Thomas's Church Newport Joint £100	213	33 6 8			
	Portsmouth Sailors' Home, Joint £500		100			331 17 1
						1301 19 9
1856						
Jan 5	Commercial Travellers' Library	220	100			
20	Plymouth School of Art	223	25			
Feb 28	Kilkenny Archaeological Soc.	224	25			
	Royal Naval School Swimming Bath Fund		10			
Mar 1	Cambridge Image Collection		50			
31	Windsor British Schools Joint £25	225	8 6 8			218 6 8

12. Some donations to institutions from Prince Albert's accounts.

the early 1850s. But after improvements in book-keeping took effect, Albert's accounts show that he was giving away about £2,000 in donations and subscriptions to sixty or so institutions each year.[46]

Prince Albert's role was ill-defined, but he 'seized the key positions—morality and industry—behind which the monarchy was safe'.[47] With the coming of the railway, it was easier to carry the crown's social message into the regions, and the Prince reached parts of the country and sections of the population which had been little known to William IV, Queen Adelaide and other members of the royal family. Factories, building sites, ports and dockyards 'drew him like a magnet', and his visits to them brought the monarchy into greater contact with the common people.[48] He was an enthusiastic supporter of mechanics' institutes, housing charities, schools and libraries, but not temperance societies. Increasingly, he patronized the great centres of manufacturing, where the citizenry often felt jealous of the level of royal attention lavished on London.[49]

The 1840s was a dangerous decade for European monarchies; hence, Albert's voluntary work must be seen in the context of Chartism at home and revolution on the continent. Indeed, the Prince's charitable enthusiasms can often be directly related to his nervousness about political affairs. In 1843, he visited Birmingham, against the advice of the Prime Minister, Sir Robert Peel, who felt that the Chartist sympathies of the mayor and the municipal authorities might cause disturbance.[50] The stated purpose of the Prince's trip was to inspect factories and to visit a leading charity school in the city.[51] The underlying purpose was to test the political terrain in a part of the country little cultivated by the monarchy.

Members of the royal family had always been sensitive to the way in which they were received by the public, and this was notably so in the 'hungry forties'. George Anson, the Prince's Private Secretary, took notes of the excursion to Birmingham, and was pleased to report that 280,000 loyal, good-humoured people turned out in the city: 'All vied with each other to do honour to the Prince's visit, which they have taken as the greatest compliment. The mayor, who accompanied the Prince in the carriage, is said to be a Chartist, and to hold extreme views. He said that the visit had created the greatest enthusiasm—that it had brought into unison and harmony opposite political parties who had shown the deepest hatred towards each other, and that it had been productive of the happiest results in Birmingham.'[52]

The presence of Prince Albert was 'universally desired', as his Victorian biographer Sir Theodore Martin remarked, 'whenever any new institution was to be founded for the advancement of the comfort, intelligence, or welfare of the people'.[53] Soon after his marriage the Prince began to shoulder a growing share of the monarchy's charitable burden, sometimes standing in for Queen Victoria. He gave public addresses, inaugurated institutions and opened new hospital wings. As Hermione Hobhouse has shown, the laying of foundation stones by members of the royal family was by this time a commonplace, and the Chest Hospital, Brompton (1844), St Mary's, Paddington (1845) and the Seamen's Hospital, Dock Street, London (1846) were among the many charities that the Prince graced with a commemorative trowel.[54]

In 1846, the Prince laid the first stone of the Sailors' Home for the Port of London. The authorities in Liverpool, not to be outshone, persuaded him to perform the same service for their city. Furthermore, they invited him to open the new docks, which they had named in his honour, and to visit the local charity schools. The occasion was a telling one for the monarchy and for Liverpool, and it well illustrates the reciprocal benefits of royal philanthropy. In his speech to the city dignitaries, the Prince said that the object of his visit 'was a work of charity—a work reflecting the greatest credit on your liberality and good feeling, as it manifests that you are desirous of promoting the comfort of those who, by constant toil and labour, are contributing to the prosperity which I have this day seen'.[55]

The Prince's tribute to Liverpool's happy mix of prosperity and charity was a theme that worked its magic on the civic dignitaries. The language of the mayor in proposing Prince Albert's health at a grand banquet in his honour must have warmed many a courtier's heart. 'You need not be told', he said, 'what zeal the Prince has always shown in promoting the best interests of mankind. . . . You need not be told how promptly he comes forward to promote the worthiest and noblest objects, especially when benefits are to be conferred upon the humbler classes. His presence today is a magnificent proof of the interest he has taken in our welfare.' Nor were the people of Liverpool, as the mayor added, likely to forget 'the lustre' which the Prince added to their 'mercantile speculations and enjoyments'.[56]

The chairman of the Committee of the Sailors' Home paid his own handsome tribute to the Prince the following day: 'Allow me most respectfully and most sincerely to congratulate your Royal Highness for having endeared yourself to the people of this nation, by associating your name with institutions formed for religious, scientific and philanthropic purposes, by these means securing the triumphs of peace and the blessings of Christianity, and for having this day added to your well-deserved popularity.'[57] The Prince replied with a few polite comments on the objects of the Home, and after the Masonic ceremonies were over, he returned to the railway station. To him, it was just another day's work, perhaps a respite from more arduous duties; but he left behind him a city whose citizens felt uplifted by the occasion. Needless to say, the Sailors' Home did not want for supporters. The Queen wrote to Baron Stockmar on the same day: 'I glory in his being seen and loved.'[58]

★ ★ ★

The uses of royal philanthropy are more apparent to the Palace in times of social unrest, and the desire of the royal family to be 'seen and loved' mounted in the late 1840s. There is no better illustration of Prince Albert's worries and how they turned his mind to charitable solutions than a look at extracts from his diary for the revolutionary spring of 1848. 6 March: 'Apprehension that they [the Chartists] would come to Buckingham Palace.' 7 March: 'Riots in Glasgow and in Trafalgar Square. . . . The property of the French Royal family is sequestered at Paris.' 10 March: 'Riots at Munich.' 17 March: 'Great riots amongst the peasantry in Swabia.' 18 March: 'News of revolution at Berlin.' 24 March: 'King of Prussia in the hands of the Burghers.' 4 April: 'Disquieting views from Ireland.' 11 April: 'Increase of anarchy in Germany.' 18 April: 'A long conversation with him [Lord Shaftesbury] as to what can be done for working classes.'[59]

The Prince could do little to influence continental affairs, but he was determined to do something to ameliorate the condition of the British working classes, in whom he took a 'parental' interest, as one of his aides put it.[60] As the Chartists gathered on Kennington Common on 10 April, he wrote to the Prime Minister, Lord John Russell. He was confident that good sense would prevail, but he was anxious that a 'commotion' be avoided because 'it would shake that confidence which the whole of Europe reposes in our stability at this moment'. Most importantly, it was not a time 'for the taxpayers to economise upon the working classes', and he hoped that the government might do something to promote employment, especially in London.[61]

The Kennington Common demonstration passed off without incident. Reassured, the government felt little disposed to heed the Prince's advice. Few ministers, after all, shared his enthusiasm for working-class causes. But the propertied classes of London, 'in deep gratitude to Almighty God' for sparing the capital 'from the horrors of anarchy', opened subscription lists to build a free hospital and erect baths, washhouses and other institutions for the benefit of the poor. Albert received the charitable circular in the middle of April, and he put the Queen's and his own name down for £500.[62] The Chartists failed to achieve universal manhood suffrage, but they did receive a public bath.

Prince Albert had much more success with philanthropists than he had with politicians, though when the politicians were wearing their philanthropic hats he found relations with them much improved. The Queen, badly shaken by the Chartists, remained as nervous as the Prince about the political situation in 1848. Having no desire to play Louis Philippe, much less Marie Antoinette, she held a ball in aid of Spitalfields weavers and required that court ladies wear only British-made clothes in her drawing-rooms. 'There must be some better way of helping the poor,' remarked Prince Albert.[63] After the Kennington Common demonstration, the Queen invited Lord Shaftesbury to Osborne to discuss what might be done 'to show our interest in the working class'. Shaftesbury, having satisfied himself that he could speak frankly, advised the Prince to put himself 'at the head of all social movements in art and science, and especially of those movements as they bear upon the poor, and thus show the interest felt by Royalty in the happiness of the Kingdom'.[64]

Lord Shaftesbury vied with the royal dukes when it came to presiding over charitable meetings, and he always had a scheme of social betterment up his sleeve. He suggested that the Prince visit a slum tenement and then take the chair at a meeting of the Society for Improving the Condition of the Labouring Classes at Exeter Hall. The Prime Minister, Lord John Russell, and the Home Secretary, Sir George Grey, thought it risky and tried to dissuade him. The Prince wrote to Russell that he felt it his duty to risk inconvenience in showing an 'interest and sympathy for the lower orders'. He was particularly anxious to dispel any notion that the royal family was 'merely living upon the earnings of the people' without any feelings for their welfare. 'We may possess those feelings and still the mass of the people may be ignorant of it because they have never heard it expressed to them or seen any tangible proof of it.'[65] In the end, he chaired the meeting of the Society on 18 May, with the blessing of the Queen, though not of her ministers.[66]

Prince Albert's speech to the Society was a revealing statement of the monarchy's social gospel. Carefully constructed, and rehearsed with the Queen, it was attuned to the needs of the poor, yet reassuring to the privileged. It endorsed the charity's commitment to the development of lodging houses, loan funds and allotments, but it put a premium on working-class self-help and application. 'Depend upon it,' he said, 'the interests of classes too often contrasted are identical, and it is only ignorance which prevents their uniting for each other's advantage. To dispel that ignorance, to show how man can help man . . . ought to be the aim of every philanthropic person; but it is more peculiarly the duty of those who, under the blessing of Divine Providence, enjoy station, wealth, and education.'[67]

In keeping with his belief in market economics and business principles, Prince Albert wished the propertied classes 'to avoid any dictatorial interference with labour and employment, which frightens away capital, destroys that freedom of thought and independence of action which must remain to every one if he is to work out his own happiness, and impairs that confidence under which alone engagements for mutual benefit are possible'.[68] This remark reveals why the Prince was so popular with the manufacturing and commercial classes. Victorian charity may be seen as liberalism turning its attention to social questions under religious pressure. Prince Albert, like Sir Robert Peel, whom he admired, had the mind of a business gentleman, active and absorbent.[69] He simply reminded middle-class capitalists that acquitting their social obligations was a form of enlightened self-interest. Prince Albert was Samuel Smiles with a German accent. His philanthropist was the welfare equivalent of the entrepreneur.[70]

The Prince's appearance on behalf of the Society for Improving the Condition of the Working Class was another episode in the development of the crown's social policy. But its meaning was potentially divisive, for it was seen by some as simply a scheme designed to dish the cause of political radicalism. The Tory paternalist Lord Shaftesbury revelled in its underlying message. 'Aye, truly this is the way to stifle Chartism. . . . Rank, leisure, station are gifts of God, for which man must give an account. Here is a full proof, a glowing instance!'[71] A disgruntled socialist lamented: 'if the Prince goes on like this he'll upset our apple-cart'.[72] In so far as people saw royal charity as an antidote to radicalism, it created a problem for the monarchy. Would radicals and socialists accept that the crown's interest in welfare causes was genuine and not simply an expedient to save itself? It was a variation on a theme which first appeared in 1789 and remains an issue for some on the left in British politics today.

In 1848, few members of the public deceived themselves into thinking that Queen Victoria and Prince Albert were sympathetic to political turmoil. A notable exception was Robert Owen, who sent a memorial to the Queen in June 1848 through Lord Brougham. In it, he explained to Her Majesty that what was taking place in the world was 'the greatest revolution that has ever occurred in human affairs; a revolution not to be dreaded, but one that will be highly beneficial to all, in every country and for ever'. He reminded her that her father was among his 'disciples', asked for her support, and signed off 'your Majesty's best friend in this period of coming revolutions'.[73] Queen Victoria, who had been putting up the tearful King and Queen of the French in exile, did not reply. Prince Albert wrote to Lord Brougham, drily: Socialist theories 'could only be tested by their practical adaptation. Unfortunately, such practical experiments have always been found to be *exceedingly expensive* to the Nations in which they have been tried.'[74]

In 1851, the Prince remarked to a meeting of the Society for the Propagation of the Gospel that the great constitutional issue was to reconcile 'the two antagonistic principles which move human society . . . the principles of *individual liberty and of allegiance and submission to the will of the community*'.[75] The Prince spoke vaguely of the 'earnest zeal and practical wisdom' which made Britain's political stability the envy of the world. The 'zeal' and 'wisdom' of a voluntary society, as he was well aware, contributed mightily to the reconciliation of antagonistic forces and to the ordered freedom which he so admired. Philanthropy was an expression of both *individual liberty* and the freedom of minorities; but because it so often linked the interests of individuals and minorities to the interests of the wider society, to '*the will of the community*', its net effect was to encourage social reconciliation.

Whatever the state of British society, molten or at peace with itself, the monarchy's support for charitable campaigns promoted social harmony, while creating allegiance to the crown. Whenever constitutional monarchy was thought to be in danger, well-wishers encouraged members of the royal family to identify publicly with charitable causes and suggested ways in which they might do so. In times of political crisis, they deemed that royal voluntarism was an effective way of preserving the continuity of British institutions, keeping republicanism at bay, and preventing what Prince Albert called the 'practical adaptation' of socialism. A visible philanthropic role was by now one of the best tools in the monarchy's survival kit. But it needed to be handled with delicacy and discrimination. A feature of the crown's charitable administration was the care taken over individual applications. Queen Victorian and Prince Albert, advised by Palace and Home Office officials, scrutinised each one, mindful of the effect their patronage might have on public opinion.

It was widely appreciated that royal benevolence acted as an antidote to revolution. Take the example of the Servants' Provident and Benevolent Society, which invited Prince Albert to chair a meeting in May 1849. The Society wanted to encourage domestic servants to invest in annuities, and to build a home and a model lodging house.[76] These were objectives in keeping with the Prince's belief in working-class self-help and discretionary charity. The *Weekly Chronicle*, along with other newspapers, praised the part played by the Prince in the proceedings:

> Whilst, in every other part of Europe, we see political passions and party animosities, setting rich and poor by the ears, convulsing society, paralysing trade, and engendering intense distress and misery, it is a proud and gratifying spectacle to behold, in our own country, all classes combining harmoniously to work out little by little, *real* reformation, and to accomplish by united efforts that genuine and durable progress, which only union can achieve, and which domestic broils and foreign warfare serve but indefinitely to adjourn.[77]

The *Globe* took a similar view of the Prince's work on behalf of servants. One of the blessings of British life, it proclaimed, was having a monarch distinguished by

> those amiable virtues which adorn the peaceful retirement of the fireside, and shed a lustre on . . . an Englishman's home. And when we see the Consort of such a Queen distinguished by similar virtues and excellencies, the tie of attachment to the Throne becomes so strong, that there is not the remotest chance of its being weakened by any sympathetic feeling with the democratic spirit that has lately convulsed . . . the neighbouring nations.[78]

To the editor of the *Globe*, royal support for the Servants' Society (the Queen and the Queen Dowager joined the Prince as patrons) was inspired by nothing less than the noble desire to spread the values of family life. In his view, the monarchy kept the revolutionaries at bay by holding itself up as a model of domestic tranquillity and familial virtue, which radiated to the wider society. By implication, political radicalism went hand-in-hand with indecency.

A policy of popularizing the monarchy was in full swing in the 1850s. Against the background of recent troubles, the crown desired to show itself to be sensitive to public needs and aspirations. Loyalty in the shires could be counted upon, so the Palace focused its attention on centres of civic culture and manufacturing where deference to the crown was less entrenched: Dublin and Belfast (1849), Liverpool (1851), Manchester

13.   The Queen drives by the Manchester Royal Infirmary, 1857.

(1851 and 1857), Birmingham (1855 and 1858), Glasgow (1859) and
Edinburgh (1861). Charitable visits and initiatives punctuated the round
of levees and receptions. The royal party fine-tuned each and every detail.
In Belfast, the Queen and Prince Albert studiously avoided the Deaf and
Dumb Institution because it was overtly sectarian, and they distributed the
royal bounty to 'the least divisive bodies'.[79] At the end of the tour, the
Prince wrote to Stockmar: 'Of the enthusiasm that greeted us from all
quarters you can form no conception. . . . The Catholic clergy are quite
as loyal as the Anglican, the Presbyterians, and the Quakers.'[80]

Laying foundation stones, knighting mayors, and encouraging
working-class industry were by now *de rigueur* on tour. Assisted by Home
Office and Palace officials, the royal family monitored the public mood
and the size of the crowds. In Salford in 1851, mechanics and working
men lined the streets, and in Peel Park 82,000 school children assembled
and sang 'God save the Queen'. The Prince took a side trip to Bolton to
inspect Thomas Bazley's factory and was pleased to discover that the
cottages were comfortable, the schools excellent and a cooperative store
established, all working in directions that he had encouraged. Between
Salford and Manchester they were seen by a million people according to
one eye-witness, a judgment that delighted the Queen. Three days later
the Prince had returned to a more normal routine and was distributing
the prizes of the Windsor Labourers' Friends' Association.[81]

During the tour of Birmingham in 1858, rewards for and inducements
to civic duty were much in evidence. The Queen knighted the mayor for
services to the city, and the royal party then continued to a people's
museum and park at Aston Hall, paid for largely by working-class

88

subscriptions. Displaying a common touch, the Queen spoke to several working men and then appeared on the balcony with the Prince to witness the opening of the park. The Queen wrote in her *Diary*:

> We went downstairs, and through the Exhibition rooms, and walked once down and back along the terrace, the people cheering us very warmly. Dear Albert is so beloved here—as, indeed, everywhere—having been here, I think, on three previous occasions for different purposes, and his love for the Arts and Sciences, and the moral improvement of the working and middle classes, and the general enlightenment of all, being so well known.[82]

With Chartism exhausted and trade revived, Britain was going through a phase of unparalleled prosperity and political tranquillity. In such circumstances, the world can be very agreeable for the privileged if they leave it alone. Yet Prince Albert continued to promote schemes of social improvement. It was proof, if proof were needed, that his interest in social reform was not simply an expedient to crush political radicalism, or what remained of it. The weight of public business was exhausting and sometimes gave him cause for complaint. He wrote to his brother Ernest in 1855: 'In the morning I have to be present at the inauguration of a hospital, and in the evening I have to preside at dinner in Trinity House, which will last five hours and where I have to hear six addresses.'[83]

At Trinity House, the Prince took up the cause of ballast-heavers, who suffered from the 'truck-driving system', by which employers allocated work through public houses. He had a word with the President of the Board of Trade with the result that a fresh clause appeared in the Merchant Shipping Act, which gave Trinity House the power to overturn the practice in the Port of London. The men paid generous tribute to the Prince for his timely intervention: 'We appealed to men of all classes, and opened an office ourselves; but we got no real help till we sent an appeal [to the Prince as new Master of Trinity House], he at once listened to us. He could put himself down from the throne he shared to the wretched home of us poor men, and could feel what we and our wives and children were suffering from the terrible truck-driving system.'[84]

Prince Albert sometimes used his influence to bring about legislative solutions to social distresses, as in the case of the ballast-heavers. But he generally preferred voluntary remedies to political ones. He had a particular enthusiasm for small-scale projects which addressed large themes. This was very much in tune with the nature of voluntary activity generally, which tended to break problems down into pieces and to seek local solutions. He was in a privileged position to experiment. Windsor, with its pliable population and longstanding charitable traditions, provided a test bed on which he could lay out a social problem for investigation. No other community of its size in Britain had so many charitable institutions or so many with royal patronage. In the 1860s, the Queen alone subscribed to no fewer than twenty-five of them.[85]

Under Prince Albert's direction, the monarchy was beginning to develop a more elaborate social policy. In the past it had concentrated on giving assistance to charitable schemes promoted by the privileged classes. Now it sought to reach the working classes more directly in order to enable them to join in the general prosperity. The 1850s were arguably the golden age of working-class self-help and voluntarism, and Prince Albert, who assumed a tutorial responsibility for the poor, wanted to accelerate the process and share the benefits. In a letter to Sir Charles Phipps in 1849, the Prince outlined four ways in which the conditions of the working classes might be improved: educate children with industrial training, improve dwellings, provide allotments with cottages, and encourage savings banks and benefit societies, preferably managed by the workers themselves.[86] There was nothing original in these ideas. They had been promoted by institutions like the Society for Bettering the Condition of the Poor since the 1790s, but they were given a new impetus by Prince Albert's sanction.

Over the years, quite a few working men noted the Prince's views and approached him for support. Factory operatives, mechanics, servants, printers, butchers, bookbinders, gardeners, soldiers, sailors, seamen and watermen all received his patronage.[87] In 1850, for example, he was asked by a group of London's journeymen tailors to advise them on the formation of a guild, which was to include charitable relief for those in distress. 'There can be no higher duty than that of mutual assistance,' replied the Prince, 'and to enable men to afford each other such assistance when it is needed, the principle of association is indispensably necessary.' But while he was happy to contribute towards the society's charitable objects, he warned that 'mutual assistance' might easily be converted into 'mutual interference', and consequently lead to idleness and improvidence.[88] It was another example of how far the Prince had imbibed a belief in philanthropic free enterprise and the dangers of interfering with the conduct of trade.

Philanthropy and manufacturing, the gospel of Christ and the gospel of work were interwoven in the Prince's thinking, whatever the project at hand. When he founded the Windsor Royal Association, a self-help scheme on the royal demesne, he hoped it would enliven the labouring classes and local industry.[89] When he encouraged charitable education for the poor, he sought to arouse the 'honest industry' of the children but also to make their parents identify with the schools through contributing fees.[90] When he promoted model cottages for the Society for Improving the Condition of the Working Class, it was to create a home environ-

14.   Model house for families, by Prince Albert, 1851.

ment that would produce industrious, independent men and women. And when he paid to have a pair of the cottages put on display at the Great Exhibition in 1851, his object was to persuade developers and manufacturers to translate his ideas into bricks and mortar.[91] The Great Exhibition itself should be seen in the light of the development of Prince Albert's charitable doctrine, which aimed to promote social reconciliation, based on those prime values of a commercial society—prudence and self-reliance.

★   ★   ★

It is instructive to compare Prince Albert's charitable role with that of Queen Victoria. There was considerable overlap in their patronages, but their emphases and enthusiasms were of a somewhat different character. The Prince was more comfortable with ideas and public speaking, and his interests extended to the private sector as well as the voluntary one. Even though most of his projects were small in scale, they dealt with large public issues. He had a special relationship with working men, particularly skilled workers, the 'aristocracy of labour'. Like Queen Charlotte and Queen Adelaide before her, Queen Victoria had a special interest in causes relating to women and children, although she was unsympathetic to women's rights.[92] Unanalytic and less interested in statistics than her husband, she enjoyed her parochial rounds among the poor.[93] This was in keeping with nineteenth-century views about women's roles, which placed personal service and compassion high on the list of distinctive female qualities.

Royal women commonly reflected and reinforced the prevailing idea that the female sex had a particular calling or social purpose. This applied especially to Queen Victoria, who was seen to embody national character and virtue. She was typical of much female philanthropy in favouring personal and practical solutions to immediate problems. Apart from dropping in on poor cottagers, she attended ladies' sales and annual fêtes at Balmoral, sometimes sitting in a Bath chair in old age, carrying out Bagehot's advice to be visible. She maintained a child orphaned in a shipwreck, bought sewing machines for needy widows, and had artificial limbs constructed for men who came to her attention on hospital visits.[94] Further afield, she was kept informed of disasters in Britain and famines in India, responded to personal appeals and sympathized with the suffering families. Compared to Prince Albert, her charity was more susceptible to calls on the emotions.

Like women of the middle class, the Queen had taken on board the conventional attitudes about 'woman's nature and mission'.[95] Indeed, she helped to establish conventional attitudes, with the result that she became enslaved by them. Queen Victoria was a strong personality, stubborn, kindly and impetuous by turns; but in many essentials, she and Prince Albert lived their lives in harmony with the doctrine of the two spheres, the most eloquent exposition of which was to be found in John Ruskin's *Sesame and Lilies*. 'Man's power is active,' Ruskin wrote in the chapter 'Of Queens' Gardens': 'He is eminently the doer, the creator, the discoverer, . . . his intellect is for speculation and invention; . . . But the woman's . . . intellect is not for invention or creation, but for sweet ordering, arrangement and decision. She sees the qualities of things, their claims and their places.'[96] Queen Victoria and Prince Albert are not the only royal couple who have personified Ruskin's views.

The separate spheres of men and women in the nineteenth century sheltered Queen Victoria from criticism and placed her in a unique political realm.[97] She often said herself that politics was a male arena, and the fact that she was a woman contributed to the removal of the crown from party politics. This is not to say that she ignored affairs of state, far from it. But because of her sex, she was able, and encouraged, to give more time to it than she might otherwise have found for a philanthropic role. Her charities were less visible and less didactic than Prince Albert's, but they were nonetheless considerable. She took a particular interest in the work of other female philanthropists, among them Mary Carpenter, who worked with ragged children, Agnes Weston, the 'sailor's friend', and Florence Nightingale.[98]

15. A royal visit, including the youthful Prince of Wales, to soldiers wounded in the Crimea, Chatham, 1855. From the painting by Jerry Barrett.

The monarchy and the military were deeply interconnected, and the Queen, herself the daughter of a soldier, maintained a lifelong interest in the plight of men at arms. Characteristically, she sent £10 and a framed portrait of herself to a Cornish woman who had seven sons in the Crimea, and dispatched articles of her own making to the front.[99] Prince Albert worried about the nutritional requirements of soldiers and the need for convalescent depots to be set up outside the war zone.[100] The Queen sent a message to the sick, which chaplains read out on the wards at Scutari: '*no-one* takes a warmer interest or feels *more* for their suffering . . . than their Queen.'[101] In England, she received invalids and distributed gifts to privates and non-commissioned officers.[102] On a visit to the wounded at Chatham Hospital, she found the conditions cramped and the atmosphere of fatality offensive; but the effects of the 'royal touch' partly compensated. 'It is very gratifying to feel [that what] one can do easily, gives so much pleasure,' she wrote in her Journal. 'It is one of the few agreeable privileges of our position & it certainly repays us for many disagreeable ones.'[103]

At the end of the war, the Queen laid the foundation stone of the Royal Victoria Hospital at Netley for the military and, not without trepidation, invited Florence Nightingale to Balmoral. As Disraeli once said to Matthew Arnold, when you flatter royalty 'you should lay it on with a trowel'.[104] Nightingale needed no such reminder and paid lavish tribute to the Queen for her marvellous skills with wounded soldiers. As ever with philanthropists in search of royal patronage, the applause was the prelude to the introduction of wider purposes. As her biographer put it, she seized the opportunity 'to convince the Queen and, equally important, the Prince Consort of the urgent necessity for immediate army reform'.[105] Her plan was to get their support for a Royal Commission into the administration of the Army Medical Department. Knowing the Prince's reputation, she worked up her statistics.

In September 1856, Nightingale put her plans for the reform of military hospitals before the Queen and the Prince Consort. The Queen, who remarked that Nightingale had 'a man's intelligence', wrote to George, Duke of Cambridge, who had just become Commander-in-Chief: 'We are delighted . . . with her wonderfully clear head. I wish we had her at the War Office.'[106] The Prince, who especially admired the charts and tables, wrote in his diary that Nightingale had put before us 'all the defects of our present military hospital system, and the reforms that are needed'.[107] Although the Queen and the Prince applauded the scheme, they did not have it in their power to establish a royal commission. But they used their considerable influence in Nightingale's campaign to persuade the Secretary of State for War, Lord Panmure, that a commission was necessary. They got their way.[108] The campaign resulted in the Royal Sanitary Commission on the Health of the Army. The subsequent reforms illustrated the blurred boundary between voluntary and political action.

★ ★ ★

Back at the Palace itself, the office of the Privy Purse was being reorganized in the 1850s, partly because of the expansion of charitable business. An extra secretary was appointed to run a patronage department. One of his duties was to administer the Queen's and the Prince's rights to nominate candidates for admission to the benefits of charities, in particular schools, orphanages and asylums. This right was taken very seriously, for it was an excellent method of finding places for aged retainers, or the children of tradesmen and others known to the royal family.[109] The administration of begging letters was another responsibility of the patronage department, and it was felt necessary to provide indices to determine whether or not someone had previously applied for assistance. By 1854 there were over 800 reports on begging letters alone.[110]

The reform of the Privy Purse office eventually led to the creation of a revealing set of guidelines on charitable donations. The 'General Rules and Principles Observed in the Offices of Privy Purse and Private Secretary to the Prince', endorsed in 1858, was to provide a coherent policy on patronage and pecuniary relief and to regulate the crown's spending

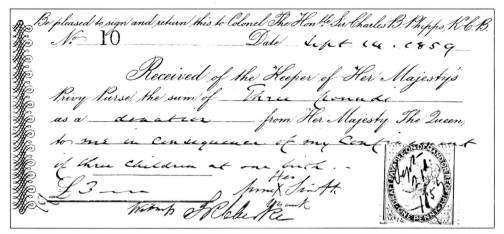

16. A receipt for triplet payment, 1859.

on philanthropic causes. The thinking behind the document recalled the charitable philosophy of Thomas Chalmers and anticipated the social casework of the Charity Organisation Society. All applications for assistance from individuals were to be investigated, as long as they bore the appearance of a 'deserving' character. Palace officials vetted them carefully and referred them to the Mendicity Society, to local clergymen, or to others with relevant knowledge.[111] The custom of giving £3 to a woman giving birth to triplets was continued, provided that the case was 'well attested'. In 1867, a good year for triplets, eighty-two mothers requested payments.[112] These grants became widely known as king's or queen's bounty.

Whatever the hardship, a successful applicant might expect £5 if he or she were from 'a better class', and £1 or £2 if working-class. As a general rule, applicants were to be relieved only once, for the sums available could hope to do little more than see poor people 'through temporary difficulties'. Preference was always given to those who would be expected to provide for themselves in the long term, which was another way of saying they were 'deserving'. This was allied to the conventional wisdom about charity's relationship to government poor relief: 'Where the destitution is absolute and hopeless, a donation is quite thrown away, as it only postpones for a short time, the resort to Parish relief, which must, in the end, be made.'[113]

The Privy Purse 'Rules and Principles' covered virtually every aspect of crown patronage and gave formal recognition to traditional practices. There were guidelines to cover: the proper method of application to the Palace (direct to the Queen or to the Prince Consort); the use of the titles patron and president (the former was employed where the Prince could not be expected to take up active duties); voting for charitable officials (the right never taken up); presents to the Queen (not accepted); the dedication of books to the Queen (only by established authors); the patronage of bazaars (the Queen's contribution usually to be expended on purchases); and handling threatening letters (to be sent to the Home Secretary). In conclusion, the rules stipulated that 'all letters are answered, and all are registered'. And, perhaps most tellingly, it was stated that 'it is right that all the Queen's subjects should consider it to be their privilege to apply to Her Majesty in distress and difficulty; and the poorest person . . . has as much the privilege of a subject, as the richest'.[114]

In the early decades of Queen Victoria's reign, the 'privilege' was being taken up by more and more citizens, who were coming to expect royal support for their societies and for themselves. Charitable promoters, whose eyelids registered pound signs on the very mention of royalty, imagined their institutions in perennial credit through monarchical association. How else can one explain the repeated applications to the Queen from the Leeds Mechanics' Institution.[115] Some societies worried about their rivals scooping local subscribers through royal patronage. On discovering that another charity had received it, they could move quickly to get a piece of the royal cake. When the Queen sent the West Cowes Relief Fund £20, the East Cowes Relief Fund took its chance, applied to the Palace, and duly received the same amount.[116] Some institutions were less calculating, but nonetheless felt obliged to apply to the royal family because it was there, a social Everest that had to be climbed.

There had been a few charities named after members of the royal family, Queen Charlotte's Hospital and Queen Adelaide's Fund among them; but after mid-century, philanthropists looked increasingly to the monarchy for inspirational titles to give to their societies. The sheer growth in the number of rival institutions triggered the search for venerable names. A thousand or so voluntary hospitals alone were set up in the second half of the century across Britain and the Empire.[117] To set up a specialist hospital, complained the *British Medical Journal*, it took only an aspiring surgeon with a spare house, aristocratic patronage and a 'striking speciality', such as the treatment of 'inverted eyelashes'.[118] Whatever the speciality, from foreign missions to local hospitals, the proliferation of institutions created a degree of muddle that would eventually come under attack. In the 1850s there were eight eye hospitals in London alone, all of them north of the Thames. Several of them boasted the royal prefix.[119]

In an era when charitable society came 'to full, indeed almost rankly luxuriant bloom', the search for attractive, high-profile titles became something of an obsession.[120] In the competitive atmosphere of charitable enterprise, voluntarists began to name scores of institutions (eventually hundreds) after the Queen or the Prince Consort, and they did not always bother to apply for the privilege. From Windsor to Adelaide, there were Queen Victoria hospitals, infirmaries, almshouses, maternity homes, memorial cottages, lunatic asylums, pension funds, schools of industry and

institutions for every other cause imaginable. From Waitak
Borioboolaga, there were royal homes and royal dispensaries, or wha
royal else took the locals' fancy.[121]

Untold numbers of institutions named a ward or an extension after a
member of the royal family, or simply put up a picture of the Queen or
the Prince Consort in the belief that it would raise the charity's social
tone. There was no shortage of pictures for sale after Prince Albert's
death. Businessmen sought the Queen's permission to reproduce photographs of the Prince, and while she had little control over what they
manufactured, her more relaxed attitude to the commercial reproduction
of royal images after Prince Albert's death stimulated a vast outpouring of
memorial prints and photographs to satisfy the intense public demand.[122]
The relative dearth of royal commemorative pottery in the 1860s may
have been because commercial firms noted Queen Victoria's aversion to
seeing her face on a plate.[123]

When Prince Albert died in 1861, worn down by his unrelenting sense
of duty, a cult appeared. Grieved philanthropists popped up across Britain
and the Empire like mushrooms after a damp night. In his memory, they
erected at least seven new hospitals alone, in Bishop's Waltham,
Devonport, Greenwich, Guildford and Lancaster in England, and at
Tenterfield and Wollongong in Australia. Across Britain, local dignitaries
set up Prince Albert funds, built almshouses and museums, schools and
orphanages, laid memorial tablets, and installed Albert bells, screens
and windows in their churches. At Welham Green, Hertfordshire, the
Butchers' Charitable Institution, of which the Prince had been a patron,
put up almshouses. At Bagshot, the Queen laid the foundation stone of
the Albert Orphan Asylum.[124] *The Builder* noted, sarcastically, that 'any
project, however ridiculous or incongruous, is justifiable and recom-
mendable if it only be useful. A set of people *want* this or that; and
forthwith they tack on to their real requirement a *false pretence* of erecting
it *to the memory* of a popular Prince.'[125]

If only a small portion of the population received any direct benefit
from royal philanthropy, many more shared in the expanded charitable
services that the monarchy made possible. In the process, millions of
subjects saw the Queen, the Prince or one of their relatives on charitable
parade. In Prince Albert's day, there was a more comprehensive range of
recipients of royal patronage than ever before, from foreign seamen in
Sunderland to Old Etonians, from distressed operatives in Coventry to
gentlefolk in Bognor. They spread the message that the monarchy took
an active interest in the nation's welfare. The Queen repeated the
message in her parliamentary addresses. In words written for her by her
government, she identified the crown with 'a comprehensive regard for
the interests and permanent welfare of all classes of my subjects' (1842),
and 'the more effectual application of charitable donations and bequests'

17. The Prince of Wales laying the first stone of the Lambeth School of Art, July 1860.

(1845), and the 'loyal spirit of my people and their attachment to institutions during a period of political revolution' (1849).[126]

In familial partnership, the Queen and the Prince Consort encouraged greater charity in all classes, and they fully expected it to produce civic improvement, respectable behaviour and deference to the crown. In an age when the demand for rights and benefits from government was at a relatively low level, they radiated a religious ethic, at once conservative and ameliorative, that invigorated civic life and promised greater social harmony. In an age of free trade, the Prince Consort promoted a social economy in which charitable enterprise, working with commercial interests, complemented government provision for the poor. State intervention in the social sphere excited relatively little monarchical enthusiasm, for it raised the spectre of regulation, which troubled philanthropic free-traders like Prince Albert. The crown, having imbibed the parochial idealism of the day, assumed that local charitable remedies were more likely to be effective than national bureaucratic ones. Voluntary measures, unlike government ones, engendered loyalty to the crown.

In political terms, the free development of voluntary institutions was thought indispensable to a liberal society. The Queen's speech to Parliament at mid-century closed with the line: 'By combining liberty with order, by preserving what is valuable and amending what is defective, you will sustain the fabric of our institutions as the abode and the shelter of a free and happy people.'[127] John Stuart Mill elaborated the political significance of voluntary institutions in that testament of liberalism, the *Principles of Political Economy* (1848). Citizens 'have their faculties only half developed,' he wrote, without the habit of spontaneous voluntary action. 'The only security against political slavery, is the check maintained over governors, by the diffusion of intelligence, activity, and public spirit among the governed.'[128] If Mill and his fellow-liberals were right, the royal family was a check on arbitrary government when wearing the crown of charity. When handing out prizes to artisans and agricultural labourers for their industry or when exciting the middle classes to civic duty, the monarchy was a force for liberal values.

The crown in the mid-nineteenth century was not a friend of democracy as understood by political radicals or Chartists, but through its voluntary work it encouraged 'subscriber' democracy and local decision-making, self-help and social pluralism. In step with middle-class society, which it did much to shape, the Victorian monarchy distrusted notions of majority rule and the trend towards bureaucratic government. Yet, unintentionally, it encouraged democratic aspirations among the lower classes by its diffusion of a liberal social vision. Along with its charitable allies, the crown offered a helping hand to individuals who sought to climb up the slippery social ladder through the steady application of their moral and intellectual faculties. It summoned rich and poor alike to assert greater control over their lives and to adopt a uniform moral code, which eroded the distinctions between the 'two nations'.[129] Could independent, self-disciplined working men, who shared the same values as the middle classes, then be denied political rights?

In 1867, the year in which parliamentary legislation added nearly a million new voters to the electorate, the Queen wrote to the Princess Royal: 'The lower classes are becoming so well-informed—are so intelligent & earn their bread & riches so deservedly that they cannot & ought not to be kept back.'[130] Although unable to influence events, Queen Victoria approved of the concession to political democracy that the Reform Bill produced, particularly as she believed the middle classes to be largely sympathetic to it. She remained hostile to universal suffrage, but she identified increasingly with the loyal and respectable working class, an identification that royal philanthropy helped to bring about. She saw the nation, as Elizabeth Longford put it, 'reshaping itself in forms ever more favourable to a benevolent Monarchy'.[131] The crucial issue for the future, not without importance for a 'benevolent Monarchy', was whether a voluntary culture, with its traditions of pluralism and *local* democracy, would prosper in a *parliamentary* democracy with an ever more ascendant central state.

4

The Late Victorian Royal Family: The Cult of Benevolence

By the late nineteenth century, philanthropy was not only a sign of individual worth and civic virtue but of national standing. Indeed, the Victorians equated their civilization with the proportion of national activity given over to benevolent causes, just as a later generation would equate it with the Welfare State. When Podsnap boasted to his foreign guest in *Our Mutual Friend* that 'there is not a country in the world, sir, where so noble a provision is made for the poor', he was trying to show his country to best advantage. When *The Times* announced in 1885 that London's charitable receipts exceeded the budgets of several European states, it was a source of national and imperial pride.[1] Ten years later the Charity Commissioners gloried in their report 'that the latter half of the 19th century will stand second in respect of the greatness and variety of the Charities created within its duration, to no other half-century since the Reformation'.[2]

Queen Victoria had assumed the leadership of the philanthropic movement by endorsing its values. And the monarchy's charitable administration, which was rarely in advance of public opinion, nourished expectant voluntarists across the Empire. The patronage work of the Privy Purse Office carried on after Prince Albert's death with little interruption, and the Queen and other members of her family indulged in a cult of benevolence that delighted civil society. Over the years the monarchy had built up a great fund of strength and credit with the citizenry through its social work. Its support for local sentiments and initiatives symbolized national virtue while empowering the crown. The reverential public felt grateful for the monarchy's beneficence, even if members of the royal family could not fathom what it was they were bestowing.

The evident benefits of royal philanthropy to the monarchy excited little comment in Palace circles after Prince Albert's death. In the 1860s, a decade of prosperity and stability, the crown's advisors had little need to consider philanthropy as a strategy for survival. In any case, Palace officials were accustomed to dealing with cabinet ministers and heads of state, and they must have thought the royal family's charitable work rather humdrum. A visit from the Shah of Persia, after all, did more for their self-esteem than a visit from some provincial worthy. Transfixed by images from the past, the Queen's staff, like the Queen herself, adjusted slowly, and reluctantly, to the monarchy's loss of political power. They spent a fair proportion of their time answering the 'flood of letters' on social questions and administering patronage, but for them public affairs still meant high politics.[3]

Constitutional writers, who showed little regard for the royal family's points of contact with civil society, abetted such attitudes. In *The English Constitution* (1867), Walter Bagehot turned some fine, misleading phrases, which have besotted monarchists and constitutional writers ever since. He was not insensitive to the 'salutary influence' of the monarchy's social power, or its ability to make sovereignty understandable to the masses through presenting itself as a *family*. He saw the crown as a focus of religious and moral sentiment, and he noted that it was 'an accepted secret doctrine that the crown does more than it seems'.[4] For all his insight, however, Bagehot failed to mention what the crown was doing in civil society, where it was certainly doing 'more than it seems'. This may have been because he was a political journalist, little attuned to social issues or the problems of the poor. Though an opponent of American slavery, his name did not appear on subscription lists, perhaps because of his melancholy doubt, as he put it, 'whether the benevolence of mankind does most harm or good'.[5]

The English may have been untheoretical, as Bagehot believed, and 'so snobbish and envious that without a hereditary head of state they would trample each other to death in a Gadarene stampede for social pre-eminence'.[6] But they were not as dim as Bagehot gave them credit for being; and their reverence for kingship was based on more than wonder. By the death of Prince Albert, the monarchy's popularity may have had more to do with its penetration of civil institutions and its provision of social goods and services than its mystique. To be sure, the nation's charities themselves created an atmosphere of acquiescence to the crown, but they were also expressions of the power of communities. By its participation in so many voluntary campaigns, the monarchy illuminated the popular will and, through it, expressed a will of its own.

Bagehot's emphasis on the monarchy's appeal to the imagination, its capacity to satisfy people's emotional longing for splendour and serenity, dazzled a generation that had grown up on a diet of dry constitutional theory. But his accent on the monarchy as the symbolic, 'dignified' part of the constitution encouraged many people, perhaps even Palace officials, to discount what he himself discounted—the 'efficient' part of monarchy. As many nineteenth-century voluntarists would attest, the royal family's charitable policy was enabling and ameliorative; and while it profited from the mystique that attended royalty, it was implemented

18. The Prince of Wales receiving silk purses at St Mary's Hospital on the occasion of laying a memorial stone of a new wing, 1865.

with an eye to results, and not simply an eye to the royal image. The monarchy's charitable administration was often carried out behind closed doors, and the results could be inversely proportional to the display. When Bagehot conjured up that famous phrase, 'we must not let daylight in on magic', he seemed to be in the dark himself.

Magicians, even royal ones, have to work at their trade. And while the monarchy cultivated its charitable patronage in a dimmer light after the death of the Prince Consort, the royal family did not relax its philanthropic routine. The Queen's reluctance to put on the robes of state did little to undermine the monarchy's influence in civil society. In hours free from the demands of politics, the Queen added fresh touches to her philanthropic activities. She preferred opening a hospital to opening Parliament. She may have weakened her tenuous relationship with government by opening Parliament only seven times in the last thirty-nine years of her reign, but she rarely failed her constituents in the voluntary sector.[7] The recipients took notice of this beneficent labour and those who saw it performed, believed. But the recipients who did not see it performed knew that in the charitable world the power of royalty could be felt without being seen.

In the ten years after Prince Albert's death, her blackest decade, Queen Victoria assuaged her grief with hospital and prison visits. At Windsor, she inspected the workhouse and oversaw the activities of the Prince Consort's Association. At Balmoral, in a bout of philanthropic estate management, she oversaw the erection of new housing and set up the

19. Silk purse presented to Princess Alexandra on a visit to the Hospital for Sick Children, Great Ormond Street, in 1893.

'Balmoral Bursaries', an educational trust in memory of Prince Albert. Paid for out of the proceeds of her book, *Leaves from the Journal of a Life in the Highlands*, the bursary scheme was the first time, though far from the last, that the royalties of royalty were used for charitable purposes.[8] Farther afield, the Queen took a sympathetic interest in a range of voluntary appeals and causes, including the Lancashire cotton famine,[9] the administration of St Katharine's Hospital,[10] the cholera epidemic of 1866,[11] several colliery accidents,[12] the Indian famine of 1868,[13] and Mary Carpenter's work on behalf of schools in India.[14]

To be interested in such matters was perhaps less eye-catching than dissolving Parliament or forming a ministry, but it had its compensations. Arguably, Queen Victoria contributed more to the nation's health and happiness through her charitable administration than through her political one. She preferred her money to be spent on specific local projects, rather than given to 'overlords driving serfs to build cathedrals'.[15] Like a latter-day Hannah More, she seemed happiest when left to her parochial rounds. Good works brought her into communion with the poor, whom she admired for their fortitude, while setting a challenge to the rich, whom she condemned for their frivolity.[16] There were moments when her cult of benevolence drove her into maudlin flights of fancy: 'More than ever,' she wrote to Queen Augusta of Prussia in 1865, 'I long to lead a private life, tending the poor & sick.'[17]

In 1868, Queen Victoria laid the foundation stone of St Thomas's Hospital, and she returned in June 1871 to open the new building, which was situated across the river from the Parliament she preferred to avoid. The opening was a grand occasion, of great moment to hospital voluntarists in London. The royal family turned out in such strength that onlookers may have confused it with a funeral. The Queen's party included the Prince and Princess of Wales, the Duke of Edinburgh, Princess Louise and the Marquis of Lorne, Prince Christian, Princess Beatrice, the Prince and Princess of Teck and the Duke of Cambridge. Among the other guests were a host of hospital officials and civic dignitaries, the Archbishop of Canterbury, Lord Shaftesbury and Disraeli. Gladstone was also present, but the police failed to recognize him and kept him standing out of sight during part of the proceedings.[18] Presumably this would not have happened had the Queen been across the river for what for him was a more important opening.

Surrounded by a guard of honour of Surrey Volunteers and a detachment of Foot Guards, the Queen, attired in black silk, entered the entrance hall and mounted a dais, on which there was a throne with its canopy festooned with crimson draperies. She listened to a loyal address, which referred to Prince Albert's work for the hospital, and knighted the treasurer. In a brief speech delivered on her behalf, she paid tribute to her friend Florence Nightingale, whose self-confidence must have surged on being singled out for praise. After a tour of the building, on which the Queen named one ward 'Victoria' and another 'Albert', she declared the hospital open. In memory of her two visits, the governors had a marble statue of the Queen erected in the entrance hall. It rested on 'a new species' of building material used in the hospital's construction, appropriately called 'Victoria Stone', made of 'petrified concrete'.[19]

Despite the Queen's intermittent public engagements, there was mounting criticism of her retirement from public life. It seems that her appearances on behalf of charity, however beneficial, did not count for much with politicians and journalists. *Punch* had set the tone in 1865 by depicting the Queen as a veiled statue: 'Descend; be stone no more.'[20] *The Times* echoed this view soon after the Queen's opening of St Thomas's.[21] Gladstone, who believed the monarchy to be in danger, complained to Lord Granville in December 1870 that 'the queen is invisible, and the Prince of Wales is not respected'.[22] Bagehot, too, spoke in terms that would have alienated the Queen had she taken notice of him. 'The Queen', he wrote in July 1871, 'has done almost as much to injure the popularity of the monarchy by her long retirement from public life as the most unworthy of her predecessors did by his profligacy and frivolity.'[23]

Although she made more public appearances in 1871 than in previous years, it was an *annus horribilis* for the Queen. To some she appeared, in Longford's words, 'like one of Landseer's red deer at bay'.[24] There was, of course, more to what Gladstone called 'the Royalty question' than the Queen's reluctance to turn up for ceremonies of state. Abroad, the Franco-Prussian War had ended with the fall of Napoleon III and the declaration of a French republic. The news shook Buckingham Palace like a mild tremor and aroused English republicans to voluntary association. Meanwhile, a few radicals, including Charles Dilke and Joseph Chamberlain, turned their minds to the Civil List. The Etonian radical, Henry Labouchere, claimed that the Queen had lost all respect by her incessant financial demands on behalf of her children. 'What does she do with it?' asked Macaulay's nephew, G.O. Trevelyan, in an anonymous pamphlet of that name. Why should the nation be expected to stump up so much money if she were not performing her public role?[25]

Bagehot, whose 'dignified' part of the constitution had seemingly disappeared into cloistered widowhood, chimed in: 'The Queen has been little seen in public, and it is of the essence of the showy parts of the Constitution to acquire importance and popularity by being seen.'[26] Gladstone too believed that the nation 'ceases fully to believe in what it does not see'.[27] Agitated by the appearance of republican sentiments, he told the Queen's Private Secretary, Henry Ponsonby, that Her Majesty's retirement from public life gave him the 'blue devils'.[28] Unlike the Prime Minister, Ponsonby was too tactful to thrust his views on the Queen, but he worried about her isolation from affairs of state: 'If . . . she is neither the Head of the Executive, nor the fountain of honour, nor the centre of display, the royal dignity will sink to nothing at all.'[29] The Prince of Wales was also apprehensive. He wrote to his mother in September 1871: 'The people are really loyal; but it is feared in these Radical days that, if the Sovereign is not more amongst them, and not more seen in London, the loyalty and attachment to the Crown will decrease, which would be naturally much to be deplored.'[30] Two months later the Prince contracted typhoid fever.

English republicanism proved far weaker than the constitution of the Prince of Wales, and, if we are to accept received opinion, it collapsed when he rose from his bed in 1872. The National Thanksgiving at St Paul's Cathedral to celebrate the Prince's 'miraculous' recovery, which Gladstone believed to be a service of moral purification, perhaps even for the Prince himself, signalled the monarchy's revival. Revival is perhaps too strong a word, for its suggests a level of disillusionment with the crown that seems far-fetched. Victorian republicanism was a poor thing. By the 1870s, as a latter-day republican notes, it 'had steadily weakened among the middle classes, leaving most of their backbones in chronic and (by this time) complacent curvature'.[31] Whether crippled by deference or not, respectable society identified with a social hierarchy headed by the sovereign. This was just as the Prince Consort, who believed that subjects should be conservative and Princes liberal, would have wished.[32]

When the Prince of Wales recovered, he was in need of employment, or so Gladstone and others believed. Unable to settle into a 'proper' job and identified with the idle pleasures of high society, he dismayed many of those closest to him, including his mother. His personal failings increased the pressure on the Queen, whose isolation so agitated loyalist politicians and courtiers alike. Bagehot called the Prince 'an unemployed youth'.[33] Gladstone, critical of the Prince's behaviour and his doubtful companions, complained to the Queen in 1871: 'I am convinced that Society has suffered fearfully in moral tone from the absence of a pure Court.'[34] His plea for reform at the top, which he believed would result in virtue trickling down the social order, suggested that aristocratic turpitude remained entrenched despite decades of evangelical cleansing. Gladstone wanted the Prince in for a moral refit.

Like a moored battleship, the heir to the throne needed an assignment worthy of his status. As ministerial responsibility was inappropriate, a host of other possibilities suggested themselves to Gladstone and Palace officials. During the Prince's illness in 1871, Ponsonby had drawn up a memorandum after talks with the Queen. Five fields came under review: philanthropy, art and science, the army, foreign affairs and India.[35] Gladstone responded with his own ideas, which included philanthropy, art and science, and a post for the Prince as representative of the Queen in Ireland, an idea which Gladstone particularly favoured. The Queen and the Prince rejected Ireland, however, as wholly unsuitable. The Prince, who did not wish to leave Britain, also rejected India. A military career was also a non-starter, for as Ponsonby remarked, the very idea of the Prince living in Aldershot was 'absurd'. Gladstone considered the Foreign Office a secondary employment, for it was unlikely to provide 'the attraction of freshness'.[36] This was a polite way of saying the Prince was indiscreet and his powers of concentration limited.

After eliminating the more conventional and, to the political mind, more important possibilities, philanthropy, art and science remained. Gladstone argued that 'it is hardly possible for the Prince to make a worthy pursuit out of philanthropy; I do not mean one worthy in itself, but of adequate magnitude'. Philanthropy, art and science were not insignificant pursuits for a future king, he explained, but they did not 'give him a central aim and purpose, which may, though without absorbing all his time, gradually mould his mind, and colour his life'.[37] Francis Knollys, the Prince's Private Secretary, did not believe the heir to the throne had the aptitude for charitable work.[38] Ponsonby dismissed it in the bluntest terms: 'Art, science and philanthropy were all no use.'[39] The remark suggests that he attributed little importance to the charitable side of the monarchy's role. But then Ponsonby ruled out almost all other potential employments for the Prince. As seen from the Palace, the chief problem was that the heir to the throne preferred amusement to business. He had abundant charm, but his social skills were 'a screen for official ignorance'.[40]

Gladstone wanted the Prince of Wales to take on responsibility without power; the Prince wanted power without responsibility. What Gladstone had in mind was an occupation that would test the Prince's abilities and eventually give him experience useful to the continuity of government. This seemed rather pointless to the Prince, who wanted to be kept informed of events but without inconvenience to himself. As the Queen told Gladstone, the Prince was happy to take on employment only as long as it did not tie him down 'to one particular spot or country'.[41] After much discussion, the causes of disagreement between the Queen and Gladstone proved insurmountable, and the issue, which had been 'a matter of cardinal importance', gradually fell into the background. The Prince would just have to take on board whatever turned up. But whatever did turn up would have an air of impermanence about it, for to many people the singular purpose of the heir to the throne was to wait upon events.

Still, the Prince's incongruous position offered him a freedom of action denied the Queen. Given his abilities and personal requirements, the most appropriate employment was one that needed personal skills more than concentrated effort; one that could be fitted into the Prince's social life or, better yet, form part of it. Of the occupations discussed by the Queen, Palace officials and the Prime Minister, philanthropy had advantages which went unrecognized. It was in many ways an ideal employment for the Prince, as it was for other members of the royal family, not least the female members. Charitable work made few intellectual demands on patrons and was compatible with a busy calendar. It would bring the Prince into popular view without tying him down to any particular place or institution.

No one mentioned it in the discussions, but a philanthropic role for the Prince of Wales would enhance the monarchy's reputation with its growing constituency in the voluntary community. It would not only reinforce the links between the crown and the diverse elements of civil society, but it would bring the Prince under the benign influence of respectable opinion. With his effortless social superiority and skill in public speaking, he would be the focus of admiration and emulation, and

20. The Prince of Wales on a visit to the Foundling Hospital in Moscow, 1866.

he could indulge his taste for official dinners, prize-giving and the distribution of honours. Through philanthropy the Prince might even do some good, for there was goodness in him. And if he made a mess of it, who was likely to complain? Certainly not those whom he honoured with his patronage. Not the government either, for voluntary activity, despite its implied political meaning, was relatively safe ground and its disputes isolated.

Given that philanthropy was employment that the Prince could fulfil after his own fashion, it seems rather surprising that it was so peremptorily rejected. But Gladstone typified the general view when he argued that philanthropy 'does not form a plan of life. It does not lay a firm or adequate foundation for habits of business.' The proper 'business' of princes, it seems, had to have reference to high politics, even though, as Gladstone admitted, 'political responsibility cannot indeed be made applicable to the Heir Apparent'.[42] It is one of the curiosities of British life that politicians transformed the crown into what Philip Magnus called a political 'rubber stamp', only to perpetuate a belief that the crown's first duty had to do with high politics.[43] The monarchy did retain a residual political role, but the obsession with it on the part of politicians and the Palace was blinkered and atavistic.

It is the fate of princes that few people tell them when they are wrong, but there is no shortage of advisors who will discourage them from doing good. But while the Palace and the Prime Minister rejected a philanthropic career for the Prince, he was already a presence to voluntarists. When Bagehot called him 'an unemployed youth', the Prince had an

21.   The Prince of Wales speaking at St Bartholomew's Hospital, 1868.

established charitable role. The Queen had made sure of it. For a start, she had contributed nearly £3,000 on behalf of the Prince of Wales to fifteen leading charities before he was ten years old.[44] She ensured that he would eventually have to take an interest in them, because the patronages brought nomination rights with them. Before his marriage to Princess Alexandra of Denmark in 1863, he was a contributor to over 130 charities and actively promoted many of them, albeit in a desultory fashion.[45]

Between his marriage and his illness in 1871, the Prince of Wales increased the number of his philanthropic engagements, and he began to attend bazaars more often, a sure sign of his wife's influence. It was typical of him that when he took the chair at a meeting or laid a foundation stone, he felt obliged to make an unofficial inspection in advance. At St Bartholomew's Hospital, for example, where he became Patron in 1867, he attended six official functions in 1867–68, but dropped in 'on many other occasions'.[46] In the late 1860s, he spent between twenty-five and thirty days a year on official charitable business, often accompanied by Princess Alexandra.[47] Such duties may not have constituted a job to most people, certainly not to the indefatigable Gladstone, but for the Prince of Wales, who spent three months of the year abroad and only dabbled in foreign affairs, charity was as close as he ever came to one. The fact that the Queen refused to let him participate in her political work gave him more time for philanthropy.

Ironically, just as the discussions were taking place about the Prince's need for employment, the Prince himself began to feel that his charitable work was becoming a burden. In April 1871, a few months before his illness, he complained to the Queen that his social duties were 'very numerous', not least because he and Princess Alexandra had to stand in for her so often. 'You have however no conception', he added, 'of the quantity of applications we get in the course of the year to open this place, lay a stone, public dinners, luncheons, fêtes without end; and sometimes people will not take *no* for an answer—and certainly think we must be made of wood or iron if we could go through all they ask—and all these things have increased tenfold since the last 10 years.'[48] In the light of his charitable duties, Gladstone's criticism of the Prince's idleness and impropriety must have seemed fanciful to the Prince.

Whatever Gladstone and others believed, the failings of the Prince of Wales and Queen Victoria's retreat from political life did not represent a serious danger to the crown. Certainly the Queen never thought so. We should be sceptical of measuring the monarchy's popularity by reference to the number of the Queen's parliamentary appearances or the feverish imaginings of Palace officials or metropolitan journalists. The troubles associated with the Queen's isolation were largely the creation of over-heated monarchists, not least the Prime Minister. After 1871, Queen Victoria did not open Parliament regularly or attend to the duties of state with her enthusiasm renewed. The Prince of Wales never settled into a 'proper' job, nor did he give up his unseemly friends and habits. Yet the popularity of the monarchy went from strength to strength in the late nineteenth century.

Gladstone and his political allies had their own motives for taking fright in the early 1870s. They were loath to admit it, but when Queen Victoria was on ceremonial duty she gave *them* a return with the electorate, especially the middle-class electorate. When she appeared in public as head of state, or presided over a state banquet, statesmen were part of the ceremony and a little of the monarchical magic rubbed off on them. The Queen's retreat from her official duties weakened the crown's relationship with government, but it also weakened the government's relationship with the crown. Her refusal to open Parliament damaged the symbolic link between the cabinet and the nation and reflected badly on Parliament. The monarchy, although politically neutered, still conferred legitimacy on a government; and, in so far as the monarchy was esteemed, it radiated esteem to those in its orbit.

Gladstone, a campaigner for charities himself, albeit an eccentric one, was sensitive to what he called 'the moral and social resources' of the monarchy, and the 'deep debt' that the country owed the Queen for her philanthropic labours.[49] But royal appearances on behalf of charity, like the Queen's audiences and drawing rooms, were rarely of national political significance. In contrast to occasions of state, they offered few rewards to government. Still, the royal family's association with welfare causes added greatly to the monarchy's popularity; and ministers basked in the glow of so incandescent an institution. Having extinguished the monarchy's political role, they were drawn irresistibly to its ceremonial trappings and social pre-eminence.

Queen Victoria's visit to the London Hospital in March 1876 gives a clue as to why she, at least, remained confident of the loyalty of her subjects. Invited to open the new Grocers' Wing extension, she travelled across the capital to the East End in a coach with Princess Beatrice, the Duchess of Wellington, and Lady Waterpark, a lady-in-waiting. Everywhere large enthusiastic crowds turned out. The Queen, always sensitive to the mood of the populace, noted the banners and inscriptions along the route, among them, 'Welcome Victoria, the Friend of the Afflicted' and 'I was sick & Ye visited me'. Inside the hospital, she received a loyal address, heard a chorale composed by Prince Albert, and a benediction given by the Archbishop of Canterbury. She named wards 'Queen Victoria' and 'Princess Beatrice' and visited burns cases and sick children.[50] In the hospital's history it was a turning point, enhancing its reputation among medical men and, importantly, City financiers.

The royal outing to the East End reassured the Queen about her popularity, but there was one upset, which was not recorded by the press. The Queen wrote in her Journal of one small child who had been run over in the street. The girl 'said she would get well if she could see me & and she smiled & and I shook hands with them all & stroked their little cheeks, poor little dears'.[51] *Punch* captured the scene in a drawing captioned 'Her Best Title—"Queen of the East"', in which the Queen is seen stroking the sick child's forehead. In her diary, Lady Waterpark alluded to the rapturous welcome given to the royal party and noted the royal attentions to the little girl, who had such hopes of survival after meeting the Queen. There were still people in Britain who believed the Queen had the power to cure by her proximity, but the royal touch did not always have miraculous effects. 'Alas,' Lady Waterpark lamented, 'the poor child died.'[52]

★ ★ ★

It might be said that all that remained for an emasculated monarchy was ceremonial and the promotion of voluntary service. Precluded from politics, commerce and the professions, members of Queen Victoria's extensive family had to carve out what careers they could in the restricted world in which they moved. Yet we should not conclude that this represented so dismal or so inconsequential a prospect. The Prince Consort exerted a powerful hold over his children, not least in death, and his

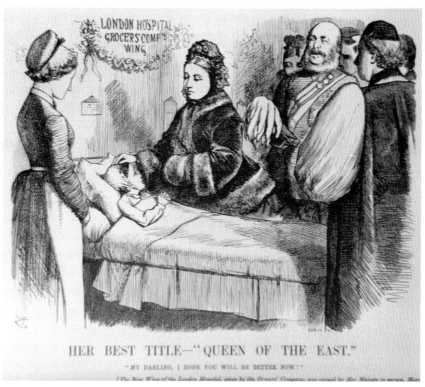

22. Queen Victoria at the London Hospital, 1876, from *Punch*.

belief that leadership in the world of philanthropy was a noble calling left a memorable impression. To the Victorian mind, and more specifically Prince Albert's, paternalism began at home.

Arguably, Queen Victoria's and Prince Albert's greatest contribution to the 'Welfare Monarchy' was having so many children. The nine royal offspring entered a privileged world in which they 'shone as a race apart, denizens of a red and gold Valhalla'.[53] Yet the Victorian Valhalla was homely, virtuous by the standards of royalty, and burdened with the cares of the world. This was as Queen Victoria and Prince Albert desired. They nurtured their miscellaneous brood of four sons and five daughters on an austere morality before releasing them into the expectant world. Under the oracular spell of Baron Stockmar, Prince Albert grandiloquently remarked that 'upon the education of princes . . . the welfare of the world in these days greatly depends'.[54] But as he recognized, the monarchy's heroic age was over. Consequently, members of the royal family, however imperious or pleasure seeking, were obliged to be sensitive to social issues. Respectability had them by the throat; the regal bearing belied a middle-class outlook.

It was highly beneficial to the monarchy that a large family was waiting in the wings to take up an active patronage role after the death of the Prince Consort and the semi-retirement of Queen Victoria. As a friend of the Queen's youngest son, Prince Leopold (Duke of Albany), put it: 'Assuredly there is work here—work earnestly demanded and gratefully welcomed by the nation—for as many public-spirited princes as any reigning family can supply.'[55] Whatever their inclinations, the Queen's children had little choice but to take up some cause or other, for public expectations of royal benevolence were so great that a refusal to fulfil a philanthropic role was simply inconceivable. Unlike most children, they had a built-in reverence for age and history, and they had to accommodate their individuality to ancestral vocations and a fixed inheritance. The family shrine was Frogmore, where they worshipped their father, and the family catchword was duty. So often repeated, it had hypnotic effects, like a mantra that took the place of thought, but which absorbed princely individuality in the interest of the monarchy's greater good.

The 'great object' of the royal princes, wrote Queen Victoria after the death of Prince Albert, was 'their steady development in everything that is great, virtuous, and useful, and that will render them good sons, brothers, husbands, citizens, and benefactors of mankind'.[56] The remark was an illustration of just how far aristocratic values had metamorphosed into a utilitarian philosophy of goodness. Royal descent had become not so much 'a title to enjoyment' as 'a summons to duty'. It was a consolation that the Victorian mind took such pleasure from the performance of a duty. In the autograph book of Prince Leopold the lines of Archbishop Trench appear:

> O righteous doom, that they who make
>   Pleasure their only end,
> Ordering the whole life for its sake,
>   Miss that whereto they tend.
> But they who bid stern Duty lead,
>   Content to follow, they
> Of Duty only taking heed,
>   Find Pleasure by the way.[57]

The royal children received an education that left them with the conviction that philanthropy was essential to the welfare of the nation and an antidote to hazardous social experiments. The Queen and the Prince Consort prepared them for a life of public service by taking them on charitable visits, introducing them to leading philanthropists, and locking them into patronages from an early age. Members of the royal family inherited charitable responsibilities the way poor children inherited clothes, but the Palace paid scrupulous attention to the quality of the goods handed down. To the philanthropic establishment, which had an eye for new recruits and old blood, heredity was a most admirable tradition.

If the children of Queen Victoria were born with silver spoons in their mouths, they also arrived with silver trowels in their hands, the better to lay all those foundation stones. Though often authoritarian, and sometimes meddling, they spread their charitable cement in every direction, all the while making those endearing connections between the monarchy and civil institutions. But while they were involved in virtually every movement for social betterment in the late nineteenth century, very little attention has been paid to their work, especially that of the sons. As the royal biographer David Duff remarked in 1940, the crown's power in the charitable world would prove of little interest to historians of the Victorian period, 'for their interest lies, and will lie, with those who wielded another category of power'.[58] Duff's insight has proven true even in an age when 'class and society' have shot up the historian's agenda.

The charitable work of Queen Victoria's family would constitute a book in itself; here it can receive only passing mention. Like women of the middle classes who found paid employment closed to them, the Queen's daughters assuaged their boredom with philanthropy. In some respects, the higher a woman's status the greater the constraints, and the life of a Princess, while uniquely privileged, could also be uniquely stifling. The housing reformer Octavia Hill said of Princess Alice: 'the paraphernalia of her position has again and again thrown her back.'[59] It could have been said of all of Queen Victoria's daughters. Voluntary work offered them one of the few escapes from the refined idleness and rituals of court life; it heightened self-confidence and self-respect and provided a degree of status that was earned rather than accorded automatically to those of royal blood.

Arguably, the talented Princess Victoria, Princess Royal and later German Empress, was the daughter in greatest need of purpose and self-respect. A liberal suffocated by German conservatism, she took refuge in voluntary activity. The wars with Austria (1866) and France (1870) freed her from conventional routine and brought out her powers of organization. She took the greatest satisfaction from her hospital work. She designed a new type of hospital building, a bungalow with a roof that rolled back, which was 'cheap to build and easy to run'. Over the years, she initiated a host of charities, including schools, infirmaries and 'Victoria Haus', a retreat for aged British and American governesses. Like her mother, she moved among the poor and the dying without embarrassment. Unlike her mother she supported women's rights, particularly female higher education.[60]

Princess Alice, later Grand Duchess of Hesse, also found that charity was the only career open to her in the constrained court circles of Germany, and during the wars of German unification developed a reputation for nursing and hospital work comparable to that of Florence Nightingale.[61] She kept abreast of charitable campaigns in Britain and invited leading female philanthropists, including Mary Carpenter, to Darmstadt. She translated Octavia Hill's *Homes of the London Poor* into German, and, perhaps remembering her father's advice to visit the poor, penetrated the London slums incognito on several occasions. Hill, who arranged these outings, found her 'as acute an observer as an experienced . . . rent-collector'.[62] On her return to Germany the Princess sent Hill a life of her hero, the Prince Consort.

Back in Britain, Princess Helena, later Princess Christian of Schleswig-Holstein, laid foundation stones, visited hospitals, set up a children's holiday home and founded the National School of Needlework in Sloane Street. At a meeting of the Ladies' Association for the Care of Friendless Girls she once declared: 'I know that I am the Queen's daughter, but really I cannot help it, and you must try not to mind me at all.'[63] Still, she pulled rank in committees, cutting through difficulties with an imperious 'we all agree on that point, don't we?'[64] When she organized the British Nurses' Association, which received a royal charter in 1893, she even had the audacity to reject the advice of Florence Nightingale.[65] As Lady Roberts said of her: 'Princess Christian has always personally administered her nurses and I have been told that if any one ventured to disagree with H.R.H. she has simply said "it is my wish that is sufficient" which always ended the discussion. The Princess Christian would never consent to be a mere figurehead.'[66] The history of nursing in Britain, which was much influenced by German practices, had much more to do with Princess Christian and the rest of the royal family than is commonly imagined.

Princess Louise, later Marchioness of Lorne and Duchess of Argyll, was also on charitable call, visiting hospitals and homes and raising money for scores of needy institutions.[67] Unhappily married and childless, she alleviated her loneliness through philanthropic work as well as through art (she was a sculptress). Women's rights attracted her in particular, and though the Queen disapproved, she served as the first President of the National Union for Higher Education of Women. She gave her name to several female societies, including a Salvation Army home for unwed mothers in Clapham and a refuge for young girls in Surrey. Few initiatives, however humble, were rejected out of hand. In the 1880s, she became the President of the 'Gordon League', a society which offered rest and recreation to working people on Sunday evenings.[68] Such schemes brought the royal family into closer association with the working classes, and carried forward the Prince Consort's policy of bridging the class divide through crown patronage.

Sharp and often out of temper, Princess Louise might have alienated many philanthropists had she not been so useful. Octavia Hill, who knew better than most the advantages of royal patronage, found her 'friendly and kind' and with an 'intelligent interest' in the Open Space movement and the National Trust. She *asked* to be President of the National Trust.[69] When Hill proposed to set up a park in Lambeth, she wrote to the Princess that her appearance 'would ensure' a favourable response.[70] The Princess obliged, the money appeared, and at the formal opening of the park (Vauxhall Gardens) she brought along the Prince and Princess of Wales, which guaranteed publicity and a crowd.[71] The royal family's role in the provision of open spaces and playing fields, and the protection of historic houses, though not necessarily their own, deserves more systematic study.

Queen Victoria's youngest daughter, Princess Beatrice, later Princess Henry of Battenberg, became her mother's companion and secretary. Though shy and withdrawn, she accepted the round of openings, prize-givings and concerts as part of her inheritance. Her public duties mounted up after her marriage. They could be a source of embarrassment. She once caused 'enormous offence' by withdrawing before the little girls were able to present their purses at the opening of a new wing of the Royal Chest Hospital.[72] Charity bazaars were more the Princess's line, and while they served many a useful cause, they added to the clutter of her own drawing rooms. Her passion for bazaars sometimes irritated Palace officials, who did not enjoy having their meetings with the Queen interrupted because the Princess wanted to paint a flower for a ladies' sale.[73]

Bazaars are a leitmotiv of royal benevolence, and when one thinks of them one invariably thinks of the Queen's cousin, Mary Adelaide, Duchess of Teck. The Duchess was a notable presence in the charitable community, not least in terms of physique. The imperious daughter of Adolphus, Duke of Cambridge, she was well known for her benevolence, her passion for objects and her inability to pay for them. (In emergencies Baroness Burdett-Coutts came to her aid.) She increased her overdrafts by giving away at least 20 per cent of her annual allowance of £5,000 granted by Parliament.[74] At any given time, she was likely to have six or more bazaars on the go. She enjoyed the part of shopwoman, but stipulated that when she attended a sale, she expected someone else to purchase the goods.

In her prime, the Duchess of Teck was perhaps the hardest working member of the royal family. She toured hospitals and orphanages by the score and handed out school prizes by the thousand. She left an indelible impression at the North London Collegiate School, where Miss Buss drilled her girls for a fortnight on 'the correct method of approaching and receding from royalty'.[75] Dr Barnardo's, the National Society for the

Prevention of Cruelty to Children, the St John Ambulance Brigade, and a dozen London hospitals were among her many patronages. She was particularly assiduous in her work for the Needlework Guild, which recruited large numbers of middle-class women to make clothes for the poor. She had the common touch with the working classes but could be sharp with ladies who obstructed her charitable administration. Highly visible, she played a significant role in encouraging deference to the crown in that most sensitive part of London, the East End, where she was known affectionately as 'Fat Mary'.[76] Not the least of her services to the 'Welfare Monarchy' was the inculcation of charitable habits in her daughter, Princess Victoria Mary, later Queen Mary.

Though it has rarely been noted, the sons of Queen Victoria fulfilled their social duties, and they attended so many bazaars that one might conclude that they enjoyed them as much as their sisters did. Prince Alfred, later Duke of Edinburgh, pursued a naval career, but he cut his charitable teeth helping Princess Alice organize bazaars in Darmstadt. He was probably the first male member of the royal family to take a stall.[77] (How exquisitely low for a prince to be identified with shopgirls and trade.) Arthur, Duke of Connaught, a military man *par excellence*, carried the tradition further. He once wrote to Lady Holland to secure her help with a bazaar he was organizing himself on behalf of one of his army charities.[78] Nor was the Prince of Wales a stranger to the ladies' sale. A month after his marriage to Princess Alexandra of Denmark, he opened one in aid of Oxford's Radcliffe Infirmary.[79] Over the years he attended scores of bazaars.

Presumably, the princes had not expected to be cutting ribbons and selling trifles when they turned their minds to useful employment. But they did it. The bazaar, part commerce and part amusement, was a characteristic nineteenth-century institution. Queen Adelaide, as mentioned, added to its lustre by her patronage. In the Victorian years, it swept all before it, for even its critics had to admit that 'large sums are frequently raised by these means'.[80] Both cause and effect of the growing feminization of philanthropy, the ladies' sale played a part in the feminization of the monarchy as well. What does it tell us about the idea of princely virtue, once identified with masculine power? The susceptibility of royalty to the bazaar, and female philanthropy generally, suggests that a transformation of some importance had taken place. Stripped of those manly pursuits of war and diplomacy, the princes of the blood had collapsed into niceness.

Bazaars were at best an amusement, at worse an annoyance, to Queen Victoria's sons, who did not dwell on their underlying meaning. The Dukes of Connaught and Edinburgh, with their military and naval careers to pursue, did not rate their voluntary work highly. Nor were they of a disposition to think much about its implications for the monarchy. Like the sons of George III, they usually found it easier to say yes than to say no to charitable applications from respectable individuals and institutions. In other words, middle-class voluntarists had them pretty much where they wanted them. The princes knew they were being used as advertisements, but it was not exacting work. From time to time they even contributed more than was expected of them.

The Duke of Connaught gave publicity to scores of voluntary agencies over his lifetime. The Boy Scouts and the Girl Guides, Masonic hospitals, the British Red Cross and a host of institutions in the colonies did not ask him to analyse his generosity; they simply wanted his support, which they used to extract money from others. Along with his highly charitable wife, whose death he commemorated by presenting the people of Bagshot with a nursing home, he gave time and money to just about any scheme devised for the benefit of soldiers and their families. When serving as Governor-General of Canada during the First World War, charitable duties took a more significant turn. But wherever he found himself abroad, whether posted there or simply on tour, philanthropic work was customary.[81]

It was on tour that Prince Alfred discovered the power of royal philanthropy, and the risks in pursuing it. His visit to Australia in 1867–8, though not the first royal tour overseas, was nevertheless memorable. Between kangaroo shoots and formal banquets, the Prince laid foundation stones, visited schools and inspected lunatics. At the Melbourne Lunatic Asylum the banner 'Welcome to our Royal Guest' gave his aides some little amusement. At Sydney things got out of hand. While at a picnic to raise money for a proposed Sailors' Rest Home, an Irish revolutionary shot him in the chest. He was thus the first member of the royal family to be wounded while performing a charitable duty. But as events surrounding Prince Charles's visit in 1994 illustrated, he was not the only member of the royal family threatened by violence while carrying out a public engagement in that city.[82]

The attempted assassination of Prince Alfred and his lucky escape had repercussions for Australia of some real benefit. To commemorate the royal recovery, the citizenry set aside their sectarian rivalries long enough to promote two new charitable appeals. The 'Alfred' hospitals in Sydney and Melbourne were the direct result of the unhappy incident, enduring tributes to the Prince's injury. The mixture of joy, fear and embarrassment that Prince Alfred left in his wake was not an uncommon feature of later royal tours. Expressions of colonial philanthropy, which identified the crown with isolated communities, proved a most satisfactory, and beneficial, way of smoothing relations between the crown and its dominions.

The haemophiliac Prince Leopold, the Duke of Albany, had to find consolation in his study rather than Australia. Unlike his brothers Arthur and Alfred, he did not follow a military or naval career, though, like them, he invested uniforms with a near-religious significance. Although not a public figure like his brothers, he discovered, rather to his surprise, a career beckoning. It was represented by the multitude of begging letters on his desk. At first, he restricted his charitable interests to those appeals in keeping with his personal tastes, such as literary societies; but eventually he began to enter into the spirit of philanthropy more generally. According to his friend Frederick Myers, who interested him in the Society for Psychical Research, Prince Leopold felt under the sway of his father whenever the cause of charity came up.[83]

In the years before his early death in 1884, Prince Leopold began to speak on behalf of charitable causes. Compared to the happiness of doing good, other triumphs were 'insipid', he pronounced at Frith College in 1879.[84] At a meeting of the Deaf and Dumb Institute in the same year, he rejoiced in the 'network of organized charitable effort' across the country.[85] In language reminiscent of the Charity Organisation Society, he told a group of Liverpool schoolchildren that the best way to improve the condition of the poor was to compel parents 'to send their children to school, keep down outdoor relief, and check indiscriminate almsgiving'.[86] And at the opening of University College, Nottingham, in 1881, he revealed what could be seen as the monarchy's simple strategy for survival: 'there is nothing which the Royal Family values more than the goodwill of their fellow countrymen; and there is nothing they will not do to legitimately deserve that goodwill.'[87]

★   ★   ★

Spreading 'goodwill' was the speciality of the Prince of Wales. He could not be called a spontaneous philanthropist, and he sometimes complained of being used simply as 'a puff to the object in view'.[88] But after his recovery from typhoid in 1872, he stepped up his patronage work, perhaps feeling the need to do something to placate Gladstone and his mother. He also began to place greater emphasis on causes relating to the sick and the poor, perhaps because of his own illness. Henry Burdett, Britain's leading expert on philanthropic institutions, noted that 'while it would be unjust to say that the Prince did not care for hospitals or orphanages before his illness, it is undeniable that his interest in these has become deeper and more practical since that time'.[89]

While the Prince of Wales developed his patronage role at home, a notable feature of his philanthropy was its expansion into the Empire. In the tradition of George IV's visits to Ireland and Scotland, and Prince Alfred's tour of Australia, he included charitable duties in his itinerary on his trip to India in 1875–76. Though his many biographers prefer to dwell on the tiger shoots, he inspected a host of institutions, including three hospitals and an orphanage in Calcutta. At schools, missions, hospitals and

23. Queen Victoria, Empress of India, keeping famine at bay, 1877, from *Punch*.

"DISPUTED EMPIRE!"

prisons across the sub-continent the populace received him with acclaim. In turn, he left the impression that the welfare of India's people, whether princes or peasants, was an imperial priority.[90] It was an exotic variation on the theme of class cohesiveness and social harmony that the monarchy invoked at home.

The Prince of Wales was the incarnation of the British Raj, and everywhere he went his hosts treated him like a god; and like a god he aroused the worshippers to civic duty. When he passed through Aden the merchants commemorated the visit by building 'The Prince of Wales's Charitable Dispensary'. At Lucknow, the Maharajah of Kashmir gave over £50,000 for the promotion of charitable and religious causes as a tribute to the royal guest.[91] As on all later tours, the royal party left a trail of new schools and hospitals behind, which served as a justification of Empire and gave a social and political return to the monarchy.[92] Philanthropy was the human face of the Empire, which made imperialism palatable and con-

120

24. The Prince of Wales delivering his speech on housing in the House of Lords, 1884. By T. Walter Wilson.

genial to subjects in Britain and the colonies alike. Royal benevolence, it was sometimes argued, did more to honour the British Raj than the triumphs of statesmanship or war. Such a view was easier to justify when the reigning British monarch was a woman, for the title 'Empress of India', which Queen Victoria adopted in 1877, suggested maternal softness compared to the military hardness of the title 'Emperor'.

Whether at home or overseas, the Prince's greater willingness to comply with the wishes of voluntarists had much to do with the burden of his inheritance and the number of requests which he could not refuse as heir to the throne. Some causes compelled attention because they were former interests of Prince Albert. One of these was working-class housing, which became an issue in 1883 with the publication of *The Bitter Cry of Outcast London* by the nonconformist minister Andrew Mearns. The Queen, the champion of oppressed crofters, wanted something to be done and wrote to Gladstone. He showed little enthusiasm for immediate action, but agreed to set up a Royal Commission into housing the poor. With the Queen's approval, the Prince of Wales joined the Commission in 1884 as an ordinary member.

In preparation, the Prince accepted the invitation of Lord Carrington, another member of the Commission, to explore the tenements of Clerkenwell and St Pancras in disguise. It was another royal glimpse into the abyss, a variation on his sister Alice's secret visits to the London slums arranged by Octavia Hill. The Prince was unnerved by the experience, especially the sight of a starving woman and her three children lying on a heap of rags in an unfurnished room. 'We visited some very bad places,' Carrington reported, 'but we got him back safe and sound to Marlborough House in time for luncheon.' Four days later, on 22 February 1884, the Prince made a speech in the House of Lords, the only one he ever made in that chamber of any substance. Referring to his own efforts at building new dwellings for the poor at Sandringham, he called for 'drastic' measures to be taken by Parliament, but on the condition that they should not endanger the work already underway by the housing charities.[93]

The Royal Commission on the Housing of the Working Classes provided 'a battleground for conflicting social philosophies', but it did not set off a revolution in housing policy. Nor was it intended to.[94] The Prince attended on sixteen of the thirty-nine days set aside for the examination of witnesses, and would have been more in evidence had he not been distracted by the death of his brother, the Duke of Albany. He asked a few questions and acquitted himself without mishap. He appeared impartial as philanthropists and municipalists staked their respective claims to superiority in housing reform, though his wish to see Octavia Hill on the Commission suggested a preference for voluntary effort over state intervention. As with so many Royal Commissions, the final recommendations were anodyne. Still, it was excellent publicity for the Prince, and it carried forward the royal association with housing and homelessness that dated from Prince Albert's time.

There was a curious episode during the Royal Commission's proceedings, which might have been embarrassing to the Prince: the examination of his own land agent at Sandringham, Edmund Beck. With the Prince in attendance, Beck was asked whether His Royal Highness was a responsible landowner. As an exercise in diplomacy the land agent's answer was masterful; it may even have been true. Before the Prince purchased Sandringham, the estate was 'little better than a rabbit warren', Beck reported. 'He [the Prince] knows exactly the condition of . . . every hole and corner of his estate of 8,000 acres; and certainly no cottage tenant or labourer is ever forgotten in this general knowledge by the Prince.' The tenants were so 'exceptionally well provided for', according to Beck's testimony, that the problem was 'to prevent their being spoiled'.[95] No one mentioned it, but there were forty-one royal charities at Sandringham, which provided virtually cradle to grave coverage for labourers and tenants.[96]

The Prince acquitted himself with ease and competence on public occasions, as the Royal Commission on housing illustrated. As a consequence, he accepted an invitation from Gladstone to join the Royal Commission on the Aged Poor in 1892. It sat for two years, and the Prince put some effort into it, attending thirty-five out of the forty-eight sessions. The majority report published in 1895 rejected the idea of state pensions, but there were dissenting voices, which recommended pensions either on a contributory basis or as of right without contributions. The Prince wished to avoid the political controversy the report aroused. He believed that the state could do more to relieve the aged poor, but he preferred self-help and private philanthropy. To his mind, the notion that the poor should receive state benefits as of right smacked of socialism. Like his mother, the Prince equated socialism with riot and the collapse of civilized life. He was never one to risk damaging 'the organic structure of a hierarchical society, which he regarded as divinely ordained'.[97]

By the time the Prince sat on the Royal Commission on the Aged Poor, Palace officials had changed their minds about his capacity for philanthropic and social work, and they were beginning to see the benefits in flying the standard of royal benevolence. Francis Knollys and his colleagues played a crucial role behind the scenes by their astute management of the Prince and his public engagements. Palace advisors played their part as well, especially Henry Burdett, who became the Prince's consultant on all matters charitable. While the philanthropic paperwork carried out by the Prince of Wales himself should not be underestimated, he preferred the less burdensome functions: chairing annual meetings, opening new buildings and attending anniversary dinners and festivals, all of which took considerable planning.

The Prince's charitable career had much to do with the women in his life. As noted, Queen Victoria put his name down as a subscriber and encouraged his charitable inclinations when he was only a boy. His marriage to Princess Alexandra engaged the Prince in a host of causes which he would have neglected if left to himself. Even his adultery had benign effects. Certainly the time he spent with Frances Maynard, Countess of Warwick, was not all voluptuous immobility. The Countess was an eccentric example of aristocratic social conscience (later a socialist), who persuaded the Prince to join her on her charitable rounds.[98] Whether he enjoyed visiting aged cottagers, signing workhouse visitors' books or sponsoring many of her other pet projects, we shall never know. But in order to be with her, he did it. With regard to philanthropic activity, the great womanizer was womanized.

25.   Princess Alexandra attending one of her dinners for poor children at the People's Palace in the East End, accompanied by the Prince of Wales.

In the 1890s, the Prince was carrying out about forty-five philanthropic engagements a year, which he supplemented with unofficial visits to favoured charities. By then he had contributed tens of thousands of pounds to nearly 1,000 institutions or appeals, including over fifty benefit societies, which provided annuities to members of virtually every trade or profession in the country.[99] Many of his societies were small in scale, including the seventy or so royal charities in Windsor and Sandringham. But he took care to cultivate the most powerful institutions as well, including seventy-five leading hospitals across the country.[100] As Burdett remarked, he did not patronize every charity, but 'the range of the Prince's work is so very wide as to include probably all the most important institutions'.[101]

The Princess of Wales was more benevolent than her husband. Capricious and feather-headed, she pursued charity to the point of reck-lessness. Before becoming Queen she made hundreds of charitable visits, and, like the other females in her family, she favoured the causes of women and children.[102] The Hospital for Women, Soho Square, the Great Ormond Street Children's Hospital and nursing institutions received special attention. She once pulled £2,000 out from under a sofa cushion and gave it to the chairman of the London Hospital.[103] In 1899,

26. Princess Alexandra presenting certificates to nurses at Marlborough House, 1899.

she brought the Finsen Light to the Hospital, an invention of her fellow Dane, Dr Niels Finsen, which proved of benefit in the treatment of tuberculosis of the skin. It was also at the London that she befriended Joseph Merrick, the Elephant Man. Where the Princess dared to go others followed. According to Sir Frederick Treves, the London Hospital surgeon, Merrick's room soon became so cluttered with nicknacks that it might have been occupied by an opera star.[104]

The Elephant Man was not the only distressing case attended by Queen Alexandra. As Mary Gladstone, the daughter of the Prime Minister, noted: 'if she happened to go to a window and any distressing object met her eye, she could not rest until she had sent out to enquire and discover what help could be given.'[105] Once, passing through a port town, she saw some way-worn horses being shipped to France for slaughter, and she compelled her lady-in-waiting to write a letter of complaint on the spot.[106] Her organizational skills did not match her sympathies, but when aroused she could be a powerful advocate and fundraiser. During the Boer War the Council of the Soldiers' and Sailors' Families Association raised £1,389,000; over £200,000 of it was due to a special appeal which Queen Alexandra made as President of the charity.[107] Though not an impartial witness, Burdett credited her with successfully reorganizing the Red Cross Society, an institution whose royal associations have never been fully documented.[108]

The influence of Queen Alexandra on the nursing world was phenomenal, though not always of certain benefit. At least six nursing bodies had her name affixed, including the Queen Alexandra Nursing Board, the Queen Alexandra Imperial Military Nursing Service and the Queen Alexandra Military Nursing Service for India.[109] She took a detailed interest in them, right down to the buttons on the uniforms. The Secretary of State for War, Lord Haldane, thought her a nuisance when he tried to improve the nursing services under the Territorial system. 'We had better dispense with royalty,' he wrote to his sister in 1908. 'She [Queen Alexandra] is about the stupidest woman in England. Can't we organise this business without a royal President?'[110] He could not. As the historian of nursing, Anne Summers, remarks: 'It is not easy for the late twentieth-century reader to appreciate the extent of royal influence in so vital a state interest as military medicine in this period.'[111]

★　★　★

What did the multifarious institutions attached to the Prince and Princess of Wales and other members of their family want from royal patronage, apart from respectability and a boost in revenue? Voluntarists greeted a visit or a cheque from their most august patrons like manna from heaven, but those attuned to large social and political issues wanted more from them, especially more in the way of leadership. According to Frederick Myers, a founder of the Society for Psychical Research, the public did not expect a royal opinion to represent an individual preference. 'A princely supporter of schemes of public welfare will carry permanent weight only if the public feels that it can count on his position as a real guarantee of impersonality, of detachment. . . . His business is not to be a special pleader, but an arbitrator; . . . not to lead revolutions in opinion, but to confer a *de jure* title on opinions which are rapidly acquiring a *de facto* sway.'[112]

This was lofty stuff, but it ignored something about royal patronage which rarely surfaced in public. In the combative world of organized charity, many voluntarists used the prestige of royal association to dish rivals, to settle old scores or to push through a contested policy. Henry Burdett used the Prince and Princess of Wales most effectively to carry forward nursing schemes which his many enemies in the medical world opposed. It was not unknown for one charity to petition the Queen in the hope of dashing a rival charitable initiative. Charles Loch, the Secretary of the Charity Organisation Society, tried this option when Burdett put forward plans to set up the League of Mercy in 1898.[113] Failing with the Queen, he appealed to the Prince of Wales for a meeting over the issue. It was refused. By then, Burdett had the royal family stitched up.

The stampede to secure royal patronage often had to do with institutional and personal rivalries, but there were deeper ideological considerations at work as well, which began to surface towards the end of the century. In a sermon preached on the occasion of the Prince's recovery from typhoid in 1872, the Reverend Archer Gurney, a former English Chaplain in Paris, had put the philanthropy of the Prince of Wales in a political context understandable to monarchists with voluntary leanings. 'We are no friends to benevolent despotisms in this land of ours. We like, in most ways and as far as may be, to administer ourselves. So private charity is with us an all-important agency. And who so ready as the Prince of Wales to give gold, and time, and trouble, at all seasons, to all useful undertakings?'[114]

To Gurney, loyalty to the crown meant loyalty to Britain's voluntary institutions and vice versa. He saw the Prince of Wales following in Prince Albert's footsteps, devoting himself to 'all good schemes for the union of classes, and the removal of social discrepancies in the commonweal'.[115] In serving good causes, the Prince would also serve the wider cause of civil liberty, which Gurney, like most Victorians, believed to be intrinsic to voluntary activity. Such a royal agenda, based on the needs of civil society, would seem quite a departure for a monarchy little identified with a defence of individual liberty. It was certainly something outside the ken of most constitutional writers and journalists. But philanthropists, who were coming under attack for their failure to eradicate distress, were beginning to see the monarchy in a new light, as a bastion of individualism against collectivism.

Henry Burdett always thought the monarchy fulfilled a quasi-political purpose through its voluntary work. He abhorred socialism or what he sometimes called 'municipalization', which was attracting converts in Britain from the 1880s onwards. In his mind, the royal family, through its voluntary role, was a most valuable defence against it. As a Tory with a passion for Empire (he stood unsuccessfully for Parliament as an Independent Conservative in 1906), he believed democratic authority to be immanent in institutions. Like Thomas Chalmers or Samuel Taylor Coleridge, he preferred local solutions to centralized bureaucratic ones. The institution which perhaps best summed up his beliefs was the cottage hospital paid for by voluntary subscriptions. To a man of Burdett's persuasion, citizenship was inconsistent with a dependence on the state

27. Sir Henry Burdett
(1847–1920).

for social benefits. In this he accepted the mid-Victorian commonplace that if government provided benefits as of 'right', it would corrode civic culture and divorce morality from poverty, thus making poverty respectable.[116]

An awesome presence in the philanthropic world, Burdett did more than anyone else, with the possible exception of Edward VII's 'indispensable' advisor, Reginald Brett, Viscount Esher, to shape the monarchy's social policy at the turn of the century. Burdett, the son of a Leicestershire clergyman, had an unprepossessing background but made up for it by an astonishing capacity for work. Esher, the son of a former master of the rolls, was an old Etonian, a favourite of Queen Victoria and an expert on military affairs. Monarchists and voluntarists to their fingertips, both men were content to influence events from behind the scenes. Their differences were more ones of personality than opinion, for Esher had all the charm and subtlety of a Renaissance diplomat, while Burdett, more than 'a little noisy', steamrollered anyone audacious enough to disagree with him.[117]

Burdett began his career at that royal institution *par excellence*, the Queen's Hospital in Birmingham. In 1874, he was elected Secretary of the Seamen's Hospital in Greenwich, where he transformed the charity's management and finances. In an exceptional change of career, he joined the Stock Exchange as Secretary to the Shares and Loan Department in 1881, where he remained for seventeen years. There he found time to compile charitable statistics and publish an annual register of philanthropic societies. All the while, he was making connections in the City of London which would help to bring to fruition the various schemes his fertile mind devised. An avid sportsman and gambler, he was said to have broken the bank at the casino in Monte Carlo. He once placed a bet on the Prince of Wales's lucky number and, characteristically, cabled the winnings to the Prince.[118]

In his book *Prince, Princess, and People*, published in 1889, Burdett chronicled the charitable activities of the Prince and Princess of Wales in massive detail, showing the same thoroughness as in his work on charitable institutions. To Burdett, they *were* charitable institutions. The book was a testament of voluntarism, which Burdett admired for its capacity to promote humanity without upsetting the social order. He believed the royal couple to be uniquely placed to give national prominence to charitable work, while marking its local significance. His purpose in writing about royal benevolence, apart from ingratiating himself in palace circles, was to study 'how far the heir to a constitutional monarchy may influence the development and administrations of the various institutions and social movements in the British Empire at the present day'.[119]

Irrepressible, Burdett answered his own question. He believed that history would record that the voluntary association of individuals under royal leadership had done more to improve national life in the mid-Victorian years than all the legislation which had been enacted in the same period. 'If this be merely or partially true—and what fair and intelligent observer will dispute it?—then it would be difficult to over-estimate the enormous advantage accruing to the people, from the course which the Prince of Wales has adopted, by placing himself at the head of every useful movement of a practical character.'[120] Burdett may have been right, yet few historians have ever taken his views on the monarchy's charitable role seriously. He does not even appear in the *Dictionary of National Biography*.

In the 1890s, Burdett relentlessly flattered the Prince and Princess of Wales and their entourage. Without a formal position at court, he penned a steady stream of letters on charitable and business affairs to the Palace, which he supplemented with flowers, perfumes and cigars. Whenever an opportunity presented itself, he dispatched copies of his books on philanthropy and hospital management. He even struck up a friendship with the Prince's mistress, the Countess of Warwick, whose charitable and financial interests overlapped with his own. His cultivation of the royal family betrayed a high level of obsequiousness, but Burdett had calculated, like other philanthropists before and after him, that the monarchy could promote charitable services more effectively than any other institution in the country.[121]

By the end of the nineteenth century, charities in need of money were well advised to look to plutocrats rather than to aristocrats, and Burdett sought to bring the royal family and the City into philanthropic partnership. Such a partnership would not only enliven the charitable establishment but would keep socialism at bay and provide a human-itarian justification for the Empire. Burdett's financial wizardry and City connections stood him in good stead. He brought financiers into Palace circles, and, along with his friend Ernest Cassel, advised the Prince of Wales about investments. As one of Burdett's colleagues remarked, he was 'chosen as the medium through which these splendid gifts have been made to charity by the merchant princes and members of the Stock Exchange in the City of London.'[122] Recognizing Burdett's unique place in the voluntary sector, the Prince and Princess of Wales sought his advice on patronage and consulted his *Year Book of Philanthropy* for information on worthwhile causes. If Burdett raised a query about any particular institution it could lead to an inquiry and the withdrawal of royal support.

Institutions favoured by Burdett tended to succeed. In 1889, for example, he recruited the services of the Prince and Princess to one of his own charities, the National Pension Fund for Nurses, which soon added the 'royal' prefix. The society's investments had reached £300,000 by 1896, thanks partly to Burdett's success in enticing Princess Alexandra to attend receptions and distribute certificates to nurses.[123] As the Fund for Nurses illustrates, one royal engagement a year was enough to keep a charity in the public eye and to stimulate subscriptions and benefactions. It also had the advantage of warding off criticism. The Pension Fund, it should be said, not only had royal sponsorship but also that of Burdett's associates in the City, the bankers Junius Morgan, Lord Rothschild and Everard Hambro, men well known to the Prince of Wales.[124]

In 1896, Burdett persuaded the Prince of Wales to join the Sunday Fund, the charity which coordinated and distributed church collections to the voluntary hospitals. Within weeks, the institution's receipts rose sharply, which convinced Burdett, if he needed convincing, that in the charitable sector almost anything was possible with royal involvement. At a special meeting of the Sunday Fund at the Mansion House, the Prince of Wales, accompanied by the Duke of York, presented Burdett with a photo album for his services. In his speech, the Prince mentioned Burdett's influence in the City and declared that his charities would ensure that his name would 'go down to posterity as it is at present—a household word'. Burdett replied with the philanthropist's characteristic flattery of princes: 'Your Royal Highness's invariable readiness to help the hospitals of this country has often inspired others like myself to fresh efforts.'[125]

The effects of royal intervention on a charity's administration, often carried out behind the scenes, could be dramatic. The Guy's Hospital Appeal of 1896 is a case in point. Guy's was going through a financial crisis because of the decline in its agricultural estates. An ambitious fundraising campaign was proposed, which was to culminate in a festival dinner. The official history of Guy's gives the impression that the campaign was a straightforward success. Invited by the hospital to attend the dinner, the Prince of Wales accepted, and at the same time accepted the presidency of the hospital upon the retirement of Lord Aldenham. In June, he chaired the hospital's great banquet at the Imperial Institute and attended a reception with 4,000 guests, many of them from the City. Thus, the official history concludes, Guy's Endowment Fund began with a spectacular success and reached its ambitious financial target.[126]

The events surrounding Guy's festival dinner were rather more complicated. A memorandum left by Burdett tells an intriguing story of the machinations leading up to the banquet.[127] It points to problems common in charities and the way in which they can be resolved by royal intervention. That the memorandum is in accord with Guy's Hospital records gives it the ring of truth. So does the Prince's festival-dinner speech in which he paid special tribute to Henry Burdett, 'one of the greatest philanthropists . . . to whom they were indebted for the trouble he had taken to make the hospital dinner a success'.[128] For some the tribute must have left a bitter taste, only a little sweetened by the vast sum, put at £150,000 raised on the hospital's behalf, the equivalent of about £7 million at today's prices.[129] It was probably the greatest result from a dinner the world had ever seen.

According to Burdett, the Prince of Wales sought his advice in regard to the invitation from Guy's. Burdett candidly told the Prince that the opinion in the City was that the management of Guy's Hospital was inefficient, owing to the age of the President, Lord Aldenham, and the inertia of the Treasurer, Edward Lushington. When Aldenham called on Burdett at the Stock Exchange, he was presented with a proposal that had the backing of the Prince of Wales. If he and Lushington were prepared to resign, the Prince would replace Aldenham as President, preside at the banquet and guarantee a successful appeal. 'Everything should be done to save the front and feelings' of the two resigning gentleman, Burdett added. A few days later the two men lunched with Burdett at the Bank of England, reluctantly accepted his conditions and approved a letter intimating their retirement from office.[130]

At the time of the Guy's appeal, Burdett and others were turning their minds to the Queen's Diamond Jubilee. By 1897, jubilees had acquired the trappings of grand state ceremonial, as David Cannadine has shown.[131] But their ceremonial power was only one aspect of their appeal. The Jubilee of 1809 and the Coronations of 1821 and 1838, as we have seen, had harnessed royal rituals to popular campaigns; and they resulted in expressions of civic pride and charitable zeal which produced lasting social benefits. In celebrating such royal occasions, the public could feel that something more was on offer from the crown than a vaporous royal progress in antique clothes. Despite the decline in its political power, the Victorian monarchy was not the impotent institution that Postmodernist historians believe it to have been. And its popularity rested on more solid foundations than royal rituals, however attractive they might be to a public enchanted by the magic theatre of monarchy.[132]

The traditional rituals of the crown have always been of interest, especially to royalists, but historians now argue that Palace officials, most notably Lord Esher, began to 'invent' them in the late nineteenth century to symbolize consensus and foster deference.[133] There is something to be said for such a view, though much turns on definitions. Clearly, Esher was an innovator who wanted to bring the monarchy's ancient practices into line with modern conditions. But innocent of social anthropology and the deconstruction of language, he would probably have been amused by the weight of interpretation put on his activities, and perhaps surprised to discover that he had such a gift for invention. It is worth recalling his own views, which he put to Knollys in 1901, apropos of the Coronation:

> I think there is great advantage in following, as far as possible, ancient precedents, so long as they are not hopelessly inconsistent with modern conditions. So much of the power and dignity of the monarchy is derived from its antiquity, and the strict adhesion of our forefathers to "precedent", that one cannot view, without regret, departure from ancient practices, which, although they would be absurd if allied with modern institutions, appear natural to the subjects of our ancient monarchy, scattered as they are all over the world.[134]

The Jubilee of 1887 drew on historical precedent, while setting a new benchmark for royal commemoration. Britain and the Empire were not content to show their affection for the Queen in a transient manner, and the celebrations saw a dramatic rise in amenities and social services, not to mention its impact on local trade. From British Columbia to Zanzibar, philanthropists erected Jubilee almshouses and hospitals. In India 25,000 prisoners were released and a host of new charities established.[135] The Queen also added a new class to the Order of the Indian Empire and honoured, among others, Indian philanthropists.[136] In Britain, as any traveller can see today, cottage hospitals, memorial halls, statuary and parish pumps appeared. There were not enough members of the royal family to open a fraction of the projects set in train. Still, they turned out in force, from Whitechapel, where the Queen laid the foundation stone of a proposed technical school at the People's Palace, to Saltaire, where

Princess Beatrice opened the Royal Yorkshire Jubilee Exhibition, complete with a model village.[137]

Two projects in particular suggested the national mood in 1887. Over two million women contributed £80,000 as a 'Women's Jubilee Offering' to the Queen, most of which was used to set up Queen Victoria's Jubilee Institute for District Nurses.[138] Though not certain that more nurses were needed, the Queen approved of the idea of aligning the new institution with St Katharine's Hospital, one of her ancient charities.[139] For his part, the Prince of Wales wanted to link the imperial pageant with a scheme of permanent public usefulness, and he promoted the Imperial Institute (now transformed into the Commonwealth Institute in Holland Park). Though supported by financiers and maharajahs, the Indian and colonial governments refused to contribute, and the project failed to realize the Prince's ambitions for it as a showpiece of imperial resources.[140]

Planning the Diamond Jubilee of 1897 took nine months and was, if anything, more frenzied than planning the Golden Jubilee. Lord Esher, then permanent secretary to the Office of Works, played a signal part in organizing the celebrations, and in that capacity built up a fund of credit with the Prince of Wales. Esher combined an extraordinary historical sense with a flair for meticulous arrangement, and he ensured that the festivities were a triumph.[141] But Esher was more than a stage manager. Among other things, he was a thoughtful devotee of voluntarism. As he put it in his book, *The Influence of King Edward*: 'there is so fine a flavour about voluntary effort, so exhilarating an atmosphere about the men and women who sacrifice time and wealth, and sometimes life, in the voluntary service of others.'[142] To Esher, the philanthropists who exploited the Golden Jubilee for their own purposes were confederates of the crown, spreading the message of royal benevolence far and wide. The greater the symbolic meaning of royal occasions the greater the scope for charitable commemoration.

In 1897, as ever, local worthies and rival institutions jostled for public favour and subscriptions. *Punch* pointed to the compassion-fatigue induced by the stream of begging letters received for worthy causes, such as 'Self-Supporting Orphans' and 'Homes for the Affluent', which no one had heard of before but which sought to take advantage of the auspicious occasion.[143] Burdett put the number of appeals under consideration at 4,000.[144] When the tension created by competing schemes subsided a general sense of well-being prevailed.[145] And with the years communities large and small erected many a beneficial monument. In Bristol, there was a Jubilee Convalescent Home; in Lewes, a library and recreation ground; in Newcastle, a new Infirmary; in Cape Town, a new wing for the Somerset Hospital; in New Zealand, a Jubilee Institute for the Blind.[146]

28. The Queen's New Year present of chocolates to her soldiers in South Africa.

In the run-up to the Diamond Jubilee, various projects were put before the Queen by her Private Secretary, Arthur Bigge (later Lord Stamfordham). It was the source of some embarrassment when Bigge reported that something might be done to rehabilitate the worst hovels in Windsor, which were called 'Victoria Cottages'.[147] But the two great projects that received the Queen's imprimatur in 1897 were the Prince of Wales's Hospital Fund for London, the brainchild of Burdett, which will be discussed in Chapter 5, and the Indian Famine Fund. As with other nineteenth-century famine funds, the Queen's patronage was deemed essential to its success. In 1897, she contributed the modest sum of £500, but it triggered an appeal which eventually reached the remarkable sum of £2 million.[148] (In purchasing power this figure far exceeded the amount raised in the mid-1980s in Britain to relieve the African famine.)[149] As the Viceroy wrote to the Queen, the English had a natural desire to contribute towards the relief of their 'fellow subjects' in India.[150]

The Victorian mind thought it beyond the capacity of government to get people to love one another, and both statesmen and voluntarists justified the charitable campaign for India on grounds of natural human sympathy. Philanthropists also believed that government relief was prone to bureaucracy and consequently not elastic enough to reach the localities, a view that must have delighted Treasury officials, who wished to keep the charges on government to a minimum. Whether charity could deal with distress on such a scale was doubtful. Nevertheless, the Queen's leading role in the campaign left an impression on the ground in India. She had a genuine concern for the East, and Indians returned her affectionate regard. In one bizarre demonstration of their esteem, the people of Jodhpur commemorated her birthday with a whip round to feed their starving cattle. Lord Curzon, the new Viceroy, wrote to the Queen that the recuperating cattle rested 'with as grateful an appreciation of your Majesty's Birthday, in their dumb unreasoning fashion, as can any of Your Majesty's human subjects have done on the same night'.[151]

By the time the cattle of Jodhpur were on their feet, the charitable attentions of the aged Queen had moved on to South Africa. The Boer War brought out all her motherly instincts. She knitted scarves to be awarded to colonial private soldiers. When an American received one of them, he was allowed to keep it for reasons of diplomacy.[152] Against advice, the Queen ordered tins of chocolate to be dispatched to 'Her troops' as a Christmas present. There was enormous national interest in these parcels. Chocolate manufacturers and railway companies vied for contracts. But the War Office had the unenviable task of delivering the 120,000 tins of melting chocolate to the front. It was less than happy when the troops, delighted with their mementoes, wanted them sent straight back home to their families. As one soldier said, 'they will fetch a good bit in a year or two's time'.[153] When a large number of the returning parcels were lost at sea off Cape Town, disgruntled relatives lodged compensation claims. The Queen was not told of the candied mess her imperial sympathies created. But she died in the knowledge that a soldier had been saved when a bullet hit his chocolate tin instead of his spleen.[154]

Never have there been more tributes to a philanthropist than on the death of Queen Victoria. Was there anyone who failed to hear about her benevolence, that most urgent of Victorian values? Certainly not in the churches or in the charities. Historians of civil society are spoiled for choice. But perhaps the eulogy which the officials of the Ragged School Union included in their history, itself written in tribute to the Queen's memory, will suffice. It came from Canon Henson's sermon at Westminster Abbey on 27 January 1901:

> Every clergyman, philanthropist and social reformer has had, these sixty-three years past, an ally and sympathizer on the throne of his country. Look through history and see how few are the periods, and how brief, in which this could be said. When we consider all these things, our sorrow, great as it is beyond words, passes into another and more religious sentiment. We thank Almighty God for the gift of that gracious and serviceable life, we add to our national treasures the priceless jewel of a pure and lofty tradition bound about the ancient and famous English Crown, and henceforth we connect *our civic duty* with a dear and honoured name.[155]

The Victorians never doubted that their 'dear and honoured' Queen had a role, at once practical and symbolic, beyond the rituals of politics and state.

5

Edward VII:
The Plutocracy and the Poor

The very attainments of Victorian philanthropy made people more conscious of the social evils that remained and less willing to tolerate them. Growing charitable receipts raised expectations of their successful application. But the persistence of poverty, particularly in its urban guise, was an acute embarrassment in a society of obvious wealth that prided itself on social improvement. The doubling of the population over the reign of Queen Victoria and the intermittent periods of economic depression after the 1870s put additional pressure on voluntary services, exposing their patchiness and lack of coordination. With its marked local character, philanthropy was most effective in a prosperous society characterized by vibrant and variegated provincial traditions. Towards the end of the century, it had not only to operate in a harsher economic climate, but in a culture growing more homogeneous and national.[1] In the late Victorian years critics began to question whether charity had the capacity to carry the primary burden of social responsibility.

It may be said that philanthropists were their own worst enemies. They tended to the vocal rather than the contemplative, and their charities had the unhappy tendency to fall out of repair or into dispute. Rivalries and muddle proliferated across the country. Hundreds of institutions worked over the same ground without cooperation. In parts of London, four or five competing district visiting societies besieged poor households each week. Some families, changing their religion from visitor to visitor, found themselves attending different church services each week in exchange for cash or coals.[2] As one Yorkshire beggar told a lady visitor when asked if he could read or write, 'No Ma'am, I can't . . . and if I'd known as much when I was a child as I do now, I'd never have learnt to walk or talk'.[3] Such stories kindled criticism of philanthropy as amateurish and misguided, while they propelled charitable activists into an examination of aims and practices.

Attempts to organize and rationalize the resources of voluntary societies were longstanding, but in the late nineteenth century grew ever more urgent. The Charity Organisation Society, the Liverpool Central Relief

Agency and other institutions made a valiant effort to coordinate charitable services and make them more efficient. They took to social statistics
when they became the rage with a naive enthusiasm born of former
factual deprivation. Self-help was to be invigorated by social casework,
Christian kindness tempered by statistical investigation. What the 'organizing' societies brought to customary practice was greater system and a
few principles of political economy. By grafting the methods of social
science on to religious precept and parochial organization, they encouraged the more efficient use of available resources. Yet charitable supply
could not keep pace with demand and the changing perceptions of what
constituted poverty.

Just as the advocates of philanthropic organization were giving charitable workers a more professional outlook, assumptions about the causes
of poverty were shifting, and the government began to take a greater
interest in social matters. Investigations of urban deprivation, including
Andrew Mearn's *Bitter Cry of Outcast London* (1883), Charles Booth's *The
Life and Labour of the People of London* (1889–1903) and Seebohm
Rowntree's survey of York, *Poverty: A Study of Town Life* (1901), made
charity's critics, and the public at large, increasingly sensitive to the
conditions of working-class life. So, too, did the reports from Select
Committees and Royal Commissions on subjects such as unemployment
and the aged poor. The Boer War, which highlighted the wretched health
of many recruits, created further anxiety and fuelled calls for action.

The growing body of social data about the physical condition of the
poorer classes, to which philanthropists contributed, provided ammunition for those who were coming to different conclusions about the
causes of social distress and the most effective way to remedy it. In an
industrial economy under strain, people began to take the view that
poverty was not simply a product of individual or familial breakdown, as
charity's advocates had long assumed, but of faults in the economy and
the structure of society. Increasingly, the focus was on national efficiency
and social reconstruction, on poverty and what could be done to abolish
it, not on the poor as a set of individual cases in need of personal
reformation.[4] From such a perspective, the efforts of charity seemed not
only inadequate but misconceived. The parochial idealism that had been
so compelling to respectable mid-Victorians appeared a bankrupt philosophy to tidy-minded collectivists in a culture growing more urban
and national.

If philanthropists flourished in diversity, their collectivist critics sought
to create a greater sense of national community. Consequently, they
looked to government to provide it through more uniform and comprehensive social services. Many of them believed that their more 'scientific'
appreciation of the causes of poverty would lead to its elimination. By a
sleight of mind, they began to assume that all that was needed was the

will of government and a vanguard of expert officials. They took it for granted that the poor themselves wished for an extension of statutory provision and that taxpayers would happily pay for it. In their writing they helped to create the illusion that the government could transform society, as if by magic. (Were they investing in the state what others invested in monarchy?) In time, this impersonal approach to welfare, the belief in the efficacy of legislation and state intervention, became as compelling to its advocates as personal service had been to the Victorians. What they inherited from the Victorians was a paternalism, often more extreme in form than that of the philanthropists they repudiated.

Central government had been drawn into the social arena in the Victorian years by its financial assistance to charitable societies, by its commissions and inquiries, and by its consequent intervention in such important matters as sanitation, factory life and education. Specialized facilities provided by the Poor Law had become more numerous as well, most notably in the fields of health and workhouse schooling. By the 1890s, there were over 350 public hospitals for infectious diseases alone.[5] Such institutions still suffered from the stigma associated with the Poor Law. Compared to the voluntary hospitals, which provided a premier service to the 'deserving' poor, they were little esteemed. Their lack of royal patronage confirmed their low public standing and exacerbated the divisions between charitable and state provision. When, in an unusual departure, the Prince of Wales did open a hospital run by the Metropolitan Asylums Board in 1897, it gave the institution 'the impress of social acceptability'.[6]

By the Edwardian years, government measures in health, education and welfare helped to trigger an assumption that further state involvement was inevitable, if not desirable. It was against this background that the Liberal government passed the pioneering, albeit piecemeal, social legislation in the early years of the century, which included school meals (1906), old age pensions (1908) and compulsory insurance for certain categories of employee against illness and unemployment (1911). The *ad hoc* legislation did not represent a stage in an inevitable progress towards the 'Welfare State', but it sent out the signal that government posed a serious challenge to charity's pre-eminence. And as government programmes came on stream, there was a case, compelling to the bureaucratic mind at least, to see them extended, if only to fill the gaps.

The Liberals' social legislation, though limited in scope, troubled many voluntarists and prompted them to reappraise their role. Some of them feared for their jobs, others for subscriptions. Those motivated by religion worried about a decline in moral activism if people turned to the state for salvation. Would the growth of government responsibility for welfare contribute to the devitalization of Christianity? The fiercely individualistic Charity Organisation Society believed that government benefits would divorce poverty from morality and 'happiness' from 'duty'. For his part, Sir Henry Burdett took particular exception to Lloyd George's National Insurance Act. He denounced the measure for meddling in the affairs of the voluntary sector and acidly remarked that 'politicians were the curse of the sick'.[7] He and his allies remained unconvinced by the Liberal logic that such legislation would make socialism less likely. They believed muddled legislative enactments to be part of the trend towards collectivism, despite the disavowals.

The ideological battle taking place between voluntarists and the votaries of mass politics in the Edwardian years may be seen as part of the wider debate between the proponents of competing political visions of Britain that were often associated with classes or parties.[8] Voluntarists turned up in all classes and parties. Some of them welcomed greater government intervention and set aside any worries about its effects on civic responsibility. For them, partnership with the state brought the prospect of augmenting their financial resources.[9] At the other extreme were those voluntarists, Charles Loch among them, who thought an electorate clamouring for rights and entitlements from government would soon deride the duties of citizenship. Burdett took comfort in the view that the citizen, as taxpayer, would prove a reluctant subscriber to further state provision.

As a result of the growth of government responsibility in the social sphere, philanthropy found itself on the defensive. Fragmented by parochialism, traditional campaigners, many of them middle-class women, were at a disadvantage in an age of social science, mass politics and declining religious enthusiasm. They often assumed that distinctions between the rich and poor were God-given and likely to persist. Conditioned by the Christian view that humanity was corrupt and poverty ineradicable, they found it difficult to compete with secular philosophies that offered visions of mankind perfected. In the new century, charitable activists looked old-fashioned to many social reformers in the Liberal and Labour parties. They laid themselves open to attack from intellectuals and socialists by their moral distinctions and their lack of social theory. To Marxists, with their dialectical eye on utopia, bourgeois philanthropists looked like the tired remnants of feudalism.

In 1910, the Fabian Sidney Webb wrote an elaborate essay on the shift in ideas taking place in Britain. He took it for granted that collectivism, which he blessed as 'the mother of freedom', would ultimately triumph in social administration as in economic policy.[10] The state would streamline social life by a progressive takeover of those activities formerly provided by voluntary associations. In his idealized relationship between the individual and the state there was little need for intermediaries, for the interests of state and society were identical. Committed voluntarists resented being told that their traditions were heading towards the historical dustbin. More than a few of them, alarmed by such sentiments, looked to the monarchy and the plutocracy to defend their interests against what they believed to be the menace of socialism.

There was more than a touch of enmity between philanthropists and their critics in this period, reminiscent of the divisions between philanthropists and radicals in the 1790s or the 1840s. Often amateurish and sectarian, charitable campaigners were open to ridicule as Mrs Pardiggles and Drusilla Clacks, people of privilege who propped up both an outmoded social order and the Empire to boot. Conflicts of opinion and personality broke out over whether the individual or the community should take responsibility for distress. There was no love lost between the defenders of charity and the Fabian Beatrice Webb on the future of social policy in the august chambers of the Royal Commission on the Poor Laws (1905–9). On the issue of philanthropy's place vis-à-vis the statutory authorities, the divide between the 'Beulah Land' of voluntarism and the Webbs' 'Heavenly City' of socialism proved unbridgeable.[11]

From the dizzy heights inhabited by Beatrice Webb, even Edward VII and his charities looked ridiculous. She sat near to him at a school prize-giving ceremony in 1897, when he was still Prince of Wales. She described him in her diary as a 'well-oiled automaton' who was 'unutterably commonplace'. Having just read in the papers that he was to commemorate his mother's reign by founding a charity to free the London voluntary hospitals from debt (The Prince of Wales's Hospital Fund), she added that it was 'the sort of proposal one would expect from the rank and file of "scripture readers" or a committee of village grocers intent on goodwill on earth and saving the rates'.[12] The remark not only illustrates her disdain for royal initiatives, but her ignorance of charitable affairs. As we shall see, Edward VII and his influential friends who created the Hospital Fund had a more cogent agenda than Beatrice Webb imagined.

The monarchy had become so formidable during Queen Victoria's reign that the supercilious ridicule of Beatrice Webb simply washed over it. The patriarchal King Edward inherited a crown that was 'a symbol of national honour and a link of empire', and he and other members of the royal family were by now popular figures, seen by millions.[13] Yet beneath the royal calm, many of the social and political currents that troubled philanthropists also troubled the monarchy. With the aristocracy in decline and Labour on the march, the social equipoise that the crown had done so much to create was under threat. Moreover, the Liberal government's intervention in social affairs, invigorated by the trend towards democracy, challenged the voluntary principles with which the monarchy now identified itself. In the fluid politics of the early twentieth century,

OUR NEW KNIGHT-HOSPITALLER.

29. The launch of the Hospital Fund as seen by *Punch*, February 1897.

the crown needed a strategy for survival more urgently than at any time since 1848.

On virtually every front, from trade unionism to female suffrage, from social policy to the House of Lords, the trend of politics gave Buckingham Palace cause for concern. Many trade unionists, distressed by a decline in real wages and politicized by radicals and syndicalists, were rejecting the conventions of deference and respectability in favour of a new militancy. The truculent MP James Keir Hardie, the founder of the Independent Labour Party, took pleasure in cocking a snook at the monarchy. He was prominent among those who attacked the generous settlement granted by Parliament to the royal family in 1901. A few years later, when it was announced that there was to be a royal visit to Russia, he accused Edward VII of condoning tsarist atrocities.[14] Highly sensitive to incendiary language, Palace officials made a mental note of Keir

Hardie's outbursts and kept a watch on any MP whom they believed to be unsympathetic to the crown.

The Palace monitored speeches by leading politicians and trade unionists, and the slightest whiff of republicanism could trigger a reaction from it. When John Burns, a former London labour leader and President of the Local Government Board, made some 'extreme comments' about the House of Lords early in 1906, the King complained directly to the newly elected Liberal Prime Minister, Sir Henry Campbell-Bannerman.[15] When Lloyd George used the King's name in a speech attacking the House of Lords in 1906, Campbell-Bannerman was asked to discipline his colleague for 'breaches of good taste and propriety'. Lloyd George apologized.[16] And when the Prime Minister himself used the phrase 'to give effect to the will of the people' in a speech, the King's Private Secretary, Knollys, told him accusingly that such expressions savoured 'more of a republican than a monarchical form of government'.[17]

As these royal complaints suggest, the Liberal landslide in the election of 1906 put Buckingham Palace on red alert. From the perspective of the crown, the Liberal Party had been out of power for so long that it had become unaccustomed to dealing with the monarchy. Palace officials looked in vain for members of the government with strong royalist sympathies. In a letter to Knollys, Lord Esher, who was now Lieutenant and Deputy Constable of Windsor Castle, castigated Campbell-Bannerman for his ignorance of precedent and his inability to see 'the immense value to the State of this great function of dispassionate criticism by the Sovereign'.[18] Certainly, the Prime Minister was perfunctory in telling the Palace of his government's intentions, but this may have been due to Edward VII's reputation for indiscretion. Palace officials were well aware of the King's failings, but they believed that if the cabinet took irrevocable decisions without informing him it weakened the monarchy. Esher wrote to Knollys in 1907 that Campbell-Bannerman had the 'indolence of senility' upon him.[19]

Frustrated by the drift of parliamentary affairs, the monarchy turned with relief to the private and voluntary sectors where devotion to the crown was more entrenched. Edward VII and his aides felt more comfortable mixing with plutocrats and philanthropists than with ministers. Such men advised the King on his investments and offered lucrative business deals to Palace officials. The King's great friend and financial advisor, Ernest Cassel, recruited Esher as a business associate in 1901.[20] Several members of the royal household, including Knollys, came in for sharp criticism in the press on one occasion when they accepted directorships of a Siberian gold-mining company formed by what one traditional aristocrat labelled 'Jew speculators'. Still, Horace Farquhar, the Master of the Royal Household, made a fortune out of the shady transactions.[21]

Edward VII was perhaps the only man in England who was not a social climber. Nor was he a snob, though he attracted snobs like a magnet. Taking after his father, he did not have a contempt for 'trade'. And, free of the anti-Semitism that characterized many aristocrats, he opened up the monarchy to outsiders and the 'smart set', who had been ignored by his mother. From the crown's point of view, the King's social openness had more to recommend it than just access to stimulating company and top financial advice. It also frustrated any inclination that the *haute bourgeoisie* might have had to become anti-monarchical.[22] In the expanding world-economy at the turn of the century, business magnates were men to cultivate and watch, whether cosmopolitans, like Cassel and the diamond merchant Julius Wernher, or native Britons, like the brewer Edward Cecil Guinness (later Lord Iveagh) and Lord Revelstoke, the head of Barings.

Though many plutocrats were of obscure social origins and sometimes tainted by scandal, they increasingly set the tone of Edwardian high society.[23] But they commanded little respect in landed circles, despite their large houses in Park Lane and the country. Ambitious and socially conventional, they were anxious to pay, to work or to marry their way into the landed elite. But imitating the English aristocracy could lead to embarrassment. Cassel, for example, could not keep his seat on a horse. He found that sitting on charitable committees proved a less hazardous means of improving his social standing. The more such men sought social acceptance, the more likely they were to wish to be seen to be philanthropic. The King's advisors, most notably Burdett, effectively brought the moneyed and the charitable into communion. It was a natural alliance, for many in the charitable establishment were entrepreneurial, imperialist and hostile to socialism.

In an unwritten social contract, Edward VII offered good shooting, respectability and honours to the moneyed elite, but at a price; and the price was, more often than not, support for his favoured charities. In 1899, for example, he had a whip round of twenty-four of his friends, including Cassel and Henry Bischoffsheim, when his bridge-playing friend Agnes Keyser sought to turn her house into a hospital for officers returning from the Boer War (it later took the name the King Edward VII's Hospital for Officers). Rosa Lewis, the Cockney proprietor of the Cavendish Hotel, remarked that the Prince 'got his snob friends to dole out'.[24] As many of the royal family's friends were pleased to discover, charitable donations could be a short cut to a shooting party at Sandringham or a Palace investiture. Edward VII was quick to lavish gifts and honours on his entourage in exchange for voluntary service and contributions.

Nothing arouses a philanthropist more than the expectation of a knighthood. As the worldly Lord Esher ruefully remarked: 'in these days everybody expects that for every effort he makes in the cause of charity, he should be rewarded.' Nor could he imagine 'why every time the King is kind enough to say that he will open something or lay a foundation stone—the mayor or the "impresario" or somebody should expect a decoration'.[25] Still, Esher believed that honours produced 'great public benefit', and he fully appreciated that they were immensely valuable in consolidating traditional allegiances. Honours were an increasingly important element in the crown's oblique campaign to counter republicanism in a time of socialist advance, but to be effective they had to be judiciously administered and kept within bounds.

· The pressures on the crown to hand out decorations indiscriminately were genuine, but they were less severe than the pressures on politicians with honours to distribute. Princess Christian once asked Esher to press the claim of a leading charitable worker in Windsor on the King. Esher wrote to Knollys: 'I believe that every tradesman in Windsor who is elected to the Town Council lives in expectation of Knighthood at the hands of the Sovereign, but this ambition is fortunately kept within limits.'[26] Unlike the political honours in the Prime Minister's gift, the honours in the gift of the sovereign aroused relatively little public interest or indignation. A prime minister without security of tenure had debts to pay and the next campaign to manage. By contrast, the monarch, removed from party politics and with a job for life, could cultivate a more circumspect and settled policy of rewarding friends and public servants.

Honours, decorations, medals and badges proliferated from the late nineteenth century onwards, and a large number of them were granted for charitable services, often to quite humble recipients. In 1883, Queen Victoria instituted the Royal Red Cross for services to nursing, the first British Military Order solely for award to women. In 1886, she created the Order of the Indian Empire, with three separate classes. Two years later the Order of St John of Jerusalem, which promoted ambulance and hospital charity, received its royal charter. The Royal Victorian Order appeared in 1896 on the eve of the Diamond Jubilee to reward personal service to the sovereign. Expanded by Edward VII, it had five classes and no limit to the number of members. The growth in the number of orders made honours, high and low, 'a legitimate object of public ambition' and put them within reach of many subjects who, in the past, only dreamed of the royal embrace.[27]

Less celebrated, but still coveted, were the medals and badges liberally dispensed by royal charities for services rendered. The Royal National Life-boat Institution used George IV's head on its silver medal, with the King's permission, until it was replaced by Queen Victoria's.[28] Queen Victoria provided a photograph to be used on the RSPCA's 'Queen's Medal', which the institution presented for conspicuous service (when she noted the absence of a cat in the design it was duly added).[29] In 1895, Princess Alexandra introduced a new badge to members of the Royal National Pension Fund for Nurses. Each nurse ceremonially received an armlet of red silk, bordered with white, ornamented with Alexandra's monogram and coronet. In the words of the Princess, the badges were to remind the nurses that she was thinking of 'every member of the Fund and that she hoped that this knowledge might increase their self-respect and stimulate them to greater exertions in the noble work to which they were devoting their lives'.[30]

The League of Mercy, which was set up in 1898 by the Prince of Wales to assist the voluntary hospitals, was another institution which had the distinction of its own 'Order'.[31] A society based on the power of social attraction, it was rich in ceremonial functions. It had a particular charm for the Prince, who revelled in the annual garden parties or receptions at Marlborough House. Captivated by the decorative and seductive trappings of royalty, he awarded the Order of Mercy to officials of the League for conspicuous service. Though the status of the 'Order' was unclear, the decorations delighted, and animated, the recipients.[32] As Prince Alexander of Teck, a Grand President of the League, remarked, 'to those of us, who receive decorations in profusion, such Orders as the L[eague] of M[ercy] may appear somewhat ridiculous', but those who received it were 'proud of it'.[33]

If charitable decorations, badges and medals stimulated humble workers to greater effort and loyalty to the throne, knighthoods could have been designed to make the more ambitious social outsider charitable. Those of the Royal Victorian Order were particularly coveted, for they were bestowed as a mark of the sovereign's personal esteem. Many of the GCVOs and KCVOs awarded in Edward VII's reign were for donations to charity and unspecified good works. Burdett, the provincial clergyman's son, received his KCVO for charitable services in 1908. Cassel, of humble Jewish stock, was one of philanthropy's great paymasters, contributing millions to charity over his lifetime. He celebrated the accession of King Edward by giving the King £200,000 to use for benevolent purposes.[34] Though far from mercenary, he collected honours, including a KCVO and a GCVO, with the same enthusiasm that he collected dividends.

So did the charitable grocer, Thomas Lipton, who rose from a Glasgow tenement to become a personal friend of the King. Lipton first came to the attention of the royal family in 1897 through the timely donation of £25,000 to Princess Alexandra's Fund to feed the London poor. According to his biographer, 'it was the single most important act of his life'.[35] The donation not only resulted in a knighthood in 1898, at the personal request of the Princess, but brought a wealth of free publicity to Lipton tea. After further contributions to royal charity, Lipton found himself invited to Sandringham. In 1901, he received a KCVO and the following year a baronetcy. Thus an anonymous businessman, who formerly dined alone and lived only for his work, became the toast of high society. As the case of Lipton illustrates, nothing puts a person more quickly in the court calendar, or on the social map, than signing a big cheque for a royal cause. Lipton's knighthood cost him the equivalent of a million pounds in today's money.

The extension of honours was a reflection of the less exclusive nature of British society and meritocratic and professional trends. When Edward VII pinned a medal on a nurse or knighted a benevolent parvenu, it was an example of what Lord Curzon called the 'democratisation of honours'.[36] Such acts signalled the shift from a patrician culture to a culture open to talent and to outsiders. As we have seen, the monarchy had been rewarding the middle classes for their voluntary services for a century or more. The knighting of civic dignitaries, especially mayors, and the distribution of royal medals had become customary. The increase in honours from the late nineteenth century on allowed the royal family to give formal recognition to a larger number of its friends and supporters. But while the monarchy satisfied the claims of a wider public to a share in the honours system, it did not decorate the citizenry to promote a classless society but to cushion a hierarchical one.

The monarchy's readiness to open out the honours system was rather remarkable when we consider that its historic prejudice had been to favour the ancient and the noble. But the bestowal of honours was a domain for innovation, easily adaptable to changing conditions. The crown had long experience of distributing honours, and it had become highly proficient at the art of investiture. In an age of growing egalitarianism, the object was to create a system of rewards that oiled established institutions and maintained the vertical ties of society. The crown's reverence for rank dictated the 'graduated' character of the awards, which in turn reinforced the social pyramid. Honours were a subtle way of keeping a hierarchical society in working order, with the royal family firmly at the top. Tailored to the Englishman's love of titles and social distinctions, they made recipients stoop and others wait expectantly.

In so far as political honours were concerned, King Edward pressed the claims of his rich friends on the Prime Minister, but not always with success.[37] For their part, ministers confused the monarchy with a machine for conferring political honours. When nominating individuals for an honour, the Prime Minister was obliged to consult the King. But when Campbell-Bannerman did so, the reply was often unenthusiastic. In 1906, Knollys told the Prime Minister that the King disapproved of the creation of an 'excessive' number of peerages. Men should be selected, he added, not simply to strengthen the government, but to make the House of Lords more 'useful'.[38]

It was not in the crown's interest for 'the fountain of honour to become a pump'.[39] And while the King primed it, he did so with misgivings. Like all monarchs, Edward VII had an obsessive interest in titles, and he could be sharp about individuals. On one occasion, he was 'stuck' at the suggestion of an honour for such a 'violent and mischievous man'.[40] On another, he rejected the proposal to elevate a nominee to a peerage on the grounds that his eldest son was a bounder; several years later he was willing to give his approval owing to the fact that the son had become 'reputable'. In the peerage, the sins of the son could be visited on the father.[41]

The King's conferring of titles on his own friends excited some criticism, but it was a most pleasing arrangement to the beneficiaries. The plutocrats revelled in their freshly minted status; the royal family enjoyed the association with fresh blood and new money. And as often as not, philanthropic bodies received an injection of cash as part of the process. But money was not all the plutocrats gave to charity. They served institutions as committee men and councillors, providing a high degree of business acumen. This was no small matter to those charities with capital investments like the Imperial Cancer Research Fund, founded in 1902 and granted royal patronage in 1904.[42] The institutions that recruited the City's financial elite tended to be highly businesslike, with methods and procedures that would rival the most entrepreneurial charities of today.

If philanthropy gave the plutocracy respectability, the plutocracy encouraged the expansion of philanthropy. Most of the nation's charities, it should be said, never received a penny from the rich friends of Edward VII. They carried on as before with local subscriptions. But the tens of millions of pounds donated to charity by the plutocracy before the First World War had considerable impact, particularly in London. Generosity on such a scale, which anticipated the charitable foundations to follow, changed the shape and character of philanthropy, and made it more attuned to politics. It fostered powerful secular institutions with more parliamentary influence than charities with local subscribers and sectarian aims. Significantly, it identified charity, to socialists at least, with wealth, privilege and Tory reaction.

The monarchy and the plutocracy rallied round philanthropy partly to dish socialism and to defend the Empire. The King and his rich friends, with their massive investments overseas, were avid imperialists; and they wedded a call to Empire with traditional paternalist doctrine. The parochial ideal was to be enlarged and enlivened by an imperial ideal, which would extract personal service from disparate peoples and cement the bonds between them. In hospitals, schools, female emigration societies and missions with links overseas imperialism took on the character of religious truth. When the Prince and Princess of Wales laid the foundation stone of the New Hospital for Women (the Elizabeth Garrett

Anderson Hospital) in 1889, it was celebrated as an imperial event, for the institution would train female doctors for service in India.[43] To Burdett, London was the metropolis of the Empire, 'the Mecca for its sick', and its hospitals, which treated so many soldiers and patients from overseas, were essential to national efficiency and imperial defence.[44]

Imperialism had the capacity to promote unity across class and party boundaries.[45] And a working class made healthier and more secure through charitable provision would not only be more receptive to imperialism but less disposed to radical social experiments. At home and abroad, the great charitable army carrying its banner 'supported by voluntary contributions' was an antidote to socialism. If little Englanders and socialists alike equated the Empire with greed, the King and his imperialist allies equated it with charity and self-help. They would have applauded the pronouncement by the head of the Girls' Friendly Society, a royal institution with a passion for Empire: 'I look upon Imperialism as a means of eradicating the selfishness of the individual which socialism teaches, self for self.'[46] In a quaint political symmetry, both socialists and capitalists accused each other of selfishness.

The monarchy, as we shall see in the case study to follow, used leading businessmen in its philanthropic campaigns with great astuteness. Like them, the Palace worried about what it saw as threats to the Empire and the drift towards socialism, state compulsion and the growth of an impersonal bureaucratic state. Queen Victoria, who vowed 'never to be the Queen of a democracy', had equated socialism with disrespect for authority and godlessness.[47] Voluntarism, on the other hand, or so Lord Esher argued, was synonymous with traditional values and a beneficent oligarchy.[48] When Esher entertained democratic principles, it was within the nineteenth-century conservative meaning of participation in local institutions and local government. In his view social progress was most effectively achieved within the framework of a traditional hierarchical society. The notion that it could be delivered by an elite of civil servants, so dear to the Webbs, was abhorrent to him, just as a regulatory state was abhorrent to a business magnate.

For his part, Edward VII did not see far into the political future or much beneath the social surface, but with his strong Tory views he did not like the prospect of state compulsion, which to him had sinister implications for the country and the monarchy. As ministers had taken away the power of the crown, it would have been masochistic on his part to have wanted to have seen more authority vested in central government. In the charitable sector he was uniquely placed to influence policy and shape administration. Indeed, he could even influence government policy through the lobbying of royal charities. Esher's defence of voluntarism would have been greeted with royal approval:

30. Reginald Baliol Brett, 2nd Viscount
Esher (1852–1930).

We have lived splendidly and comfortably under an oligarchy and under
a voluntary system. . . . No man in his senses could desire, in order to
square with some theory of government or live up to some political
dogma, to change a system so rooted in our habits and so beneficial to the
nation in its results. . . . No one, in fact, but a dry theorist, would dream
of substituting compulsion for voluntary effort so long as the latter could
be relied upon to produce average results, whether in education, sanitation, or military service.[49]

Esher, Burdett and other Palace advisors recognized that in health and
education, as elsewhere, the 'shadow of compulsion' had crept into the
national life, and that many working people looked favourably on state
pensions and other government social measures. But having built up its
welfare role over 150 years, the crown did not wish to give 'compulsion'
further encouragement. Members of the royal family, like other philanthropists, had lobbied for government legislation on social questions, but
they looked on government dominance in welfare rather like the curly-
haired boy in *Nicholas Nickleby* looked upon Mrs Squeers's brimstone
and treacle spoon. Arguably, the crown had more to lose than most

philanthropic institutions from state intervention. If government absorbed charity's health and welfare functions, it would eliminate the most substantive role remaining to the monarchy.

At issue, as Esher saw it, was 'whether "voluntarism" is compatible with "democracy" in the functional activities of a modern State'.[50] Behind that question lurked another related one, rather more crucial to Buckingham Palace. Was the monarchy itself compatible with majority rule and a 'modern state', or would it collapse in the maelstrom of a materialistic democracy? Few people outside Palace circles thought in such stark terms. But then they had not lost so much to government already or had so much left to lose. Confidants of the King believed that more was at stake than the narrow issue of the sovereign or his successor. It was the crown that mattered, not the transient who wore it.[51] To them the monarchy was the institutional and constitutional anchor of a nation adrift.

One of the great dilemmas for twentieth-century rulers, whether cabinet ministers or kings, has been how to cope with disillusioned workers. Esher wrote in 1910 that 'the great problem of the future for England and the English race, lies in the answer to the question whether or no the artisans, the labouring classes, will develop an altruistic ideal'.[52] Given the monarchy's limited room for manoeuvre, its strategy to deal with rising working-class demands had an obviousness about it. In 1918, Esher ventured to call it 'the "democratization" of the monarchy'.[53] In practice, the democratization of the monarchy meant that the royal family would open out socially to sections of the community relatively little known to Queen Victoria, from the plutocracy to the proletariat. The crown would stay true to its traditional allies in civil society, but it would seek to shift more of its attention to industrial workers whose political views were inchoate. When Edward VII visited a humble dwelling, he wanted to see a picture of himself on the wall, not one of Keir Hardie.[54]

The 'democratization of the monarchy', which picked up momentum in the reign of George V, was little more than a populist version of Prince Albert's ideal of civic duty, which had been successful in encouraging deference among artisans and skilled workers. To those members of the royal family on charitable auto-pilot, who already moved among the poorest classes, it could hardly be described as a new strategy, if a strategy at all. But whether they thought seriously about the crown's voluntary role or not, Esher, Burdett and others did. And they knew from the Diamond Jubilee celebrations that a 'democratized' monarchy, visibly sensitive to the welfare of the proletariat, was a perfect complement to an imperial monarchy of spectacular display, for which Edward VII had such a gift.

Edward VII much admired historical landmarks and associations, and at the beginning of his reign he took over most of his mother's patronages. The Office of the Privy Purse was, however, anxious to avoid any connection with societies that fell into debt or disrepute.[55] It was also now more sensitive to the explosion in the number of 'royal' charities. So many applicants, from orphanages to potato growers, requested to use the title 'Royal' or 'King Edward' that the Home Secretary became alarmed in 1903.[56] No one doubted the value of the royal sanction. When Queen Victoria died, the Ragged School Union feared that King Edward might refuse patronage. When he granted it, the society's relief was palpable. Its secretary expressed the deepest gratitude to the King 'for assuming a position that has great influence upon the financial fortunes of the society'.[57]

During his reign, Edward VII was the patron of about 250 charities, and made contributions to another 250 or so causes each year at a total cost to his Privy Purse of around £9,000 annually.[58] Queen Alexandra's contributions are more difficult to assess because she was prone to handing out large sums of cash, but in 1902 she gave away £2,240 to 72 institutions and individuals.[59] The King's charitable expenditure was roughly on a par with his mother's, but he divided it between a larger number of institutions. His donations constituted just over 10 per cent of his Privy Purse income, excluding the money added to it from the savings from other categories of his Civil List.[60] Given that the King had a history of indebtedness, he might have been tempted to reduce his charitable expenditure; but he was locked into it by long tradition, and he recognized that relatively small donations reaped disproportionate benefits to the monarchy. In any case, the sums he spent on charity could not seem all that significant to him when he earned more in stud fees during his reign than he gave to good causes.[61]

The Office of the Privy Purse operated on the basis of precedent and consequently Edward VII's patronages and donations bore a close resemblance to those of Queen Victoria. But there were differences of emphasis. Given his love of European travel, the King supported more continental charities, including the poor of Naples and the necessitous bandsmen of Marienbad. In Britain, schools, orphanages and the charities of Sandringham and Windsor did very nicely, but the King spread his largesse widely, if not deeply, and he added the odd golf club, yacht club and scientific society to his list. In a donation that may be seen as having a measure of calculation in it, he contributed £2,400 in 1904–5 to the Unemployment Fund, a hybrid scheme which brought voluntarists into partnership with local authorities.[62] Queen Alexandra also made a public appeal on behalf of the unemployed in 1905, which raised £150,000.[63] She added to it 'a large sum' from the sale of her bestselling book *The Queen's Christmas Carol*.[64]

If one charitable cause took precedence in the King's thinking, it was that of the sick poor treated by the voluntary hospitals. Improvements in medical and surgical practice had long been of interest to him. As a boy

31. King Edward VII and Queen Alexandra at the London Hospital, June 1903.

he had attended Faraday's public lectures on natural science and, influenced by his father, he sought to encourage the practical application of science. He cultivated the society of leading physicians and surgeons and kept himself informed of the latest research. He hosted medical congresses and chaired meetings on specific diseases When he discovered that Joseph Lister, the pioneer of antisepsis, wanted to advance bacteriological research, he promoted the foundation of the British Institute of Preventive Medicine, established in 1891. In appreciation of his services, the Royal College of Physicians offered him an honorary fellowship in 1897, which he accepted.[65]

One of Edward VII's initiatives had important repercussions for medical treatment, reminiscent of the monarchy's support for vaccination in the reign of George III. 'My greatest ambition', the King wrote to the London Hospital surgeon Sir Frederick Treves, 'is not to quit this world till a real cure for cancer has been found.'[66] Having undergone radium treatment for an ulcer on his nose in 1907, he concluded that radium was the cure. Aware of the work of the Radium Institute in Paris, he pressed Ernest Cassel and Lord Iveagh to found a similar centre in London. Thanks to their generosity the Radium Institute in Portland Place opened in 1911.[67] As a consequence of the King's nose, other medical charities developed an interest in radium as well, not least the King's Fund. In the 1920s, Sir Otto Beit, the philanthropic plutocrat, gave the King's Fund £50,000 for the purchase of radium.[68]

★   ★   ★

The King's Fund was, and remains, a charity with intimate royal associations. A study of its early years provides a revealing glimpse into the monarchy's charitable operations and purposes. Established to commemorate Queen Victoria's Diamond Jubilee, it started life as the Prince of Wales's Hospital Fund for London. It should be seen against the background of the hospital crisis in the 1890s, which was largely brought about by the new demands which public expectations were placing upon medical services. Its aims were to ensure the financial stability of the capital's voluntary hospitals and to improve their performance through the coordination of their services. Still an influential body today, with Prince Charles as its President, it is arguably Edward VII's most significant permanent memorial. Few other charities at the turn of the century better illustrate the near-magical attractions, and effects, of royal philanthropy.

The Hospital Fund was Burdett's idea, and he cleverly exploited the occasion of the Jubilee to get it underway. Such an ambitious scheme would have been inconceivable without his Palace and City connections.[69] He persuaded the Prince of Wales, with a little help from the Prince's mistress, the Countess of Warwick, that the scheme was a viable one and would do credit to the crown. A letter addressed to the inhabitants of London, signed by the Prince of Wales and published in all the leading newspapers, made the appeal public. It outlined the financial anxieties of the hospitals and concluded with a pronouncement that declared the ideological sympathies of its royal President: 'if these institutions are to be saved from the State or parochial aid, their financial condition must be secured.'[70] This was the letter noticed by Beatrice Webb, who dismissed the proposal as befitting 'a committee of village grocers'.

The Fund's governing council, hand-picked by the Prince of Wales, bore little resemblance to 'a committee of grocers'. No other voluntary society of the day brought together the monarchy, the great and the good, and the not-so-good but rich, in such profusion. Lord Rothschild and the Governor of the Bank of England rubbed shoulders with Lord Lister and the Presidents of the Royal Colleges, the Chief Rabbi and the

Bishop of London with the millionaires Ernest Cassel and Julius Wernher. These men were determined to make a success of the institution, not least because the Prince of Wales had put his trust in them. At the meeting which launched the Fund, the Prince turned to Burdett and one or two other confidants and expressed his earnest support for the project and reminded them of his reliance on their judgment.[71]

The Fund took little action in the early days without the authority of the Prince of Wales. Burdett kept him informed about sensitive issues such as methods of fund raising and the distribution of income.[72] Recommendations of the executive committee regarding policy and appointments were sent to him for approval through Knollys. Moreover, the Prince's participation at meetings of the council, which he never missed as President, kept him in touch, while at the same time lifting morale and guaranteeing publicity. The records of these meetings demonstrate that the Prince was informed, involved, and strong-minded. His views, however, were not always translated into policy. He tended to get his way on financial questions, for example the size of the annual grants to hospitals, but when he suggested that new wards brought into existence through the Fund's good offices might be called 'Victoria Wards' the idea was quietly dropped.

To achieve its large ambitions, the Fund developed what was then an unusual financial policy for a charity. The Prince of Wales insisted that the charity create a sizeable endowment. On the Fund's own reckoning, it required capital reserves in the region of £2 million. An endowment income, it was argued, would not only give permanence to the institution as a memorial to Queen Victoria, but would enhance its authority over the London hospitals. The Prince of Wales was particularly eager that the Fund should not fritter away its capital on transitory objects. As he made clear to Burdett, he did not wish to feel under pressure to go cap in hand to the public each year.[73] As he recognized, mounting the most ambitious hospital campaign the world had ever seen would require more than a little assistance from the royal family.

To set an example, the Prince instituted a plan whereby he and each member of his family gave an annual subscription to the Fund by standing order. (Between them, Edward VII and Queen Alexandra gave £2,000 over the years.)[74] The Prince then had a word with his friends, many of whom were on the Council. They responded with generosity. Cassel contributed £66,000, Guinness £60,000; the Jewish financier Edgar Speyer, who along with Cassel and Alfred Beit founded the Anglo-German Union Club in 1905, donated £25,000. The Fund's Treasurer, N.M. Rothschild, contributed £15,000 through his merchant bank. With the years the list of benefactors boasted an array of Edward VII's plutocratic friends, especially his German-Jewish friends. In 1912, Julius Wernher left the Fund a huge bequest of £390,000.[75]

The businessmen who came together at meetings of the Fund in Edward VII's lifetime oiled the wheels of the institution and gave it acumen and a hybrid character. They were a diverse blend of foreign-born and established British plutocrats. Cassel, Everard Hambro, Speyer and Wernher were among the former; Guinness, Revelstoke and John Aird, the civil-engineering contractor, were among the latter. In the City, as in the Fund, public confidence and personal contacts were essential. It is worth remembering that Burdett, from his years on the Stock Exchange, was intimate with many of these men and received consider-able financial support for other of his charities from them.

The business connections between the councillors and committee men of the Fund can only be touched upon here, but they are intriguing.[76] When he wished to sell his family business to the public, Guinness approached Rothschild and then Barings, headed by Lord Revelstoke. Hambro was an associate of the Barings and the Morgans, who were represented in the Fund by J.P. Morgan Junior. Hambros Bank eventually gave the Fund £7,000. Revelstoke was a close friend of most of the leading bankers and financiers associated with the Fund, especially Cassel, with whom he made some handsome profits at the turn of the century.[77] As a Director of the Bank of England, he cemented the Fund's ties with that body. He succeeded Lord Rothschild as the Fund's Treasurer in 1914 and left the institution £100,000 at his death in 1929.

In the Fund's early history, Cassel's connections are particularly fasci-nating. A dominant figure in the City, he had extensive dealings with many of his colleagues in the Fund, most notably Edward VII himself, who ascended the throne free of debts because of his advice. Arguably, Cassel was the shrewdest of the plutocrats. In 1897 he agreed to provide the finance for the construction of the Aswan Dam, which was built by John Aird and Co., a firm which appeared among the Fund's more generous subscribers. He also invested heavily in the South African mines developed by Wernher, Beit and Co. The German-born diamond merchant Alfred Beit and his brother Otto eventually gave over £125,000 to the Fund. Wernher, as noted, left it £390,000. Cassel also had longstanding connections with the London merchant bank, Bischoffsheim and Goldschmidt. The Bischoffsheims gave a handsome sum to the Fund. It is not clear whether Cassel put pressure on his business associates to contribute, or whether his own generosity aroused their interest. But as the closest male friend of Edward VII and an initial contributor, his role in the Fund was significant.

To what extent the Fund's meetings and social occasions promoted the business affairs of its band of Edwardian plutocrats can only be imagined. None of them relied on charitable connections to stimulate business. They often met socially elsewhere, sometimes in the company of Edward VII. Certainly, the Fund benefited enormously from their profits, especially those derived from expanding markets in the Americas, Egypt and South Africa. In turn, the Fund reinvested much of its capital abroad, not least in mines, railways and American securities.[78] It is obvious that the plutocrats would not have been so generous without the knowledge that Edward VII desired it. His friends the Bischoffsheims were quick to admit as much, for they contributed to the Fund on the precise understanding that it was a gift to the King, to be 'invested as His Majesty may direct'.[79]

In the history of the King's Fund, the tapping of the honours system is a subterranean theme. Few charities received more in the way of royal recognition in the early years of the century. As honours are awarded for unspecified good deeds, it is difficult to know just how many of them were given exclusively for services to the Fund, but large benefactors and dutiful Honorary Secretaries often received a KCVO. In later years, the Fund's Treasurer could expect one. Those who served in more humble capacities might hope for a CVO or an MVO. As Burdett argued, a knighthood enabled the recipient to be more useful and attracted favourable publicity to charitable institutions. Honours were given for faithful service, but the anticipation of an award kept many a volunteer at his post.

We should not conclude that the Fund's benefactors and officers served the institution simply, or primarily, in anticipation of honours. Undoubtedly, social snobbery and ambition played a significant role in the plutocrats' decision to contribute. But just how easy was it for a rich friend of the Prince of Wales to refuse the Prince when he asked for a donation to a good cause? The Fund's supporters outside the royal enclosure had innumerable reasons for their charities. Sickness or death in the family often triggered an interest in hospital work, as in the case of Edward VII himself. Others had religious or humanitarian motives. For others still, charitable work broke the monotony of normal business and opened up possibilities of wider experience and usefulness.

Most of the Fund's subscribers were far-removed from the honours system. But, in keeping with the monarchy's strategy of raising money from all social classes, the charity complemented its royal persuasions with a range of standardized appeal letters and thank you notices, carefully graded to suit individual cases. Here, as elsewhere, the royal hand was visible. Those who contributed £5,000 or more received personal letters from the Prince of Wales, and sometimes invitations to parties or royal events. Others who contributed time or money received gifts of game from Sandringham, in a hierarchy from pheasants to rabbits, with a tag attached headed 'From the Prince of Wales'.[80] The survival of these tags reveals both the importance of royal gifts to their recipients and the subtlety with which the crown graced the lives of its subjects while reaching into their pockets.

The Fund's initial mass appeal might be seen as a model for other charities; it certainly exploited its royal connections to the hilt. At the launch of the Fund, *Punch* gave it a puff with a cartoon in which the Prince of Wales, 'Our New Knight-Hospitaller', was seen on horseback holding a banner which read 'Loyalty' and 'Charity'. Another drawing in the press showed the Prince wearing a southwester about to man a lifeboat, with the shipwrecked hospitals in the distance.[81] Whether approaching City companies, workshops, churches or the citizenry directly, the message was unmistakable: subscriptions to the Fund were symbols of 'love and loyalty to the throne'.

Burdett devised the ingenious idea of a Hospital Fund stamp. He recruited the Prince and Princess of Wales to see the stamps being printed and the Duke and Duchess of York to witness the ceremonial destruction of the plates. Based on a picture of Charity by Reynolds, the stamps came in different colours and denominations, each bearing the Prince's signature and neatly packaged with a royal message. The image of a woman surrounded by her children served as badge of innumerable charities and expressed an underlying theme of the Fund and the monarchy—the promotion of healthy family life. The stamps raised over £40,000, mostly from humble contributors.[82]

The stamp was a variation on the truism in charity that subscribers may have to be approached indirectly, by means of gimmicks or entertainments. As one wit put it, a philanthropist is a person who can make you grin while picking your pocket. There was a superabundance of ideas. Among the more traditional were benefit concerts with a member of the royal family in attendance. The sale of Diamond Jubilee programmes raised over £2,000. Another clever use of the royal association was the

32. Commemorative stamp to raise money for the Hospital Fund.

photograph album, in which 100,000 children were to have their pictures taken set beside a picture of the royal princes. Though supported by Princess Alexandra, who appealed for 'every child in the land to contribute to their poor afflicted brothers and sisters', this scheme came under attack.[83] As the *Daily News* put it, parents 'run the risk of turning their offspring into little snobs and hypocrites'.[84]

In 1897, the Fund missed few opportunities to extract money from the public, from the proverbial widow's mite to the large sums donated by plutocrats. Still, the overall receipts fell short of the amount needed to create the desired capital reserve. Moreover, the original appeal had failed to reach large sections of its potential support among the poorer classes, despite the small sums contributed by gypsies, labourers and servants. A fear of social unrest, heightened by the miseries of the poor in London, haunted Burdett and others at the end of the century.[85] Working-class subscriptions would not only reduce the miseries, but provide a demonstration of self-help and good citizenship. They were valuable ammunition in the propaganda war against the municipalists and socialists, who looked at the voluntary hospitals with suspicion and envy. The Fund looked forward to a time when people gave a hospital subscription as automatically as they paid their rates, but 'with all the difference in cheerfulness'.[86]

Disappointed by the Fund's receipts for 1897–98, Burdett and the Prince of Wales came up with an innovation designed to tap the incomes of the respectable working class. This was the League of Mercy, which was designed as a money-gathering auxiliary of the Fund. Like other charitable auxiliaries, such as the NSPCC's League of Pity or the RSPCA's Band of Mercy, it was intended to bring local traditions of community service to bear on a wider cause, in this case the voluntary hospitals. Ideally, it would attract sorely needed cash and publicity to the Fund, but it would also bear witness to the friendly, reciprocal relations between the hospitals and the principal users of their services, the sick poor. It would also illustrate the esteem in which the monarchy was held by the humbler classes.

Burdett's proposal for a League of Mercy was not universally admired. Some saw it as unworkable and feared that it might embarrass the royal family. Charles Loch of the Charity Organisation Society, unenthusiastic about the Fund itself, called it a 'bold measure' of 'a wrong type', which would congest the already overcrowded field of charitable provision.[87] He tried to alert the Prince of Wales to the dangers in the hope of stopping the project in the planning stage, but he was refused an interview. Loch was doubtful about any scheme associated with Burdett. So was Sydney Holland, Chairman of the London Hospital, who wrote to Loch that the Prince did 'see through' Burdett, but 'admires his energy, his cocksuredness—which saves trouble—and his organizing powers'.

Holland fully expected the League to fail, and when it did, he suggested, H.R.H.'s 'admiration' for Burdett would end.[88]

Holland and Loch were frustrated, for Burdett had the ear of the Prince and they did not, and, far from dishing their rival, the League enhanced his reputation with the royal family. The Prince of Wales rallied behind the scheme. He wrote to his sister Victoria in December 1898 that a preliminary meeting to set up the League had been very promising. The following March he wrote to her again: 'We had a large meeting at Marlborough House and you will doubtless have seen an account of it in *The Times*.'[89] At the end of March 1898, the institution received a royal charter, establishing it as an auxiliary of the Hospital Fund. Burdett remembered the occasion vividly, for the Prince handed him the document with the words, 'There is your charter; now go and work it'.[90] Nominated Treasurer by the Prince, Burdett's dogged determination paid off, and, despite a few initial difficulties, the charity grew, as Loch lamented, like a 'gigantic snowball'.

The organizational model behind the League was a simple social pyramid. Below the Prince and Princess of Wales were presidents and lady presidents. Drawn from the royal family or titled aristocracy, each was appointed to head a district based on parliamentary divisions. Princess Victoria of Schleswig-Holstein and Princess Alexander of Teck were among the first members of the royal family to serve. As such luminaries were unavailable to fill all the sixty-five districts canvassed by 1902, MPs, senior churchmen, and friends of Edward VII, including Cassel and Hambro, volunteered. They nominated an upper-middle-class Vice-President and Lady Vice-President, who in turn enlisted middle-class members with roots in the locality. Within a decade, 20,000 officers and workers were collecting money in London and the Home Counties. Each of them secured twenty subscribers of one shilling or more. Tradesmen and domestic servants came under particular pressure. Thus through an institutional hierarchy which mirrored the social order, the League extracted small sums from local communities.[91]

The League depended on the power of social aspiration, particularly among the middle classes, which, as noted earlier, it cleverly cultivated by the creation of its own 'Order of Mercy'. The hospitals were an attractive issue on which to campaign, but the League was further proof of the accuracy of Burdett's view that success in charitable fundraising is largely determined by the prestige of the person you can get to support it at the top. To the King's Fund, the League proved a useful ally and one of the principal means by which it extended its tendrils into neighbourhoods in London and beyond. Before it was wound up in 1947, it had given over £600,000 to the Fund for the benefit of the capital's voluntary hospitals. It also awarded an additional £250,000 to hospitals outside London under its own name.[92] Many

33. A collector for the Coronation Appeal, 1902.

of those much-loved cottage hospitals dotted across Britain owed it a great debt.

Even with the assistance of the League of Mercy the Fund did not achieve its financial target in its first five years. By a fortuitous turn of events, however, the charity's prospects improved dramatically in 1902. Just as Queen Victoria's Jubilee had triggered the creation of the Fund, her death offered the opportunity of its resurrection. As King, Edward would no longer serve as the Fund's President, and the office passed on to the new Prince of Wales, who had been prepared for his responsibilities by his father. Relations between the King and his son George were exceptionally close, even 'unique in the annals of the royal family'.[93] This was crucial to the Fund, whose fortunes were so dependent on the continuity of its royal leadership. As it transpired, George's enthusiasm for voluntarism in general and the charitable hospitals in particular, first as Prince of Wales and then as King, proved exceptional.

160

CORONATION GIFT TO THE KING

KING EDWARD'S HOSPITAL FUND FOR LONDON.

34. The Coronation Appeal promoted in the *Graphic*, January 1902.

One of King Edward's services to the Fund was the appointment of a committee in 1901 to launch a 'Coronation Appeal'.[94] Its object was to solicit fresh revenue and inform the public of the work of London's voluntary hospitals. To the public, it was loosely seen as a means of putting the hospitals in a position of financial security, which the Fund had not been able to accomplish in its early years. The appeal committee, chaired by Lord Duncannon (later Earl of Bessborough), quickly realized that the Coronation offered the Fund a once-in-a-lifetime opportunity. As the Jubilee appeal had shown, the public was more inclined to part with its money in the happy atmosphere of a royal occasion. As Edward VII's Coronation was the greatest royal event since 1837, it could, with a little flair, result in enormous benefits for those with the right cause and the right connections.

No charity was more attuned to the advantages in royal commemoration than the Hospital Fund, and it devised a scheme by which contributions would be collected for a 'Coronation Gift' to King Edward.

"FIT FOR A KING."
Henry VIII., Act 1, Sc. 2.

HOLBROOK'S
SAUCE

Have you yet sent your Contribution
to the
**Coronation
Gift?**

KING EDWARD'S HOSPITAL FUND, 81 CHEAPSIDE, E.C.

35. Advertisement, *The Lady*, April 1902.

The King, in turn, graciously declared his wish that the gift should be devoted to the Fund. This elegant idea tied the institution ever closer to its royal founder, who oversaw the campaign in some detail, despite his new responsibilities. The decision to rename the charity 'The King Edward's Hospital Fund for London' as from January 1902 may be seen as part of this campaign. The King's willingness to consent to this change in name showed his esteem for the institution and his growing confidence in it. And the willingness of the heir apparent to take up an active role in its management was a guarantee of continuity and a further boost to morale.

The Coronation Appeal drew on the traditions of the initial Jubilee appeal, but had a distinctive character suited to the particular royal occasion. The sale of seats along the Coronation route proved highly rewarding. Another new twist, sanctioned by the King, allowed companies to associate themselves with the campaign. Thus, carefully selected

162

businesses, including Bovril, Pears Soap and Holbrook's Sauce, took out advertisements with the Fund's Coronation Appeal notices included. Tellingly, the Managing-Director of Bovril Ltd, George Lawson Johnston (later Lord Luke), was on the appeal committee. The association of monarchy, charity and business was a clever variation on the tradition of Royal Warrant holders.[95] It gave the crown's seal of approval to the best of British trade while showing royal philanthropy side by side with popular brand names and, by implication, dynamic entrepreneurial skills.

Lord Esher wanted the Coronation to have an imperial dimension.[96] A feature of the 'Coronation Gift' was that it was thrown open to the whole of the Empire. As Burdett never tired of pointing out, the London hospitals treated patients from all over the world: 'Our countrymen who have gone out to fight the battle of Empire all over the world, in a great measure depend upon the men who have received their medical training in the great hospitals and medical schools of London.'[97] The occasion called forth 'the expression of the deepest loyalty to the throne by the whole Empire, and in the circumstance that the words "Supported by Voluntary Contributions" redound to the credit of the British nation all the world over'. With a neat imperial symmetry, the object of the appeal was to involve 'every resident within the British and Indian Empires, however humble in station, to assist King Edward's great scheme to benefit directly all the London hospitals, and indirectly every inhabitant . . . under the protection of the British flag'.[98] As a vicar from Devon wrote to Burdett, the Fund 'must bring the whole English-speaking race into closer unity and sympathy'.[99]

In raising money, as in other matters, the Fund was fortunate in its new President. Unlike his father, Prince George was a diffident man with little worldly experience, but his strong sense of social duty, combined with the awe in which he held his father, reinforced his enthusiasm for the Fund. In the Coronation Appeal considerable sums came from abroad, including donations from the Maharaja of Gwalior and the Maharaja of Jaipur. Most notably, the Prince buttonholed the Canadian railway magnates Lord Mount Stephen (George Stephen) and Lord Strathcona (Donald Alexander Smith), whose charitable work he had admired while on an imperial tour in 1901.[100] In 1902 each of them gave £200,000 to the Fund to be added to the endowment. 'These two donations', wrote Knollys to Burdett, 'have done much to place the undertaking on a sound foundation.'[101] Coronation year was an *annus mirabilis* in the history of the Fund, for it saw over £600,000 added to its capital.[102]

Just as his father had done before him, Prince George brought his friends and contacts into the Fund, and nurtured their interest by rewards, honours and his companionship. They fully appreciated that their expressions of social conscience increased his affection for them. Mount

Stephen, who lived at Brocket Hall in Hertfordshire, was a frequent guest of the Prince and Princess of Wales. His second wife had been a lady-in-waiting to the Princess's mother, the Duchess of Teck. He appealed to the Prince's decided preference for down-to-earth, unpretentious country gentlemen like himself. Over the years Mount Stephen became a pillar of the Fund. He advised on investments and chased up his rich friends on the Fund's behalf, including Andrew Carnegie, who contributed £100,000 in 1907.[103] A man of quixotic generosity, his own contributions were on a grander scale. Eventually, he and his wife gave the charity £1,315,000, which should be seen as a personal tribute to George V and Queen Mary.[104]

The way in which the royal household handled contributors and potential contributors to the Fund was not left to chance. The case of Mrs Samuel Lewis is most revealing. Mr Lewis, a Jewish financier of humble origins, had left the Fund £250,000 upon his death in 1901, subject to his wife's life interest in the capital. Anxious to extract the £10,000-a-year interest in the capital, the Fund received Prince George's approval for a scheme whereby one of its councillors, Lord Farquhar, the Master of the Royal Household, would 'manage' Mrs Lewis. Farquhar happened to be one of her neighbours and with the assistance of her solicitor, Algernon Sydney, persuaded her to part with the £10,000 a year on the eve of the Coronation. (Sydney soon joined the Fund's council.) Mount Stephen followed the negotiations with the 'old lady' with consuming interest. He wrote to the Prince's Private Secretary that her 'splendid gift' had 'set the pace' and that it should be acknowledged in the press, for 'she is a woman'.[105]

Acknowledgement of Mrs Lewis's generosity had already been sent in the form of gracious letters from both the King and the Prince of Wales, a seat in Westminster Abbey for the Coronation, a Coronation medal and the inevitable parcel of game from Sandringham. Given her husband's background and profession, such attentions were perhaps exceptional, but they reveal the Edwardian court's openness to people with money, especially those willing to give it away. When she died in 1906, Ada Lewis left the King's Fund half the residue of the estate, and by the time it was wound up decades later, the Lewises' contribution to the charity came to over £565,000. In an address to the Fund's Council in 1906, the Prince of Wales paid tribute to this 'charitable lady, who was one of our most liberal supporters'.[106] Sir Arthur Bigge remarked, with wry amusement and a hint of contempt, 'certainly the Hospital Fund have benefited by the money lending business'.[107]

Prince George served as patron or president of over 400 voluntary societies, but few of them received the personal attention he gave to the Fund.[108] He applied himself to its administration with characteristic thoroughness. The nature of the institution was such that his power was virtually absolute. This had advantages in a charity which contained so many large personalities accustomed to having their own way. No one dared contradict the Prince and his decisions were accepted with good grace by all parties. At a word from the Palace, committee members quietly resigned and more congenial ones appeared. When there was a battle of wills between the Finance Committee and the Executive Committee in 1906 over the size of the annual distribution to the hospitals, the Prince intervened and the tensions subsided.[109]

The problems of financial management in the Fund raised fundamental questions about its organization, which had an air of amateurishness about it. The upshot was an inquiry into constitutional issues in late 1906 by the Prince of Wales and his colleagues.[110] The choice put before the Prince, who was an avid reader of official documents, was to have either a royal charter or an act of incorporation. After taking legal advice, the Prince decided that an act of incorporation was the best way to protect past investments, give sufficient powers for future investment and protect the interests of the crown. He sanctioned a draft bill to be presented to Parliament. The King was kept informed.

The Prince's chief worry revolved around the question of financial control. He took the view, put most forcefully by Mount Stephen, that there must be 'no representative control. . . . The money is given to the Prince of Wales and he appoints whoever he chooses to administer it.'[111] The Fund, as one of its internal memoranda stated, 'expresses the loyal sentiment of the contributors toward our King and the Heir to the throne'.[112] The fear, as Bigge put it, was that 'if Parliament places restrictions on the President's power as to investments or disposals of money, many of the most liberal friends of the Fund will shut up their pockets'.[113] Clearly, the plutocrats often opened their pockets because of royal persuasion and with a view to royal favour, and they were happier to see their money under the control of the heir to the throne than a committee of charitable managers.

Both inside and outside Parliament there was opposition to the proposed changes in the Fund's constitution, especially in regard to the President's powers. The British Medical Association, which was excluded from the Fund's council, sent out an alarm. Dr Henry Langley Browne, the Chairman of the BMA, took particular exception to the Prince of Wales as sole trustee. The Prince took a look at his extract from the *Medical Directory* and decided that he was not distinguished enough to pose a threat.[114] Opposition in Parliament was more worrying, for the Liberals had a parliamentary majority, but they were not much in evidence in the Fund. 'Where do the people come in?' asked one MP, who felt that subscribers required representation.[115] Unlike most charities, the King's Fund was not a subscriber democracy, but rather an expression of what social Tories called the 'best interests'. As one of its officials later

36. Visit of the Prince and Princess of Wales to St Bartholomew's Hospital, July 1907.

described it, it was 'a surprisingly autocratic body, a sort of limited monarchy'.[116]

Someone attached to the Fund, perhaps the King himself, had a word with the Prime Minister, for when the bill came up for debate in July 1907 Campbell-Bannerman described the charity as a 'model' of management with low running costs. And he reminded the critics that the King had created the institution and that 'it was to him that the money was given—money which would not have been obtained' otherwise. It was therefore not unreasonable to expect that the President wished to have some say in the management of the money.[117] The Bill passed with minor amendments, including a clause that any future president had to be either a son, brother or grandson of the Sovereign. Typically for the day, no one questioned the exclusion of women. The Act gave the royal President extraordinary, if not absolute, control over the institution. Delighted with the result, Prince George thanked the Prime Minister for steering the bill through 'stormy' waters.[118]

Prince George served as President of the Fund until he ascended the throne, and he maintained a lifelong interest in its affairs. Although his biographers have ignored the subject, he had a unique knowledge of hospital administration. Like his father, he did not hesitate to make his views felt. Virtually every hospital scheme proposed in London received his attention through the offices of the Fund, and his disapproval of a building programme was usually sufficient to stop it. The guarantee of royal patronage, on the other hand, was often enough to compel hospital governors to accept a proposal. More than one amalgamation of London

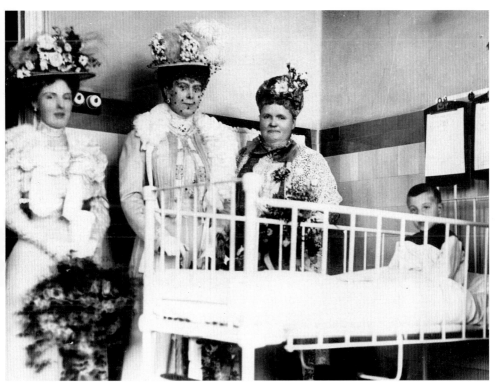

37. The Princess of Wales with Helen, Duchess of Albany (right) and Alice, Princess of Teck (left) visiting Royal Waterloo Hospital, October 1908.

hospitals turned on subtle royal pressures.[119] As President of the Fund and the patron of so many health-related charities, including fifty London hospitals, he was to become the single most influential friend the medical establishment ever had.[120]

With a little help from his son, Edward VII lived to see his favoured institution surpass the financial goals which he had set it. No other coordinating charity had ever raised such sums before. In 1910, the year of the King's death, the Fund's total assets were nearly £2 million and it was distributing about £150,000 a year to the voluntary hospitals of London, which was over 10 per cent of their combined income.[121] By the time of the First World War, the society was acting as a central board for London's charitable hospitals. Its administrative reforms had brought medical expenditure under tighter control, and its grants and practical work had humane and beneficial effects. It is now forgotten, but in the early decades of the twentieth century London's voluntary hospitals were the envy of the world.

Over the years, the King's Fund became a prototype for other schemes of hospital coordination, including one instigated by the Emperor of

Japan. Those English innocents, the Webbs, commented on the Emperor's project when they visited Japan in 1911, describing it as a form of 'extorted benevolence' worthy of the Tudor sovereigns.[122] They seemed blissfully unaware that it drew on the experience of the very Edwardian institution that Beatrice once ridiculed as worthy of village grocers. But then the Webbs were never generous to the monarchy. When Edward VII died Beatrice decried the 'slobbering over the lying-in-state and the formal procession. Any collective thought and feeling is to the good; but the ludicrous false sentiment which is being lavished over the somewhat commonplace virtues of our late King would turn the stomachs of the most loyal of Fabians.'[123]

'Loyal' Fabians often looked down their noses at royalty and philanthropy; yet the monarchy and its allies, especially the plutocratic ones, had contributed mightily to the voluntary sector in the Edwardian years, and not without an eye to its effects on the socialist cause. Well over 1,000 charities were now in receipt of crown patronage, and in a difficult climate they looked increasingly to members of the royal family for leadership and financial support. The King made little impression on high politics, but as a catalyst of benevolence in Britain and the Empire he was unrivalled and unimpeded. His interventions on behalf of philanthropy bolstered public confidence in voluntary principles and reinvigorated the charitable sector. This was no small achievement in an era of state expansion and mounting doubts about the viability of voluntary provision.

In the ideological struggle between voluntarists and collectivists, health and welfare were fast becoming a battleground. The crown gave funds, publicity and a more prominent voice to the charitable establishment. But it also made philanthropy more susceptible to criticism and a focus of resentment. In the context of an emergent democracy, the monarchy perhaps did it a disservice by associating it more closely with privilege and the plutocracy. When Lord Esher and Sir Henry Burdett espoused the voluntary cause, they coupled good works with paternalism and imperialism. And when business magnates picked up the bills, they further alienated those critics of philanthropy who saw capitalism as the cause of social distress, not its cure. Still, charitable societies were open institutions, which could ill-afford to turn away support. Nor could the monarchy. It had no wish to retrench or to expire in the name of progress. In a political no man's land, it had to avoid clashes with modernity and proceed by stealth.

6

George V: The Spectre of Socialism and the Uses of Philanthropy

George V's many admirers believe him to be the most knowable, and likeable, of British monarchs, a King without the mask of royalty, who magnified those public and domestic virtues that the British regard, or at least once regarded, as so much their own. Peering into the crown's 'enchanted glass', they have discovered a patriot of duty, decency, common sense, and gruff good humour, an unpretentious family man resistant to the tinsel glamour of high society. Harold Nicolson, who suppressed his reservations about the King, varnished the official portrait, which later biographers have touched up with modest alterations.[1] George V is drawn from a palette of gold, honest and true, tolerant and coura- geous. Tapping the barometer of state in an age of stormy transition, the King is a great conciliator sailing above class and party, 'a strong benevo- lent patriarch personifying the highest standards of the race'.[2]

Not everyone has taken such a flattering view of the King's character and constitutional correctness. Socialists, bound by grievance and despis- ing privilege, carried the tattered flag of republicanism into the new century. But their attacks on the crown were more often rhetorical abuse than reasoned argument. The more strident among them saw George V as a dim-witted lackey of the reactionary classes. On the birth of the King's eldest son, later Edward VIII, Keir Hardie declared that 'the life of one Welsh miner is of greater commercial and moral value to the British nation than the whole royal crowd put together'.[3] George Lansbury, the left-wing Labour leader and newspaper editor, though usually more circumspect, thought George V 'a short tempered, narrow minded, out of date Tory' given to meddling in matters beyond his brief.[4] The leader of the London County Council, Herbert Morrison, also thought the King an unbending Tory of the *Daily Mail* variety, who believed in his divine right to keep commoners in their place.[5]

As such divergent testimonies suggest, it is difficult to disentangle George V from the spin of politics. There seems little doubt that he was a dutiful, if old-fashioned, patriot, with more than a passing resemblance to Queen Victoria. Like her, he was intemperate and intolerant of dissenting opinion; and though devoted to domestic life, he mistook parental responsibility for a variation on naval drill. The majority of his subjects, who knew nothing of the tensions in the royal family, believed the King to be honourable and sound. He returned the favour, unless, of course, someone disagreed with him. Given his upbringing and the weight of his inheritance, he may be forgiven for confusing his views and prejudices for those of the country at large. But ill-educated, unimaginative and rarely contradicted in social intercourse, he too easily assumed that his conception of the world was an expression of some hierophantic truth, which all right-minded people accepted as self-evident.

George V's aides did not shelter him from bad news or unpleasant criticism, and he developed an excellent long-term memory for those who let down the side or who dared to criticize. When Hugh Dalton, the son of the King's tutor, returned from Cambridge with his head full of socialism, the King dismissed him as an anarchist, a view which he passed on to George VI.[6] The royal family had a generic dislike of socialists, but George V and the ultra-Tory Queen Mary indulged a particular contempt for Keir Hardie, whom the King privately mocked as 'that beast'.[7] This was perhaps understandable given Hardie's description of George V as 'no better than a street-corner loafer' and 'destitute of even ordinary ability'.[8] Such insults disposed the King and Queen to see all socialists as enemies of the crown. It was a mistaken assumption, but it deeply influenced thinking in the royal household.

The surge in the number of industrial disputes heightened the crown's view of socialism as irresponsible and dangerous. From the perspective of the 1990s, it may be difficult to understand the horror with which the monarchy regarded trade unionism and the labour upheavals in the early years of George V's reign. But, as Nicolson noted, the Palace saw them as 'the presage of a rising proletariat and the injection into our political life of the dangerous Continental theory of syndicalism, with its battle cry of "they who rule industrially will rule politically"'.[9] If the monarchy was the fount of traditional values and social hierarchy, the labour movement was by contrast raising the red flag of progress and social equality. The ideological fault line was clear and seemingly unbridgeable.

The delicacy of the crown's constitutional role, combined with the Labour Party's growing popularity, compelled the royal family and its advisors to keep their political sympathies under wraps and to carry out their policies with discretion. The Labour Party had its own political ambition to consider. Although the role of a monarch in a classless society might be an enigma, it was not a Labour priority to produce a manifesto on the future of the royal family. After the collapse of republicanism in the 1870s, gratuitous attacks on the crown were impolitic. Keir Hardie's ejaculations did not receive parliamentary applause and embarrassed many in his own party. Yet any marked decline in the popularity of the crown might awaken the republicanism latent in Labour ideology. Socialists and monarchists shadow-boxed with mutual incomprehension.

The reduction in the power of the House of Lords, the troubles in Ireland, and industrial unrest preoccupied the new King and were taken as ominous portents by the monarchy. Lord Esher, still a formidable presence behind the throne, worried deeply about working-class disaffection. A letter to Queen Mary early in the reign revealed his anxieties: the 'darkest point, however, on our horizon is the growing antagonism between Labour and Capital. It looks as if, during the next five years, great prudence and foresight will be required from those entrusted with the government of the country, if a struggle which might be fraught with disastrous consequences, is to be avoided. No outlook has been quite so gloomy since 1848.'[10] With little confidence in the determination of the government to maintain order, Esher encouraged a more active policy of getting the King and Queen out among the poor. While there might seem to be little difference between opening an orphanage, inspecting a regiment, or visiting a mining town, Esher knew that the latter was likely to produce a greater return for the monarchy in sensitive working-class districts.

Other well-wishers brought advice similar to Esher's to the Palace. Within days of the death of Edward VII, the celebrated writer Hall Caine, a friend of Queen Alexandra, approached George V through a courtier. A mining disaster at Whitehaven on the Cumbrian coast precipitated his remarks:

> King George comes to the throne at a moment of most momentous difficulty. How can he best overcome the enormous problems of the inevitable situation? By bringing the Throne and the people into line. This will make him more powerful than any Ministry and place the Monarchy on the pinnacle of power in the Empire. . . . If the King could find it possible to set aside for 24 hours the tyranny of his work in London and go to Whitehaven and say, 'The Palace is in mourning but the cottage is in mourning too, and I come here because King and People are at this great moment bound together by a common bond of sorrow and fate'— if he could do this, he would do the greatest thing any English Sovereign has ever had the chance of doing, and place himself at the absolute head for the rest of his reign.[11]

Preoccupied with pressing events in London, the King did not catch the first train to Cumbria, but Queen Alexandra, now the Queen Mother, wrote a letter of sympathy which, according to Caine, made 'a profound impression' in Whitehaven.

Hall Caine's advice to the King to bring 'the Throne and the people into line' was very much in keeping with the strategy being elaborated by the Palace to deal with industrial unrest. There was nothing new about the proposition that members of the royal family should visit mining villages and factory towns. Prince Albert was a familiar figure around factory gates, and Edward VII 'made a point of spending three or four days once a year, during July, in some pullulating industrial centre'.[12] For their part, George V and Queen Mary had experienced the industrial cauldron as Prince and Princess of Wales. In June 1909, for example, they had visited the Phoenix Tin Mines near Cheesewring in Cornwall. Large crowds witnessed the Prince descend into a mine shaft in oilskins and later console an injured miner, actions reported in *The Times* as a welfare mission to a depressed industry.[13] Such missions were an ideal accompaniment to patronage work, for they extended the monarchy's welfare role to people often beyond the reach of royal charities. They became more urgent with the deterioration in industrial relations and the rise of the Labour Party.

The precise role of George V in the formulation of Palace strategy is unclear. On the available evidence, he set the general tone but left the ideas and details to others. (Queen Mary was more likely to have ideas than George V.) Certainly, the King's defenders, who do not wish to suggest that he was at odds with expressions of the popular will, are inclined to acquit him of political calculation or ulterior motives. The official view, to which the King subscribed, was that whatever he did, he did from a sense of duty. But George V and Queen Mary did not visit the nation's black spots simply out of altruism, without regard to its meaning for their personal standing. They were both greatly agitated by industrial disputes and highly attuned to their political implications. Horrified by the outbreak of strikes in the summer of 1911, Queen Mary blamed the Liberal government: 'I do think the unrest is due to their extraordinary tactics in encouraging Socialism all these years & in pandering to the Labour party.'[14]

The King and Queen had their limitations but naiveté was not among them. Well-informed and sensitive to opposition, they knew their interest. In their view, it was synonymous with the nation's. They lamented that they were not in a position to do much to help on the political front. But assisting the poor was a royal prerogative. Plainly moved by the distress caused by unemployment, they contributed to its relief. In return for this material assistance, they expected that the beneficiaries would be more likely to reject the slogans of radical ideologues and accept the traditional order of things. From their perspective, charitable work not only ameliorated distress, it was a way of squaring deference with democracy and enticing the labouring classes into the royal camp. If the worst happened and the socialists came to power, the Labour Party must at least first be shorn of its republican tendencies.

Feeling besieged by strikers, Irish agitators, tiresome suffragettes and sneering socialists, the monarchy decided to give greater priority and

38 (*above*). George V and Queen Mary, when Prince and Princess of Wales, down a tin mine on a visit to Phoenix Mines, Cheesewring, Cornwall, June 1909.

39 (*left*). Queen Mary when Princess of Wales on the surface at Phoenix Mines, Cheesewring, Cornwall, June 1909.

publicity to its social role. As ever, the Palace monitored conditions in the distressed areas as well as the political reactions to them. During the great coal strike in the spring of 1912, Esher spoke to a group of miners in Bannockburn. He reported to the King that the men were tired, hungry, and 'dreadfully bored' by the strike. They were 'simply sheep', he added, 'although they are very intelligent, and are driven by agitators. . . . Whatever their "leaders" may be, it is absurd to think of the mass of the miners as revolutionaries or socialists. They are simply decent men, waiting for proper guidance, and hopelessly misled.'[15] In Esher's mind, there was no doubt where the guidance should come from.

Esher's letter must have struck a chord, for a few weeks later, in June 1912, the King and Queen visited south Wales, using a motor car to reach the more out of the way areas. They inspected the Seamen's Hospital in Cardiff, laid the foundation stone of the National Museum of Wales, and penetrated the colliery districts of Glamorgan and the Merthyr Valley, what Queen Mary called 'the heart of Keir Hardie's constituency'.[16] Keir Hardie was on their minds, for in an open letter to *The Times* he had opposed the trip as a 'ruse' to 'whitewash' the mine owners.[17] The couple visited the pitheads and examined the stables. The King picked out a lad for special attention. The Queen, perhaps remembering those Blue Books on social conditions that she had read as a girl, asked to see the inside of a typical cottage. She found it airy and clean, complete with her picture on the wall. She pronounced it a model dwelling.

The King addressed a group of miners in a speech that was characteristic of those he delivered on his tours: 'We wish to express our sincere admiration of the courage and devotion which are the proud traditions of the mining population, and to assure you that we have very much at heart the success of every effort to lessen the perils and alleviate the hardships of underground labour.' He varied the message at another colliery: 'The safety and welfare of those engaged in coal mining have always been a matter of great solicitude to me. . . . I look forward to the time when conflicts of industrial interests will be solved by the co-operation and good will of all concerned.' In a reply to the mayor of Merthyr, he linked the miners 'With the defence and well-being of the Empire' and concluded with the leitmotiv of the trip, the royal family's 'deep interest in the welfare of every toiler, however humble and remote his place in this great arena of industry'.[18] Queen Mary wrote to her aunt Augusta in Strelitz: 'We are assured on all sides that our visit wld do more to bring peace and goodwill into the district than anything else & that we had done the best days work in all our lives!' Keir Hardie, she added, 'will not have liked it!'[19]

The following month the royal couple went on a tour of industrial Yorkshire, visiting mines, mills and factories.[20] George V went down a coal pit and shook hands with a crippled worker, to whom he had presented a pair of artificial limbs some years before. Drawing on the philanthropic training imbibed from her mother, Queen Mary mixed easily with the cottage wives. While they were staying at a nearby country house, there was a disaster at Cadeby Colliery, in which seventy miners lost their lives. It brought a sudden change of plan and a late-night drive to the scene. Consoling the bereaved relatives, the Queen lost her usual 'adamantine' self-control. 'Too tragic,' she wrote afterwards. The tour proved a great success. 'We had a most wonderful reception in Yorkshire in the most radical parts,' Queen Mary wrote to her aunt.[21] On returning to Buckingham Palace, the King noted in his diary that 'we must have seen at least 3,000,000 people'.[22]

Not every outing went so well. Accompanied by the Scottish peer Lord Balfour of Burleigh, the King and Queen once made a surprise visit to some properties in Kennington, which would eventually come into the possession of the Prince of Wales. Inadvertently, they knocked on the door of the Labour MP for Whitehaven, Tom Richardson. One of Richardson's daughters kindly showed them round the house. Hanging on the wall was the family icon, a portrait of Keir Hardie. The King spotted it and said something under his breath to Lord Balfour, who commented: 'Yes, a terrible man that!' Overhearing the remark, the self-possessed Miss Richardson coolly replied 'that is the portrait of one of the best men I know; and if anyone does not like him they need not stay in our house'. Lord Balfour did his best to mollify the girl, but the royal party did not stay to tea.[23]

A tour of the Potteries in 1913 demonstrated a surer royal touch. Esher, who took every opportunity to congratulate the King and Queen on their 'progress' through industrial Britain, observed that they were 'really at home' with the humbler classes, 'so like Queen Victoria'.[24] Unlike Edward VII and Queen Alexandra, they saw themselves as a team and worked in effective social partnership. In the early years of their marriage, patronage work took up a large part of their time, though Nicolson, who took the view that the King, when Duke of York, 'did nothing at all but kill animals and stick in stamps', failed to notice it.[25] The tours, like their patronage work generally, brought out and publicized their better qualities, while giving shape to the Queen's role as Consort. The King and Queen were not to know it in 1913, but their long experience in the charitable field would be the most fitting preparation for the cataclysm to come.

★   ★   ★

The First World War made unprecedented demands on royal philanthropy, as it did on philanthropy generally. It allied the monarchy and charity to national purpose to a degree unknown since the Napoleonic wars; but in accelerating social change, it unsettled charitable institutions and voluntary impulses. By disrupting the rituals of parish life and eroding religious faith, it struck at the roots of philanthropic activity. As a generation of men went to the front, those who filled their jobs had less time to spare for voluntary work. As health and welfare shot upwards on the political agenda, the war exposed the shortcomings of voluntarism and pointed to the need for greater state involvement. It encouraged closer relations between philanthropic bodies and the expanding state bureaucracy, but not always to the advantage of the former.

During the conflict, 10,000 new societies were founded, from King George's Fund for Sailors to Miss Gladys Storey's Fund for Bovril.[26] Yet the war severely tested charitable finances and resolve. Institutions old and new were zealous in their support of the British cause, and they demonstrated their patriotism by promoting the sale of war bonds, making articles for men at the front and attending to the casualties. Charities with imperial sympathies thrived, although in the long term the war undermined the ideological basis of the Empire, a change which would have serious implications for the culture of voluntarism. Though rarely keeping pace with the demand, the public generously supported the societies and funds set up for servicemen and their families. The Red Cross alone raised £21 million through war-time appeals.[27] The King's own charitable donations doubled during the war. In addition to the £8,484 allocated for distribution to institutions and individuals in 1915, he contributed £8,436 to charities directly connected with the conflict.[28]

What did the King do in the years 1914–18? Royal biographers, with their high political interests, have difficulty with the role of constitutional monarchs in modern wars. As Harold Nicolson admitted, George V had no executive responsibility for the war effort, which posed 'a problem of composition'. A straightforward narrative of the campaign was inappropriate, for the King did not raise 'his baton against a background of fleets and armies'.[29] Nicolson nevertheless concentrated on the conduct of the war, domestic politics and foreign affairs, rather than risk boring the reader with an analytical narrative of the King's day-to-day activities. The King's work succouring the wounded and raising morale among the troops and war workers constituted significant responsibilities, but is hardly considered to be the stuff of bravura royal performance, or bravura biography.

A bare summary of the King's actual duties during the war is telling enough. Apart from overseeing the administration of his many charities, several of which were set up because of the emergency, he made goodwill tours of the industrial areas and inspected munitions factories and food distribution centres. On occasion, the cabinet asked him to extend the trips because of fears of industrial unrest.[30] King George paid seven visits

40. King George V and Queen Mary visit Sunderland, June 1917.

to naval bases, toured the armies in France on five occasions, and held 450 inspections.[31] The 300 hospital visits he carried out in four years proved the most harrowing and exhausting of his activities, for he had to smile and to control his emotions amidst the gassed and mutilated. With Queen Mary, he also entertained the wounded at Buckingham Palace, providing as many as three parties a week in the Riding School. When the bombing started he travelled to the scene of devastation and spoke to the injured in the wards. 'You can't conceive what I suffered going round those hospitals in the war,' he later confided to a lady of the court.[32]

The King must have found that decorating his subjects was less onerous than visiting hospitals, and during the war he bestowed 50,000 awards.[33] He was reluctant to create new orders, but whoever convinced him of the virtue of the Order of the British Empire, which he instituted in 1917, deserved a KBE. (It may well have been Lord Esher, who had suggested before the war that voluntary workers merited greater recognition.)[34] Subdivided into five classes, the new Order was given in recognition of non–combative services rendered in connection with the war. As a tool to instil deference and to take the republican edge off the labour movement it was a masterstroke. As A.J.P. Taylor observed, 'its holders went over the top for the governing class, just as the officers had done for the generals'.[35] A look at the first list of OBE's shows that trade unionists, including the syndicalist sympathizer, William Appleton, Secretary of the General Federation of Trade Unions, and Ben Turner (later Sir Ben), President of the General Union of Textile Workers, accepted their awards with as much alacrity as any courtier.[36]

As a recent critic of the honours system argues, 1917 was 'a busy year' for King George. While the revolutionaries in Russia were tearing down their regime, he was 'shoring up the British establishment'.[37] That, of course, was a king's job, as George V saw it. The OBE, as David Cannadine puts it, 'was deliberately instituted to be the order of chivalry of British democracy'.[38] It was not accidental that the Order appeared at the very moment that extending the suffrage was under political discussion (the Representation of the People Act received royal assent in 1918), and it signalled the monarchy's ingenuity in adjusting to the new voting public. While some ridiculed the new Order for debasing the honours system, it proved highly popular with factory workers, charitable campaigners and trade union officials. It caught on wonderfully well. There were 22,000 recipients by the end of 1919.[39]

While King George redecorated the monarchy by decorating his subjects, Queen Mary was busy elsewhere. Like women of every class and background, the war offered her fresh opportunities for self-expression. While she sometimes complained of the drawbacks of philanthropic work, 'the constant bowings, the strain of looking pleased, the noise', she seized every opportunity to be useful and welcomed the favourable

41.   Silver Wedding 'shower' of gifts for soldiers and sailors, St James's Palace, 1918.

attention her usefulness elicited.[40] Her distinguished biographer, James Pope-Hennessy, described her 'dominant characteristics' as 'patriotism, a love of order, an earnest desire to relieve distress and a concern about social conditions'.[41] Never content with symbolic patronage, she had always shown enterprise, whether uncovering inefficiencies in charitable administration on one of her inspections or marshalling teams of middle-class needlewomen in support of poor and disabled children.

Like her mother the Duchess of Teck, Queen Mary was a charitable bulldozer, clearing a path for hundreds of thousands of volunteers. Within twenty-four hours of the outbreak of hostilities, she wrote to her friend, Lady Mount Stephen: 'Both of us are heart and soul trying to do our level best for our beloved country at this supreme moment of trial. We have the feeling of being supported by the people which is the great and glorious thing.'[42] She was already laying her plans. On 6 August 1914 she wrote in her diary: 'Very busy seeing people about the various Relief schemes.'[43]

At first glance, one might conclude that the relief effort of women was synonymous with needlework. Sewing took on a quasi-religious character for British women during the First World War, as in the Napoleonic and Crimean campaigns. The ladies of the Needlework Guild, now called Queen Mary's Needlework Guild, took up the cause with frenzied determination. The King gave his permission to turn the state apartments at St James's Palace into a warehouse, and they were soon piled high with gifts for distribution. In touch with the efforts of other formidable charities, including the Red Cross and the St John Ambulance Brigade, the Queen joined a host of ambitious schemes. An imposing presence, she not only inspired others to contribute time and money but served as a one-woman coordinating body for the administration of wartime charity.

One of the most significant projects which Queen Mary assisted in was the National Relief Fund. It was popularly known as 'The Prince of Wales's Fund' because the Prince issued the initial appeal. (King George contributed £5,000 and the Prince £3,000.)[44] Though the Prince received a good deal of favourable publicity from the project, which raised £250,000 in twenty-four hours, he had no control over the distribution of the agency's money.[45] And he had little, if anything, to do with its administration. The Fund worked closely with government departments and eventually channelled nearly £7 million into military, naval and civil relief through existing charities before it was wound up in 1921.[46] When it closed, there were those on its committee who thought that the Prince of Wales might have thanked them for their services.[47] Their irritation suggests that when the royal family becomes associated with a campaign, it has to follow through. Unlike her eldest son, Queen Mary followed through.

An unemployment crisis, albeit temporary, was one of the first conse-quences of the war, and the Queen, taking soundings from industrial experts, concluded that women needed jobs more than they needed anything else. She thus formed the Queen's Work for Women Fund as a female branch of the National Relief Fund. She informed the Prime Minister of her scheme and secured the appointment of a government Committee on Women's Employment. An unlikely ally was Mary Macarthur, the Secretary of the Women's Trade Union League, with whom she formed an effective partnership. Macarthur wrote to the Queen in August 1914: 'May I venture to express to Your Majesty on behalf of the working women whom I have the honour to represent the deep gratitude which we feel we owe to your Majesty at this time.'[48] Given the Queen's view of trade unionism, it must have been a pleasing tribute and may even have softened her view of socialism. But what would she have made of Macarthur's view, put to a colleague, that 'the Queen does understand and grasp the whole situation from a Trade Union point of view'?[49]

Raising money and visiting the many projects associated with her Work for Women Fund identified the Queen with a sensitive working-class cause during the national emergency. But it was only one of countless projects which filled the Queen's diary during the war years. Practical work was the priority, whether organizing nursing services, ladling soup, or providing more effective artificial limbs for disabled soldiers. A Lady of the Bedchamber, the Countess of Airlie, noted that the number of the Queen's engagements trebled during the war. 'Every day there were visits to hospitals—sometimes three or four in an

12. Princess Mary's Christmas gift to the troops, 1914.

afternoon—munitions factories and soup kitchens. Over and above these, the many relief schemes in which the Queen was actively interested necessitated an immense amount of correspondence.'[50] Like many of the ladies at court, Airlie herself was an active charitable campaigner. A word in the Queen's ear could prove invaluable in getting things done.

Virtually every member of the royal family played a part in wartime voluntary work, though the women, having no military duties, were most in evidence. The surviving daughters of Queen Victoria, Princesses Helena, Louise and Beatrice, raised funds for their respective charities, planned hospitals and visited convalescent homes. Princess Alexander of Teck and Princess Victoria of Schleswig-Holstein, among their many war-related duties, joined the committee of the Queen's Work for Women Fund. The Duke of Connaught, Governor-General of Canada when the war broke out, formed a body of leading Canadians to relieve the families of those who volunteered for active service. Arguably, his presidency and chairmanship of the executive committee of the Canadian Patriotic Fund was the most beneficial activity in his long career of public service. By the time he left Canada at the end of 1916, the appeal had raised over $18 million.[51] Such work helped to mitigate the criticism directed at the royal family for their German connections.

Queen Alexandra, growing old and deaf, no longer took pleasure from public appearances, but her charitable handouts reached such a pitch during the war that her devoted Comptroller Sir Dighton Probyn worried lest she bankrupt herself. 'Nobody knows what the Queen has paid away from her own private income on war charities since this war began,' he wrote to Horace Farquhar despairingly in 1915.[52] Princess Mary, the only daughter of King George and Queen Mary, must have inherited some of her grandmother's financial recklessness, for she devised a scheme to send a personal Christmas gift to every soldier and sailor out of her allowance. When someone pointed out to her that her allowance was insufficient to meet the cost, she launched a national appeal, the first to be associated with her name, which ultimately raised £162,000. The shipment of nearly half a million brass boxes, containing pipe tobacco, cigarettes, and a Christmas card from the Princess, was reminiscent of Queen Victoria's gift of chocolate to the troops in the Boer War. The problems of administration proved equally nightmarish.[53]

★   ★   ★

Despite the monarchy's well-publicized war work and the change of family name to Windsor in 1917, Palace officials grew increasingly nervous about the prospects for the crown as the war drew to a close. The spectre of the Russian revolution and class war petrified the King and his court. British socialists hailed the downfall of the tsarist regime. Ramsay MacDonald, the future Labour Prime Minister, praised Lenin and attacked the government for sending troops to Archangel.[54] The ex-Fabian H.G. Wells wrote a letter to *The Times* urging the overthrow of 'the ancient trappings of throne and sceptre'. And in 1917 left-wing socialists called for a convention of Labour delegates 'to do for this country what the Russian Revolution had accomplished in Russia'.[55] The King took soundings from labour leaders, including Will Thorne the union agitator, but he seems not to have appreciated that militant socialists were then in disarray. He did not like them better when the Bolsheviks shot the Tsar in 1918.

Palace advisors expected that when the war ended and the troops returned, a tide of disenchantment would sweep the country, with alarming repercussions for the crown. They looked around Britain and saw disaffection and oligarchic values in decline. They looked around Europe and saw a once great monarchical system in ruins. They looked to America and saw President Wilson, a democratic busybody who was making republicanism 'the Fashion'. Esher suggested that 'the Strength of Republicanism lies in the *personality* of Wilson'.[56] Lady Airlie, who was in waiting when the President visited Buckingham Palace in 1918, believed that the President was 'determined to undermine the prestige of the British Monarchy'.[57] Nor was the King himself impressed by Wilson. When he asked him to send the American army into Russia to save the country from Bolshevism, the President refused. 'After that I never thought very much of the man,' he later told Lady Airlie.[58]

The American President was not the worst thing on the horizon at the end of the war. Everyone expected demobilization to be painful, perhaps provoking violent disturbances. Esher wrote to Stamfordham that 'unless tact and sympathy are pronounced features of the demobilization of the vast horde of men and women now employed under government, Bolshevism is inevitable'.[59] A few days later he wrote again, seemingly obsessed by the prospect of unemployed industrial workers, conscious of their misery, turning to Bolshevism.[60] He had long believed that the working classes did not much care who ruled the country. In 1914 he had argued that patriotism 'is a luxurious habit of mind of the well-to-do'.[61] Still, he did not despair for the monarchy at the end of the war, although he believed that 'imagination and boldness will be required, necessitating the abandonment of many old theories of Constitutional Kingship'. Influence in imperial affairs and the inculcation of deference and patriotism in the British poor were crucial to the crown's survival.[62]

Stamfordham pored over the newspapers and was in close communication with journalists, churchmen and others with their fingers on the working-class pulse. His views on the proper function of the monarchy, while in keeping with 'Constitutional Kingship', were in line with Esher's. He wrote to the Bishop of Chelmsford, the Reverend John Watts-Ditchfield, in November 1918:

> We must, however, endeavour to induce the thinking working classes, Socialists and others, to regard the Crown not as a mere figurehead and as an institution which, as they put it, 'don't count', but as a living power for good, with receptive faculties welcoming information affecting the interests and social well-being of all classes, and ready not only to sympathise with those questions, but anxious to further their solution. . . . If opportunities are seized, during His Majesty's visits to industrial centres, in conversation with the workmen to show his interest in such problems as employers and employed will have to solve, these men will recognise in the Crown those characteristics—may I say virtues?—which I have ventured to enumerate above.[63]

Few men of their day were more attuned to the uses of royal philanthropy than Stamfordham and Esher. A week before the armistice was signed on November 11, Esher suggested to Stamfordham that the whole of the charitable money remaining in the Prince of Wales's Fund (the National Relief Fund) be used to address the problems of demobilization on the basis of individual cases: 'If . . . the Queen would act as *President* and *really* preside, you would be getting the Monarchy on to the track

43. King George V and Lord Stamfordham in the grounds of Buckingham Palace, June 1918.

that alone leads to safety in the future.' The inevitable objections to giving more functions to the King and Queen must be overridden, he added, for 'we stand at the parting of the ways. . . . The Monarchy and its cost will have to be justified in the future in the eyes of a war-worn and hungry proletariat, endowed with a huge preponderance of voting power.'[64]

The reference to 'voting power' was apposite. In June 1918 Parliament had enshrined the radical, democratic principle of 'one man, one vote' in the Representation of the People Act, which enfranchised more citizens, including women over twenty-eight, than all the earlier reform acts combined. Precisely what the King and Queen thought of the Act is unclear. Their official biographers do not even refer to it, a singular omission for what was probably the most important piece of legislation in the reign of George V. We may assume that when the Act was passed the royal couple did not break into a jig. The day after the armistice, Esher wrote to the King: 'As Your Majesty well knows, Ambition, Vanity, Tyranny, and a "Swelled head" are not the characteristics of monarchs

184

only, as it is the fashion of the moment to suppose, but are equally the privilege of Statesmen and Journalists and other leaders of that curious superstition which men called democracy.'[65]

Like so much else that was new and unpalatable, the monarchy would have to adjust to the 'curious superstition which men called democracy'. On five successive days during armistice week, the King and Queen drove through the poorest parts of London in an open carriage. George V noted in his diary that 'waves of cheering crowds' greeted them.[66] Esher wrote to Stamfordham, not without a certain irony, praising ' "democratization" of the Monarchy' that these journeys represented. He warned that the King must avoid 'any relapse into the old "display" . . . until the people begin to settle down, and they see prosperity reviving. It is the modesty and simplicity of the King that wins hearts.' And he ended the letter with a plea for the King to offer clemency to a conscientious objector, 'a man with much influence with the most *dangerous* sections of the Working Class. He must be let out sooner or later. It would be good policy if he thought that the King had a hand in his release.'[67] In the new age of Labour Party ascendancy, Palace advisors believed that royal benevolence must extend to socialists, even to those they deemed the most obnoxious.

Just as trade unionism and industrial unrest had given shape to the crown's social policy before 1914, the war and its aftermath led to a greater degree of calculation in Buckingham Palace. Expressions of sympathy for Russia in 'Red Clydeside' and south Wales, combined with the distinct possibility of a Labour government, made matters seem perilous indeed. The King hoped that socialists would become more responsible as their power increased and trade improved.[68] But as unemployment rose, so did the King's fear of insurrection. Advisors fanned his worries. Given the fate of the German, Russian and Austrian royal families, a degree of paranoia would have been an understandable reaction in the Palace. Where in the post-war world could the monarchy look to for the reassurance that Queen Victoria took for granted?

George V's views about the state of the nation vacillated, but after 1917 he was always looking over his shoulder for extremists. At a football match in the spring of 1921 he was happy to report to his mother that 'there were no Bolsheviks there!'[69] Some years later, he seemed to think that Bolshevism might even interrupt 'the cheery contentment' of New Zealand.[70] Monarchs feel secure in proportion to the loyalty of their subjects; for a King so used to obsequious adoration, open dissension was unsettling. Cheering hordes at the Palace gates were all to the good, but the memory of such scenes was apt to fade when news broke of 'sulphurous speeches' attacking the crown, policemen on strike, or communists hissing the King's name at a meeting at the Albert Hall to celebrate the anniversary of the Russian revolution.[71] Though generally popular, George V was socially isolated and politically neutralized. He felt exposed.

The 1920s was a turbulent decade, in some ways reminiscent of those pre-war days when the King could think of little else but social unrest and called on God to help him out of his despair. When God failed, George V looked to the politicians. In September 1921, he instructed Stamfordham to write a series of trenchant letters to ministers. These graphically illustrated the King's nervousness about unemployment, which had reached over two million by the summer of 1921, and his desire to see something done about it before the coming winter. Stamfordham informed Lloyd George of the King's fear of discontent spiralling out of control and agitators taking charge and fomenting revolt.[72] He informed the Home Secretary that the King believed that communists, backed by Russian money, were 'doing their utmost to bring about revolution'![73] And he informed the secretary of the cabinet that the King wanted work not dole for the unemployed and appealed to the government to meet the crisis.[74]

Like God, the politicians disappointed. Palace officials had little faith in the will of governments to address post-war problems seriously. And they would have been right to doubt that ministers much considered the interests of the crown in the determination of policy. Political trends were such that the role of the monarchy was now only of marginal interest to politicians. As the power of the crown waned, ministers became less and less sensitive to its views, a habit encouraged by the decline of the aristocracy and the widening of the franchise. One portent was the Labour Party's constitution of 1918, which called for the 'common ownership of the means of production'. Another was the greater centralization of power brought about by the First World War, which led politicians to pay less regard to those local voluntary traditions so beloved of the crown.

'Parliamentary Sovereignty' had replaced a formerly powerful monarchy, and under the new constitutional arrangements authority was beginning to be concentrated in the office of prime minister in a manner reminiscent of Tudor sovereigns.[75] The King could deal with his boxes, and he could 'consult', 'encourage' and 'warn' as much as he liked, but politicians were under little obligation to take notice, though it sometimes suited them to do so. When Ramsay MacDonald formed the first Labour government in 1924, he found it easy enough to deal with George V, because the crown would not present an obstacle to his policies. MacDonald had written in 1909 that 'the political reformer may pass it [the monarchy] by without notice, even though on theoretical grounds he may be a republican'.[76] King George, though he sometimes tested the limits of his authority, knew that there was more to be gained from accommodating and charming ministers than from alienating them.

For the monarchy, the political high ground was largely outside high politics.

The crown did not itself lack initiative or resolve; it could do something positive, beyond the reach of politicians, to defend itself. If during the war the royal contribution to charity had been linked to national survival, it was more closely linked to the monarchy's survival at the end of it. Social malaise and the drift of politics galvanized the monarchy into a more vigorous policy of self-help. In view of the constitutional constraints, royal self-help meant forging bonds of affection at home and across the Empire. Clive Wigram, the King's Assistant Private Secretary, was among those who wanted greater publicity given to imperial tours and welfare missions to working-class communities; he also sought closer links with Labour Party representatives. A master of propaganda and 'imaginative gestures', he proposed that the gardens of Buckingham Palace be opened to convalescing officers and suggested that clergymen should be seen more often in the company of the royal family: 'Preachers propagate better than most people the gospel of devotion to the throne.'[77]

Not everyone in Buckingham Palace agreed with such ideas, some of which were rather novel. Wigram described a court divided between reformers and 'Troglodytes who shudder when any changes are proposed, and consider any modification of the present Court functions as lowering to the dignity and status of the Sovereign'. Presumably, Frederick Ponsonby, Keeper of the Privy Purse, was a Troglodyte, for he told the Prince of Wales that if members of the royal family became too accessible they would lose the element of mystery.[78] In Ponsonby's view, there was no romance in seeing the King step out of 'a dust-laden motor car'.[79] On that issue, and others, Ponsonby was defeated.

Palace reformers believed that providing information on the day-to-day work of the monarchy was essential in the campaign against republicanism. The appointment of a full-time press secretary in 1918 reflected the change in mood and tempo. But the policy of letting a little light in on the crown required not only the cooperation of the press, but also the cooperation of the royal family. For a King who was said to have hated public relations, George V was rather good at them. One royal biographer argues that 'the "selling" of the image of the family firm to the people who would have to pay for it was to be a major royal preoccupation in the post-war years'.[80] This was so, but we should not conclude that the creation of the caring royal image that gained ground in the 1920s was simply an invention of the media. There was more to the monarchy's survival strategy in the interwar years than salesmanship and insubstantial pageant. With its extensive network of patronages, the monarchy was well placed to assist the voluntary sector to deliver an array of much-needed social services.

44. Queen Mary visiting the Rachel Macmillan baby camp, Deptford, April 1919.

45.   Queen Mary visiting Shoreditch, March 1922.

Despite the growth in wartime state intervention, there was no consensus on the best way to mitigate the level of social distress in the post-war years. The King himself sometimes advocated increased government action. In 1927, he asked the Minister of Health, Neville Chamberlain, to encourage the local authorities to alleviate the problems of slum housing.[81] The pressure on the social services, whether state or voluntary, was intense, and public expectation of provision grew faster than the nation's capacity to provide it. Labour activists often favoured more collectivist measures, but in general the labour movement was divided on the best way to proceed with regard to the social services. The new electorate, and many of those who spoke on its behalf, displayed a widespread resistance to change. If people expected more of government, they did not usually overrate its capacity to deliver.

Victorian habits of self-help and personal service, though under strain during the war, persisted despite higher levels of taxation. In London, at least, voluntary contributions were picking up by the mid-1920s. 'Universalism', that rallying cry of post-1945 social policy, was far less attractive in the interwar years. Most people, still deeply imbued with 'Victorian values', did not wish to make a decisive break with a familiar liberal society in which localism and selectivity were deeply ingrained. As a leading scholar has argued, 'the embodiment of corporate life remained for most men and women in Britain . . . his or her voluntary association, trade union, family, local community, church, place of work, public house'.[82]

In common cause with the voluntary and commercial sectors, the monarchy cleverly responded to social issues and turned them to its own advantage. Everyone in Buckingham Palace was conscious of the need for vigilance, though one or two members of the royal family had to be persuaded to perform their duty. It seems unlikely that the King gathered his entire family and his advisors around him at the end of the war to devise a strategy in detail. But the post-war activities pursued by members of the royal family suggest no small degree of calculation and forward planning. Esher believed that the popularity of the Prince of Wales 'might be a great asset' when the war ended, and he had told the Queen as much in a lengthy meeting with her.[83] Queen Mary wrote to the King at the end of 1918: 'I think David ought to return home before *very* long, as he must help us in these difficult days.'[84] Highly sensitive to the dangers to the monarchy at the end of the war, she had 'some capital talks' with the Prince of Wales, and she noted that 'he is quite ready to do anything we want'.[85]

The Prince of Wales was not a social crusader by temperament, but he was susceptible to parental pressure. Hitherto he had supported a few projects on behalf of the homeless and unemployed, paid for by the income of the Duchy of Cornwall. But in June 1919 he made the first of those goodwill tours of south Wales which were to do so much for his reputation. There, as later elsewhere, he inquired into housing conditions and the welfare of ex-servicemen, and he hammered home the message that he had the interests of the poorer classes 'very much at heart'. On a visit to the left-wing stronghold of Glasgow, he was well received by the men in cloth caps, with only a smattering of boos. The family obsession with Bolshevism had rubbed off on the Prince. He reported to his mistress, Freda Dudley Ward: 'I do feel I've been able to do just a little good propaganda up there and given Communism a knock.'[86] He could take further consolation in the fact that, after his visits, the public houses in the 'red villages' put up his picture.[87]

The 'provincial forays', as the Prince put it in later life, 'were minia-tures of my Imperial tours'.[88] Lloyd George is credited with the idea of sending the Prince on the series of foreign trips that began in 1919, for he was worried that pent-up demands for reform threatened the Empire with disintegration. The Prime Minister was perhaps not fully aware just how well his own political concerns dovetailed with the worries of Palace officials, who believed that the monarchy should cultivate the Empire for its own ends. The King was not altogether convinced that his son was up to the job of royal ambassador, and Lord Stamfordham solemnly reminded the Prince of Wales: 'The Throne is the pivot upon which the

Empire will more than ever hinge. Its strength and stability will depend entirely on its occupant.'[89] Politicians and the Palace took what comfort they could from the tours, but not necessarily the same comfort.

While the Prince of Wales propped up the Empire in Toronto and Delhi, his younger brother, Prince Albert (later George VI), discovered that he had a liking for factories and shipyards in Glasgow and Liverpool. The shy, stammering Prince had been ill during part of the war, but in early 1919, the King, after considerable thought, gave his consent for his son to accept an invitation from the Reverend Robert Hyde to become President of the Boys' Welfare Association (soon to be renamed the Industrial Welfare Society).[90] 'I'll do it provided that there's no damned red carpet about it,' the Prince remarked.[91] He accepted the job, which lasted for sixteen years. Entirely dependent on voluntary contributions, the institution profited from the Prince's capacity to recruit new members and to extract donations. In turn, the Prince, who was created Duke of York in 1920, developed an unusual knowledge of factory conditions and industrial relations.[92]

The Industrial Welfare Society sought to humanize industry by improving the physical conditions of the workplace and by bringing employees into closer communion with their employers. Such practices could hardly have been better suited to the monarchy's goal of reducing class bitterness and promoting social cohesion. Inevitably, there was opposition to the Society. Some trade unionists argued that it simply 'bolstered up an outworn capitalist system'. At a meeting in Blackpool, miners accused the Society of 'patching an old pair of trousers', when a new pair was needed. Some industrialists, on the other hand, accused it of 'promulgating the worst form of socialism'.[93] The Prince did his share to overcome such prejudices by quietly getting on with the job. His assiduity earned him the nickname 'the foreman' from his brothers.[94]

The Duke of York's Camp, which brought together thousands of teenage boys from factories and public schools, emerged in 1921 out of the Industrial Welfare Society. As its organizer Robert Hyde remarked, if anybody but a member of the royal family had started it, the 'average parent of a public schoolboy would have been a little timorous about the advisability of allowing Claude to associate with Bill, lest he should "catch" something detrimental to his health, or far worse, to his manners'.[95] To the Duke of York, who took a great personal interest in the scheme, the camps played 'a part in oiling the wheels of industry with good-fellowship and understanding'. And while breaking down class barriers, they would, to use Hyde's phrase, 'tame young Bolshevists', which was no small recommendation to a member of the royal family. The value of the camps was, as George VI's biographer observes, 'more symbolic than real', but they did offer a distraction to working-class boys in some pretty grim years, while promoting a positive royal image.[96]

Just a few days before his wedding in 1923, the Duke of York became the first member of the royal family to visit a trade union, the Amalgamated Engineering Union. *The Times* reported that 'the Duke might suppose that in coming to the headquarters of a great trade union he was visiting some sort of Bolshevik organisation more concerned to promote strife than peace'. *The Times* need not have worried, for the Union's President, James Brownlie, had accepted a CBE in 1917. After an obliging tour of the headquarters, Brownlie invited the Duke into his office, offered him refreshments and enthused about the royal wedding: 'Take my assurance that you are perfectly safe in the hands of a Scots lassie.'[97] So it turned out.

The marriage of the Duke of York to Lady Elizabeth Bowes-Lyon was propitious. The monarchy was more dependent on its female members for its popularity than even it realized, and the introduction of another woman willing to undertake public duties was highly desirable. By the mid-1920s there was a shortage of royal females available for patronage work and welfare tours. With Queen Alexandra in her dotage (she died in 1925), Princess Helena dead (she died in 1923) and the Prince of Wales and the royal dukes wifeless, the pressure on Queen Mary and Princess Mary mounted. The Duchess of York offered a measure of relief. She took over Princess Helena's patronage list, which included the National Society for the Prevention of Cruelty to Children and the Young Women's Christian Association, expanded it, and soon established herself as one of the most formidable charitable campaigners in the history of the British monarchy. Like so many other royal wives, she specialized in causes relating to women and children, which complemented her husband's interest in boys' camps, working men and industry.[98]

One of the Duke of York's most successful patronages was the National Playing Fields Association, which received its royal charter in 1925. Few royal charities made such a visible, and lasting, contribution to working-class welfare and public amenities generally. The movement to establish children's playing fields, as opposed to gardens and public parks, dated from the 1890s. It should be seen in the context of the concerns about national efficiency and industrial performance. As one supporter pronounced: 'A man who plays cricket on Victoria Park would face the bloodiest battle with absolute indifference.'[99] Another argued that 'the boy without a playground is father to the man without a job'.[100] Playing fields fitted neatly into the thinking of the Duke of York and the Prince of Wales about the shortage of factory amenities and the physical and moral decay that flowed from it, and they consented to support the charity.

Admiral Lionel Halsey, Comptroller to the Prince of Wales, and General R.J. Kentish, Honorary Secretary of the British Olympic

Association, were the Association's leading advocates, and they cleverly exploited their royal connections. In the mid-1920s charitable appeals were like aeroplanes queuing up for takeoff. Finding the right moment to get one off the ground was crucial, as was finding a member of the royal family to pilot the plane. While they waited, Halsey and Kentish put together a list of millionaires to be approached, and cultivated the Lord Mayor of London, who they believed would be unable to resist a scheme which had enlisted the support of the Prince of Wales.

When they finally lined up the Prince to broadcast an appeal in 1927, Halsey remarked that 'it would be impossible to exaggerate the effect of such a message'. In response to the Prince's appeal the Carnegie United Kingdom Trust donated £200,000 alone. Another donor sent a cheque for £10,000 on the grounds that the appeal had royal backing, which elicited a letter of thanks from the Duke of York.[101] The King himself contributed two of the royal paddocks in Bushy Park, which were then turned into playing fields. The royal family's promotion of the National Playing Fields Association, like so many other institutions, was crucial to its success. In the lean years after the Second World War, Prince Philip revitalized the charity, which now acts as guardian trustee for hundreds of sites across the country.[102]

Like Queen Victoria and Prince Albert, George V and Queen Mary kept a close watch on their children and monitored the level of their philanthropic activity. George V did not warm to backsliding, and he kept a map in Buckingham Palace which chronicled his family's public work, complete with little flags showing locations. In ten years, the King and Queen and the Princes carried out 3,000 engagements.[103] Ultimately, George V even went to the lengths of having a chart, compiled by Robert Hyde and brought to him at Sandringham each Christmas, that listed the family's public appearances over the year.[104] As the younger children reached an age at which they could take up a public role, their names were added.

The King pored over his charts like a sea captain over his logbooks. He would have given special attention to the performance of the Prince of Wales. Princess Mary's output was satisfactory. She went to work at the Great Ormond Street Hospital in 1918, and in later years she made hundreds of visits to institutions as various as the Girl Guides and unemployment centres. The King would also have noted with approval the eighty or so functions carried out each year by the Duke of York, a figure which increased after his marriage. He took for granted Queen Mary's charitable output, which set a benchmark for the rest of the family. Has a minister of health ever visited more hospitals or child welfare centres? In 1921, Sir George Newman, the chief medical officer at the Ministry of Health, said that the Queen's philanthropic work was 'invaluable' and her

46. Queen Mary and Princess Mary, Viscountess Lascelles, inspecting Girl Guides, May 1923.

social influence 'sound and statesmanlike'. And he noted, in passing, that her beneficent labours were 'enormously strengthening the influence of the Crown with the people'.[105]

★ ★ ★

In this cursory survey only a few of the causes actively promoted by the royal family in the interwar years can be dealt with in any detail. Medical charity was, as we have seen, a primary royal concern, and in the early 1920s it was undergoing one of its periodic crises. The voluntary hospitals were volatile institutions, which threw together officious patrons, aspiring professionals and uninvited guests. The war had unsettled their traditions and depleted their finances, while stimulating clinical advances and increasing medical costs. It had pointed to health as a national asset, which some easily translated into a national responsibility. Hospitals and health had become politicized as never before, and the stage was set for a propaganda battle between voluntarists and state-interventionists that would last for decades.

With its longstanding doubts about the viability of voluntary hospitals, the Labour Party was now discussing a national health service under state control. Imperceptibly, modes of expression shifted, which suggested a growing predisposition to collective action. The formation of the Ministry of Health in 1919 was seen as symbolic of changing attitudes towards medical provision, and it probably contributed to the perception that government would increasingly meet the costs of hospital care, or introduce a programme of municipalization. The fact that Labour flirted with such notions put the voluntary hospitals on political alert and in turn they alerted the King.

In 1920, the Ministry of Health appointed Bertrand Dawson, who had served as a consultant in France during the war, to chair a consultative council on medical services. Though far from being a socialist, Dawson accepted that a greater degree of state intervention was necessary to improve British medical services. His ideas, published in the Dawson Report of 1920, outlined a reorganization of hospital provision that had much in common with a plan supported by the Labour Party. As part of the scheme, the great charitable hospitals were to be introduced to regional planning and subject to outside supervision. Such schemes, anathema to hospital voluntarists, did not find favour in Buckingham Palace. In a matter perhaps not unrelated, the King doubted the wisdom of raising Dawson, who was his Physician in Ordinary, to the peerage in 1920.[106]

George V was apt to see a red under every state hospital bed. The voluntary hospitals, on the other hand, were particularly dear to him, and his response to their plight illustrates the high level of coordination between the monarchy and the charitable sector when the interests of the medical profession were at stake. The King's Fund, which now served as a central board for the London voluntary hospitals, informed George V of the dangers represented by Dawson's proposals. In turn, the King instructed Stamfordham to inform the Minister of Health, Dr Christopher Addison, that he was opposed to government intervention.[107] Some weeks before Dawson's scheme appeared, the minister reassured the King that the government had no intention of taking over the hospitals.[108] The strength of the charitable sector and worries about the potential cost of implementing the proposals were sufficient to dash Dawson's report.

But the collapse of Dawson's proposals did nothing to resolve the hospital crisis. Consequently, the Minister of Health appointed a committee, chaired by Viscount Cave, to investigate voluntary hospital finances. The final report of the Cave Committee, published in June 1921, vigorously defended the charitable system, which, it argued, was suffering the inevitable aftershocks of the war. Its chief recommendation was that Parliament should make a temporary grant of £1 million to help the voluntary hospitals get through the crisis. But when Parliament, now fierce in its pursuit of cuts in public expenditure, looked at the figure, it reduced it by half; and the Treasury attached the condition that fresh money from charitable sources must be raised to match government grants pound for pound.[109]

The government's decision triggered the greatest hospital drive of the interwar years, led by a host of royal charities. In London, the King's Fund was given responsibility for directing a 'Combined Hospitals Appeal' which brought together the Joint Council of the Order of St John and the British Red Cross, the Sunday Fund, and the League of Mercy. The omens were unfavourable, for the appeal was launched against the background of trade depression and high taxation. The King's Fund assumed that, for the campaign to succeed, the royal family's active participation was crucial. It immediately cabled its president, the Prince of Wales, who was in India, to ask his permission to give his name to the appeal and to invite him to preside at a grand dinner at the Mansion House upon his return to England.

The Prince's response was dispiriting. He refused most of the Fund's requests with the excuse that he would be out of the country at the launch of the appeal. This somewhat 'blunt refusal' was explained further in a telegram from Godfrey Thomas, the Prince's Private Secretary. The Fund's officials probably never saw this cable; if they had, they would have been deeply disturbed. The Prince's reluctance to involve himself in the appeal, apart from allowing his name to appear in the literature as president of the Fund, was not due simply to the fact that he would be absent during part of the campaign. He also had grave doubts about its success. 'He is of the opinion', wrote Thomas, 'that all who can afford to give money and are disposed to do so would have already contributed as far as their means permit to the touching appeals which every individual London Hospital has for so long been making, and cannot help thinking that this general appeal which is presumably last effort to save voluntary system is therefore foredoomed to failure.'[110]

The Prince's attitude was an extraordinary departure for a member of the royal family, which for so long had been devoted to the charitable hospitals. It is intriguing to speculate on how the Prince came by the opinion, prophetic in hindsight, that the voluntary hospital system would not survive. Of course, he may have simply wanted a good excuse to beg off, for there were always more interesting things for the Prince of Wales to do than spend time with do-gooders and the sick. But he may have come under the influence of Lord Dawson, who became one of his physicians in 1923. Clearly, his refusal to cooperate was another example of his cavalier rejection of the values of the older generation. Charitable hospitals were part of a pre-war Victorian world, a world inhabited by his father.

To George V, the expansion of state hospital provision at the expense of the voluntary system would be tantamount to a national moral disaster; and he whipped his family into line to rescue his favoured institutions.

47.   A poster to promote the Hospitals of London Combined Appeal, 1922.

'The people of London have generously resolved to save their Hospitals,' he wrote in an open letter on behalf of the appeal. 'It is impossible to contemplate the closing of any of them, for in character & organisation our Hospitals are unique among the charitable institutions of the world.' He diplomatically excused the absent Prince of Wales: 'I know that my son, the President, would have taken an active, personal part in this great effort had circumstances so permitted.'[111] When the prodigal son returned, the King must have had a word with him, for the Prince's enthusiasm for the voluntary hospitals miraculously revived.

The Combined Appeal displayed a high level of entrepreneurial flair. The object was to reach all classes of the community, to impress on local residents that the hospitals were 'their' hospitals and that they relied on neighbourhood support. The devices used to extract contributions were as ingenious as ever, with new twists suited to the 1920s. That perennial ally and victim of royal charity, the game bird, played its part: pheasants shot by the King sold for over £3 a brace. Prize-winning posters, which displayed the royal crest, bedecked railings and buildings all over the metropolis. Collecting boxes adorned shops, hotels and pubs. Fifty thousand women volunteers rattled tins on the streets. Cinemas, theatres and music halls hosted events. A film, *When George was King*, celebrated the advances in hospital care. Queen Alexandra starred in a cameo role. Shown in cinemas, it was said to have brought in 100,000 new hospital contributors.[112]

The level of royal participation in the appeal was impressive. George V and Queen Mary turned out, as did virtually every member of their extended family. Among the many royal outings, the King and Queen attended a 'Revue of Revues' at the Hippodrome, the Duke of York a display of physical exercises at the Albert Hall and a dinner at the Guildhall, the Princess Royal a Children's Choral Festival and a ball, and Princess Alice, Countess of Athlone, a garden party at Kew Gardens. For his part, the Prince of Wales appeared at the 'Revue of Revues' and attended an Open-Air Schools' Festival at Chelsea Football Ground, a ball at the Albert Hall, and a film *When Knighthood was in Flower*. At a ceremony at County Hall in March 1923, he accepted a cheque for £50,000 collected by schoolchildren.[113]

The Combined Appeal eventually raised nearly £500,000, well in excess of the sum required to earn the government grant for London. For a time, at least, it put the hospitals back on financial track. The chairman of the appeal's organizing committee argued that the success of the campaign was largely due 'to the exceptional measure of support given by H.M. the King and many members of the Royal Family'.[114] This was not far-fetched, for the presence of members of the royal family at many of the events brought distinction, fashion and enlarged receipts. With its rich brew of commerce and entertainment, sport and education, the

BUCKINGHAM PALACE.

I am following with the closest interest the progress made by King Edward's Hospital Fund in organising this combined appeal on behalf of the Voluntary Hospitals of London & I congratulate the Organising Committee on the results already achieved.

My family have been intimately associated with the Fund from its inception: & I know that my son, the President, would have taken an active, personal part in this great effort had circumstances so permitted.

His happiness in returning home will be increased by the knowledge that the people of London have generously resolved to save their Hospitals. It is impossible to contemplate the closing of any of them, for in character & organisation our Hospitals are unique among the charitable Institutions of the world.

June 12th 1922.

George R.I.

48. An open letter from King George V in support of the Hospitals of London Combined Appeal, 1922.

49.   King George V and Queen Mary visiting the site of Queen Mary's Hospital, Stratford, June 1923.

50.   A visit by the Duke and Duchess of York to open the Princess Elizabeth Ward, Queen's Hospital for Children, Hackney, March 1931.

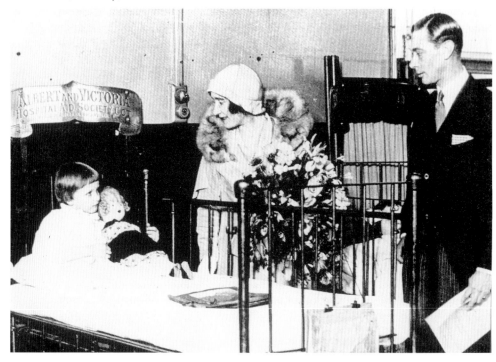

Combined Appeal was in step with social change. Where it was most effective it made the act of charity natural and diverting, a part of everyday life. At the same time it was part of the pattern of introducing the royal family to an increasingly wide social circle. All in all, the appeal made no small contribution to the weaving of charitable traditions, visibly led by the royal family, into the life of the community.

The Prince of Wales must have been surprised by the success of an appeal that he had assumed could end only in failure. Indeed, by 1924 the post-war hospital crisis was over, and with industrial production back to pre-war levels and trade improving, the future looked brighter. So much brighter, in fact, that the Prince felt able to say at a meeting of the King's Fund in July 1924 that he looked forward to voluntary hospital expansion. In a line written by one of his aides, he pronounced: 'I wonder if there is any one who still thinks the voluntary Hospital System is dead, or dying.'[115] It was a pointed reminder to the Prince that he had been mistaken to underestimate the vitality of charitable traditions. In the interwar years a host of voluntary hospitals, several boasting royal titles, were built or expanded, many of them in the working-class suburbs.

★ ★ ★

In his ghosted autobiography, *A King's Story*, published after his abdication and creation as the Duke of Windsor, Edward recalled his days as Prince of Wales: 'The job . . . as I tried to interpret it, was, first, to carry on associations with worthy causes outside politics and clothe them with the prestige of the Prince's high position; and, second, to bring the Monarchy, in response to new conditions, ever nearer to the people.'[116] It was an accurate assessment of his duties (it would serve equally well for the present Prince of Wales). But Edward VIII both as Prince and King proved a more reluctant philanthropist than the statement implies. In 1918, in keeping with Palace strategy, he had received a letter from Lord Stamfordham outlining the various offices that his father expected him to assume, including the presidency of the King's Fund. As his biographer Philip Ziegler observed, the 'dismal catalogue' of duties 'must have chilled the Prince's heart'.[117]

Given the distractions of his private life, his dislike of ceremony and his ambivalence towards voluntarism, the Prince of Wales seldom looked forward to the demands that patronage made on his time. Unlike his father, he rarely took the initiative in defending the voluntary sector. A charitable secretary who worked with him remembered him as a 'pathetic' figure, who could not effectively chair a meeting.[118] Locked into his patronages and under pressure from his parents, the Prince nevertheless carried out many of the duties asked of him by his charities. He read the interminable speeches, entertained charitable workers, wrote thank you letters to large-scale benefactors, and made innumerable appearances at special events. No man ever danced more for charitable purposes.

Looking back on the interwar years, Edward argued that 'whenever there was a necessity for a public drive for funds, my services were always called upon and most willingly given'.[119] This was disingenuous. Certainly institutions often called on his services, but he did not always 'willingly' oblige. As he was aware, his refusal to turn up for an fundraising event could threaten a society's very existence. More than one local charity 'fizzled out' for want of an appearance by the Prince. When he did appear, he contributed more in the way of time than money. In the late 1920s, he paid less than £1,000 in subscriptions to a total of about 125 charities each year, plus a few donations.[120]

The appearance of the Prince could have memorable results, and when the spirit moved him he had a deft touch at extracting money from others. His very presence at a charitable engagement put the well-to-do under terrific pressure to contribute. In 1932, for example, he opened a new wing at the Worcester Infirmary and received purses. Sir William Morris (later Lord Nuffield), a native of Worcester, was among the honoured guests. During the proceedings, it was announced that the charity was in serious debt. Morris, a golfing partner of the Prince, whispered something in the Prince's ear. The Prince, there and then, announced a contribution of £26,000 from Sir William to cover the deficit. George V soon granted the hospital the title of the Worcester Royal Infirmary.[121]

With his good looks and surface charm, the Prince of Wales was a dazzling front man for interwar charities. On the whole, they handled him effectively and conspired to cover his tracks when necessary. Millions of people, many of them jobless, saw him on tour, heard him on the wireless or attended one of his set-piece events. Most were charmed, and not a few spellbound. One admirer wrote to him: 'It causes the greatest delight imaginable to me to write to you because I love you and have done so since I read that account of your visit to the military hospital narrated in the book *Christ of the Open Road*.'[122] The displays of deference and affection helped Palace aides through the embarrassments that they sometimes had to endure, as on the occasion when, in a temper, the Prince kicked the superintendent's dog on a visit to the Cardiff Royal Infirmary.[123]

With the onset of the Depression, charitable officials, mayors and other local worthies were more assiduous than usual in cultivating the monarchy's good offices. Voluntary bodies provided the royal family with fresh thinking and administrative backup. The Prince of Wales was the Patron of that prominent coordinating body for charities, the National Council of Social Services, founded in 1919 (now the National Council for Voluntary Organisations). In a manner typical of royal charities, the

Council bombarded him with proposals, hoping that one of them would arouse his interest. But it took the catastrophic effects of unemployment to put the Prince in a mood to contribute personally to its initiatives on jobs and national reconstruction.

The Prince agreed to deliver a speech on unemployment at the Albert Hall. Enormous care went into the address, which was written by the Secretary of the National Council, Captain Lionel Ellis, and the Secretary of the Pilgrim Trust, Thomas Jones. The Prince's Private Secretary, Godfrey Thomas, asked the Conservative leader Stanley Baldwin for ideas. The speech had to strike the right note, needing to encourage something more potent than a bazaar but also to stop short of provoking a revolution. The politics of the address were well understood by the Prince's staff. It was timed to come after the election at the end of 1931 that returned Ramsay McDonald's National Government. 'After the election there will be greater need than ever of some call to the country that will tend to unite people,' remarked Ellis to Godfrey Thomas.[124]

The Prince personally wanted to avoid 'political issues', but in the circumstances this was difficult. The Area Commander of the British Fascists wrote to the Palace warning of a communist plan to wreck the Prince's speech. The Palace uncovered a leaflet by the Young Communist League denouncing the Albert Hall meeting and informed the police. On a different front, the Secretary of the Women's National Emergency Movement asked the Prince to 'proclaim Christ's coming' and rely 'upon Divine intervention as the ultimate hope for national and world deliverance'. She had to be discouraged from coming to see the Prince. The Transport and General Workers' Union took the view, which it put to the Prince after the speech, that private schemes to relieve unemployment were 'bound to fail' and only its new National Government policy of 'rationalization and concentration' could hope to succeed.[125]

The Prince delivered the speech, which was broadcast across the country, to a packed audience at the Albert Hall on January 27, 1932. There was a timelessness about the message, despite its being tied to the immediate issue of unemployment. Much of it would have been unexceptionable to Prince Albert. It was a restatement of charity's first principles directed at the nation's youth. The Prince applauded 'the wonderful voluntary work' that was already being done in connection with countless good causes, but he stressed that the problems of unemployment and social dislocation needed to be broken 'into little pieces' by personal service and local solutions. It was an explicit critique of collectivist remedies and a reminder that a sense of 'community' had little reference to politics or the engine of the central state:

> You should not think of social service purely as State action. . . . The wide provision of State social services has perhaps lessened in some of us the

sense of the need, the duty, of personal service, and has encouraged a tendency to take all these things for granted—encouraged a readiness to receive without at the same time inculcating that readiness to give which is the only justification for the privileges of citizenship. . . . There is no central machinery here in London . . . that can provide a substitute for the good neighbour.

He ended with some remarks about his own role in promoting good neighbourliness in the Empire, just the thing to please his father.[126]

Whether or not the Prince believed the words put into his mouth is questionable. But the speech elicited an immediate and remarkable response. On the day of the broadcast, 260 meetings sponsored by local voluntary groups were held at centres around the country, including two in Sheffield attended by Princess Mary, who was now the Princess Royal.[127] Within a year, 2,300 projects had appeared, including visiting schemes, clubs, settlements, workshops, canteens, nursery schools and playing fields, some of them started by the unemployed themselves. They catered to 250,000 people.[128] Such initiatives were proof that those Victorian remedies of personal service and self-help still had a great attraction, especially when actively encouraged by the royal family.

The Prince followed his speech by stepping up his schedule of tours to depressed industrial and rural areas.[129] He moved more easily among the working classes than he ever did among professional people who often saw through him. His image in the press was positive: a future King spreading the message of self-help and good neighbourliness, sharing the concerns of those he called 'his fellow-men'. George V preferred the usage 'my people'.[130] There was little to suggest publicly that the Prince's visits to the slums and mining villages sometimes left him depressed. Looking back, he remarked: 'I had the feeling that empty as was my mission, my appearance among them was in large measure appreciated and taken as a sign that the Monarchy had not forsaken them in their misfortune.'[131] When one considers the many useful schemes he helped to establish, it was perhaps less 'empty' than he imagined it to be.

There were those less than happy with the monarchy's role as the vanguard of the proletariat, and not only the Young Communist League. The General Council of the Trades Union Congress declined to cooperate with any of the schemes launched by the Prince. The decision aroused one journalist to reproach the TUC for its opposition 'to a movement of disinterested welfare simply and solely because that movement does not spell Socialism'.[132] When the Ministry of Labour under the National Government agreed to make grants available to projects sponsored by the National Council of Social Service, the Labour left denounced the decision as a cheap and devious way of buying off the

51.   The Prince of Wales visits Liverpool slum replacements, July 1933.

unemployed.[133] Richard Crossman, Labour Secretary of State for Health and the Social Services in the 1960s, summed up the collectivist view of interwar philanthropy as an 'odious expression of social oligarchy and churchy bourgeois attitudes. We detested voluntary hospitals maintained by flag days.'[134]

The collectivist wing of Labour despised do-gooding voluntarism, even of the working-class variety. Its preferred 'road to freedom' was, after all, grounded in central planning and a 'scientific' redistribution of wealth. Collectivists were right in thinking that voluntary work would never bring about the millennium. Philanthropists lacked a political dynamic, apart from the negative ones of maintaining social order and dishing socialism. They had no ideological vision, though Christianity still imparted a sense of social responsibility. Yet the charitable were willing to deal *personally* with the never-ending job of coping from day to day with an awesome level of unemployment, endemic disease and other social ills. One is reminded of the Salvationist, General William Booth, who once said that he had nothing against utopianism, collectivist or individualist, at the same time observing that 'here in our shelters last night were a thousand hungry, workless people. . . . It is in the meantime that the people must be fed, that their life's work must be done or left undone for ever.'[135]

★   ★   ★

In the mid-1930s, the division between voluntarism and collectivism remained profound, especially in the hospital sector, where longstanding medical traditions and valuable properties were at stake. Still, socialist leaders rarely criticized the monarchy openly for its alliance with the charitable sector. They saw little profit in attacking the crown, for there were few votes in it. This had become clear in 1923, when the Labour Party Conference put the motion 'Is republicanism the policy of the Labour Party?' The republicans were defeated by a vote of 3,694,000 to 386,000.[136] The figures were not simply a tribute to the royal family's mystique, but to its cultivation of the Labour constituencies. Just as the crown intended, the slum visits, the dispensaries and cottage hospitals, the youth clubs and playing fields, the training schemes and workshops, the consoling words at the pit heads and in the canteens, had taken the republican edge off socialism.

As far as the Labour left was concerned, royal social work simply deflected the lightning from striking the Palace, while palliating evils which might otherwise be entirely removed. Yet the monarchy had won the hearts and minds of the working classes more effectively than socialism itself, not least because it delivered so many well-publicized social amenities. For a host of reasons, including economic realities, interwar Labour governments had little success in providing social benefits. (As head of the National Government in 1931, Ramsay MacDonald actually reduced unemployment benefit.) Perhaps the greatest contribution that the Labour Party made to welfare causes in the 1920s and 1930s was to remind the crown of its social responsibilities, thereby frightening the royal family into good works. This was no small achievement, although it appears to have been based on the crown's misunderstanding of British socialism.

Along with its charitable work in the socialist heartlands, the monarchy's cultivation of Labour MPs and trade union officials took hold in the interwar years. In a world in which ideology was a danger to the crown, the practical politics of the royal family meant winning over potential enemies by granting them some of their minor wishes. As the Palace had to win its battles without appearing to fight, artifice and civility were essential. In the manner of clever King Magnus in George Bernard Shaw's *The Apple Cart*, George V dropped a kind word here, an invitation there, and scattered honours everywhere. It all helped the cause of disarming the socialist strongmen, absorbing them into the political system and moderating any criticism they might have of the crown. Perhaps Shaw was right in his belief that 'in conflicts between monarchs and popularly elected ministers the monarchs win every time when personal ability and good sense are at all equally divided'.[137]

Meetings with the King and Queen tended to be 'lovingly recollected' by Labour politicians and trade unionists in their memoirs, even class warriors such as Will Thorne, who 'delighted' to 'walk with Kings'.[138] John Hodge, the President of the Iron and Steel Trades Confederation, titled his autobiography *Workman's Cottage to Windsor Castle*. After dining at Windsor, he praised the King and Queen for their intimate knowledge of trade unionism and applauded the Palace aides, who 'made you feel as if you were one of them'.[139] Philip Snowden, the Labour Chancellor and an evangelical socialist in his youth, became a Viscount and took tea at Sandringham. In his *Autobiography* he skirted over his views on the Russian Revolution, preferring to talk about the charm of the King and Queen, who presented him and his wife with a reading table and a tea table, 'gifts we shall always treasure'.[140]

The incorruptible Beatrice Webb lamented: 'This romancing about the royal family is, I fear, only a minor symptom of the softening of the brain of socialists, enervated by affluence, social prestige and political power.'[141] She had Ramsay MacDonald upmost in her mind. The Labour leader proved highly susceptible to the royal embrace, and when he kissed hands with the King he forgot his former admiration for Lenin. (Whether the King forgot it is another matter. His refusal to accept MacDonald's resignation as Prime Minister in the dark days of 1931, when economies unpalatable to the proletariat were unavoidable, may be seen as a brilliant royal stroke to discredit socialism.)[142] And what would Beatrice Webb have made of Walter Citrine? As the General Secretary of the Trades Union Congress, he received his KBE in Jubilee year, an award that may have given the King more pleasure than the recipient. After Citrine's knighthood (he later became a baron), the TUC overwhelmingly rejected a resolution that leaders of the trade union movement should refuse honours.[143]

The Silver Jubilee of 1935, which Ramsay Macdonald compared to a 'Holy Communion', must have made Beatrice Webb long to return to the Soviet Union.[144] King George and Queen Mary appeared on the balcony of Buckingham Palace every night for a week to rapturous applause. They attended a service at St Paul's, and the King noted that there were 'the greatest number of people in the streets that I have ever seen in my life. The enthusiasm was indeed most touching.'[145] They drove through the East End and the dock areas and through Battersea, Kennington and Lambeth. Everywhere the working classes greeted them with jubilation, their houses decorated with flags and streamers, and banners bearing loyal messages. In his diary, the King commented favourably, if laconically, on these decorations 'all put up by the poor'.[146]

Wigram, now the King's Private Secretary, had never seen George V in such good form. (Wigram was made a peer in Jubilee year.) He described the affection for their Majesties during Jubilee week as 'like a dream—a miracle arranged by Providence'. He reported that even the federation of pickpockets had stopped all activities out of loyalty. In one of the worst slum streets 'was hung a blue overall with the inscription "lousy but loyal"'.[147] George Orwell also noted the expressions of loyalty at the Jubilee: 'It was even possible to see in it the survival, or recrudescence, of an idea almost as old as history, the idea of the King and the common people being in a sort of alliance against the upper classes.'[148] Shaw may have had a point when he said that kings were 'made by universal hallucination'. Yet the triumph of 'popular monarchy' in 1935 cannot be explained simply by reference to spectacle and illusion. It demeans the British working classes to think so. They had better reasons to admire the royal family.

During the Silver Jubilee, the philanthropic classes could hardly contain themselves. It was their first royal celebration since George V's recovery from illness in 1929, when they raised £700,000 for charitable causes in 'thank offerings'.[149] Most charities launched special appeals, and they wheeled out members of the royal family, including the Duchess of York and the Duke of Gloucester.[150] The King's Fund made £11,000 simply by selling seats at Jubilee processions.[151] Schemes and proposals arrived at Buckingham Palace from across the Empire: Canada launched an appeal for a Silver Jubilee Cancer Fund which raised £250,000 within weeks; South Africa a King George Silver Jubilee Tuberculosis Fund; Australia a King George V and Queen Mary Maternity and Infant Welfare Memorial; India a general fund to provide money for existing charities; and Bermuda just sent a cheque for the King to dispense with as he wished.[152]

In his Empire Speech in May 1935, the King thanked his subjects for their loyalty and love and dedicated himself anew to their service: 'I grieve to think of the numbers of my people who are still without work. We owe to them, and not least to those who are suffering from any form of disablement, all the sympathy and help that we can give. I hope that during the Jubilee Year all who can will do their utmost to find them work and bring them hope.'[153] He ended with a call to voluntary service, and he made a special plea for the commemorative fund that had just been launched by the Prince of Wales, whom *Punch* lovingly described as 'Wales King-of-Alms'.

The Prince of Wales had decided on a national appeal to 'promote the welfare of the younger generation'; this became the King George's Jubilee Trust. Some people refused to support it, including leading socialists and communists who derided the scheme as capitalist folly.[154] Still, money and ideas poured into the Trust's offices from mayors, businessmen, boy scouts, working men and the jobless. Many of the suggestions were helpful, others cranky or self-serving. A few wanted to promote eugenics, others to increase old age pensions.[155] In the end, the Prince of Wales decided that the Trust should provide clubs, camps and other recreational facilities for the young, which built on work already set in train by members of the royal family. The initial appeal raised £1 million and would have been more successful had the Prince not succeeded to the throne within a year of its launch. Most of the money was divided between established youth organizations, such as those arch-royal institutions the Boy Scouts and the Girl Guides.[156]

Whatever the Trust's achievements, it was a triumph of self-advertisement for the monarchy. *Punch* promoted the cause with a drawing of the Prince wearing a herald's coat blazoned with the arms of the sovereign, blowing his trumpet for donations. It was followed a month later by a revealing cartoon, in which an agitated Herr Hitler is seen taking notice of the Jubilee Trust in a headline in the *Daily Mail*. He laments: 'I thought I had the best youth movement in Europe.'[157] The Jubilee Trust, which conspicuously identified the crown with the next generation, was part of a long royal tradition. From George III's educational charities to the Prince's Trust today, the monarchy has continually acknowledged that the future lay with the nation's youth.

The Jubilee Trust, like the Jubilee celebrations generally, was a tribute to the King's personal popularity. Over a long reign, George V had set a standard of rectitude and benevolence that had endeared him to the British public. A large part of his life had been taken up by political administration, but it is doubtful whether his dutiful attention to his boxes had much to do with his popularity. He always recognized that there was more to being a king than politics. Indeed, George V's industrial tours, hospital work, visits to poor cottagers, speeches, broadcasts, subscriptions and fundraising were better known to the common man than his opinion of the Versailles Treaty or the gold standard.

George V inherited most of his patronage and social work, which recommended it to him. But he did innovate from time to time. In 1932, inspired by Princess Marie Louise, the daughter of Princess Helena, he reestablished the monarch's active participation in the Maundy distribution.[158] The tradition had been neglected since the end of the seventeenth century, though members of the royal family occasionally attended the service. The King also delivered the first Christmas broadcast in 1932 in the depth of the Depression. It closed with a succinct and revealing statement of his purpose as sovereign: 'to arrive at a reasoned tranquillity within our borders, to regain prosperity without self-seeking, and to carry with us those whom the burden of past years has

52. *Punch* celebrating King
George's Jubilee Trust for
youth, 1935.

WALES KING-OF-ALMS.

disheartened or overborne'.[159] It was characteristic of George V that when
'the burden of past years' caught up with him he thought of others. On
his deathbed, when his 'private war with the twentieth century' was at
last over, he dispatched a cheque for £20,000 to benefit the sick poor of
London.[160]

Edward VIII, by contrast, was too distracted, and too mercenary, to
contribute very much to philanthropic causes during his brief reign.
Although 776 institutions appeared on his patronage list, including a large
number of golf clubs, his subscriptions to charity were well down on
those of his father.[161] Nor was he so dutiful in meeting his commitments.
On one notorious occasion, not long before his abdication, he excused
himself from opening a new hospital in Aberdeen. He sent the Duke and
Duchess of York instead, offering the lame excuse that the court was still
in mourning for his father. But on the same day he was seen in Aberdeen

210

THE LEADER.

53. Hitler's response to the Jubilee Trust, as seen by *Punch*, 1935. 'I thought I had the best youth movement in Europe, but I begin to think I'm mistaken.'

on his way to pick up Mrs Simpson. To the intense embarrassment of the Palace, a local newspaper took up the story, publishing photographs of the two events. One courtier remarked, rather melodramatically: 'This has done [the King] more harm than anything else and has lost him Scotland.'[162]

Despite his many charitable labours as Prince of Wales, Edward VIII had never been wholly committed to voluntary traditions. Indeed, their traditionalism made them less palatable. His 'smart set' was a world away from the 'smart set' of Edward VII, not least in shedding its social conscience. Would Mrs Simpson, as royal consort, have taken on the duties of Queen Alexandra, Queen Mary or Queen Elizabeth? As Edward VIII had made clear as early as the 1922 Combined Hospitals Appeal, he was more inclined than George V or any other previous British monarch to look to government to take the lead in welfare causes. When he said 'something will be done' to an unemployed shop assistant in south Wales

211

in November 1936, he meant someone else would do it.[163] In the end, the King of modernity, vanquished by love, preferred to shift the responsibility for 'his fellow-men' on to others, as indeed he did. The abdication was the greatest betrayal of royal duty in modern British history.

7

George VI:
War and the Welfare State

If it had not been for the abdication, George VI would probably have led a quiet, privileged life in the country, leavened by a little light work cultivating his rhododendrons and his voluntary bodies. Perhaps his wife would have made more of him, but the world would have been largely content to leave the unobtrusive Duke in peace. He was not without qualities, for, as Sarah Bradford has pointed out, he shared many with his father: 'an innate sense of decency and duty, a capacity for hard work, common sense and sympathy for his fellow human beings'.[1] He was also short-tempered and unintellectual like his father, although a better listener. Had he read a book for every brace of birds he bagged, he would have been the best-read man in Europe. A poor student at Dartmouth Royal Naval College and lacking a taste for literature or art, he was decidedly lowbrow. But he was not the 'moron' that the American ambassador in Paris, William Bullitt, believed him to be.[2]

Reserved and insecure, George VI felt most at ease in his natural habitat, at home surrounded by his family. He enjoyed a happier domestic life than his father, but his excursions into the public arena caused him greater anxiety. He was out of his depth on the world stage and, for that matter, in the sectarian world of British politics. His traits would have been the ruin of an aspiring statesman, but in a sovereign without ambition, bounced into kingship by the Fates, these obstacles could be overcome by that dogged-as-does-it mentality which is so beloved by the British. Had he been clever, he would have been censured for meddling. Had he been highbrow, he would have aroused resentment. The public came round to George VI precisely because he was vulnerable, unpretentious, decent and dogged. He was king-as-anti-hero, well suited to a political democracy, for his subjects could match him in everything but station. Ultimately, he earned their affectionate regard.[3]

How did George VI measure up in civil society at his accession? The abdication shocked the nation, but left the voluntary establishment crestfallen. Many charitable officials had invested heavily in Edward VIII, and they recoiled in horror at his errant behaviour, for anything that brought royalty into disrepute had implications for royal institutions. The new monarch was something of an unknown quantity, lacking his elder brother's high profile and presentational skills. Nor was he so well provided with contacts in the charitable sector, for his voluntary work had been rather specialized. Consequently, many royal societies worried about their standing at the Palace. With every incoming royal administration, as with every political one, there are winners and losers. At the end of 1936, charitable administrators looked to George VI like so many expectant children watching the fireplace at Christmas, but with less faith.

Frustrated, yet loath to criticize, some institutions sought guidance from the Palace. The National Society for the Prevention of Cruelty to Children wanted to know whether the ex-King would continue as its patron as Duke of Windsor, and if so, where his name should appear on the list of royal patrons.[4] Sister Agnes Keyser, still running the King Edward VII's Hospital for Officers, wanted a royal replacement straight away, preferably Queen Mary. In the event, the Palace decided that George VI was more appropriate, given the character of the institution. Keyser's comment on the abdication summed up a general feeling. She wrote to Wigram, who had been called out of retirement to help the new King to settle in: 'How sad it has all been. Poor little Ex-King. What a terrible awakening when he realizes what he has done.'[5]

Most charitable campaigners who wished to keep in with the Palace drew a veil over Edward VIII and waited upon events. The treasurer of the King's Fund, Sir Edward Peacock, was Edward VIII's chief financial advisor at the time of the abdication crisis. He and his colleagues in the Fund adopted a policy of dignified silence and turned their gaze on the royal dukes. One of the last communications from Edward VIII to the Fund was a letter in which he pledged to watch the society's progress and welfare 'with feelings of genuine and unabated interest'. Such a letter, signed by a king, would normally be prized by an institution, but this one has only recently been redeemed from a pile of unimportant papers in an attic in the Fund's headquarters.[6]

The charitable sector expected a shift of social emphasis with a new monarch, perhaps even a little gentle pruning of the patronage list. But with Esher and Stamfordham dead and Wigram on the sidelines after his brief spell as Private Secretary, the value the King's advisors placed on voluntary work appears to have been reduced. Palace correspondence suggests that by the late 1930s the King's Private Secretary had less to do with patronage work and that the Keeper of the Privy Purse took on greater direct responsibility for discussing donations and applications with the King. George VI knew that he would inherit many institutions, but, preoccupied with more pressing matters, he demurred at the prospect of taking responsibility for all of Edward VIII's societies, especially as he had his own list as Duke of York to consider.[7]

The beginning of a new reign was always a time for considering patronages and ensuring that the 'standard of merit' of individual societies, to use Wigram's phrase, had not slipped. Though well informed about youth and industry, George VI was unfamiliar with many voluntary causes. In particular, his knowledge of hospitals and medical charity was much poorer than George V's. Partly on the basis of information provided by the Home Office, the Palace dropped a host of institutions from the patronage list. With the years, however, new societies were added to it, and by 1943 the King's donations to charity stood at over £6,000 a year, which was comparable to the annual distributions of George V at the end of his reign. George VI's patronages, which, in addition to charities, included professional bodies, service associations and the quaintly named Lucifer Golfing Society, eventually numbered over 700.[8]

For those institutions in which links to the monarchy disappeared or declined in quality the results could be unsettling. Subscriptions waned, honours dried up and the cause of voluntarism suffered politically. The King's Fund continued to receive the King's largest annual subscription (£1,000), but it lamented the deterioration in its relations with the Palace. Along with the League of Mercy and many hospitals, it looked back on the reign of George V with nostalgia. Beset by the political demands of a job for which he was unprepared, George VI could not sustain the level of active support for philanthropic causes that leading institutions had become accustomed to from their foremost patron. Moreover, he lacked the speaking skills and the easy charm that voluntary bodies required of royalty. Those institutions in the political front line would miss George V when they had to deal with the Labour Party in 1945.

A period of mourning on the death of a sovereign offered a break from normal routine, but with the abdication it was thought crucial to proceed with business as usual. Given their anxieties, voluntary bodies turned to other members of the royal family, who came under greater pressure to increase their charitable duties. With the best will in the world, the monarchy's level of patronage could never keep pace with demand. But in 1936 the royal family had lost its most glamorous member, and while the Dukes of Kent and Gloucester stepped up the number of their commitments, they were no substitute for a Prince of Wales, even a distracted one. Their marriages in the mid-1930s, to Princess Marina of Greece and Lady Alice Montagu-Douglas-Scott respectively, provided a measure of relief from the incessant charitable demands.

Institutions with royal patronage could be compared to properties in a game of Monopoly, and each member of the royal family received a large number to play with. The Duke of Kent inherited a handful with the abdication, including the presidency of the King's Fund and some hospitals; the Duke of Gloucester held, among others, the Metropolitan Drinking Fountain and Cattle Trough Association, and King George's Jubilee Trust.[9] For her part, the Duchess of Gloucester took up her first patronages in 1937, with the St Johns Ambulance Association and the 'Invalid Kitchens', a forerunner of 'Meals on Wheels'.[10] The Duchess of Kent picked up the Royal National Life-boat Institution and several other societies.[11]

Queen Elizabeth, who had carved out a charitable niche as Duchess of York, proved to be one of the best patronage players the royal family ever produced. This proved all the more significant given her husband's preoccupations. She had no constitutional duties as Consort, and like Queen Mary before her she recognized that social service constituted her primary work for the monarchy. The transition from Duchess of York to Queen Consort was awkward and perplexing. The side of it dealing with charitable administration, carried out behind the scenes, required tact and discretion. Queen Mary wished to continue with many of her patronages, as did other members of the royal family. Thus Queen Elizabeth's household had to sort out which hospital, orphanage, society or fund was to be taken on board or given up. To the monarchy, charitable attachments had long been the spoils of the liberal social polity, and it is not far-fetched to picture the two Queens sitting down with their aides dividing them up.

A decision about an individual charity, though sometimes made casually on the advice of a lady-in-waiting, often turned on personal preference or historical precedent. A new queen usually became patron of national institutions, sometimes at the expense of local associations. But as an early biographer noted, 'this did not meet with Queen Elizabeth's approval at all', and she retained a connection with as many small charities as possible.[12] The Queen had a well-developed parochial sense, combined with a unique gift for public relations. After watching her performance at the opening of some new buildings at Morley College, Harold Nicolson remarked that she had an 'astonishing gift for being sincerely interested in dull people and dull occasions'.[13]

George VI did not concentrate on social issues before the outbreak of the war. Nor did he make public pronouncements that would suggest that he understood the strategic value of voluntarism to his cause. His first Christmas broadcast in 1937 emphasized the need for goodwill in a world in which the 'shadows of enmity and fear' were on the rise.[14] (The Not Forgotten Association, which provided entertainment for disabled exservicemen, received the proceeds.) With international affairs in crisis, the King felt the pull of high politics and the pressure of his own inexperience. The politicians who queued up to have a word with him were little interested in boys' camps or playing fields, and they steered him towards his boxes and their own anxieties. When the Prime Minister turned up on matters of great political moment, thoughts of attending a bazaar on behalf of the Girl Guides receded, even when the bazaar offered a better prospect of success.

In the late 1930s, high politics and formal duties preoccupied the King, though he did tour the depressed regions and make appearances on behalf of charities. In 1938, for instance, he and the Queen visited Glasgow to open the Empire Exhibition. They combined the opening with a tour of the welfare schemes and housing projects in Renfrewshire and Lanark-shire, areas of heavy unemployment.[15] There were also excursions to hospitals, housing estates and Ministry of Labour training programmes, which irritated the odd socialist. Beatrice Webb, who now had the distinction of having looked down her nose at five British monarchs in succession, detested the 'extreme deference' and 'worshipful emotion' that royalty elicited on such visits. She dismissed the King and Queen as 'ideal robots'.[16]

Although preoccupied by politics, the King was kept in touch with patronage work by the Queen, the Keeper of the Privy Purse, Ulick Alexander, and Robert Hyde, the longstanding Director of the Industrial Welfare Society. (Hyde offered to carry on the tradition of making an annual map of royal visits for the King's information but did not follow through with it.)[17] There was no let up in royal activity. Few members of the royal family had ever worked the poor neighbourhoods as effectively as Queen Elizabeth. Even the Duchess of Teck, 'Fat Mary', a pioneer of the monarchy's East End social work, would have been impressed with the Queen's common touch and brilliantly orchestrated informality.

Other members of the royal family were beginning to find their charitable feet. In 1937, the Duke of Kent carried out about 100 official charitable engagements.[18] Suave and diplomatic, with his drug problem behind him, he proved an effective fundraiser and advocate. At every opportunity, the voluntary hospitals exploited his good offices in their propaganda battle with the municipalists. The Duke of Gloucester also proved a more assiduous charitable worker than might have been expected, given his regimental duties and the call of the grouse moors. In May 1938, he received widespread attention when he proposed that a national fund be set up to finance all of Britain's voluntary hospitals.[19] But his exclusion of the municipal hospitals, which he believed to be inferior institutions, did not go down well with municipal socialists.

The tensions between voluntarists and their rivals were never far beneath the surface in the 1930s. Despite a growing level of cooperation, government officials and charitable campaigners continued to fight their respective corners. When, for example, the members of the London

54 and 55. George VI and Queen Elizabeth on a visit to Great Ormond Street Children's Hospital, 1938.

County Council met the representatives of the London Voluntary Hospitals Committee to discuss rationalizing the services of the municipal and charitable hospitals in the capital, the LCC officials sat themselves on a dais from which they could look down on the voluntarists.[20] Such affronts only encouraged the more politically exposed voluntary bodies to step up their lobbying of Parliament and to increase their propaganda activities. Meanwhile, they played their royal patrons like trumps.

A world apart from the voluntary sector were the idealists who dreamed of a 'socialist welfare state' and looked to 'planning' to produce it. It is easy to overstate the influence of collectivist opinion in the Labour Party in the 1930s. At the local level, on issues such as child welfare, socialists and voluntarists often worked in harmony. But the opinions of the Party's *avant-garde*, men like Hugh Dalton, Hugh Gaitskell and Douglas Jay, were making headway.[21] Deeply influenced by Soviet planning, they dismissed the myriad traditional associations based on the family and civil society as irrelevant. Nor did they have much regard for the traditions of mutual aid within the Labour movement. Friendly societies and

cooperatives lacked centralizing power, and having been integrated into the mixed economy could do little to challenge social injustice and the corruption of British political life.

Collectivists bowed to Clause Four and the administrative state, and they sent out the message that individual freedom and national well-being turned on central control. Douglas Jay's *The Socialist Case* (1937) and Richard Crossman's early essays, later brought together under the title *Planning for Freedom* (1965), exemplified their thinking. As Jay famously declared: 'In the case of nutrition and health, just as in the case of education, the gentlemen in Whitehall really do know better what is good for the people than the people know themselves.'[22] In this highly charged atmosphere, collectivists saw themselves as representatives of a new age, and like other radicals in the past they believed it was their mission to reject tradition and introduce a rational order into society. They did not address the point, put by Bertrand Russell in the 1930s, that the wish to create a planned society had less to do with idealism than a desire for power.[23]

Given the background of Labour's growing attachment to planning, the economic slump and the pusillanimous politics of the 1930s, anxieties mounted in the charitable sector. Increasingly, there were voices claiming that the liberal vision of society was defunct. Many civil servants, transfixed by state social action and their part in its promotion, took the view that charity was demeaning. Perhaps the most worrying trend to the cause of voluntarism was the sheer growth of the public sector bureaucracy, much of it a result of piecemeal social legislation. The number of established civil servants rose from 168,000 in 1914 to 387,000 in 1939.[24] By 1939, public sector employees made up nearly 10 per cent of the working population. Whether in their Whitehall bastions or in their local government offices, civil servants in the health and welfare departments tended to dismiss perceptions of social need which differed from their own. As their strength and numbers grew, their disregard for voluntary traditions increased, a trend greatly encouraged by the Second World War.

Voluntarists had survived the First World War, the Depression, higher rates of taxation, and the vicissitudes of politics, but only the more sanguine among them expected their cherished institutions to survive intact once the war broke out. Aerial bombardment, mass evacuation and war work took their toll of both local and national societies. While the number of civil servants rose sharply to over 700,000 during the war, charities had to cope with the continual calling-up of their personnel for the forces.[25] But the bombing was the most serious issue for many of them. In the Ragged School Union alone, thirty-eight missions suffered war damage.[26] As in the First World War, charities suffered or died, while others came into existence, often with royal assistance. The effect of war on voluntary traditions did not engage George VI at the outbreak of hostilities, despite its importance to the crown. The King, like his subjects, was swept up by events over which he had little control.

The Second World War was in many respects a reprise of the First for the monarchy, but with a different royal cast in the leading roles. The story is familiar terrain.[27] Princess Elizabeth moved effortlessly from the jollity of the Girl Guides to the rigours of the Auxiliary Territorial Service (ATS). The Princess Royal, Controller Commandant of the ATS, travelled the country visiting welfare agencies and war canteens. The Duke of Kent made tours abroad and visited bomb sites at home before he died in a plane crash in 1942. Queen Mary moved to Badminton, where she visited evacuees, opened hospitals and salvaged scrap.[28] She also executed a carpet in *gros point* needlework, which became celebrated at the end of the war when it was sold to a Canadian women's organization for $100,000. She gave the money not to charity, as advised by her friends, but to the national exchequer, an artful act of benevolence which elicited

56. Queen Mary, the Duchess of Kent and the Duchess of Beaufort with soldiers at the YMCA canteen, Badminton, 1941.

not only great publicity but a letter of thanks signed by the entire Labour cabinet.[29]

Without ceremony or pretentiousness, but with due publicity, the King and Queen turned Buckingham Palace into a royal war office. Gas masks at the ready, they ate spam and took target practice, becoming symbols of national resistance. Though frustrated by the lack of a 'definite job', unlike his cousin Lord Louis Mountbatten who became Chief of Combined Operations, the King carried out the unpleasant tasks assigned to royalty in wartime with doughtiness. He inspected the troops and toured the factories and hospitals. One should not underestimate the boost to morale provided by royal visits, even when the consequences were less than charitable. After the King and Queen had toured the Globe Works, an aircraft factory in Accrington, the company's chairman wrote to Buckingham Palace: 'In our workshops our output rose an overall twelve per cent for the week after the Royal visit.' The result, he concluded, was that 'their Majesties sent two extra Lancaster Bombers over Germany'.[30]

57.   The King and Queen inspecting bomb damage at Buckingham Palace, September 1940.

The mass bombing of British cities in the Second World War was unlike anything delivered by the Germans in the Great War. The attacks on London in the autumn of 1940 and the spring of 1941 caused thousands of civilian casualties and destroyed or damaged vast numbers of properties, including, catastrophically, seventy-three voluntary hospitals.[31] But the bombs that hit Buckingham Palace on 13 September 1940 missed the King and Queen by ninety feet and gave the monarchy its greatest propaganda coup since George V's Silver Jubilee. The Ministry of Information, sensitive to complaints by East Enders that 'it is always the poor that get it', despatched forty journalists to the Palace to report the damage.[32] Even hereditary monarchs, it seems, are made or unmade by chance. As Bradford remarks, recalling a line by Churchill: 'It was the shared experience of the Blitz on London in September 1940 which more than anything forged a bond between the King and his people.'[33] If so, George VI's finest hour was spent not in Coventry with the shell-shocked nor at Churchill's side in the cabinet war rooms, but surveying the Palace rubble.

The celebrated remark by the Queen, 'I'm glad we've been bombed. It makes me feel I can look the East End in the face', was made in the knowledge that she would be a frequent visitor there. Indeed, the King and Queen toured the East End to inspect the bombed areas during the

222

week of the attack on Buckingham Palace. With its poverty and potential for discontent, and ease of access from Buckingham Palace, the royal family had long used the East End as a test of the monarchy's popularity. How many institutions had received more royal visits than the London Hospital (now the Royal London Hospital)?[34] But the destruction and suffering caused by the bombing made visits there more poignant and distressing. The Minister of Food, Lord Woolton, whom the Queen encouraged to become the Chairman of the Red Cross, said they were 'very nice people doing a very human job'.[35]

Queen Elizabeth was supremely conscious of her public role. And with a mind of her own, she was not a government cipher. In 1939, the Ministry of Information wanted her to deliver a personal address to British women, written by the children's author A.A. Milne. It is hard to imagine a more patronizing document. 'Men say we gossip,' the Queen was to tell her listeners, 'perhaps we do. It is nice sitting cosily with a friend and saying "did you hear this?" and "did you hear that?" But please, please, don't let us gossip now.' The Director General of the BBC thought the draft address 'generally admirable' and it was sent to Buckingham Palace for approval. It was not delivered.[36] But in 1943, the Queen delivered a broadcast with a very different message and tone to the women of the Empire.[37]

'With the stamina of a show business trouper', the Queen performed brilliantly at the bomb sites and feeding centres, in the shelters and the factories. Day after day, always on the move, she consoled the weary and the afflicted. Arguably, the tours during the blitz to the East End and the docks, Swansea and Plymouth, did more to impress on the public the caring and compassionate role of the monarchy than all her patronage work put together. Still, she found time to visit her struggling charities and take on additional patronages, including the Women's Land Army. Her attention to journalists and cameramen, in marked contrast to Queen Mary, set the standard for other members of the royal family. With a talent for 'imaginative gestures', she dispatched sixty suites of furniture from Windsor Castle to families who had lost their possessions through bombing, sent a message to each foster parent of an evacuee, and, in 1941, paid for eight ambulances as 'a symbol of that fellowship which unites all of us who share danger today'.[38]

The shared danger resulted in another royal initiative. In time of war, a king's mind turns to medals, and the Second World War proved no exception. Like most of his family, George VI had a passion for things sartorial. But as we have seen in regard to the creation of earlier decorations, such as the Order of the British Empire, the royal impulse to honour cannot be explained simply by reference to a love of fancy dress. The blitz prompted the King to think of gallantry on the home front, and with civilians primarily in mind, he instituted the award of the George

58. Visit of George VI and Queen Elizabeth to air raid shelters in Bermondsey, 1941.

Cross and the George Medal for acts of heroism and devotion to duty in September 1940.[39] The awards were a very human response to what the royal family often witnessed. But given the usefulness of decorations to the crown, George VI would have been neglecting his duty not to have created an addition to the honours system at the time.

★ ★ ★

As A.J.P. Taylor remarked, 'the *Luftwaffe* was a powerful missionary for the welfare state'.[40] Planners thrive on unhappiness, and the suffering and devastation on the home front made their proposals for a post-war transformation in welfare provision more popular and compelling. Politicians took notice. At their disposal was the expanded public administration that the war had created. The monarchy had an early warning of the shift in government attitudes about the control and direction of social policy in 1940, when Robert Hyde informed George VI of the difficulties the Industrial Welfare Society was having with Ernest Bevin, the new Minister of Labour in the war cabinet.

Hyde's organization, in which the King played such a prominent part, had worked with employers and trade unionists in improving health and safety within factories for many years, but now Bevin proposed to shift such responsibilities to his Factory Department. He left Hyde in no doubt that the future of industrial welfare would be a government responsibility, but if voluntary bodies 'cared to help him in *his* campaign he would make full use of that help'.[41] Hyde found Bevin 'blustering', with a penchant for elaborate bureaucracy, a man 'dazzled by a row of shining buttons any one of which he need but press to set in action schemes and movements and reforms which require instead much careful thought'. He wrote to Buckingham Palace that the Minister's plan was 'an utter waste of time and little more than a stupid piece of window dressing'.[42]

Meanwhile, the Palace was well aware of the likelihood of change on the hospital front. The issue came up early in 1942, when the Royal National Throat, Nose and Ear Hospital asked the King to grant his patronage as a replacement for that of the late Duke of Connaught. Ulick Alexander, the Keeper of the Privy Purse, turned to Lord Dawson for advice. Dawson said that the municipal hospitals had improved over the years and should not be discounted, a point he had been making to the Palace for some years. He noted that the Duke of Kent, on the advice of the King's Fund, had made a speech extolling the courage of doctors and nurses, but referring only to charitable hospitals. It caused 'a rumpus' in the London County Council and protests from the municipal hospitals.[43]

Dawson assumed that the voluntary and municipal hospitals would have to come into a scheme of greater coordination at the end of the war, if only for economic reasons. (He had said the same thing in 1918.) Thus he reasoned that the monarchy would be wise to cultivate the municipalists. 'Lesser members of the royal family' should feel free to patronize the smaller voluntary hospitals, Dawson argued, 'but with the conflicts of opinion and interest ahead of us, I think you will agree the King and Queen would prefer to be independent.' On these grounds, he advised George VI to refuse patronage to the Royal National Throat, Nose and Ear Hospital. The King accepted the advice.[44]

Alexander told Dawson in 1942 that he felt the time had come for the King and Queen to consider granting patronage to municipal hospitals, but personally did not see how it could be done, 'since it would be rather on the same lines as if the King was granting his patronage to a Government department'.[45] In fact, a few municipal hospitals had applied for royal patronage, but they were turned down for the reason given by Alexander. Before the war was over, however, the question of hospital reorganization came to the fore, heightening the rivalries between municipalists and voluntarists. The White Paper of February 1944, which promised a 'comprehensive' health service with control vested in the Minister, looked decidedly ominous to entrenched voluntarists.

The charitable hospitals looked to the monarchy to defend their interests. George VI's support showed restraint, as befitted the constitutional delicacy of his position. But he sent a message to the King's Fund in 1944, which was read to its General Council: 'I feel sure that whatever arrangements are made for the future hospital service, there will still be ample room for voluntary work and voluntary support.'[46] The Duke of Gloucester was more forthcoming. *The Times* quoted a speech in which he said that whatever scheme was implemented, it must 'preserve the freedom of the medical profession and of voluntary hospitals', and that 'no vote or public moneys could replace the personal affection and collective interest which had been lavished on the voluntary hospitals of London and the provinces'.[47] Meanwhile, Princess Elizabeth began to play her supporting role in hospital history when she accepted the presidency of the Queen Elizabeth Hospital for Children in Hackney, which had been named after her mother. On a visit to the institution in May 1944, she wished 'to assure' the governors that her service would be given 'wholeheartedly to what we all know to be a good cause'.[48] It was her first public address.

It was increasingly difficult to defend the preservation of voluntary institutions independent of government, for 'Total War' emphasized the deficiencies in charitable provision and accelerated the extension of state power. In creating and exposing scarcity and deprivation, the war made traditional philanthropic remedies look more and more inadequate. Charitable donations, for example, could never pay for the emergency medical services or rebuild the large number of voluntary hospitals that

59.   Princess Elizabeth making her first public speech at the Annual Court of Governors at the Queen Elizabeth Hospital for Children, Hackney, May 1944.

60.   Princess Elizabeth with dockyard workers on a visit to a northern port to launch a battleship, December 1944.

had been damaged or destroyed by the end of the war. On every domestic front, the government was on the march, from the command of the economy and labour controls to rationing supplies and evacuating children from the cities.

With each year that the national emergency dragged on, it made further inroads into erstwhile voluntary services and encouraged people to think of comprehensive solutions. Evacuation, ration cards, and the state direction of labour 'nationalized' daily life as never before. Against this background, the Beveridge Report on social security, published in 1942, became a bestseller. With their longstanding reservations about uniform state provision, voluntarists with something to lose put the report under a microscope. To not a few of them, Beveridge was just another liberal doing the dirty work of collectivism. To the King's Fund, his proposals were 'a mechanistic solution', which 'in the long run would be a mistake'.[49] Voluntarists, including members of the Friendly Society movement, preferred local control of social insurance and less red tape. But, compared to the prospect of universal state provision, their emphasis on local initiative did not look very compelling, nor did appeals to self-help in the context of the sacrifices the war itself demanded.

The war and the dramatic shift in social policy that it encouraged threatened to devastate community life and all it represented. The civic life of localities had been under threat for nearly a century. The voluntary ethos, and the religious belief that so often sustained it, had undergone repeated shocks in the increasingly mobile and materialist age. Was there a future for parochial charity in a world in which more and more women went away to work, where children lived apart from their parents, where families were no longer buried in the same churchyard? Was there a future for religion in a world in which people, including churchmen, looked increasingly to the state for salvation on earth? Was there a future for the cooperative traditions of mutual aid in a world in which the very idea of community was being redefined?

The problems of reconstruction experienced in 1945, among them housing shortages, demobilization and the return to peacetime production, were not unlike those in 1918. But if members of the public had wanted a return to 'normalcy' at the end of the First World War, they were more in a mood for change in 1945. Memories of the 1930s, with its social divisions and high unemployment, were often unhappy. By contrast, the war brought people from different social backgrounds into closer contact and encouraged egalitarian hopes for the future. The Labour landslide in the election of 1945 suggested widespread support for the changes prefigured by wartime planning, though perhaps not as much as historians have led us to believe. A great issue for the future was whether the extension of government controls during reconstruction would destroy those traditions of duty and personal service that had nourished civil society in the past.

Proposals for a vast expansion of government-directed health and welfare services after the war threw voluntarists into disarray. In the light of state intervention, and the sorry state of many of their institutions, they could no longer make exaggerated claims about their own pre-eminence in British life. In the extraordinary atmosphere of social experimentation, central government was seemingly sweeping all before it. State spending on the social services dwarfed the funds available to charities. Those institutions that had forged a relationship with government departments during the war found they were disregarded or relegated to the role of 'junior partner'. Some of them received government money, which threatened to undermine their cherished independence. Charitable administrators had to ask themselves whether the ascendant state would endanger their flow of funds from traditional subscribers, or even make their institutions unnecessary.

★   ★   ★

Unlike the voluntary establishment, the monarchy came out of the war with its popularity undented, even strengthened. But while the war was the making of George VI as a king, it exhausted him as a man. No sooner was it over than a fresh set of problems appeared that had serious implications for the crown. In a manner reminiscent of his father in 1918, the King felt uneasy about social deprivation, high taxation and the Empire. But unlike the end of the First World War, there was little domestic unrest. Nor was there a Russian revolution, with its attendant fears of Bolshevism at home, to worry about. Instead, a headstrong Labour government came to power and sought to transform public life and nationalize welfare provision. Apart from the monarchy's suspicions about the republicanism latent within the Labour movement, trouble loomed in those ringing phrases of Clause Four, which called for the 'common ownership of the means of production . . . and the best obtainable system of popular administration and control of each industry and service'.

For a monarchy that looked to precedent and the past, the Labour programme of reconstruction and renewal appeared decidedly audacious, if not extremist. If implemented, it would not only weaken friends in the financial and commercial sectors, but subdue and dispirit those civil institutions from which the monarchy drew so much of its strength. What was the point of royal philanthropy if the government nationalized welfare provision? What was left for the monarchy to provide if the state provided for all human ills, from the cradle to the grave? If civil society collapsed, the implications for the monarchy were ominous. Presumably, its popularity would depend more and more on mystique, insubstantial spectacle and a constitutional role that even monarchists had difficulty defining.

There is little to suggest that such thoughts agitated the tired and ailing King; conceivably they did not much engage anyone else in his entourage. As we shall see, George VI and his family had views on government social policy at the end of the war, though they felt obliged to express them obliquely, often through their charitable associations. According to the governess Marion Crawford, the King and Queen 'never spoke' about the Labour Party's programme in her company. But this had more to do with prudence than a want of opinion. As Crawford observed: 'In the Palace, discretion and self-control—and I feel I must add genuine self-sacrifice—are carried to lengths quite unbelievable to the world outside.'[50]

If there was a Lord Esher in the wings at the end of the Second World War, he kept his secrets. Old Lord Wigram knew the ropes well enough, but he had retired from the lieutenant-governorship of Windsor Castle in 1944 and had moved to London before the 1945 election. The King's Private Secretary, Alan Lascelles, was another traditionalist with a wide knowledge of public life, but whether he appreciated the importance of civil society to the crown is questionable. He barely mentioned patronage work in his posthumously published *Letters and Journals*, but this may have been because it was the Keeper of the Privy Purse who dealt more directly with the King on charitable matters by the late 1930s.[51] Voluntary societies kept the loyal Keeper of the Privy Purse, Ulick Alexander, informed. More than others, he could hardly be innocent of the significance of charity in the affairs of the crown. His correspondence with Lord Dawson in 1942, in which he discussed the granting of patronage to municipal hospitals, suggested as much.[52]

Arguably, the most influential inhabitant of Buckingham Palace was the Queen, who, as Chips Channon remarked, was the King's 'will power'.[53] Social work was her forte, and while she did not criticize government policy directly, her many comments and public statements on the post-war world dwelled on the continuing need for voluntary service in a materialistic, over-administered society. Speaking at a meeting of Toc H, for instance, a royal charity founded in 1915 to promote Christian social service, she concluded: 'In a world where the individual may sometimes seem almost to lose his individuality, submerged beneath the mass movements of which we hear so much, we may well be heartened by remembering that we stand here today because of the inspiration of one man.'[54]

The Queen had a marked preference for Christian kindness and voluntary service over the corporate and the abstract. Though not insensitive to the old saw that 'the hand that gives also gathers', it is questionable whether even she fully appreciated the historic importance of philanthropy to the crown. If she did, she has never mentioned it to a royal biographer. When asked years later whether the Palace had a policy of modernizing the monarchy during or after the war, which most historians believe it did, she waved away the notion: 'We never consciously set out to change things; we never said "let's change this or introduce that." Things just evolved.' She reduced the wartime monarchy to a phrase: 'everybody worked together. . . . We just tried to do our best.'[55]

Royalty never admits to mixed motives, but it seems unlikely anyway that members of the royal family fully recognized the significance of good works to their own continued well-being after the war. They had other things to distract them, from high politics to family affairs. Even if they had read history, it would have given them little insight, for such tomes rarely mentioned royal patronage. Bagehot's inventive phrases, ceaselessly invoked, were the stuff of kings, and he never mentioned charity at all. In any case, the Palace had always shown less enthusiasm for thinking about its role in times of social stability than in times of upheaval. For all the hardship of post-war Britain, the political atmosphere was peaceful.

Despite the social calm and the monarchy's popularity, the Palace did appreciate that it needed to instil loyalty to the throne in the brave new world of egalitarian aspirations. In the invigorated social democracy, it had to adjust to changing public expectations and not be too much identified with the hidebound class system that the war had undermined. In these circumstances, it would be wise to show flexibility. If government intervention was in fashion, would it not be judicious to prop up civil institutions and maintain old friendships in the voluntary sector, but without alienating ministers and government departments? One way forward would be for members of the royal family to continue to promote voluntary societies that worked alongside or in partnership with the emerging state services, while penetrating where it had never penetrated before—the welfare institutions of government itself. This is precisely what they did.

★　★　★

Before we look at Buckingham Palace's adjustment to the Welfare State, it is worth considering more closely what the monarchy made of the Labour Party's social policy, which threatened to undermine its most substantive role. It is not a question that taxed George VI's official biographer, John Wheeler-Bennett, or any historian since. Wheeler-Bennett confides that the King may have had 'personal misgivings' about the Labour victory in 1945, but he dodges the rather important issue of what the Palace thought about Labour social policy. All that he will allow is that the King told his ministers that the programme of nationalization was 'going too fast'.[56] Before moving with speed himself to the more congenial subject of foreign affairs, the official biographer Whiggishly concluded that in the reign of George VI 'a social revolution of a permanent nature' took shape and that the Welfare State 'conferred considerable benefits upon the country'.[57] The reader is left with the impression that the King can be identified in some way with the Welfare State.

Wheeler-Bennett's vagueness is reminiscent of Harold Nicolson's silence on the question of what George V thought about universal manhood suffrage in 1918. Such omissions are not simply disingenuous: they obfuscate the record for other scholars who have to rely on the official record. Arguably, they do not even serve the monarchy. The royal family can, as we shall see, be given some credit for the benefits conferred by the Welfare State, but not in the nebulous way implied by Wheeler-Bennett. Sadly, official royal biographers tend to accommodate the mind of their subject to every shift of contemporary mood or ministerial whim. Above all, modern monarchs must never be seen to be doing anything that might be interpreted as unconstitutional or against the grain of public opinion, even if it means that they are reduced to ciphers.

Let us look more closely at a piece of Labour legislation that was more crucial to the monarchy than has been apparent to royal biographers: Aneurin Bevan's National Health Service Bill. Social legislation introduced by socialists was bound to be of interest the crown. (Today some historians see the NHS as not particularly socialist, but at the end of the war the royal family would have needed some convincing of this.)[58] The King and Queen were not averse to the government doing more about health, but they did not wish it to be at the expense of voluntary service. They did not need to be social philosophers to perceive that *universal* state provision would tend to squeeze out individual responsibility, or that what people received by way of right they would soon take for granted. When George VI said in 1951, 'I really don't see why people should have false teeth free any more than they have shoes free', leading Hugh Gaitskell to call him a reactionary, he was simply stating what to him was self-evident.[59]

To the crown the central issue presented by Bevan's legislation was royal patronage. The point had been raised by Lord Dawson in his letter to the Palace in 1942. What Dawson predicted, and the Health Service Bill embodied, was a bringing together of the municipal and charitable hospitals in a unified system under central control. This was nothing less than a death sentence for the voluntary hospitals. There were about a thousand of them in Britain. Hundreds of them had links to the crown, including virtually every teaching hospital.[60] There would seem to be a *prima facie* case that the monarchy, which was obsessive about the continuity of institutions, would wish to defend those charities in which they had made so many friends and allies. Put another way, what was the royal family likely to think of a great Tory stronghold, St Bartholomew's Hospital, for centuries a royal institution, being nationalized by an upstart Welsh Marxist?

Whatever his misgivings, the King showed great discretion over the NHS proposals, if only because the socialists were in power. He did not make representations to the Ministry of Health about the proposed nationalization of the voluntary hospitals. Nor did he make controversial public statements in defence of the hospitals through the King's Fund or any other of his charities. On the other hand, in his capacity as patron, he sometimes sent general messages of support to societies that publicly opposed the government's health proposals. He could have objected directly to Bevan in conversation, but this would have been impolitic and probably counter-productive. Wheeler-Bennett, pulling his punches, tells us only that the King liked Bevan's 'effervescent personality'.[61] But the Minister for Health was not a man the royal family would have respected. According to Chips Channon, the King had difficulty conceal-ing his dislike of socialists, but he would have been civil to a minister, in a manner becoming a monarch whose training was strong on deportment.[62]

However charming, Bevan was well known for his Bolshevik sym-pathies, once dubbed 'a ritzy Robespierre' and a 'lounge-lizard Lenin' by Brendan Bracken.[63] In Parliament, he diplomatically accepted that the Labour government should make use of voluntary bodies, but he believed them to be a repugnant 'patch quilt of local paternalisms' and thus the enemy of 'intelligent planning'.[64] Soon after taking office, he wrote to his cabinet colleagues that 'the notion of the self-contained, separate, inde-pendent, "local hospital," is nowadays a complete anachronism'.[65] His dislike for do-gooding charitable campaigners was heartfelt, though he would have avoided the subject in conversation at the Palace. Bevan equated charities with a perfidious English class system and the indignity of nurses organizing fêtes on their weekends off. Such views were not in keeping with the sentiments of the royal family, with its penchant for paternalism and bazaars.

If the King was reluctant to criticize Bevan's Bill in public, a storm of protest from royal institutions blew up when the Ministry of Health unveiled its proposals. The King's Fund put the case for the charitable hospitals, particularly those in London. It may be said to have represented the royal outlook, in particular the outlook of the Duke of Gloucester, who succeeded the Duke of Kent as the charity's President in 1942. The Fund's arguments, presented from time to time by the Duke of Gloucester himself, were that the charitable hospitals were expressions of democratic pluralism, which provided local decision making and 'an independent standard' against which hospitals provided by the public authority could be measured. In contrast, a uniform, centralized service would introduce insensitive bureaucracy and the wasteful factionalism of party politics.[66]

As a national coordinating body for charitable hospitals, the British Hospitals Association, also under the patronage of the Duke of Gloucester, took a similar line against a unified health service. It was, if anything, more hostile to Bevan's scheme than the King's Fund. Bernard Docker, the Chairman of the BHA, declared that 'this mass murder of the hospitals and their replacement by State institutions is wholly unnecessary'.[67] Many of the royal hospitals, including the Perth Royal Infirmary and the Royal Halifax Infirmary, also took the 'horrified' line with the Ministry. They complained most about employment, the uncertain future of 'life' governors and the status of endowment funds.[68] The NHS would create a boom in public sector employment but losses to the salaried staff in the voluntary sector.

As the many petitions to the Ministry of Health attest, there was widespread dislike of 'state officialdom', which calls into question the assumption that ordinary citizens typically favoured government intervention. Lord Woolton had a point when he doubted that the voters knew 'what they had let themselves in for' under Labour.[69] The furore that nationalization of welfare created in the voluntary sector was partly to do with the strong personalities on both sides, partly to do with jobs and institutional allegiances, and partly to do with money and property. The capitalized assets of the voluntary hospitals were worth about £300 million before the war, which was a sum large enough to put a gleam in the eye of a minister and worth protecting by the voluntarists who had raised the money.[70]

The royal family could only watch with dismay as loyal institutions came first under government scrutiny and then control. The old guard, which included Queen Mary, Queen Elizabeth and the Duke of Gloucester, must have thought the nationalization of the charitable hospitals an act of vandalism comparable to the dissolution of the monasteries (but in the case of the monasteries a King had at least had a hand in it). The hospitals were, as *The Times* noted, in 'funereal' mood, but they had a stay of execution between the passage of Bevan's Bill in November 1946 and the 'appointed day' in July 1948, when they were to come under government control. During this period, members of the royal family made a concerted effort to bolster morale in the hospitals by visiting many of them and making symbolic donations. Conscious of the sensitivity of these events, members of the royal family avoided remarks that might have had a political interpretation put on them.[71]

The hospital tours of the King and Queen, Queen Mary, Princess Elizabeth, Princess Margaret, the Princess Royal and the Duke of

61. Visit of Princess Elizabeth to the Queen Elizabeth Hospital for Children, Hackney, 1946.

Gloucester in the spring of 1948 had great poignancy, the final gestures of royal support for the country's great voluntary hospital tradition. The Queen's visit to the Queen Elizabeth Hospital in Gateshead in March 1948 was typical. With her decided preference for the personal over the corporate, she declared that state control did 'not absolve us from the practice of charity or from the exercise of vigilance. The English way of progress has always been to preserve good qualities and apply them to new systems.'[72] In May, she was the guest of honour at the Mansion House to commemorate Hospitals Day. The effects of the National Health Service could not be predicted, she remarked, but whatever happened it would continue to need voluntary service, and she called on the hospitals to enrol charitable workers to lighten the worries of patients and 'to show that sympathy and compassion were still freely given'.[73]

As President of the Queen Elizabeth Hospital for Children, Princess Elizabeth attended the annual Court of Governors in May 1948. Her remarks about the takeover of the Hospital by the National Health Service betrayed a sense of dismay. She referred to the members of the Court, who, after years of service, would have to relinquish office under the new regime: 'I feel a very special regret because of the long connexion my family has had with this hospital.'[74] In a further attempt at keeping up the institution's morale, she visited the country branch of the same hospital at Banstead the following month, only a week before the 'appointed day'. But it was not the last visit by a member of the royal family to a voluntary hospital before nationalization. On 30 June the Duke of Gloucester visited the Royal National Orthopaedic Hospital in Great Portland Street, and Queen Mary opened a new maternity wing at the Elizabeth Garrett Anderson Hospital.[75] What they said in private can only be imagined.

The Queen and Princess Elizabeth were saying publicly what hospital voluntarists around the country were feeling as the NHS began 'its hazardous advance into an unknown future'.[76] In the former voluntary hospitals the sense of loss was palpable. The outgoing management of the Worcester Royal Infirmary, for example, did not disguise its feelings about state control. 'The voluntary system in hospitals, the Life-boat Institution, and in so many other organisations, is an expression of British character,' it pronounced in 1947. 'We may not have the wealth of Government, nor the power to command a big staff, nor the funds to build all we require; but we have got a priceless asset, that as a people we want to maintain our democracy not only in a parliamentary way, but in our social service.'[77]

Having lost the battle to save the charitable hospitals, voluntarists wanted the traditions of personal service and democratic local support to be carried over into the National Health Service. They considered royal support crucial to their rearguard campaign. After the passage of Bevan's Bill in 1946, they wrote to the Palace or spoke to members of the royal family to discover whether royal patronage was compatible with the new hospital regime. Ulick Alexander, the Keeper of the Privy Purse, wrote to the Home Office early in 1947. At issue was whether the crown could patronize an agency of the government, something it had never done before.

The reply was crucial to the future role of the royal family in the nation's welfare. The Home Office took the casuistical line that a state hospital was not a government department as such, for it was under the control of the Regional Hospital Board, and thus it would 'not exist, as Government Departments exist, to enable the various King's Ministers to perform their ministerial duties'.[78] Consequently, neither the Home Secretary nor the Minister of Health had any objection to NHS hospitals enjoying royal patronage. But there was a powerful underlying consideration at work in the decision, which became clear in a Home Office letter to the Keeper of the Privy Purse: 'to withdraw Patronage at the time of transfer from voluntary to State auspices might be construed as indicating that the Royal Family disapproved of the National Health Scheme.'[79]

In its concern about the status of its fledgling hospital service, what the Labour government did in effect was to offer the monarchy a foothold in a department of state. Alexander put the proposal to George VI, who agreed that royal patronage should continue 'to all hospitals' that passed under the control of the Minister of Health.[80] The beauty of the arrangement for the crown was that it would open up the former municipal hospitals to royal influence for the first time. But it would do more than this. As the former municipal and voluntary institutions were part of a new unified system, it would eliminate the worrying problem for the monarchy that Dawson and others had noted in the past, that of being seen to support one set of hospitals against another. No longer would members of the royal family be identified with confrontations between the older voluntary system, with its snobbery and class associations, and the municipalists. Perhaps the crown could salvage something from the NHS after all. Nationalization might be a blessing in disguise if it reduced institutional and social tensions while retaining a welfare role for the royal family.

There was, however, some difficulty for the monarchy in the new patronage proposals. The Queen was 'most anxious' that members of the royal family should, if possible, be able to continue as hospital presidents. But the Palace did not want them placed in a position where they might come, as Alexander put it, 'under the direction of the minister'.[81] In the event, a compromise was struck whereby the appointment of members of the royal family as presidents and vice-presidents would lapse, except in the case of the 'disclaimed hospitals', typically small religious institutions, not coming under the Ministry's control.[82] In state institutions, 'royal personages', as the Home Office put it, should simply become patrons. (Eventually the government relaxed this directive and members of the royal family returned as hospital presidents.)

The monarchy did not approve of the suggestion put by the Ministry of Health in 1948 that 'other suitable persons' might stand as hospital patrons where members of the royal family were also patrons. This was carrying egalitarianism too far. Queen Mary, for one, was unhappy at the prospect of seeing her name on a list alongside some obscure trade unionist. In the end the Home Office agreed: 'Royal patronage is such a high honour that the hospital which has members of the Royal Family as Patrons should be content with that honour and should not also include in their list of Patrons any of the King's subjects.'[83]

The Palace had reason to be content as well. In an age of state welfare it would not be isolated. It would have a prominent social role both inside and outside the state. In the monarchy's adjustment to hospital nationalization, its longstanding role in medical charity had paid dividends. But would royal patronage of state hospitals recreate a hierarchy of institutions within the new service? The former 'royal' hospitals were not disposed to drop the 'royal' prefix. Indeed, several soon added it, including, in 1948, the London Homoeopathic Hospital.[84] Not even Bevan, that scourge of social distinction, could bring himself to blackball the royal family from the NHS.

Like its charitable work generally, the monarchy's patronage of NHS hospitals was widely sought, usually given, and well received. Members of the royal family lived up to their word about the need to perpetuate voluntary traditions, and soon after nationalization the Queen, Princesses Elizabeth and Margaret, the Duke and Duchess of Gloucester and the Duchess of Kent began to visit the hospitals again in earnest, building up new personal and institutional allegiances.[85] There was a particularly poignant return to the London Hospital in July 1949 by Queen Mary, who had written to the institution's chairman only a year before, resigning as President. Under the NHS, she consented to become joint patron with George VI.[86]

Hospital visits represented only a fraction of the patronage work being carried out in the last years of George VI's reign by members of the royal family, but they helped to make up for losses in the voluntary medical world. Several royal institutions had disappeared altogether, including the League of Mercy and the British Hospitals Association. Others, like the King's Fund and the Sunday Fund, struggled on, changing tack as necessary. Others still, like the Leagues of Hospital Friends and the St John Ambulance Brigade, sought a foothold in what they continued to see as local hospitals. A visit by the Queen, Princess Elizabeth, or the Princess Royal, who asked the Red Cross to assist the NHS, was a terrific boost to morale and fundraising.[87] But sustaining 'the voluntary hospital spirit', so admired by the royal family, would be an uphill task in the new service.

In the early days of the NHS, relations between voluntarists and civil servants were not helped by the Ministry of Health. Bevan and his team of planning experts had convinced themselves that the cost of the NHS would *decline* as the population became healthier as a result of nationaliz-ation.[88] Consequently, they saw little need for charitable donations. Voluntarists, hardened by decades of raising money for ever-expanding medical services, were less inclined to believe in man's perfectibility. Bevan issued a circular instructing hospital staff not to accept contri-butions from patients and to refuse to cooperate with hospital charities in their activities. When a number of hospitals initiated fundraising drives in their neighbourhoods in 1948, he directed that such practices should stop. Collection boxes were even removed from post offices.[89] The Palace knew about these edicts, but could do little about them. The King's Fund denounced them as 'sheer bullying'.[90] Such developments were sympto-matic of the bureaucratic temper of centralized administration that relegated voluntarists to the sidelines.

★   ★   ★

The creation of the NHS and the torrent of regulations from the Ministry of Health signalled that in the longstanding battle between collectivism and voluntarism there seemed to be a clear winner. The ministerial, civil service state of Sydney Webb had routed the civic pluralism of Samuel Taylor Coleridge. To put it another way: indirect, representative democracy, expressed through cabinet government, now reigned supreme in social policy over the spontaneous, pluralistic form of democracy that was immanent in the voluntary institutions of civil society. Local government fared little better than the charitable sector, for the loss of its principal service, the municipal hospitals, was a crippling blow to morale and recruitment. Having subdued its rivals, central government was on its way to perfecting a form of executive democracy in which citizens were 'consumers' of government rather that its 'producers'.[91]

The Labour government of 1945–50 was profoundly influenced by the extraordinary circumstances of the war, and it did not fully appreciate where collectivism would lead or how much it would cost, financially or culturally. The war had propelled Labour's planning mentality, and under the sway of historical materialism and collectivist ideals, its leadership paid little heed to the democratic impulses and good offices of voluntary societies with their individualist ethic. Nor did Labour place much value on its own voluntary traditions of mutual aid, which gave socialism its democratic infrastructure and moral centre. Was the belief that citizens became moral agents through compulsory taxation to pay for universal benefits, which often accrued to those who did not need them, a deception? Few asked whether collective social properties existed. Socialists were so certain of it that they did not bother to provide the evidence.

There were people in the Labour Party, including the Prime Minister Clement Attlee, Herbert Morrison and Lord Pakenham (later the Earl of Longford), who spoke up on behalf of voluntary traditions and local democracy.[92] Attlee, more empirically minded than some of his colleagues, remarked in 1947 that 'we shall always have alongside the great range of public services, the voluntary services which humanize our national life and bring it down from the general to the particular'.[93] But underlying much of socialist thinking was the belief, as an official in the Ministry of National Insurance later put it, that Labour was 'creating Jerusalem'.[94] To the social prophets of the New Jerusalem, who believed that social laws offered an ideological blueprint for the reconstruction of society, philanthropists were irrelevant.

There was, in fact, nothing inevitable about the shape of the nation's social provision, but the belief that history was moving in their direction had encouraged collectivists to disregard traditional practices in favour of root-and-branch measures. It was perhaps not surprising that they discouraged popular participation in their reforms, for if the triumph of their doctrine was inevitable, participatory democracy was pointless in any case. That deceptive civil service expression 'consultation' helped to paper over the arrogance of officialdom. Yet, as Richard Crossman, the Labour Minister for Health in the 1960s, later conceded: 'The impression was given that socialism was an affair for the Cabinet, acting through the existing Civil Service.'[95] Labour ministers simply assumed that the state was the embodiment of social good. They believed, in Crossman's words, that it was 'only through state action' that a transformation of society and a sense of community could be achieved.[96] In practice, this belief was as paternalistic as the values of the voluntarists which they rejected, if not more so.

The influence of collectivist ideology in the formation of Labour's post-war welfare programme may be overstated, a point which socialists themselves were happier to concede after 1989. By the meticulous standards of Soviet planning, British collectivism was a poor thing, *ad hoc* and full of gaps. Politicians and civil servants could justify greater state intervention in the social sphere simply on the grounds that the intermediate institutions of civil society had broken down and were unlikely to recover. Still, the belief, attributed earlier to Ernest Bevin, that by the ministerial push of a button a programme of social progress would be set in train would soon become a feature of British politics. The growing identification of the central state with society in government circles not only discouraged pluralism and local democracy but politicized ever wider areas of social life. The 1945–50 Labour government introduced, for the first time in British history, the sense that virtually everything was subject to politics.

The vast expansion of government services created a hybrid form of social imperialism, in this case turned inwards on little England. Indeed, the collapse of the Empire and the need to employ overseas civil servants at home may have helped the cause of administering what, to Whitehall mandarins, was a world of underlings. Unlike their Victorian forebears, post-war ministers no longer took the view that the state was an artificial contrivance or that the Treasury was an odd ministry to bring about the redemption of mankind. They turned their attention to areas of human activity which would have stunned Gladstone or Disraeli.

While government intervention made inroads into sickness and deprivation, it excited expectations of further rights and entitlements that would place an enormous burden on later governments. Furthermore, it elevated ministerial responsibility to an unprecedented level—to a degree that one voluntarist, in 1950, called 'fiction'. 'We smile at the refinements of mediaeval scholasticism', remarked Arthur Ives, the Secretary of the King's Fund, 'but our own notions about the minister's ultimate responsibility are just about as far fetched.'[97]

Collectivism aroused spirited opposition outside the voluntary sector as well. In *The Road to Serfdom* (1944), the liberal economist Frederick Hayek indicted the planned society for its departure from liberal values. In *The Quest for Community* (1952), the American sociologist Robert Nisbet, harking back to Coleridge, saw an overbearing, impersonal state devastating traditional allegiances, leaving the individual adrift and alienated. Malcolm Muggeridge, the journalist and professional misfit, had 'a recurrent nightmare' in the early 1950s:

> in our inimitable English way we are allowing a servile State to come to pass of itself without our noticing it. . . . In the nightmare it seems clear that all the faceless men, the men without opinions, have been posted in key positions for a bloodless take-over, and that no one is prepared to join a Resistance Movement in defense of freedom because no one remembers what freedom means. . . . People swim into the Great Leviathan's mouth. He does not need to chase them.[98]

Social engineering was bound to have social costs, if only because it constituted so decisive a break with the nation's historic voluntary traditions. As a consequence of the state's ascendancy in welfare, the public, though now fully enfranchised, dealt less directly with social issues. (Was the decline of civil society a result of the growth of political democracy?) Personal service, long associated in the minds of collectivists with 'churchy bourgeois attitudes', was now widely seen as ineffectual. Even the Church of England proved susceptible to socialism's New Jerusalem. Despite the misgivings of the laity, the Church's Lambeth Conference in 1948 issued a resolution affirming the belief 'that the State is under the moral law of God, and is intended by Him to be an instrument for human welfare. We therefore welcome the growing concern and care of the modern State for its citizens, and call upon Church members to accept their own political responsibility and to co-operate with the State and its officers in their work.'[99]

Such pronouncements had little justification in scripture and compromised centuries of religious teaching in which personal reformation turned on the discretionary charity of individuals. Victorians commonly assumed that poverty was ineradicable, yet sought its amelioration through personal service. By contrast, secular socialism assumed that poverty could be abolished, but required little from the individual beyond the payment of taxes. The bishops did not wish to undermine Christian voluntary service, but they failed to appreciate that the growth of government welfare would contribute to the devitalization of Christian charity and, by implication, Christianity itself. Collectivism and the nationalization of culture were not conducive to community religious life and those myriad parish societies that provided social services for the poor and a moral training for the faithful. Rendering unto Caesar the things that traditionally were beyond Caesar's domain was a risky policy for Anglicans. It bonded the citizen to Whitehall, not to Lambeth Palace. Membership of the Church of England continued to decline after 1948.

For all the benefits, collective social action left the individual disconnected, while the nationalization of culture eroded former loyalties. Individuals were in some ways more impotent in an age of universal suffrage and parliamentary democracy than their disenfranchised ancestors had been under an oligarchic system.[100] How were they to create links between themselves and society in a political culture that placed so little value on individual effort and the intermediary institutions of civic life? Was the creation of such a bureaucratic welfare system an aberration in British history? Clearly, something fundamental was happening in a society, so voluntarist in the past, in which the burden of care shifted so radically to government, in which anonymous officials doled out the nation's capital in the name of 'the people', while individual service became characterized as a frill.

As if in compensation, politicians and social commentators sought to replace the sense of community, which people had built in the past out of family life and local institutions, with a sense of national community, built out of party politics and central administrative structures. In passing social legislation, the government acted in the name of freedom, progress and humanity. The professed aim of planning, after all, was to liberate the individual. But the more the government expanded its social role into areas formerly the responsibility of families and local associations, the more it diminished the duty, morality, and nobility of individuals. The more civil servants and politicians talked about 'the people' and the 'national community', the weaker people and communities became.

★ ★ ★

Uneasiness about the future of philanthropy led to a debate in the House of Lords in June 1949. Several peers, unsettled by the genie of big government that had been let out of the bottle, worried about 'the natural bias of the welfare State towards totalitarianism'. Voluntary action, as the Bishop of Sheffield argued, was one way of keeping it in check. The Labour peer, Lord Nathan, formerly a Liberal, joined in the paean of praise to philanthropy, describing charities as 'schools in the practice of democracy'.[101] Lord Beveridge himself, who the year before had published his book *Voluntary Action*, in which he called for 'fruitful co-operation' between the state and voluntary bodies, seemed to be having second thoughts about the impersonal bureaucracy that he had helped to shape. He was well aware of the state's capacity to destroy 'the freedom and spirit . . . of social conscience'.[102] Philanthropy would always be needed, he observed: 'Beveridge . . . has never been enough for Beveridge.' Some things 'should in no circumstances be left to the state alone', he added, or 'we should be well on the way to totalitarian conditions.'[103]

Voluntarism, though battered and diminished, survived. The state bureaucracy, though imperious, was less than monolithic, while the roots of civil society, often intertwined with the monarchy's, were so deep in British soil that nothing short of totalitarianism could destroy them. Older institutions persisted and new ones emerged partly as a reaction to the very sense of powerlessness that individuals felt in the face of an imperfect democracy and the standardizing tendencies of the state machine. Charity's critics, with their eyes fixed on the state, did not fully appreciate just how vital philanthropy would remain after the war. Mutable, restless and fertile, the voluntary sector was perpetually discovering new needs and aspirations. In the debate in the Lords, it was generally agreed that philanthropy would and must endure, for in a 'perpetually moving frontier' it was necessary, as Beveridge put it, 'to pioneer ahead of the state'.[104] With the years, one of its more pioneering roles would be to provide a critique of the state services.

Paradoxically, voluntary activity would be broadened, sharpened and enlivened by the very nationalization of welfare that voluntarists had so often opposed. State social reform held out the prospect of partnership between charities and government departments. Thus it precipitated changes within charitable bodies themselves, bringing many of them into line with modern conditions. As state provision was egalitarian and materialistic, it tended to erode those hierarchical values and sectarian pieties that had brought charity into disrepute in the past. For those reconsidering or losing faith, allegiances often shifted from church or chapel to new institutions thought to be more relevant to social need. One of voluntarism's great strengths, as a campaigner noted in 1945, is that it only takes an individual with a minute book and a few like-minded friends—and behold a new society is launched.[105]

The Welfare State affected established charities in different ways and degrees. Many societies, including those for animals and the arts, were not directly affected by social legislation. On the other hand, the surgical aid societies, which provided crutches and trusses, were left without a function, though a court order permitted the Royal Surgical Aid Society, founded in 1862, to change its objectives.[106] Other charities, like the Women's Institutes, gave greater emphasis to the social side of their activities. Others still changed their names and shifted their priorities. The Charity Organisation Society became the Family Welfare Association and concentrated on social casework. Many with a longstanding welfare role, such as the Salvation Army and the city missions, wondered about the efficacy of legislation, since so many people continued to fall through the welfare net. The Royal National Life-boat Institution, whose important local operations many thought should be taken over by the state, carried on as before. To have closed it down would have further eroded local responsibility for a local service. It would also have been costly for the public purse.

A major problem for charitable societies in the welfare field was how to adapt to the complex and compromising world of state social provision without distorting their objectives or losing their way. Another was to create a new, workable division of responsibility between voluntary and public bodies to replace those obsolete Victorian categories of the deserving and the undeserving. Fundraising emerged as the most immediate concern, for people often now assumed that as government benefits were comprehensive charitable donations were unnecessary or inconsequential. As the Save the Children Fund *Report* for 1951 put it: 'it is still sometimes necessary to explain to enquirers that the nationalisation of the social services in Britain . . . does not impinge in any way on the voluntary status of the Fund.'[107]

★ ★ ★

The monarchy played its part in the survival and adaptation of voluntary traditions after the war. It gave a much-needed boost to a section of society whose moral capital, built up in an age of faith, was trickling away. Largely above the political fray, it got on quietly with its traditional patronage work within the new context. Troubled about the nation's future, and the monarchy's, the King used his Christmas broadcasts to champion the cause of charity. Playing on that post-war slogan 'reconstruction', he called for 'spiritual reconstruction' in 1946: 'If our feet are on the road of common charity . . . our differences will never destroy our underlying unity.'[108] In 1950, he remarked that we 'must consolidate what past generations have achieved for us. . . . This inheritance of ours is not the product of any rigid system. It is something far more human than that. It is the collective expression of the lives of countless thousands of men and women, quite unknown to fame, who have laboured incessantly for the good of their fellows.'[109]

Charitable campaigners took heart from such remarks and the good works that continued to radiate from Buckingham Palace. So did institutions as disparate as the National League of Hospital Friends, the YWCA, Missions to Seamen, and the British Legion (the latter received its royal charter in 1971). Just before he died, George VI received a letter from his old aide, Robert Hyde, about a successful meeting of the Duke of York's camp in Glasgow, which had been attended by a mixture of boys, employers, headmasters and trade unionists. Kurt Hahn, the founder of Gordonstoun School and Outward Bound, had spoken at the meeting

62. Queen Mary, and Mary, the Princess Royal, and Lady Cynthia Colville at a bazaar at Sandringham Rectory, 1951.

and 'stated unreservedly that all his work with Outward Bound was inspired by the Duke of York's camp. In his words it was "pregnant with meaning" both for the Monarchy and for the future of [the] relationship between the classes.'[110]

In his letter, Hyde mentioned a further incident that he thought the King would like to know about. A trade unionist had retailed a story of a boy of 'extremely left wing views' who had been sent to a camp 'with deliberate intent and returned with a completely changed outlook and with eight snapshots of the camp, six of which were of his host. Some months ago this boy was listening to a Communist who was railing against the monarchy. The boy listened for a bit and then burst out "If you knew the King as well as I do you wouldn't talk such bloody nonsense".' The King died in the knowledge that he had converted at least one republican to the crown through his own exertions.[111]

A brief look at another of the charities assisted by the royal family, the

Save the Children Fund, is instructive. It had been set up at the end of the First World War by two sisters, Eglantyne Jebb and Dorothy Buxton, to preserve the lives of children menaced by economic hardship or wartime distress. At the end of the Second World War the demands on its services increased dramatically, but, as its officials intimated, many members of the public were under the impression that children's needs were being met by the state social services. Given the pressures on its finances, the charity needed a relaunch to boost its income and to give it a more distinctive presence.

The Save the Children Fund had little connection with the royal family before the war. It had requested 'a sign' of the King's 'sympathy' in a letter to the Palace in 1938, but the Ministry of Health advised the King against granting patronage to the institution on the grounds that its work was mostly abroad and that its views were not always politically opportune.[112] The war obviously changed perceptions, and in 1946 Princess Margaret accepted an invitation to open a new play-centre for the charity in Camden, her first 'solo' official engagement.[113] In 1948 Princess Elizabeth received a party of holiday children, and in the same year Princess Marie Louise, the daughter of Princess Helena and granddaughter of Queen Victoria, attended a benefit performance on the Fund's behalf. In 1949, Princess Marina, the Duchess of Kent, visited a play-centre in London, Princess Marie Louise chaired the thirtieth anniversary dinner and, significantly, Countess Mountbatten of Burma became the charity's President.[114] The Save the Children Fund has never looked back.

The Fund's astute publicity office made great play of the royal engagements and displayed pictures of the royal family prominently in the annual reports. Meanwhile, the management of the charity widened the work of the royal family through gentle persuasion and the offer of engagements that fitted into the Palace diary. Princess Marina opened the biennial General Council of the International Union for Child Welfare in 1950, and Princess Elizabeth visited workers in Greece in 1951. When she became Queen the following year, she agreed to become the Fund's patron, reducing the society's former patrons, the Archbishops of Canterbury and York, to the status of vice-presidents. The Save the Children Fund's report for 1952 pronounced that such an honour was 'granted only to organisations of proved worth' and that this was the first example of a children's charity with an international dimension to receive royal favour.[115] In the mid-1950s the Fund's finances improved dramatically and its membership grew, not least in the Commonwealth.

As the history of the Save the Children Fund suggests, the crown benefited from the fresh demands made on its services by charities undergoing a period of uneasy transition. The changes in voluntarism itself—its adjustment to the Welfare State, its expansion into overseas aid, and its declining class-consciousness—turned out to be a blessing for both the charities and the monarchy. Through philanthropic work the post-war royal family was able to swim with the tide of those post-war and post-imperial social currents—egalitarianism and internationalism—that helped to disengage the crown from the old ruling class in the minds of the public. A monarchy seen associating with African children and Greek peasants was in keeping with the post-war mood. Meanwhile, charities encouraged deference by playing on the royal family's unique eminence.

Philanthropy's survival into the age of planning and state provision owed more to the resilience of Britain's civic life than to the monarchy, although the monarchy was an instrumental ally. Just as noteworthy as the persistence of philanthropy was the ease with which Buckingham Palace adjusted to collectivism and changing post-war values. The royal family lost many friends in the voluntary sector, but it sustained its charitable role inside and alongside government services. It was the post-war variant of a theme dating back to the eighteenth century. After 1945, the crown nourished, and was nourished by, institutions, old and new, which filled gaps in state provision or served new aspirations. It had little need to plan its own survival after the war. It muddled through by satisfying the wishes of voluntarists and mollifying the politicians who needed the royal family to give respectability to their policies. In more than one sense, the 'Welfare State' created a compatible 'Welfare Monarchy'.

But the 'Welfare Monarchy' was potentially adversarial, for there was a final, intriguing twist in the royal family's adjustment to the Welfare State. In 1949, the Duke of Gloucester, speaking as the President of the King's Fund, criticized the NHS for maladministration.[116] The following year he said that the administrative arrangements of the Health Service remained 'on trial', and that 'some time must elapse before it could be assumed that they are providing a service that is both humane and economical'.[117] The Fund's officials put these comments into Gloucester's mouth, but he was content to deliver them. They signalled a new role for members of the royal family—as critics of departments of state. With the years, citizens would look increasingly to charities, and through them to the royal family, for mitigation of government policy.

8

Queen Elizabeth II:
The Crown and the Rediscovery
of Civil Society

The first twenty years of the reign of Queen Elizabeth II may be said to be the heyday of state-directed health and social services in Britain. Few doubted that central government had the primary responsibility for welfare provision, and most commentators assumed that it was well-equipped to administer the system devised by Parliament. The consensus did nothing to enhance the status of voluntarists, whose impulses were to decentralize, to break a problem down into pieces. Local newspapers reveal the continuing commitment to philanthropy, but from the 1950s to the mid-1970s government captured the welfare headlines. Just as the National Health Service pushed voluntarists to the periphery of the debate on health, national insurance pushed them to the periphery of the debate on social security.

The belief that only government action could conquer poverty and enlarge human freedom proved useful to politicians and civil servants of any political persuasion who wished to expand their authority. Transfixed by the role of the Welfare State in their election prospects, politicians began to narrow discussions of social policy down to government action. So did civil servants in the welfare departments. Their numbers swollen, they jealously guarded their new authority. Under the sway of collectivist ideals, post-war scholars and social commentators began to revise history in such a way as to make social reform appear coterminous with state provision. To them, charities had a quaint, Victorian air about them and were of little interest unless they prepared the ground for the state. The more they studied philanthropy simply in relation to government, the more marginal it came to be seen.

The ideal of social partnership, heralded by William Beveridge and his colleagues in the House of Lords, proved elusive for many philanthropists who wished to work with the state services. From the earliest years of the NHS, charity paid for capital projects, equipment and research, which made a nonsense of the notion that it only provided amenities.[1] Yet trade unionists and civil servants continued to treat such contributions as frills and volunteers as marginal figures, typified by the Red Cross lady running

a trolley shop. The very disparity in the scale of their respective operations made an effective partnership between bureaucratic departments
and diverse charities difficult. Small movements in government policy
required disproportionate activity from voluntarists. Like mice scurrying
around a proud and fabled lion, they had to keep an eye on every shift
in government policy for fear of being smothered. Politicians and the
press, their eyes fixed on the lion, took little notice of the proliferation of
mice, even those with royal patronage.

Charities worked in more fruitful partnership with the monarchy than
with government, and they consistently argued that voluntarists had a role
to play in humanizing state welfare provision, especially in hospitals and
residential institutions. The Secretary of the King's Fund, who wrote
those speeches for the Duke of Gloucester that criticized NHS administration, argued in the 1950s that the object of the Health Service should
be to combine the spirit of the old voluntary system with the universality
of the new. He and his colleagues assumed that the demand for medical
care would overwhelm national resources, in the same way as it had
overwhelmed charitable resources in the past. As they saw it, state social
provision was essentially materialist in conception, and in spending tussles
with the welfare departments the Treasury would not wish to cultivate a
reputation for compassion. It was the responsibility of the government to
devise financial arrangements that provided a sound 'basic' service, while
encouraging voluntarists with their 'unlimited' sense of responsibility,
moulded by Christian thought, to extend its humanity.[2]

The message went largely unheeded. In the early days of the NHS, as
we have seen, 'do-gooders' were not made to feel welcome in the
nation's hospitals. Yet by 1962, there were 800,000 volunteers in the
National League of Hospital Friends alone, a body under the patronage of
Queen Elizabeth, the Queen Mother.[3] Other royal institutions, including
the British Red Cross, the St John Ambulance Brigade, and the Women's
Royal Voluntary Service, also had close links with the hospitals. On the
research side, the great foundations and cancer charities were filling the
gaps created by government cash-shortages. Between them, the Cancer
Research Campaign and the Imperial Cancer Research Fund, both royal
charities, provided 29 per cent of all money expended on cancer research
in 1952, a figure which rose dramatically over the following two decades.[4] Still, as the King's Fund ruefully observed in 1965, the Labour
Party remained 'fiercely anti-voluntary and endeavoured to prevent hospitals from having any voluntary support'.[5]

When Richard Crossman became Secretary of State for Health and
Social Security in 1968, he was 'staggered' by the extent of voluntary
activity in the Health Service. On his rounds he could hardly fail to
notice the amount of hospital equipment and the range of services
provided by voluntary contributions, often presented or opened by a

member of the royal family. But he was 'astonished by the strength of the resistance' among his civil servants to his proposal that charitable activity should be extended.[6] He detected a particular tendency in the NHS to treat volunteers 'as cheap, auxiliary labour', while noting that the idealism in the service had drained away. Chastened by his experience as a minister, he now lamented that the post-war Labour Party's predilection for welfare provision based on centralized bureaucracy had done 'grievous harm' to philanthropy.[7] As he was aware, his Party had also done 'grievous harm' to its own traditions of mutual aid.

While voluntarists persisted with the state services, often with the active support of the monarchy, they turned more and more of their attention to less contentious areas, where government could not or dared not enter. With their longstanding connections all over the country, members of the royal family were better placed than most to know the extent of social service beyond Whitehall, much of it being performed at the community level. They continued to cultivate hospitals, homes and housing estates with visits and openings. But the most creative attachments and projects of the royal family lay in areas relatively free from politics and officialdom. With so many institutions, trusts, foundations, clubs and associations at its disposal, and so many others willing to be of service if called upon, the monarchy was spoiled for choice when it wished to promote a voluntary initiative.

Like every monarch since George III, Queen Elizabeth II inherited the headship of philanthopy. In the early years of her reign she took the time to fulfil engagements for many of her organizations, although the ones nearest to her homes saw more of her than those farther afield. According to Dermot Morrah, one of the more thoughtful royal commentators in the 1950s, her granting of patronage was symbolic, suggesting that the entire community took an interest in the work of the organizations to which she extended her patronage. But more than that, when the Queen lent her name or appeared at a charitable function she stood 'for the idea that the ultimate reality in corporate life—at the heart of what sometimes seems the chilly and soulless machinery of the modern state—is not an abstraction, but a human being of like passions with ourselves'.[8]

Despite Morrah's reference to 'like passions with ourselves', the Queen's patronage work does not reveal much about her as a person, though it might be observed that to be so widely seen yet so little known requires self-control of a high order. To date, the Queen's many biographers have treated her as though she were a public monument and not a living being at all.[9] Clearly, she likes dogs, horses, the Commonwealth and her grandchildren, but this is hardly the stuff of biography, though it will have to serve until the archives appear or another Lytton Strachey comes along. 'The heart of kings is unsearchable,' says Proverbs. A monarch's personality cannot be unaffected by its institutionalization. And the Queen, like Bagehot's royal magician, has contrived to efface herself in the relationship between her subjects and her office, leaving us to wonder and to fantasize.[10]

From the beginning of her reign, Queen Elizabeth II buttressed her philanthropic work with Christmas broadcasts, following the tradition established by her grandfather. By contrast with the Queen's speeches to Parliament, delivered on behalf of the government in fulfilment of her constitutional duty, we may assume that what she says at Christmas reflects her own beliefs. The two very different sorts of message may be seen as expressing respectively the constitutional and the social functions of the monarchy's national role: the one distanced and impersonal, the other deliberately intimate. In her Christmas broadcasts she has returned again and again to the long-established voluntary themes of Christian brotherhood and the continuing need for charitable action. In 1964, she spoke of self-discipline and the right to assemble, of freedom and its origins in 'ancient institutions'.[11] The following year she called on the young to take up voluntary work: 'We can all find some practical way to serve others.'[12] But these Christmas messages, though personal and uplifting in tone, did not at that time shed much light on how Britain's most 'ancient institution' of all saw its welfare role or how important it thought it was in its own affairs.

The Queen and the Queen Mother, according to Morrah, vied with each other to see who could fulfil the greatest number of public duties.[13] But without the political and ceremonial work of the sovereign, the Queen Mother had more time for charity, and her patronage list grew to over 300 organizations.[14] Individual charities come and go in royal favour, and with so many patronages the Queen and the Queen Mother would be hard pressed to remember half of those on their lists. Many royal institutions, of course, receive little if any direct royal involvement, though this does not prevent them from using the Palace association to advantage. An astute campaigner who knows royal predilections and how to use the Palace network can be invaluable to an organization. As in the past, it is not uncommon for more than one member of the royal family to serve a single institution, and it is possible to transfer or exchange patronages.

Since Princess Margaret is inevitably president or patron of fewer institutions than the Queen or the Queen Mother, she can give greater attention to individual cases. She has been most assiduous with the Girl Guides, the NSPCC, charities for disabled children, nursing organizations and ballet companies. Her appearance at a performance or a gala event can be worth between 10 and 15 per cent of an organization's annual income.[15] One of her early ventures in fundraising came in 1954, when she served as assistant director in an amateur theatrical production of *The Frog* by Ian Hay and Edgar Wallace. As her biographer observed, 'it was

63. Queen Elizabeth, the Queen Mother, in conversation with elderly ladies while nursing staff look on, c. 1960.

an ideal distraction, filling her off-duty hours, while also allowing her to indulge one of her strongest interests, the theatre'.[16] Noel Coward thought the production, performed by the Princess's aristocratic friends, 'one of the most fascinating exhibitions of incompetence, conceit and bloody impertinence that I have ever seen in my life'.[17] Playwrights, it would appear, have lost their monarchical zeal since the reign of George IV. Still, the event raised £10,000 for the Invalid Children's Aid Association.

The Duke of Edinburgh, whose list of foundations, associations, clubs and regiments now numbers over 800, once remarked that it was 'impossible to belong completely' to all his many organizations.[18] But having so many causes at his fingertips offers him scope to pick and choose and, importantly, to bring them together when need arises. If the female members of the royal family specialize in the caring end of the charitable register, with an occasional nod to the arts, Prince Philip favours institutions like the National Playing Fields Association, which he revitalized, and the Outward Bound Trust, the brainchild of his mentor

Kurt Hahn, the headmaster of Gordonstoun School.[19] Such institutions encourage self-reliance, competitiveness and active citizenship. Self-reliant children, the Prince might add, are less likely to be a charge on the state, or look to government for salvation in later life.

Arguably, Prince Philip's most important creation was the Duke of Edinburgh's Award, launched in 1956. Inspired by Hahn, it brought the Spartan philosophy and puritanical air of Gordonstoun to city children and sought to instil in them a sense of social obligation through community work.[20] The Prince was well known in the charitable sector as a fixer and a look at the list of benefactors of his Award scheme suggests that he took pains to extract cooperation from disparate charities and leading lights from the worlds of business and sport.[21] He also pressed the commercial world for contributions, which was in keeping with the remark he made in 1963: 'Princely gifts don't come from princes any more. They come from tycoons.'[22]

The Duke of Edinburgh's Award has much in common with George V's camps and expands the monarchy's work with youth, which has always been a charitable priority with the royal family. By the end of its first decade, nearly half a million schoolchildren had participated in Award programmes, a figure which rose to over two million in 1989.[23] Not all of the children who join a programme finish. Nor do all those who collect their awards in Buckingham Palace at the quarterly presentations, at which Prince Philip and (latterly) Prince Edward preside, leave the scheme more committed to the monarchy than when they started their training. But in keeping with all the other royal charities for the young, the Duke of Edinburgh's Award inculcates the monarchy's abiding values in the rising generation, while giving prestige and favourable publicity to the royal family.

The monarchy's support for individual initiative and voluntary association made unobtrusive headway in the early years of Queen Elizabeth II's reign, and the innumerable royal appearances at well-attended events such as award-givings, concerts, variety performances and cinema premieres added up. So much so that, when Mass Observation carried out a survey on the monarchy in 1964, it concluded that the public was three times more likely to see a member of the royal family in a 'welfare' context than in any other. As 60 per cent of adults claimed to have seen a member of the royal family this was no small achievement and confirmed that nothing was doing more to bring the monarchy into communion with the public than its social service. Not a few in the sample wanted charitable work expanded and urged the Queen to show more 'intelligent interest in social questions'.[24] Leonard Harris, who initiated this particular survey, concluded: 'The concept of welfare monarch and welfare royalty is thus implicit in much of the current activity of royal people; and it is this aspect of their behaviour which has in total, the biggest *personal* audience.'[25] Here was an early usage, if not the earliest, of the phrase 'welfare monarch'.

Bagehot had opined that 'royalty is a government in which the attention of the nation is concentrated on one person doing interesting actions'.[26] The Mass Observation report of 1964 confirmed that voluntary work constituted one of the monarchy's most 'interesting actions', for by definition an event in which a member of the public came into contact with a member of the royal family was of interest. Other findings of the survey showed that some respondents worried about the loss of democratic freedoms and saw the crown as 'a bulwark against danger'. Thirty per cent said the Queen was 'especially chosen by God'. Only 16 per cent described themselves as republicans, chiefly on economic grounds. Most of these were socialists.[27] Many of the findings were consistent with other surveys carried out in the first twenty-five years of the reign.[28] Taken together they illustrated that the monarchy had accomplished its principle mission—to remain viable in a political and social environment which had changed dramatically since the 1930s.

Palace officials would have been aware of the Mass Observation report, but did they draw any conclusions from it? The central message—the monarchy's enduring popularity—was reassuring and encouraged business as usual. As in the past when the royal family had been confident about the future, it rather took its charitable rounds for granted. Moreover, in the 1960s, the crown's patronage role, however worthy, was rarely eye-catching. Royal visits to disasters like the Welsh village of Aberfan in 1966 received widespread coverage. (According to Harold Wilson, Lord Snowdon was particularly admired for his sensitive attentions to the bereaved.)[29] But even big set-piece events, such as the Queen's visit to King's College Hospital in 1968, which took months of planning, failed to attract the level of media attention that would have been given to such outings in the 1930s. At the local level, however, they were most memorable occasions, especially for the officials who competed to be introduced to Her Majesty or the pilferers who stole the china after the Queen had taken her tea.[30]

A host of new voluntary societies had emerged in the 1950s and early 1960s that received royal patronage, including the Spastics Society, the Samaritans, Voluntary Service Overseas and the British Heart Foundation. But Palace advisors moved in metropolitan circles where charity was less under discussion than at any time in modern British history. Moreover, they had more exciting things in the court calendar to think about than a visit by the Queen Mother to a convalescent home or Princess Margaret opening a Dr Barnardo's centre. They went through the charitable motions partly because the motions had always been made. Like members of the royal family themselves, they sometimes resented the

64. Princess Margaret opens a new Dr Barnardo's Centre for handicapped children in Barkingside, Essex, October 1975.

onerous demands that philanthropy made on their own time. Despite the findings of the Mass Observation survey, the idea that the monarchy's popularity might have more to do with good works and charitable appearances than its constitutional role, or the stately ceremonial and the television coverage that it aroused, would have been waved away dimissively in the 1960s or 1970s. The idea is taken rather more seriously in the Palace today.[31] This has partly to do with the rediscovery of civil society.

★ ★ ★

The proponents of collectivism had rather taken it for granted that the Welfare State would continue to rise indefinitely. But it reached its high-water mark in the 1960s. By the mid-1970s, national and international economic problems, ignited by the oil crisis of 1973, led to a contentious reappraisal of welfare provision, which has still to run its course.

Government expenditure on the health and social services, including education and housing, had risen from 16 per cent of Gross National Product in 1951 to 29 per cent in 1975, which was half of all public expenditure in that year.[32] The expansion of the social budget resulted in higher taxation and increased borrowing, but, however much money the government raised, it appeared never to be enough to keep pace with the insatiable demand for services. As the historian of social policy Geoffrey Finlayson observed: 'Just as the appetite of charities for funds had always been virtually unappeasable, so too was the appetite of the state; but attempts to satisfy the state's appetite were much more damaging since the public expenditure involved put immense strains on productive capacity and wealth creation in the nation as a whole.'[33]

As the spiralling costs and bureaucratic inefficiencies of the state welfare services became more apparent, the strategic planning and social engineering that characterized the 1950s and 1960s came under attack. By the mid-1970s the backlash against the post-war welfare consensus began in earnest. The New Right, led by Keith Joseph and Margaret Thatcher, who became leader of the Conservative Party in 1975, castigated the social services for excessive expenditure and for failing to satisfy expectations or to deliver the promised economic benefits. Against this background, the long tradition of liberal, anti-collectivist thought, typified by economists like F.A. Hayek, returned to prominence. To the libertarian proponents of market forces, the issue was not simply whether the state *could* deliver social services, but whether it *should* do so.[34]

Following Mrs Thatcher's victory in 1979, central government became an increasingly reluctant sponsor of the Welfare State and the emphasis in social provision shifted to the pursuit of efficiency, private-sector expansion, and pluralism. Politics, it is said, is the organization of hatreds, and the 1980s witnessed a new-model Conservative Party taking its revenge on the public sector, which it equated with bureaucratic waste and national decline. There was no serious prospect of welfare provision ceasing to be primarily a government responsibility, but the controversial government changes resulted in turmoil for the health and social services. With collectivist provision under strain, if not attack, voluntarism began to be taken much more seriously by politicians, and public awareness of philanthropic influences and voluntary campaigns increased.

The ideological dog fighting and political upheaval put voluntarists under more pressure than at any other time since the 1940s. On the right, there were those more sanguine about what charity could achieve than charities were themselves. On the left, many commentators feared that the resurgence of charity foreshadowed a return to the 1930s and what Robin Cook has called a 'flag day NHS' and Gordon Brown 'a sad and seedy competition for public pity'.[35] Politicians tended to ignore just how much philanthropy itself had changed since the war. Charities were now less socially divisive than they had been in the 1930s. In addition to propping up the health and social services, they had carved out an experimental role for themselves on a range of contemporary issues: the environment, wildlife, recreation and ethnic minorities. Freed by government from many of their former thankless tasks, few welfare charities could be found in the 1980s that were nostalgic about the 1930s. What they would have liked was a little less paternalism from politicians and civil servants.

In the 1980s, voluntary agencies had no desire to be caught in a political crossfire or to be put in a position in which they were expected to provide services simply to reduce government expenditure. They welcomed the fresh publicity, but they were decidedly nervous about the added pressure on their services. That distinctively 1980s word 'privatization' suggested a primary role for voluntarism that it had been forced to abdicate under the diktat of an earlier government. In the general reassessment taking place, there needed to be greater clarity in setting the boundaries between statutory and voluntary provision. There was also a danger that the traditional meaning of voluntarism as activity free from state control was being undermined by increased government funding of charities and the granting of quasi-charitable status to statutory bodies. After decades of state supremacy in welfare, it was doubtful whether there was a cultural basis for a dramatic expansion of charity, or whether charity was a suitable way of providing basic services according to need.

Whatever the outcome for philanthropists, the expectations of collectivists had not materialized. The vast expansion of state power in the sphere of social provision had been accompanied not by charitable decay but charitable profusion. If in the first half of the century voluntarists had done their best to limit the expansion of state power, in the second half of the century they had taken on a pioneering role, often lobbying Parliament on particular issues and sometimes criticizing government policy. For its part, the public appeared to want both higher levels of welfare expenditure and lower levels of officialdom. Against the background of dependence and a desire for independence, the philanthropic pulse beat persistently, if erratically. In the 1980s, the Charity Commissioners were registering thousands of new institutions each year.[36] Many of them, it should be said, received so much of their income from government sources that they could make little claim to autonomy.

In the Thatcher years, Britain reached a stage in the evolution of social policy at which the government wanted more from the voluntary sector and the voluntary sector wanted more from the government. There were signs that the longstanding ideological battle between voluntarists and collectivists, which many assumed to have been won by the latter, was now heading towards the ropes, with the combatants holding each other up. As any residual belief that centralized state welfare might bring forth the Millennium collapsed, a more balanced view of philanthropy's potential began to emerge. The innovation and cost effectiveness of voluntary activity were most immediately obvious. With social engineering less fashionable, the attractions of welfare pluralism, which emphasized local initiative and personal service, also came back to the fore. No less important, the grassroots democracy inherent in the institutions of civil society became more apparent.

★   ★   ★

The waning of collectivism and the rediscovery of voluntary traditions were bound to have repercussions for the monarchy. The shift in thinking accelerated by the social philosophy of the New Right gave the Palace cause for thought. With Labour ideology on the wane, the monarchy's social philosophy, which might be described as deriving from Edmund Burke by way of Prince Albert, was coming back into fashion. What was to be done, if anything? The crown was secure and the forecast favourable, judging from the opinion polls. In times of peace and prosperity, the royal family did not have to show great initiative. Indeed, where it showed initiative, as in its flirtation with the media, it sometimes came unstuck. The Edwardian Lord Esher might have advised the Palace to wait for the political and social pendulum to swing and be 'modernized' by default.

Prince Philip, Duke of Edinburgh, a 'modernizer' who wished to adapt the monarchy to the changing political and social economy, saw an opportunity presented by the Thatcher phenomenon. Like the Prime Minister, his thoughts on the state and society had been shaped by the Cold War and hostility to socialism. Always outspoken, he began to express his views on sensitive social issues with greater trenchancy than in the past. Given the peculiarity of his constitutional position, he had more leeway than the Queen. Though inherited and unsystematic, his social views are nevertheless intriguing for the insight they give into Palace thinking. They were unlikely to attract applause from the left in the ideological battlefield of the 1980s and thus constituted something of a risk, even for the candid Prince.

Beginning in 1979, a year of discontent and the election of Mrs Thatcher, Prince Philip clearly felt that he could express himself without fear of a political backlash. He began to articulate in a series of lectures a social philosophy in greater detail than was possible in a Christmas broadcast or on the back of an envelope. The series brought together in 1982 in his book *A Question of Balance*, marked a departure from his earlier pronouncements. Compare, for example, 'Conflict', 'The Individual and the Community' and 'Community Health' with his earlier speeches, which tended to address uncontentious subjects like scientific work in the Commonwealth or 'Aviation and the Development of Remote Areas'.[37] An exception to the earlier pattern had been a speech he delivered in 1959 to the British Medical Association entitled 'Freedom and Organisation', in which he described the BMA as an institutional expression of democracy.[38]

Like Prince Albert and a legion of Victorian social philosophers, Prince Philip distrusted over-centralized political power and felt most comfortable with self-governing institutions, social pluralism and entrepreneurial values, especially self-help. As has already been suggested, such ideas informed his various schemes for underprivileged youth and his charitable operations more generally. Like George V, he abhorred social upheaval and those trends in philosophy and politics which conjured up 'an idealised state as the instrument' for conquering all human ills. The lecture 'One Aspect of Human Conflict', delivered at St George's House, Windsor in 1980, was a direct response to his depression over the 'winter of discontent' and the state of Britain. In it he includes a nice touch of royal revenge, a swipe at the Webbs, those icons of the left, for their 'obstinate and blind commitment' to ideology and their 'remarkable aversion to reality' in supporting the Soviet Union.[39]

In his published musings, Prince Philip worried about big government in Britain and its tendency to ride roughshod over the individual. 'Government is no longer satisfied with neutral concerns of peace and security', he argued, 'but now it is interested in morality and behaviour and legislating for the common good. The fact is that the liberty of the individual is a vital part of the common good also. . . . The trouble is that the promise of [state] benefits makes people overlook the loss of choice and responsibility, which inevitably follows.' In his view, the duty of government was to provide 'a safety net', not to obstruct the free development of family life and voluntary effort. 'Self-government of institutions is a vital element in any society which aspires to be democratic, and furthermore it has the great advantage in that it allows government to concentrate on the business for which only governments can be responsible.'[40] Intriguingly, the Prince failed to make the connection, which had been made in the nineteenth century, between the monarchy's support for self-governing institutions and the liberty of the individual.

If British collectivism came in for a drubbing, the Prince had a special antipathy to Marxism, and saw it, in Leszek Kolakowski's famous phrase, as 'the greatest fantasy of our century'. The 'greatest weakness' of Marx's historical materialism, according to the Prince,

65. Prince Philip visiting the Moss Side Youth Centre, Manchester, 1970.

is that it ignores the purely voluntary and altruistic elements in human nature which are encouraged to flourish in any civilised human society. The concept of charity (in the voluntary sense), or of obligation, or of social conscience, hardly exist in Marxist doctrine but there are vast numbers of people of all classes in this country who give money generously to charities and who give their leisure time and energies to voluntary organisations of all kinds and who respond with astonishing speed to the needs of the victims of natural and man-made disasters all over the world. This cannot be swept aside as a sort of fringe phenomenon peculiar to the bourgeoisie and unworthy of consideration by serious political and economic commentators. It is a vitally important factor in life and the very best example of individual initiative and sense of responsibility.[41]

Such comment, a rare glimpse of the monarchy's thinking on social matters, could have been delivered by Mrs Thatcher. Indeed, Mrs Thatcher spoke in glowing terms of philanthropy and Victorian values on more than one occasion. In an address to the Women's Royal Voluntary Service in 1981, she saw 'the voluntary movement . . . at the heart of all our social welfare provision' and told her audience that 'we politicians

260

and administrators must not forget that the state has a limited role' and that the 'willingness of men and women to give service is one of freedom's greatest safeguards. It ensures that caring remains free from political control.'[42] In the event, state funding of charities increased in the 1980s, but became more selective, while the cuts imposed on local government reduced the money available for local institutions.[43] Mrs Thatcher, it transpired, had a need for 'political control' that expressed itself in greater centralization, not less.

The Victorian values of Mrs Thatcher were highly selective.[44] The idea of the enabling state and the 'mixed economy of care', which coloured Tory thinking, appealed to many voluntarists, including members of the royal family. The 1980s saw a frenzy of reforming zeal and a profusion of rhetoric linking government with 'care' and 'the community'. On the other hand, the Prime Minister failed to recall that her Victorian counterparts saw little virtue in the centralization of government power for its own sake or in blurring the boundaries between the state and the charitable sectors. Moreover, she seemed to expect rather a lot from the charitable sector without really understanding its character and needs. Some thought she provided too little incentive; and others, including many churchmen and at least one Prince, disliked her hectoring and apparent want of compassion.

For decades, voluntarists had had to deal with a state bureaucracy that disregarded their activities. Now they had to deal with the ideologues of the right, who identified civil society with the market. This was unpalatable to those voluntarists who had come to distrust unfettered market forces as much as they did state planning. The term civil society, which was now becoming more commonly used in Britain, was nothing if not elastic. In the shifting social economy of the 1980s, it tended to mean a set of institutions, antithetical to the state, that counterbalanced both the state and the marketplace. Put another way, civil society consisted of a half-way house of free associations, which mitigated the atomizing effects of arbitrary, bureaucratic government, whether of the left or the right.[45] In this half-way house between state and society, between socialism and the market, the monarchy had a room with a view.

★   ★   ★

In 1966, Princess Alice, Countess of Athlone (1883–1981), the last surviving granddaughter of Queen Victoria, and in her day a great charitable work-horse, left a message for her family in her *Reminiscences*. Royalty, she reflected, was

> an arduous profession whose members are seldom granted an opportunity of opting in or out of their predestined fate. . . . Their daily tasks, for months ahead, are prescribed and set out in a diary of engagements from

which only illness can excuse them. None but those trained from youth to such an ordeal can sustain it with amiability and composure. The royal motto "Ich Dien" is no empty phrase. It means what it says—I serve.[46]

For generations, members of the royal family had this message, so redolent of Queen Victoria and Prince Albert, drummed into them. In the main, they did not disappoint. Whether they felt like it or not, they turned up for their engagements and delivered in their fashion. And when they did not, like Edward VIII, the Palace and their charities covered up for them.

Those members of the royal family who joined the charitable circuit in the 1960s and 1970s—the Kents, Princess Alexandra, and the Gloucesters among them—also delivered.[47] The public not only sees them because of their charities but largely defines them by their causes, which loom large in their calendars. Without such activities they would struggle against the syndrome that bedevilled Edward VIII after the abdication. Indeed, it might be said that Edward VIII continues to haunt members of the royal family and enlivens their desire to do something, and be seen to be doing something, more serious than shooting pheasants or playing golf. Even so, the noble motto 'Ich Dien' sounded decidedly old-fashioned in the 1960s. To live up to it, as Princess Alice recognized, required a high degree of self-denial.

The younger generation of royalty has not always taken to public service with becoming selflessness. Perhaps the most notable example of one who has is Princess Anne (created Princess Royal in 1987), who became President of the Save the Children Fund in 1970. Over the next twenty years its annual income rose from £2.5 million to over £50 million, an achievement that insiders were happy to attribute to her good offices. She had, as one of them put it, turned the institution into 'a household name'.[48] She has taken on board nearly a hundred other presidencies or patronages, including the Riding for the Disabled Association and Missions to Seamen, but the media concentration on her efforts for the Save the Children Fund has benefited her reputation as much as it has the Fund itself.[49] For all her assiduousness with each of her charities, it is identification with one that has made the most impact in turning her public image into that of a respected professional.

The high-profile role of the Princess of Wales with the British Red Cross may eventually be compared to the work of Princess Anne for the Save the Children Fund. Steered into a routine of charitable engagements by Palace aides after her marriage, a role predestined for royal females, she rebelled; but after an introspective interlude she came round to a similar set of duties. Whatever the personal difficulties of the Princess of Wales, she combines a unique glamour with a common touch; and the seventy

66. Princess Anne at one of the Riding for the Disabled Association centres, with the Blue Peter presenter Lesley Judd.

67. The Prince and Princess of Wales with Bob Geldof at the Live Aid concert, 1985.

or so charities with which she is connected will provide a willing vehicle for the publicity which she apparently enjoys. Their enjoyment is, after all, at least as great as hers. Her social work might be called therapeutic, if not redemptive like the Duchess of York's. Her position is reminiscent of that of one or two of Queen Victoria's daughters, though in their day royal marital failure was little advertised and noble reserve had not yet collapsed into tabloid confession and bathos.

The uniqueness of the Prince of Wales's position makes especial demands. His patronage list has risen to over 400 organizations, nearly half of which are explicitly philanthropic. In a typical year he fulfils 400 or so engagements, most of them with some charitable dimension.[50] His preoccupations, among them the inner cities, the causes of minorities and the environment, are well known to the public and need little further comment here, except to say that they are couched in the language of community and social partnership. Apart from the charities which he has founded himself, such as the Prince's Trust (1976), he has nudged several of his inherited institutions into areas which are in keeping with his chief concerns. One would not, for example, associate the King's Fund with alternative medicine and homelessness. But under the presidency of Prince Charles it has developed an interest in these issues.

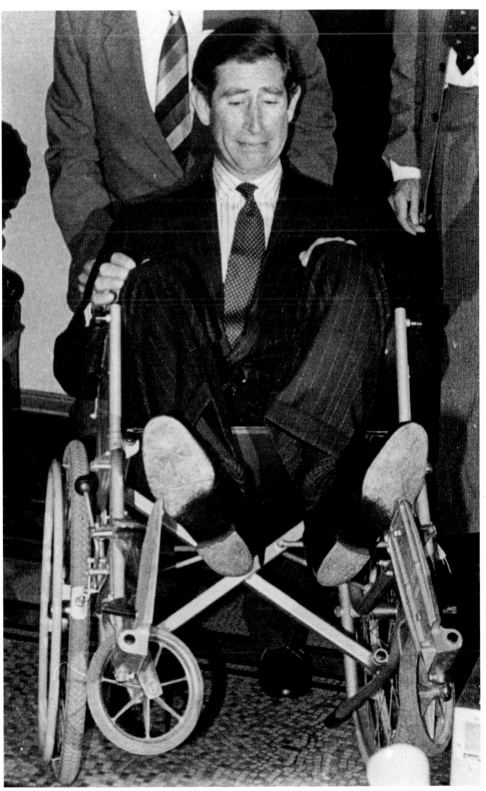

68. The Prince of Wales testing a wheelchair at the launch of a boat for disabled anglers, 1985.

The Prince of Wales disposes of considerable sums of money through his charities and raises some funds through his own efforts. His income derives not from the Civil List but from the net revenues of the Duchy of Cornwall, with its 130,000 acres of land spread across twenty-three counties. Over the years he has invested the money from the estates of deceased intestates without kin dying domiciled in Cornwall in the Duke of Cornwall's Benevolent Fund. With assets of over £1 million in 1993, it distributed £134,000 in that year.[51] In addition, Prince Charles, like other members of the royal family, has set up his own trust to distribute money, much of it raised from the royalties received on his books and films. The Prince of Wales's Charities, not to be confused with the Prince's Trust, handed out £1,367,230 in 1992 to a wide variety of projects, from health and welfare to conservation and the environment.[52]

For the Prince of Wales it is relatively easy to extract money from others, even if it is sometimes irksome; and businessmen and celebrities feel the pinch of the royal embrace just as they did in Edward VII's day. Just how much money Prince Charles has raised for charitable purposes will probably never be known, but an invitation to dinner with him can be expensive. Having him to dinner can be exorbitant. In 1985, the American magnate Armand Hammer, the Chairman of Occidental Petroleum, guaranteed Prince Charles $1 million for the United World Colleges, a movement promoted by Lord Mountbatten, simply in return for attending a gala with the Princess of Wales.[53]

The charitable demands on the Prince of Wales, some of which are inescapable, have increased because of the pressure building up in civil society. As the heir to the throne, the Prince has automatic promotion, but as he wants to leave a mark on British life he wishes to apply himself now, while the constraints on his activities are relatively few. Many people do not see voluntary work as a 'proper' job for the Prince of Wales (shades again of Edward VII), but he is in a strong position to bring about social improvements in Britain, although on a more modest scale than he might like. Despite the distractions of his private life, there is little doubt about the seriousness with which he takes his welfare role, as his biographer Jonathan Dimbleby is at pains to make evident.[54]

Dimbleby does not provide any historical background to the Prince's welfare work, but states that Prince Charles speaks out 'across a range of public issues—to an extent that none of his predecessors had ever contemplated'.[55] Edward VII would not be amused by this. One wonders whether Prince Charles himself is aware of the degree to which his family promoted charitable causes in the past? We are led to believe by Dimbleby that he sees himself as creating a distinctive welfare role of his own design. But the biographer's assertion that the Prince 'has personally contrived a significant shift in the role of the monarchy' should be taken with a pinch of salt.[56]

69. The Prince of Wales talking to Asian children on a visit to Spitalfields, East London, 1989.

The navy is perhaps not the best preparation for the life of social service the Prince of Wales now seems destined to follow. When Prince Charles left the navy, his then Private Secretary, David Checketts, rummaged through the files 'in search of guidance about the role of the heir to the throne'. According to Dimbleby, 'he drew a blank; if any wisdom had been accumulated through the ages it had not been recorded for the benefit of posterity'.[57] This episode suggests a high degree of ignorance among Palace officials about the history of the crown's voluntary work. Obviously, Lord Esher and Sir Henry Burdett were long forgotten. But Palace aides might have looked at a few books in the Royal Library, including *The Memoirs of the Duke of Windsor*. As cited earlier, the Duke of Windsor saw his role as Prince of Wales clearly enough: 'The job . . . as I tried to interpret it, was, first, to carry on associations with worthy causes outside politics and clothe them with the prestige of the Prince's high position; and, second, to bring the Monarchy, in response to new conditions, ever nearer to the people.'[58]

Prince Charles does not model himself on any member of the royal family from the past, but there are striking similarities of role, especially to Edward VII and Edward VIII as Princes of Wales. And there are striking similarities of outlook, especially to Prince Albert, who favoured 'the quiet working out of particular schemes of social improvement' and called on the rich and famous to support them.[59] Like Prince Albert, Prince Charles assumes that a sense of place and good architecture are essential to human happiness and that the commercial and charitable sectors are essential motors in the drive for social betterment. The message of many of his charities, several of which have 'community' in their title, is that social problems are best remedied by personal service, self-help and local initiative. He said so himself in a speech at the conference to launch the 'Volunteers' project in 1990. The views expressed on that occasion were entirely consistent with the address on voluntary social service, cited earlier, by Edward, Prince of Wales, in 1932.[60]

Though not enamoured of collectivism, Prince Charles is probably less hostile to the state than any member of his family in this century. Certainly, none of them has talked of partnership with government in quite the same way. Seeing himself as a catalyst in shifting ministerial thinking, he cultivated Mrs Thatcher at one time with enthusiasm. His network of contacts across the country is superior to that of most ministers, but his efforts to engage Mrs Thatcher's government in local initiatives largely failed, despite her election-night pledge in 1987 to address the problems of the inner cities. As Dimbleby points out, some matching funds were forthcoming from government for a few projects of the Prince's Business in the Community scheme, but Mrs Thatcher rejected most of the royal proposals that had implications for public expenditure.[61]

By his own account, Prince Charles wants 'to put the "Great" back into Great Britain', but is frustrated by the trail of assorted worthies and officials who are happy to eat his dinners and drink his wine but who fail to imbibe his message.[62] This suggests that he exaggerates the potential in voluntary activity and what it can achieve in partnership with a welfare bureaucracy that is given to rigidity and cheese-paring. It has been unfortunate for voluntarists that discussions about their work since the war are commonly limited to interpretations of social provision inherited from the state. Such perceptions have encouraged philanthropists to think bigger than is practicable for voluntary bodies, which are usually most effective when small and clearly focused. Furthermore, they have raised expectations of the partnership between voluntary bodies and central government to unrealistic levels.

As the Prince's own experience would imply, social partnership is more likely to work effectively when government has devolved greater responsibility for the implementation of social policy to smaller, more accountable departments and to local authorities and community groups.

But experiments in devolution, for example the creation of NHS Trusts, which were justified on the grounds of bringing hospitals closer to their communities, have not lived up to expectations. It seems that when old bureaucracies die they are resurrected in a different guise, and that decentralized organizations gravitate towards greater centralization. Attempts at reforming the health and social services in Britain suggest that as long as a higher government authority exists, it is destined to be used to stifle the very freedom of action that a policy of decentralization sets out to encourage.

Health and welfare charities cannot easily avoid government bureaucracy. Where they have made pacts with the state or taken state money they have often been let down, partly because of the comparative scale of their operations and partly because of what Prince Charles calls the 'institutionalised short-termism' endemic in British life.[63] Where they themselves grow in size, they start to show some of the same failings that are associated with government bureaucracy.[64] Charitable campaigners, royal ones included, have always been most effective where their labours are local, spontaneous and unobjectionable, in actions that prevent catastrophe or help people through it, that avert everyday disappointments or offer people the possibility of getting outside themselves into wider, shared experience. They are not in a position to move heaven and earth, certainly less so than the state.

Prince Charles is sometimes charged with lacking a coherent programme, but an approach to social ills that is based on 'community', defined here as a specific locality and not a collective abstraction, is bound to seem muddled. The philanthropic approach can rarely be called strategic, for it is essentially antithetical to social engineering and state planning. The lack of a strategic view is not so much a problem for Prince Charles as it is for the public, which has been led by successive post-war governments to assume that if it only pays its taxes it can sit back and leave the removal of social inequalities to experts. State provision has brought undoubted benefits, but has also left many members of the public with a belief in impersonal, overarching solutions. Against this background, it must be remembered that the Prince of Wales is a prince and not a minister, and what he achieves is essentially philanthropic in character. Just as his individual successes are likely to be modest, when he disappoints it is not disastrous.

★   ★   ★

The relationship between charities looking to central government and government looking to specialized charities, while often fertile, resembles a marriage in which the partners are bound to disappoint one another. It is this very disappointment that has been responsible for the criticism of government policy by so many voluntary bodies. Remote bureaucracy, cash shortages, stop-go policies, factional politics, and the further centralization of power by successive administrations have dashed the hopes of many charitable campaigners. Their complaints have been building up for years and have cut across the spectrum of government policy. And they, like other members of the public, regularly make representations to members of the royal family, on issues both great and small.

The Queen sends all politically sensitive appeals for support on to the appropriate government department. But what are her thoughts when she receives representations from endangered institutions, for example NHS hospitals with longstanding royal associations? In 1961, Her Majesty opened a set of new buildings at St Bartholomew's Hospital, including the Queen Elizabeth II Wing. 'I am confident', she said to the assembled company, 'that whatever success the future may bring, the traditions of St Bartholomew's, which reach back to the year 1123, will be carried on, as they are today, in the interests of patients.'[65] In 1992, she opened a new unit at Barts. Now a Conservative government intends to close the hospital. Built by patronage, it seems fated to be destroyed by planning.

The threatened closure of St Bartholomew's puts the Queen in an invidious position, for the crown's association with the institution goes back centuries—the government's less than fifty years. The demise of royal institutions is unusual. The monarchy has always taken care to identify itself with organizations that show signs of perpetuity. When it accepted a patronage role for state hospitals in 1948, it did not realize that they would be so vulnerable to closure; nor, it must be said, did the Ministry of Health. Does the Queen have a responsibility to Bart's and other threatened royal hospitals, including Guy's and the Queen Elizabeth Hospital for Children, which overrides the political niceties of her constitutional role? A large number of correspondents, many of them former patients, have appealed to her for support in the campaign to save Bart's. She is undoubtedly concerned about the hospital's plight; she has said so privately to the Dean of the Medical College.[66]

The Queen has not made a public statement on behalf of St Bartholomew's, although the Duke of Gloucester, the hospital's President, has rallied to its defence. She must feel it would be counterproductive to intervene, given the Conservative government's explicit disregard for historic institutions, even once-great Tory ones. It seems that ministers and their departmental planners, captivated by a managerial ethos that is insensitive to the inherited tradition, will blow out the candles to see better in the dark. As they extinguish ancient institutions like the older teaching hospitals, the monarchy itself becomes more exposed. The crown may be in greater danger from the market-driven wing of conservatism than from socialism.

70. Princess Anne and the Minister of Health, Kenneth Clarke, at a meeting to launch the Save the Children Asian Mother and Baby Campaign, 1984.

When members of the royal family do raise their heads above the parapet, it is usually prompted by representations from 'their' institutions. In 1990 alone, the year of Mrs Thatcher's political demise, Prince Charles defended the rights of pensioners and took up the plight of the disabled, Princess Anne decried the shortage of nursery places, and Prince Philip berated monetarist short-sightedness and called for a switch to renewable energy sources. Since then there have been other royal interventions. The Prince of Wales has raised the sensitive issue of homelessness and attacked government proposals for community care.[67] As mentioned, the Duke of Gloucester champions St Bartholomew's against the government. Many a minister has had a delicate meeting with a member of the royal family in recent years, or has had to write a careful letter explaining the government's position.

Intriguingly, few protested in the early 1990s when members of the royal family disregarded the constitutional niceties and pronounced on political issues. As Ferdinand Mount argues, there seemed 'to be a positive expectation that the royal family [would] give a lead, not just by the example of their lives of service, but by their ideas and opinions'.[68] This leading role is not a new one for the monarchy. It harks back to the nineteenth century, when charity, with the royal family in tow, was ascendant. The role has re-emerged because of the reinvigoration of civil society and the growing disillusionment with politics in general and Parliament in particular. In some respects the crown was filling the vacuum left by the Labour Party. In an interesting configuration of events, the Labour Party's revival took shape just at the time when royal scandals were reducing the monarchy's effectiveness and standing in public esteem.

The Labour Party has re-emerged with a greater sensitivity to voluntary traditions than at any time since the war. With ideology in decline and the Labour leader Tony Blair lamenting that his party has discounted the charitable sector and 'the citizenship of contribution', there is fresh hope for a consensus on the role of charity and its relationship with the state. 'It is by casting aside the rigid dogmas of the past', said Blair in 1994, 'that we begin to see a new and exciting role for the voluntary sector—not an optional extra but a vital part of our economy, helping to achieve many of our key social objectives.'[69] This little speech to a Jewish charity was seen by the press as a move to the 'right'. It was quite a confession by the leader of a party that had so strongly identified with state planning in the past. Much of it could have been written by Prince Charles or John Major, though they might disagree about what 'community' actually means.

It would appear that the Labour Party is shedding its collectivist zeal and is coming around to pluralism and decentralization in social policy. If so, it would be sweet news to the Palace, which expended such thought and energy in the reign of George V to emasculate Clause Four socialism. Prince Philip was quoted in the *Daily Telegraph* in 1994 as saying that the crown had helped Britain to 'get over . . . the development of an urban industrial intelligentsia reasonably easily'. He was simply stating what for him was obvious, though it seemed to upset a few MPs and journalists who perhaps knew less about the monarchy than they thought they did.[70] If Tony Blair wishes to dissociate his Party from past Labour dogma, he might pay tribute to the monarchy for helping, albeit unintentionally, to save British socialism from itself during its doctrinaire phases.

Labour's rediscovery of civil society and its own traditions of mutual aid cannot be understood without reference to the collapse of the Soviet Union. For a century, left-wing ideologues had an antipathy to voluntarism; but now that 'real existing socialism' has shown itself to be bankrupt, those 'bourgeois freedoms' offered by civil society, often derided as a deceit played on the proletariat, have more to recommend them. Once again Britain shows signs of a shift in attitude, a swing of the pendulum in social perception. No one doubts that economic dislocation creates severe social problems, yet we hear less today about the links between distress and the structural faults of capitalism. Rather, we are told about 'the crisis of the inner cities' and 'the slow collapse of the family', which are best addressed by the devolution of the 'caring services' to the localities.[71] An article in the *Guardian* argued that 'the health of the body depends on the health of . . . the parish or neighbourhood, with which people can readily identify'.[72] The remark could have come equally naturally from a Victorian drumming up support for a boot club or from Prince Charles discussing one of his community projects.

There are few people around today who still believe that government can build Jerusalem, much less ban tobacco advertising. The old socialist doctrine that the state and society are synonymous, which encouraged ever-greater centralization of power, had an element of *hubris* about it. As voluntarists had pointed out before the war, if government takes responsibility for everything only government can be blamed. But the Labour Party has no monopoly on the post-war politics of imperiousness. Under Mrs Thatcher the belief in central control and ministerial responsibility was so categorical that when an emergency bed closed or a pensioner died of cold, party officials leapt in front of the cameras in a frenzied defence of government spending on the social services.

Whichever political party is in power, the government is likely to continue to shoulder the primary burden of social provision. But for all its inventive intervention in family life, the state and its mechanisms are widely seen today as too blunt and impersonal to provide security for the British family without reinforcement from charities and volunteers. There is a growing belief, as one philanthropic sympathizer put it back in the 1950s, that 'the distress of an individual or the collapse of a family circle really *is* due to special individual misfortune or defect of character, and really *does* need an individual approach'.[73] There are signs that the Victorian emphasis on bringing out qualities of character that might help people to help themselves is coming back into prominence. In the new 'civic socialism', as in 'civic conservatism', the words 'duty' and 'self-help' are coming into focus.[74]

The question remains: can government, whatever its political coloration, develop a more beneficial social policy, less subject to factional politics and central control?[75] In other words, can it create a more balanced, efficient partnership between uniform state assistance and diverse voluntary provision, which has been so elusive in the past? If a future government should make the attempt, ministers and civil servants may find the royal family an effective ally. But oblivious to the monarchy's influence in civil society, the Labour Party proposes to reduce the number of royal family members undertaking public duties. (Among other things, this would restrict those independent royal criticisms of government policy.) The Conservatives, too, seem unaware of the royal family's historic role as an agency of social empowerment. As the experience of the Prince of Wales would suggest, they have shown little imagination in cooperating with the crown in the public interest.

Whatever the direction of government policy, the monarchy will take notice, if only because its voluntary bodies will require it to do so. *New* forms of partnership on offer between the state and the charitable sector would be of special interest. Meanwhile, members of the royal family will continue to express their views, as Prince Philip did in the Arnold Goodman Charity Lecture, entitled 'Charity or Public Benefit', in June 1994. They will also support experimental initiatives, while building bridges between charities as well as between charities and departments of state. Whether they appreciate it or not, the monarchy has an instrumental part to play, for with one foot in the state and the other in the voluntary sector, no other institution is in a more pivotal position to bring them together. The Prince of Wales wrote to John Major in 1990 that the role of government should be that of a 'strategic co-ordinator'.[76] But at present, with government reluctant to untangle the welfare knot, it is a role that the Prince himself has been trying to fill.

In some respects, the Welfare Monarchy is an underdeveloped national resource. Even Palace officials do not entirely grasp its implications. Lord Charteris, the Queen's former Private Secretary, remarked in 1995 that 'it's only the monarch who matters'.[77] The research on which this book is based suggests that other members of the royal family, the dutiful ones at any rate, *do* matter. With fewer constraints on their activities than the Queen, they play a conspicuous role in making those endearing and beneficial connections with the nation's civil institutions. A streamlined monarchy has attractions, not least for the image of the crown in a time of republican revival; but it may prove shortsighted if it results in members of the royal family withdrawing from their public duties. Already, there are 300 societies worried about finding a royal patron to replace the Queen Mother when she dies. One problem for the monarchy in the next generation may be a shortage of working members, not a superfluity.

★   ★   ★

It is worth recalling A.J.P. Taylor's remark that voluntarists, 'a great army of busybodies, . . . were the active people of England and provided the ground swell of her history'.[78] One thing that is clear is that over the centuries the crown has become inextricably linked with this 'great army of busybodies'. Has there ever been a more dynamic alliance outside politics in British history? Obviously, not all voluntarists are monarchists, including many of those individuals who have steered members of the royal family on official visits ever so politely through their charities. Indeed, some of them have had republican sympathies, which they have repressed because the crown was so beneficial to their purposes. In turn, members of the royal family have not always been enthusiastic about the causes which they have patronized. Yet they have drawn enormous strength from their charitable allegiances.

Since the Palace crises in the early 1990s, which attracted so much adverse publicity to the crown, critics have become more sensitive to members of the royal family using good causes to improve their own public image. Given the obsessive media coverage of royal scrapes and the simultaneous resurgence of republicanism, it may be said that the monarchy now needs the voluntary sector more than the voluntary sector needs the monarchy. There is no sign that the royal family is being deserted by its charitable allies. None of the Duchess of York's charities has censured her for her indiscretions. If anything, they have exploited her vulnerability to garner more attention for their causes. When the Princess of Wales announced her retreat from public life at the end of 1993, 'it sent', as one journalist put it, 'shock waves through the charity world registering at the upper end of the royal Richter scale'.[79]

Locked into its welfare role by custom and interest, the monarchy remains well placed to make the most of its voluntary associations. Its collective patronage now extends to nearly 3,500 organizations, about 500 of them foreign or Commonwealth.[80] Apart from the regiments, clubs, universities and professional bodies, members of the royal family are active in virtually every area of charitable activity, from prenatal to geriatric care, from playing fields to the preservation of ancient monuments, from housing reform to the world's wildlife. Seventy-five per cent of the top twenty fund-raising charities in Britain have royal patronage.[81] As ever, few things promote a charitable cause more effectively than a royal appearance, or, short of that, a royal subscription.

The crown has always used modest, symbolic donations as a way of giving a psychological boost to philanthropic campaigns. With notable exceptions such as George III and Queen Adelaide, members of the royal family have not given away vast sums of money, partly because those to whom they give are then enabled to raise substantial donations from others, and this in turn makes it possible for the royal family to spread the benefit of its own charity more widely. The Queen herself does not formally head special appeals, but the very association of her name with a charity gives a campaign greater weight. When an appeal is launched for a cause of national importance, she often makes a donation. So does Prince Philip, whose Edinburgh Trust, set up in 1959, distributed £49,000 in grants in 1993.[82] The size of 'the egg laid in the nest to encourage the hen to lay' is never disclosed in particular cases, for fear of incurring invidious comparisons.

71. The Princess of Wales visiting an old age centre in Hyderabad, India, 1992.

It is now possible, however, to discover how much the Queen gives away each year in total and the general pattern of her charitable giving. This information is available through the annual reports of the Privy Purse Charitable Trust, which was established in 1987 to distribute funds at the Queen's behest from her private income. In 1994, the Trust received £261,612 in donations, and its assets, which are invested mainly in United Kingdom equities and unit trusts, stood at £1,134,850.[83] At the Queen's request, the trustees, chaired by the Keeper of the Privy Purse, Sir Shane Blewitt, are responsible for making donations to a wide variety of charities. While the figures cited below suggest that the Queen has a penchant for religious and youth causes, we should not read too much into this, for she inherited many of her 800 patronages from George VI.[84]

	1994	1993
	£	£
Ecclesiastical	102,988	92,264
Youth, school, sports and institutional charities	66,944	84,828
Social, benevolent and welfare charities	16,603	7,871
Armed service and public utility charities	5,175	5,000
Medical charities	11,349	6,200
Charities for animals	2,330	2,150
Miscellaneous	2,996	12,554
	208,385	210,867

On the figures cited above, the Queen is now distributing about twenty times more than Queen Victoria did to charitable campaigns a century before; but, taking inflation into account, there has been a decline in the monetary value of the crown's charitable distribution. On the other hand, the calls on Queen Victoria's sympathies were more urgent and the government far less committed to picking up the bill for social provision.

Financial matters aside, one of the striking things about the Queen's patronage list is the large number of organizations on it that were in existence in the reign of Queen Victoria.[85] Historically, most charitable societies have not been long-lived. Many disappeared because of improvements in the trade cycle. Others became obsolete with medical or technological advance. Others still did not withstand the nationalization of welfare after the war. Yet the longevity of so many British charities is remarkable. More than a few of the Queen's patronages, including the British and Foreign School Society, the National Society for Promoting Religious Education, the Royal Humane Society and the Thomas Coram Foundation (the Foundling Hospital), have royal associations dating back to the reign of George III, if not earlier. Their survival suggests both the continuities in the human predicament and the durability of the ancient institutions.

★   ★   ★

The collapse of communism in the USSR and the West, which has had such interesting effects on British socialism, was seen by the monarchy as convincing proof of the incalculable value of historical continuity and voluntary traditions. Having despised Bolshevism since 1918, Buckingham Palace rejoiced as the old enemy sank into oblivion and civil society began to re-emerge in Eastern Europe. In her Christmas message to Britain and the Commonwealth in 1991, the Queen surveyed the momentous changes that had taken place in the world during the forty years since her accession. In a deceptively simple address she highlighted the voluntary work of 'the ordinary citizen'. She tied her speech to events in the former communist empire and reminded her audience that the peoples there had only recently 'broken the mould of autocracy'.[86]

The Queen's reference to the liberation of Eastern Europe was essentially a prologue to her principal theme, 'the elements which form the bedrock of our own free way of life—so highly valued and so easily taken for granted'. In her view, the voluntary service of ordinary citizens was the foundation of democratic life, a safeguard against oppressive regimes. As she put it in a revealing sentence, 'democracy depends, not on political structures, but on the goodwill and the sense of responsibility of each and every citizen'. Among the most important elements in a 'free society' was the willingness of individuals to play a part in the life of their community. 'I am', she added, 'constantly amazed by the generosity of donors and subscribers, great and small, who give so willingly and often towards the enjoyment of others. Without them . . . voluntary organisations simply would not exist.'[87]

The Queen concluded her broadcast with a solemn pledge to carry on the royal tradition of public service which she had inherited from her father. 'You have given me, in return, your loyalty and understanding, and for that I give you my heartfelt thanks.'[88] By linking her own voluntary service, and that of George VI, to the loyalty of her subjects, the Queen made explicit the unwritten pact that she believed to exist between the royal family and the British public, a pact characterized by reciprocal obligations and benefits. As the nation's premier voluntarist, she had illuminated the first principle of a Welfare Monarchy: in exchange for the royal family's support in a myriad social causes, the Queen asked for 'loyalty and understanding'.

Unspoken in the Queen's address was the corollary that, through its promotion of voluntary bodies, the monarchy was itself part of the 'bedrock' of civil society and a check on the arbitrary power of the state.

Was this corollary unspoken because it had not been fully thought through by Buckingham Palace? Or was it simply impolitic to suggest that Britain needed a vigilant and effective voluntary sector to keep government in check? Buckingham Palace, of course, wishes to distance itself from sensitive political pronouncements, for it believes it must appear to be above the political fray. But this speech implied that the monarch herself knows that she has a role beyond the prescriptions of Bagehot.

As we have seen, the 'dignified' part of the constitution could also make claims to being an 'efficient' proponent of a traditional form of democratic polity through its age-old affiliation with civil society. Given the decline of ideology and the recent moves by all political parties towards the centre, there are indications that the participatory democracy of voluntary association and community action may come into greater communion with the representative democracy of cabinet government. If it does, the monarchy is well placed to take advantage. Divisive political dogma, whether from the left or the right, is damaging to the monarchy, for the crown can hardly be seen to symbolize a unified nation when the nation is divided ideologically. On the other hand, a non-ideological age, which offered the prospect of a more fruitful social partnership between civil and state institutions, would augur well for British royalty. After all, nothing has done more to endear the monarchy to the public since the reign of George III than its welfare work and its cultivation of adaptive civil institutions, and latterly also of state ones.

The robustness of philanthropic traditions constitutes an improbable legacy in an age of the ascendant state.[89] But now that centralized state welfare has lost its plausibility as a panacea for the nation's ills, just as charity once did, perhaps we can take a more balanced view of the contribution philanthropy has made to British life and more fully appreciate its character. In the past, charity's proponents overrated its capacities, which encouraged collectivists to underrate its virtues. Those virtues have as much to do with the act of giving as the gift. From the diversity and principled rivalry and the love of the *ad hoc* remedy that typify voluntary action, the nation has gained immeasurable moral and democratic benefits. These may be the most enduring legacies of those philanthropists of the past, misguided or wise, whose works radiated from the slums and the suburbs, from the City and the Palace.

★   ★   ★

The emergence of a welfare role is not singular to the British monarchy, for other European courts have developed their own distinctive charitable traditions. Yet the British royal family's voluntary activity, whether through patronage or tours and outings to communities, industry and

Empire, has been on a unique, global scale. Rich in counterpoint and variation, it should be seen against the background of the waning of the crown's political power and the emasculation of those ancient ideas of nobility, which did not put a premium on social service. As the crown's political-cum-warrior traditions gave way to charitable patronage and active benevolence, kings and princes, rather reluctantly, took off their uniforms and donned middle-class dress to open bazaars and visit hospitals.

What has taken place constitutes what may be called the feminization of the monarchy. The female members of the royal family have been vital to the development of the crown's welfare role. They bear out a theme that once suffused the charitable literature. The Victorian philanthropist and feminist Josephine Butler put it directly in 1869, when she wrote that the parochial system of personal ministration, with its corollary of recreating domestic life in institutions, was essentially 'feminine' in character, while large legislative welfare systems were 'masculine'.[90] Such generalizations should not be overstated when applied to the crown, however, for the monarchy's loss of a high political role made it increasingly susceptible to voluntary causes in any case. And its social work generally, whether carried out by male or female members of the royal family, has favoured personal service over state intervention.

There has been a measure of calculation in the rise of the Welfare Monarchy in Britain. Prince Albert, whose charities were of a 'masculine' complexion, had an idea of where he wanted philanthropy to take the crown in the post-1832 constitutional settlement. That old reprobate Edward VII consciously gave the monarchy a facelift through a masterful display of charitable enterprise. So did George V and Queen Mary, in response to democratic and socialist pressures. But in general, the superscription that introduces this book, that 'a man never rises so high as when he does not know where he is going', applies to most members of the royal family over the past 250 years. When they carried out their charitable work, most of them thought of themselves as doing what was unavoidable, or doing their duty out of conscience or in response to public pressure. Essentially, the rise of the Welfare Monarchy has been the fortuitous result of the accumulating effects of a vast number of royal actions undertaken more or less in an *ad hoc* and piecemeal fashion and not as part of any grand design.

The gradual separation of the monarchy from government over the centuries is evident, and in the crown's survival its exercise of its head-of-state position should not be underestimated.[91] But the constitutional and ceremonial roles of the monarchy have tended to obscure what was taking place just below the political surface or behind the Palace window dressing. Since the Second World War, the royal family has adapted the tradition, which dates back to George III, of making the monarchy the

72. Queen Elizabeth II laying a wreath in memory of Britain's war dead at the Cenotaph, Whitehall, 1992.

head and focus of civil society through its welfare work. Beyond that, royal philanthropy serves well the monarchy's wider intention of providing the unifying symbol of the nation. Yet the significance of the social side of the monarchy's national role through its promotion of welfare causes is largely lost on the crown's defenders, who, having read little since Bagehot, continue to dwell on those familiar nostrums of magic and high politics.

When republicans assemble they too dwell on high politics and the constitution, while lingering over the costs, the scandals and the symbolism of royalty.[92] Whatever the merits of their case, they, like the monarchists, leave the monarchy's welfare role out of the equation. Certainly, the abolition of the crown would create a presidential system, turn 'subjects' into 'citizens', and save public money, though perhaps only in the short term. Beyond that lies greater uncertainty. In this debate, as in so much else in politics, temperament is fate. But if there is a lesson from the past, it is that reform usually has unforeseen and unintended consequences. For the circumspect, who share the crown's suspicion of what Prince Albert described as 'exceedingly expensive' political experiments, the dangers of republicanism seem real enough, the benefits less obvious. If Britain did become a republic, it would be an unhappy irony if its 'citizens' found themselves with fewer civil liberties than they had enjoyed as 'subjects' of the crown.

Britain's philanthropic traditions, so instrumental in civic life and liberty, are profound. The crown's contribution to these traditions has been and continues to be enabling. The abolition of the monarchy, whatever the benefits, would mark another stage in the perfection of the state monolith. Moreover, it would eliminate that part of the constitution that serves as a buffer between the state and society. It could be argued that this is a role that an elected president could not sustain nor endure. To be sure, the United States has a vibrant voluntary sector without a monarchy, but it has developed its own charitable customs within a quite different social, fiscal and constitutional context. The first lady, however many her charities, cannot be compared to the Queen as a focus of civil society.

Republicans and monarchists alike would do well to recall the line of Dr Johnson:

> How small, of all that human hearts endure,
> That part which laws or kings can cause or cure!

Undoubtedly, Britain's voluntary traditions would survive a republic, as they have survived religious decline and the ascendant state. Still, the abolition of the monarchy would destabilize thousands of existing institutions, many of them with royal charters. Where would they turn to steady their finances and to reassure their supporters and those who depend on their services—to the president? If to the state, it would only further increase its costs, and its influence, at the expense of their independence. But this is academic, for barring cataclysm or self-destruction, the monarchy is only likely to be in real danger when the begging letters cease to arrive at Buckingham Palace.

A Note on Sources

This book attempts to bring together two distinctive sets of literature, on the monarchy and on philanthropy, which in the past have been treated in isolation from each other. My object was to rescue the history of philanthropy from parochialism and that of the crown from the straitjacket of biography and high politics. Whether I have succeeded in this must be left to others to decide, but I hope at least that some of the sources for the study of British philanthropy, and royal philanthropy in particular, will be better known as a result of the research. No doubt readers will find that I have overlooked familiar institutions, or less familiar ones in which they have an interest. Looking through the notes and the index, I am acutely aware of just how many royal societies I have omitted, from Alexandra Rose Day to the Zebra Trust.

The material available for the subject is inexhaustible, and I cannot pretend to have used more than a fraction of it. The British Library provided most of the printed sources and some of the manuscripts. The Royal Archives, cited 'RA' in the notes, have given me access to a wide range of materials, including patronage books, diaries, accounts, personal letters, and the correspondence of Private Secretaries and keepers of the Privy Purse, but they contain more that is relevant to the subject than I have had the insight or tenacity to pursue. In a study that turned into something of a general reassessment of the monarchy, rather a lot in the Royal Archives seemed relevant.

Charitable records and the associated sources for the study of civil society are, if anything, more copious than the records of the crown. But one of the problems for the study of royal philanthropy, like other subjects to do with the monarchy, is the tendency of institutions to be highly protective of their royal materials. Just as a hundred-year closure rule was placed on royal files in the Public Record Office until recently, contemporary charities often require special permission to make available the most innocuous documents which relate to the monarchy. Fortunately, the Royal Archives were able to provide material on the crown's relations with many individual charities for the period up to the present reign.

Notes

I have not provided a separate bibliography, but the references to each chapter should provide a running guide to sources. The place of publication is Great Britain unless otherwise stated. References are given in full at the first citation in each chapter.

Chapter 1

1 Paul Langford, *A Polite and Commercial People: England 1727–1783* (1989), p. 481.
2 Thomas Biddulph, *National Affliction Improved: In Three Sermons* (1820), p. 57.
3 Quoted in David Owen, *English Philanthropy, 1660–1960* (1964), p. 89.
4 Pat Thane, 'Government and Society in England and Wales, 1750–1914', in *The Cambridge Social History of Britain*, ed. F.M.L. Thompson, 3 vols. (1990), vol. 3, p. 2.
5 Roy Porter, *English Society in the Eighteenth Century*, (1982), pp. 145–7; see also B.R. Mitchell, *British Historical Statistics* (1988), p. 605.
6 Frederick Morton Eden, *The State of the Poor*, 3 vols. (1797), vol. 1, p. 465; see also Owen, *English Philanthropy, 1660–1960*, p. 100.
7 Anthony Highmore, *Pietas Londinensis* (1810), p. 967.
8 Paul Langford, *Public Life and the Propertied Englishman, 1689–1798* (1991), p. 493.
9 Quoted in Owen, *English Philanthropy, 1660–1960*, p. 100.
10 For a general introduction to British charity that gives emphasis to religion, see Frank Prochaska, *The Voluntary Impulse: Philanthropy in Modern Britain* (1988); see also F.K. Prochaska, 'Philanthropy', in *The Cambridge Social History of Britain, 1750–1950*, vol. 3, pp. 357–93.
11 Owen, *English Philanthropy, 1660–1960*, p. 11; Langford, *Public Life and the Propertied Englishman, 1689–1789*, pp. 491–2. On London, see Donna T. Andrew, *Philanthropy and Police: London Charity in the Eighteenth Century* (Princeton, 1989).
12 Linda Colley, 'The Apotheosis of George III: Loyalty, Royalty and the British Nation 1760–1820', *Past and Present*, 102 (February 1984), p. 95; see also Mark Bloch, *The Royal Touch: Sacred Monarchy and Scrofula in England and France* (1973), pp. 222–3; R.O. Buchholz, ' "Nothing but Ceremony": Queen Anne and the Limitations of Royal Ritual', *Journal of British Studies*, 30, no. 3, July 1991, pp. 288–323. On the monarchy and Royal Maundy see Brian Robinson, *Silver Pennies and Linen Towels: The Story of the Royal Maundy* (1992).
13 *Gentleman's Magazine*, January 1731, p. 24. A surviving Privy Purse account book for the years 1737–49 does not record any benefactions to charitable institutions, but it does include small sums paid to distressed individuals. See British Library, Add. MSS. 27908.

14 *The Open Heart and Purse; or, British Liberality Display'd* (1740), p. 3. See Langford, *Public Life and the Propertied Englishman, 1689–1789*, p. 492.

15 *Autobiography of Mary Granville, Mrs Delany*, 3 vols. (1862), ed. the Rt. Hon. Lady Llanover, second series, vol. 1, p. 188. I would like to thank Matthew Kilburn for this reference.

16 John Watkins, *Memoirs of Her Most Excellent Majesty Sophia-Charlotte, Queen of Great Britain* (1819), p. 233.

17 *The History and Statutes of the Royal Infirmary of Edinburgh* (1778), p. 8; *The Annual Hampshire Repository* (1799), vol. 1, p. 57.

18 J. Blomfield, *St. George's 1733–1933* (1933), pp. 12, 20.

19 R.H. Nichols and F. A Wray, *The History of the Foundling Hospital, London* (1935), p. 18.

20 John Cannon and Ralph Griffiths, *The Oxford Illustrated History of the British Monarchy* (1988), p. 308.

21 Delbert A. Evans and Howard L.G. Redmond, *The Romance of the British Voluntary Hospital Movement* ([1930]), p. 199.

22 Bacon, 'On Nobility', in *Essays*.

23 *London Chronicle*, 8 September 1768, vol. 24, p. 239. I would like to thank Matthew Kilburn for this reference.

24 Lacey Baldwin Smith, *Henry VIII: The Mask of Royalty* (1971), pp. 2, 77.

25 *The Works of the Late Right Honourable Henry St. John, Lord Viscount Bolingbroke*, 8 vols (1809), vol. 4, pp. 281, 324.

26 Hannah More, *Hints Towards Forming the Character of a Young Princess*, 2 vols. (1805), vol. 2, p. 15 and passim. See also Hannah More, Preface, *Moral Sketches of Prevailing Opinions and Manners* (1821).

27 Hannah More, 'Daniel', *Sacred Dramas* (1782), p. 241.

28 *The Life of William Wilberforce*, ed. Robert Isaac Wilberforce and Samuel Wilberforce, 5 vols (1838), vol. 2, p. 460.

29 W.J. Sparrow, *Knight of the White Eagle: A Biography of Sir Benjamin Thompson, Count Romford, 1753–1814* (1964), p. 108.

30 M.G. Jones, *Hannah More* (1952), p. 109.

31 Hannah More, *Thoughts on the Importance of the Manners of the Great* (1788), p. 116.

32 Thomas Gisborne, *An Enquiry into the Duties of Men in the Higher and Middle Classes of Society in Great Britain* (1794), p. 53.

33 Colley, 'The Apotheosis of George III', pp. 104, 126.

34 There is a stimulating discussion of the changing image of George III in Linda Colley, *Britons: Forging the Nation, 1707–1837* (1992), chapter 5.

35 More, *Moral Sketches of Prevailing Opinions and Manners*, p. 85.

36 *The Works of John Wesley*, 14 vols (1872), vol. 11, p. 16.

37 John Brooke, *King George III* (1985), p. 361.

38 *The Reports of the Society for Bettering the Comforts and Increasing the Condition of the Poor*, 5 vols. (1798–1808), vol. 3, p. 66.

39 Brooke, *King George III*, p. 215.

40 *Ibid.*

41 *Ibid.*

42 The figure of £14,000 was widely cited at the time of George III's death. See Richard Grimes, *George the Third, a True Israelite: A Funeral Sermon* (1820), p. 29; Biddulph, *National Affliction Improved*, p. 57.

43 In addition to those charities mentioned in the text George III was Patron of the Royal Hospital of St Katherine's (vested in Queen Charlotte upon their marriage), the Humane Society for the Recovery of Persons apparently Drowned, the Royal Lancasterian Association, and Charterhouse. Apart from the records of the charities themselves, *The Royal Kalendar and Court and City Register* and Highmore, *Pietas Londinensis* are useful starting points to track down royal patronages.

44 Edward Jenner, *An Inquiry into the Causes and Effects of the Variolae Vaccinae . . . a Disease Known by the Name of Cow Pox* (1800), pp. vi–vii; Blomfield, *St George's*, p. 11. See also Derrick Baxby, 'A Death from

Inoculated Smallpox in the English Royal Family', *Medical History*, 28 (1984), pp. 303–7,

45   John Baron, *The Life of Edward Jenner, M.D.*, 2 vols. (1827, 1838), vol. 1, p. 572.

46   *Ibid.*, pp. 327, 495, 576; *Royal Jennerian Society, for the Extermination of the Small-Pox, by the Extension of Vaccination* (1817), p. 16.

47   J. Heneage Jesse, *Memoirs of the Life and Reign of King George the Third*, 3 vols. (1867), vol. 2, p. 59.

48   For a description of Lancaster's methods, see Highmore, *Pietas Londinensis*, pp. 773–80; *The Philanthropist* (1811), vol. 1, pp. 81–86.

49   William Corston, *A Brief Sketch of the Life of Joseph Lancaster* (1840), pp. 15–17. See also, David Salmon, *Joseph Lancaster* (1904), pp. 18–19.

50   Rev. J. Richardson, *Recollections, Political, Literary, Dramatic, and Miscellaneous of the Last Half Century*, 2 vols. (1856), vol. 2, p. 264.

51   Edward Holt, *The Public and Domestic Life of His Most Gracious Majesty, George the Third*, 2 vols. (1820), vol. 1, pp. 283–4; Watkins, *Memoirs of Her Most Excellent Majesty Sophia-Charlotte*, p. 306.

52   Brooke, *King George III*, p. 286.

53   Grimes, *George the Third, a True Israelite*, p. 20; John Howard, *The State of the Prisons in England and Wales* (1780), p. 337.

54   The statue was never erected, for Howard declined it. Jesse, *Memoirs of the Life and Reign of King George the Third*, vol. 3, p. 13.

55   William Henry MacMenemey, *A History of the Worcester Royal Infirmary* (1947), pp. 119–20.

56   Watkins, *Memoirs of Her Most Excellent Majesty Sophia-Charlotte*, pp. 390–91. See also *A Diary of the Royal Tour, in June, July, August, and September, 1789* (1789).

57   *The Times*, 24 August 1789, p. 3.

58   *Ibid*, 24 October 1809, p. 1.

59   Colley, *Britons: Forging the Nation, 1707–1837*, p. 222.

60   See advertisements, *The Times*, 24 and 25 October 1809; 8 February 1887, p. 3.

61   Holt, *The Public and Domestic Life of His Most Gracious Majesty, George the Third*, vol. 2, p. 284. See also Nichols and Wray, *The History of the Foundling Hospital*, p. 156.

62   A. Aspinall, *The Later Correspondence of George III*, 5 vols. (1962–70), vol. 5, pp. 409, 424–5.

63   Highmore, *Pietas Londinensis*, p. vi.

64   More, *Moral Sketches of Prevailing Opinions and Manners*, p. xiii.

65   Jesse, *Memoirs of the Life and Reign of King George the Third*, vol. 2, p. 12.

66   Watkins, *Memoirs of Her Most Excellent Majesty Sophia-Charlotte*, p. 391. For an eyewitness account of this event, see *A Diary of the Royal Tour . . . 1789*, p. 86.

67   Percy Black, *The Mystique of Modern Monarchy* (1953), p. 59.

68   *Ibid.*, p. 26.

69   Olwen Hedley, *Queen Charlotte* (1975), p. 90.

70   *The Times*, 7 July 1814, p. 3.

71   Hedley, *Queen Charlotte*, p. 92.

72   Thomas Williams, *A Brief Memoir of Her Late Majesty Queen Charlotte* (1819), p. 69; Watkins, *Memoirs of Her Most Excellent Majesty Sophia-Charlotte*, pp. 598–9.

73   Williams, *A Brief Memoir of Her Late Majesty Queen Charlotte*, p. 66; see also *The Royal Encyclopedia*, ed. Ronald Allison and Sarah Riddell (1991), p. 546.

74   Watkins, *Memoirs of Her Most Excellent Majesty Sophia-Charlotte*, p. 189. On the Magdalen Hospital, see Andrew, *Philanthropy and Police*, pp. 119–27.

75   *Ibid*, pp. 314–15.

76   Williams, *A Brief Memoir of Her Late Majesty Queen Charlotte*, p. 59.

77   Watkins, *Memoirs of Her Most Excellent Majesty Sophia-Charlotte*, pp. 578, 599–600.

78   Williams, *A Brief Memoir of Her Late Majesty Queen Charlotte*, p. 69–73. For further information on Queen Charlotte's will, see Hedley, *Queen Charlotte*, pp. 303–4, 321.

79   Christopher Hibbert, *George IV: Regent and King, 1811–1830* (1973), p. 124.

80   Sarah Trimmer, *The Oeconomy of*

Charity, 2 vols. (1801), vol. 1, pp. 4, 10.

81 For a glimpse into day-to-day life at court, see *Court and Private Life in the Time of Queen Charlotte: Being the Journals of Mrs Papendiek*, ed. Mrs Vernon Delves Broughton, 2 vols. (1887).

82 Rev. S. Piggott, *Female Virtue and Domestic Religion Recommended by the Example of our Late Illustrious Queen Charlotte* (1818), p. 2.

83 Lady Rose Weigall, *A Brief Memoir of the Princess Charlotte of Wales* (1874), pp. 35–8.

84 *Letters of the Princess Charlotte, 1811– 1817*, ed. A. Aspinall (1949), p. 38.

85 *The Autobiography of Miss Knight*, ed. Roger Fulford (1960), p. 133.

86 *Memoirs of Prince Leopold* (1817), pp. 12–13.

87 *Letters of the Princess Charlotte, 1811– 1817*, p. 245.

88 *Ibid*.

89 *The Times*, 22 August 1816, p. 3.

90 John Belcham, 'Orator Hunt': Henry Hunt and English Working-Class Radicalism* (1985), pp. 36, 51.

91 The Hermit of Marlow, *An Address to the People on the Death of Princess Charlotte* ([1818]), p. 6.

92 Thomas Paine, *Rights of Man: Part the Second*, 2nd edn (1792), pp. 69–70.

93 *Select Extracts and Beauties, taken from One Hundred and Twelve Sermons Delivered from the Pulpit on the Occasion of the Demise and Funeral of Her Royal Highness the Princess Charlotte of Wales* (1818), p. 1; see also *Memoirs of the Late Princess Charlotte Augusta of Wales and Saxe Coburg* (1818).

94 *A Sketch of the Life and Character of Princess Amelia* (1811), pp. 5, 44.

95 Ford K. Brown, *Fathers of the Victorians* (1961), pp. 312, 350.

96 See Frank Prochaska, 'The Many Faces of Lady Jane Grey', *History Today* 35 (October 1985), pp. 35–40.

97 RA 19033; *The Philanthropist* (1814), vol. 4, p. 329 and passim.

98 F.K. Prochaska, *Women and Philanthropy in Nineteenth-Century England* (1980), p. 2.

99 RA 19033.

100 *City of London Truss Society for the Relief of the Ruptured Poor throughout the Kingdom* (1818), p. 3.

101 L. Gluck Rosenthal, *A Biographical Memoir of His Late Royal Highness the Duke of Sussex* (1846), p. 13. The notices in *The Times* are a good source for the Duke of Sussex's charitable activities. See, for example, the advertisement for Catholic Charitable Institutions on 16 June 1820, p. 2.

102 His patronages can be traced in the *Royal Kalendar* and advertisements in *The Times*.

103 BL, Add. MSS. 27823, ff. 42–43.

104 Quoted in Rosenthal, *A Biographical Memoir of His late Royal Highness the Duke of Sussex*, p. 23.

105 Roger Fulford, *Royal Dukes, Queen Victoria's 'Wicked Uncles'* (1933), p. 318; McKenzie Porter, *Overture to Victoria* (1961), p. 102. For a list of the Duke of Cambridge's patronages see the *Gentleman's Magazine* (1850), vol. 127, p. 205.

106 *Annual Register . . . of the Year 1850* (1851), pp. 245–6; *The Times*, 15 July 1845, p. 4.

107 *Gentleman's Magazine* (1850), vol. 127, p. 206.

108 *Ibid.*; see also *The Times*, 9 July 1850, p. 5.

109 *The Times*, 20 November 1851, p. 5.

110 *Gentleman's Magazine* (1806), vol. 76, p. 473; (1850), vol. 127, p. 206.

111 Holt, *The Public and Domestic Life of His Most Gracious Majesty, George the Third*, vol. 2, p. 66.

112 Anthony Highmore, *Philanthropia Metropolitana* (1822), p. v; see also Baron, *The Life of Edward Jenner, M.D.*, vol. 1, pp. 366, 371.

113 Charles Greville, *The Greville Memoirs 1814–1860*, ed. Lytton Strachey and Roger Fulford, 8 vols. (1938), vol. 1, p. 59.

114 *The Annual Register . . . of the Year 1827* (1828), pp. 463–5.

115 Porter, *Overture to Victoria*, p. 102.

116 Brown, *Fathers of the Victorians: The Age of Wilberforce*, p. 235.

117 *Ibid.*, pp. 229–30; Belcham, 'Orator Hunt', p. 51; *The Philanthropist* (1812), vol. 2, pp. 229–38.

118 See M.J.D. Roberts, 'Reshaping the Gift Relationship: The London Mendicity Society and the Suppression of Begging in England, 1818–1869', *International Review of Social History* 36 (1991), pp. 210–31; Owen, *English Philanthropy, 1660–1960*, pp. 111–12.

119 Pierre Crabites, *Victoria's Guardian Angel: A Study of Baron Stockmar* (1937), pp. 142–3.

120 Cecil Woodham-Smith, *Queen Victoria: Her Life and Times 1819–1861* (1972), p. 4.

121 See Anne Somerset, *Ladies in Waiting from the Tudors to the Present Day* (1984), p. 305 and passim.

122 RA 19035.

123 Percy Fitzgerald, *The Royal Dukes and Princesses of the Family of George III*, 2 vols. (1882), vol. 2, p. 303.

124 Brown, *Fathers of the Victorians*, p. 356.

125 Ernest Marshall Howse, *Saints in Politics* (Toronto, 1952), p. 157.

126 Richardson, *Recollections*, vol. 1, pp. 189–90.

127 Porter, *Overture to Victoria*, p. 151.

128 *Ibid.*, p. 138.

129 David Duff, *Edward of Kent: The Life Story of Queen Victoria's Father* (1938), pp. 218–19. Twenty-two of the Duke of Kent's charities are listed in *Memoirs of His Late Royal Highness Duke of Kent* (1820), pp. 28–9. See also *The Second Annual Report of the Loan Society* (1817).

130 Quoted in Porter, *Overture to Victoria*, p. 185.

131 Erskine Neale, *The Life of Field-Marshall His Royal Highness, Edward, Duke of Kent* (1850), p. 236.

132 See RA 43253–43291; Add. 7/1165.

133 Duff, *Edward of Kent*, p. 225.

134 *The Life of Robert Owen Written by Himself*, 2 vols. (1967), vol. 1, pp. 97–8, 229.

135 RA Add. 7/1511.

136 On the son, see Henry Tattam, *A Short Memoir of the Late John Camden Neild, Esq., of Chelsea* ([1852]).

137 David Holt, *Incidents in the Life of David Holt, Including a Sketch of some of the Philanthropic Institutions of Man-* *chester* (1843), p. 39; see RA Add. 7/29).

138 *The Private Letters of Princess Lieven to Prince Metternich, 1820–1826*, ed. Peter Quennell (1937), p. 6.

139 *The Life of Robert Owen Written by Himself*, vol. 1, p. 193.

140 Giles St Aubyn, *Queen Victoria: A Portrait* (1991), p. 2.

141 *The Philanthropist* (1811), vol. 1, p. 376.

142 *Ibid*, p. 189.

143 *The Times*, 8 June 1818, p. 3.

144 See Dudley Miles, *Francis Place, the Life of a Remarkable Radical, 1771–1854* (1988) p. 39 and chapter 6; see also Alice Prochaska, in 'The Practice of Radicalism; Educational Reform in Westminster', *London in the Age of Reform*, ed. John Stevenson (1977), pp. 102–116.

145 *The Philanthropist* (1814), vol. 4, p. 168. *The Times*, 8 June 1818, p. 3; *Report of J. Lancaster's Progress from the Year 1798, with the Report of the Finance Committee for the Year 1810* (1811), p. vi.

146 *Report of J. Lancaster's Progress from the Year 1798*, pp. v, 13.

147 *The Philanthropist* (1811), vol. 1, p. 384.

148 See, for example, RA Add. 7/7, 9. For more on Kent's contribution to the British and Foreign School Society, see Highmore, *Philanthropia Metropolitana*, pp. 212–54; Salmon, *Joseph Lancaster*, p. 43.

149 Salmon, *Joseph Lancaster*, p. 20.

150 Miles, *Francis Place*, p. 86.

151 BL, Add. MSS. 17823, f. 36; Miles, *Francis Place*, p. 86.

152 Quoted in Owen, *English Philanthropy, 1660–1960*, p. 166.

153 James Sherman, *Memoir of William Allen, F.R.S.* (1851), p. 147.

154 Holt, *Incidents in the Life of David Holt*, pp. 22–3.

155 *Anti-Jacobin Review* 49 (1815), pp. 618–22.

156 D.M. Stuart, *The Mother of Victoria* (1941), p. 37; Neale, *The Life of Field-Marshall His Royal Highness, Edward, Duke of Kent*, pp. 202–3.

157 *First Annual Report of the National Society for Promoting the Education of*

the Poor in the Principles of the Established Church (1812), p. 9. See also
RA 18852.

158 In 1818, for example, members of
the royal family contributed over
£2,000 to the National Society. See
*Seventh Annual Report of the National
Society for Promoting the Education of
the Poor in the Principles of the Established Church* (1818), p. 29.

159 Highmore, *Philanthropia Metropolitana*,
p. 215.

160 Maurice J. Quinlan, *Victorian Prelude:
A History of English Manners 1700–
1830* (New York, 1941), p. 171.

161 *Substance of the Speech of his Royal
Highness the Duke of Clarence in the
House of Lords on the Motion for the
Recommitment of the Slave Trade Bill*
(1799), p. 14.

162 See *The Times*, 4 July 1814, p. 2.

163 *The Philanthropist* (1811), vol. 1, p.
383.

164 *The Times*, 8 June 1818, p. 3.

165 *The Life of William Wilberforce*, vol. 2,
p. 461.

166 Duff, *Edward of Kent*, p. 217. See also
Gisborne, *An Enquiry into the Duties
of Men in the Higher and Middle
Classes of Society in Great Britain*, pp.
41–4.

167 Highmore, *Pietas Londinensis*, pp. v–
vi.

168 RA Add. 7/27.

169 Viscount Esher, *To-day and Tomorrow
and other Essays* (1910), p. 116.

Chapter 2

1 *The Greville Memoirs*, ed. Henry
Reeve, 8 vols. (1888), vol. 1, p. 159.

2 Ford K. Brown, *Fathers of the Victorians* (1961), pp. 60–61.

3 Hannah More, *Moral Sketches of Prevailing Opinions and Manners* (1821),
p. xvi.

4 In the 1820s his Royal Bounty Payments to superannuated servants and
widows of office holders exceeded
£2,000 a year. RA 30584–86.

5 He once gave the Duke of York
£50,000 to pay off his racing debts,
and in 1826 bailed out the Duke of
Clarence with a gift of £10,000. See

Christopher Hibbert, *George IV:
Regent and King, 1811–1830* (1973),
p. 316. Henry Hobhouse put the gift
to the Duke of Clarence at £15,000.
See *The Diary of Henry Hobhouse
(1820–1827)*, ed. Arthur Aspinall
(1947), p. 122.

6 Hibbert, *George IV*, p. 316; *The Correspondence of George, Prince of Wales,
1770–1812*, ed. A. Aspinall, 8 vols.
(1971), vol. 1, p. 305; *The Journal of
Mrs Arbuthnot, 1820–1832*, eds.
Francis Bamford and the 7th Duke of
Wellington, 2 vols. (1950), vol. 2, p.
448; Percy Fitzgerald, *The Life of
George the Fourth*, 2 vols. (1881), vol.
2, p. 442.

7 Fitzgerald, *The Life of George the
Fourth*, vol. 1, p. 351; vol. 2, p. 442.

8 *Ibid.*, vol. 2, p. 363.

9 *George the Fourth, the Patron of Literature* (1831), pp. 4–5.

10 Hibbert, *George IV*, p. 265. See the
Quarterly Review 175 (December
1850), p. 143.

11 RA 30269–70.

12 This number has been compiled
from *The Royal Kalendar*, the Privy
Purse accounts in the Royal Archives
and the reports of charitable societies.

13 See the figures presented in the
annual reports of the National
Society for Promoting the Education
of the Poor in the Principles of the
Established Church.

14 *The Correspondence of George, Prince of
Wales, 1770–1812*, vol. 1, pp. 305–
6.

15 Fitzgerald, *The Life and Times of
William IV*, vol. 1, pp. 347–8.

16 David Owen, *English Philanthropy,
1660–1960* (1964), p. 166.

17 John Brooke, *King George III* (1985),
p. 215.

18 Henry James Burgess, *Enterprise in
Education* (1958), p. 212. A Royal
Letter issued by Queen Victoria is
printed in the *Monthly Paper* of the
National Society 35 (November
1849), pp. 257–8.

19 Oliver Warner, *The Life-boat Service:
A History of the Royal National Life-
boat Institution, 1824–1974* (1974),
pp. 7, 10, 22.

20 *Memoirs of His Royal Highness the*

Prince of Wales, 3 vols. (1808), vol. 3, p. 234.

21 RA 30067, 30137, 30155, 30197.

22 RA 30161.

23 RA 30578–79.

24 Warner, *The Life-boat Service*, p. 7.

25 See *The First Annual Report of the Royal National Institution for the Preservation of Life from Shipwreck* (1824).

26 RA 30221–24.

27 See E. Evelyn Barron, *The National Benevolent Institution, 1812–1936* (1936).

28 *Tour of Their Royal Highnesses the Prince of Wales and Duke of York* (1789), p. 13.

29 *The Royal Visit Containing a Full and Circumstantial Account of Everything Connected with the King's Visit to Ireland* (1821), p. 139.

30 *Ibid*, pp. 137–9. For a critical account of George IV and the use of royal pardons see V.A.C. Gatrell, *The Hanging Tree: Execution and the English People, 1770–1868* (1994), pp. 550–58.

31 Quoted in Linda Colley, *Britons: Forging the Nation, 1707–1837* (1992), p. 235.

32 Lady Knighton, *Memoirs of Sir William Knighton*, 2 vols. (1838), vol. 1, p. 196. *Account of the Royal Visit of George the IVth to Scotland* (1822), p. 21.

33 *Account of the Royal Visit of George the IVth to Scotland*, p. 24.

34 Lady Knighton, *Memoirs of Sir William Knighton*, vol. 1, p. 194.

35 Thomas Paine, *Rights of Man. Part the Second*, 2nd edn (1792), pp. 69–70.

36 John Wade, *The Black Book; or Corruption Unmasked* (1820), p. 184.

37 *Ibid.*, p. 185.

38 *Ibid.*, pp. 152–3.

39 J. R. Dinwiddy, *Radicalism and Reform in Britain, 1780–1850* (1992), p. 428.

40 More, *Moral Sketches of Prevailing Opinions and Manners*, p. xvi.

41 *The Times*, 24 July 1821, p. 2; See also, Colley, *Britons: Forging the Nation*, p. 224.

42 *The Times*, 24 July 1821, p. 3.

43 Elizabeth Longford, *Victoria R.I.* (1964), p. 26.

44 Mary F. Sandars, *The Life and Times of Queen Adelaide* (1915), p. 123.

45 *The Times*, 16 July 1820, p. 2.

46 *George IV, the Patron of Literature*, p. 3.

47 *Report of the Society for the Promotion of Christian Knowledge* (1830), p. 16.

48 Rev. R. C. Dillon, *A Sermon Preached on Thursday, July 15, 1830; Being the Day of the Funeral of his Late Majesty George the Fourth* (1830), p. 15.

49 Rev. M. Seaman, *Christian Loyalty and True Patriotism* (1880), p. 21.

50 Burgess, *Enterprise in Education*, p. 43. The *Monthly Paper* of the National Society contains information on the monarchy's role in fundraising. See, for example, no. 8, August 1847, p. 1; no. 35, November 1849, pp. 257–8.

51 *The Times*, 23 April 1830, p. 4; Owen, *English Philanthropy 1660–1960*, p. 61.

52 *The Private Letters of Princess Lieven to Prince Metternich, 1820–1826*, ed. Peter Quennell (1937), p. 372.

53 Philip Ziegler, *King William IV* (Cassell edn, 1989), p. 294.

54 *The Nineteenth-Century Constitution 1815–1914: Documents and Commentary*, ed. and introd. H.J. Hanham (1969), p. 31.

55 A.J. Maley, *Historical Recollections of the Reign of William IV*, 2 vols. (1860), vol. 1, p. 5.

56 *The Correspondence of the Late Earl Grey with His Majesty King William IV*, ed. Henry Earl Grey, 2 vols. (1867), vol. 1, pp. 126–7.

57 G. Kitson Clark, *The Making of Victorian England* (1962), p. 123.

58 Ziegler, *King William IV*, p. 294.

59 John P. Mackintosh, *The British Cabinet* (1977), pp. 72, 76.

60 Tom Pocock, *Sailor King: The Life of King William IV* (1991), p. 82.

61 Fitzgerald, *The Life and Times of William IV*, vol. 1, pp. 67–71; see also Ziegler, *King William IV*, p. 55.

62 See, for example, G.N. Wright, *The Life and Reign of William the Fourth*, 2 vols. (1837), vol. 2, appendix 2 and passim.

63 See the *London Calendar* (1817), p. 187.

64 *Report of the Society for the Promotion of Christian Knowledge* (1830), pp. 16–17; Ziegler, *King William IV*, p. 142.

65 *The Times*, 10 July 1912, p. 8.

66 Henry Moses, *Visit of William the Fourth when Duke of Clarence, as Lord High Admiral, to Portsmouth, in the Year 1827* (1840), p. 7.

67 John Watkins, *The Life and Times of 'England's Patriot King', William the Fourth* (1831), p. 771.

68 David Roberts, *Paternalism in Early Victorian England* (New Brunswick, 1979), pp. 258–61.

69 See, for example, Ziegler, *King William IV*, p. 147.

70 Roberts, *Paternalism in Early Victorian England*, p. 45 and passim.

71 *Ibid.*, p. 54. Thomas Chalmers was a leading exponent of such ideas; see S.J. Brown, *Thomas Chalmers and the Godly Commonwealth in Scotland* (1982).

72 Ziegler, *King William IV*, p. 293.

73 The use of 'Patriot King' runs through the literature on William IV. See, for example, *The Patriot King to his People* (1831); John Watkins, *The Life and Times of 'England's Patriot King', William the Fourth* (1831); Grace E. Thompson, *The Patriot King: The Life of William IV* (1932).

74 Watkins, *The Life and Times of 'England's Patriot King', William the Fourth*, p. 771.

75 RA Box 14/4, William IV, Bank Pass Book.

76 *Ibid.*

77 *The Correspondence of the Late Earl Grey with His Majesty King William IV*, ed. Earl Grey, vol. 1, p. 222.

78 Wright, *The Life and Reign of William the Fourth*, vol. 2, p. 630.

79 Marquess of Anglesey, *One-leg: The Life and Letters of Henry William Paget, First Marquess of Anglesey K.G., 1768–1854* (1961), pp. 227–30; see also Colley, *Britons: Forging the Nation*, p. 235; Ziegler, *King William IV*, p. 144.

80 Wright, *The Life and Reign of William the Fourth*, vol. 2, p. 776.

81 *Ibid*, vol. 2, pp. 628–9, 776–7, 792–3, 850.

82 Colley, *Britons: Forging the Nation*, p. 236.

83 Wright, *The Life and Reign of William the Fourth*, vol. 2, p. 540.

84 William Brockbank, *Portrait of a Hospital, 1752–1948* (1952), p. 58.

85 *Ibid.*, p. 59.

86 See *The Royal Kalendar* for details of their joint patronages.

87 Wright, *The Life and Reign of William the Fourth*, vol. 2, pp. 792–3, 850.

88 RA Box 14/4, William IV, Bank Pass Book.

89 Wright, *The Life and Reign of William the Fourth*, vol. 2, pp. 481–2.

90 *Queen Adelaide*, (1851), p. 11.

91 *Ibid.*, p. 22.

92 Christopher Wordsworth, *A Sermon Preached at Westminster Abbey . . . the Sunday after the Death of Queen Adelaide* (1849), pp. 16–18.

93 James Grant, *Sketches in London* (1838), p. 4.

94 G.M. Young, *Victorian England: Portrait of an Age* (Galaxy edn, 1964), p. 44.

95 RA Box 17C; list of applicants for assistance, 1849.

96 G. Cecil White, *Glimpses of King William IV and Queen Adelaide* (1902), pp. 62–3; see also Akihito Suzuki, 'The Politics and Ideology of Non-Restraint: The Case of the Hanwell Asylum', *Medical History* 39, no. 1 (1995), pp. 1–17.

97 MacMenemy, *A History of the Worcester Royal Infirmary*, p. 221.

98 RA 89725–89733. Queen Adelaide's Treasurer's Accounts: Donation Account, 1836–37.

99 *Dictionary of National Biography*; see also Mary Hopkirk, *Queen Adelaide* (1946), p. 171.

100 Henry Boyd, *Death of the Queen Dowager: A Poem* (1850); see also Dr Doran, *Memoir of Queen Adelaide, Consort of King William IV* (1861).

101 Sanders, *The Life and Times of Queen Adelaide*, p. 124.

102 For a general survey of the bazaar, see F.K. Prochaska, 'Charity Bazaars in Nineteenth-Century England', *Journal of British Studies* (spring 1977),

pp. 62–84. See also F.K. Prochaska, *Women and Philanthropy in Nineteenth-Century England* (1980), chapter 2.

103 *Queen Adelaide*, pp. 29–30. The British Library has a set of these hand-written texts; see Add. MSS. 38190, ff. 135–43.

104 Prochaska, *Women and Philanthropy in Nineteenth-Century England*, p. 51.

105 Charles C.F. Greville, *A Journal of the Reigns of King George IV and King William IV*, 3 vols. (1875), vol. 2, p. 383.

106 *Memoir of the Life of Elizabeth Fry*, ed. by her daughters, 2 vols. (1847), vol. 2, p. 128.

107 *Ibid.*, p. 129.

108 *Ibid.*

109 *Ibid.*, vol. 1, pp. 429–31.

110 *Ibid.*, vol. 2, p. 126; James Sherman, *Memoir of William Allen* (1851), p. 359.

111 Sherman, *Memoir of William Allen*, passim.

112 This list of 'royal' wards is taken from St George's Hospital in the mid-nineteenth century. See Blomfield, *St George's 1733–1933*, p. 67.

113 *Annual Register . . . of the Year 1840*, vol. 82, p. 176; for her London patronages, see *The Royal Kalendar*.

114 *The Royal Kalendar* is a useful, though incomplete, guide to King Leopold's charitable connections in London.

115 Dorothy Margaret Stuart, *The Mother of Victoria: A Period Piece* (1941), pp. 38–41; *The Times*, 5 August 1818, p. 3.

116 Hector Bolitho, *The Reign of Queen Victoria* (1949), pp. 19–20.

117 Gisborne, *An Enquiry into the Duties of Men in the Higher and Middle Classes of Society in Great Britain*, p. 50.

118 *Report of the Present State of the St George's German and English School* (1819).

119 *The Training of a Sovereign: An Abridged Selection from 'The Girlhood of Queen Victoria', Being Her Majesty's Diaries between the Years 1832 and 1840*, ed. Viscount Esher (1914), pp. 59–60.

120 BL, Add. MSS. 38303, ff. 8–9.

121 Cecil Woodham-Smith, *Queen Victoria: Her Life and Times* (1973), p. 75; Walter Arnstein, 'Queen Victoria and Religion', in *Religion in the Lives of English Women, 1760–1930*, ed. Gail Malmgreen (1986), pp. 91–2. On Queen Victoria's education, see also Monica Charlot, *Victoria: The Young Queen* (1991).

122 Woodham Smith, *Queen Victoria*, p. 88.

123 Quoted in Wright, *The Life and Reign of William the Fourth*, vol. 2, p. 756.

124 BL, Add. MSS. 34588, f. 215.

125 *Ibid.*, f. 214.

126 RA Queen Victoria's Journal, 1 November 1832.

127 BL, Add. MSS. 34588, f. 216.

128 John Poland, *Records of the Miller Hospital and Royal Kent Dispensary* (1893), pp. 52–3.

129 Though an incomplete guide to Princess Victoria's charities, see *The Royal Kalendar . . . for the Year 1836*.

130 F.G. Fairholme and W. Paine, *A Century of Work for Animals* (New York, 1924), pp. 71–2, 83; see also E. Treacher Collins, *The History and Traditions of the Moorfields Eye Hospital* (1929), pp. 68–9.

131 Ziegler, *King William IV*, p. 294.

132 Quoted in Longford, *Victoria R.I.*, p. 62.

133 Dr Johnson added this line to Oliver Goldsmith's *The Traveller*.

134 *The Training of a Sovereign*, ed. Esher, p. vii.

135 Edward Copleston, *A Good King the Nursing-Father of the Church: A Sermon on Death of William IV* (1837), p. 5. See also Rev. D.M. Isaacs, *Funeral Oration, Delivered on the Occasion of the Burial of His Most Gracious Majesty, King William the Fourth* (1837); Rev. C. Stovel, *National Bereavement Improved, a Sermon Occasioned by the Death of His Most Gracious Majesty King William the Fourth* (1837).

136 The royal family's patronage of the Bible Society was restricted largely to

the London auxiliaries. See *The Twenty-First Report of the British and Foreign Bible Society* (1825), appendix 1, p. 11. See also Rev. George Browne, *The History of the British and Foreign Bible Society*, 2 vols. (1859), vol. 1, pp. 83–4.

137 Burgess, *Enterprise in Education*, p. 212.

Chapter 3

1 [William Rathbone], *Social Duties* (1867), p. 14.

2 Frederick Engels, *The Condition of the Working Class in England*, trans. and ed. W.O. Henderson and W.H. Chaloner (Stanford, 1958), p. 140.

3 *Family Budgets: Being the Income and Expenses of Twenty-Eight British Households, 1891–1894* (1896), p. 75.

4 William Conybeare, *Charity of Poor to Poor: Facts Collected in South London at the Suggestion of the Bishop of Southwark* (1908), p. 6. For more information on working-class charity, see Brian Harrison, 'Philanthropy and the Victorians', *Victorian Studies*, 9, no. 4 (June 1966), pp. 368–9.

5 See F.K. Prochaska, *Women and Philanthropy in Nineteenth-Century England* (1980), p. 227 and passim. See also Anne Summers, 'A Home from Home—Women's Philanthropic Work in the Nineteenth Century', in *Fit Work for Women*, ed. Sandra Burman (1979), pp. 33–63; Brian Harrison, *Peaceable Kingdom: Stability and Change in Modern Britain* (1982), pp. 233–4.

6 R.J. Morris, *Class, Sect and Party: The Making of the British Middle Class, Leeds 1820–50* (1990), pp. 161–8. For a fascinating discussion of the nature of voluntary institutions see also Ernest Gellner, *Conditions of Liberty: Civil Society and its Rivals* (1994).

7 See Dror Wahrman, '"Middle-Class" Domesticity Goes Public: Gender, Class, and Politics from Queen Caroline to Queen Victoria', *Journal of British Studies* 32, no. 4 (1993), pp. 396–432.

8 F.M.L. Thompson, *The Rise of Respectable Society* (1988), p. 353. On respectability, see also Harrison, *Peaceable Kingdom*, p. 176; Gertrude Himmelfarb, *Poverty and Compassion: The Moral Imagination of the Late Victorians* (New York, 1991), pp. 8–10.

9 Brian Abel-Smith, *The Hospitals, 1800–1948* (1964), pp. 250–51.

10 Jose Harris, *Private Lives, Public Spirit: Britain 1870–1914* (Penguin edn, 1994), p. 18.

11 George Griffith, *History of the Free-Schools, Colleges, Hospitals, and Asylums of Birmingham* (1861), pp. 151–61, 201, 205.

12 *Ibid.*, p. 213.

13 G. Munro Smith, *A History of the Bristol Royal Infirmary* (1917), pp. 282, 322.

14 RA PP Vic 2/4/3895 (1853).

15 Morris, *Class, Sect and Party*, p. 167 and passim; see the review of Morris by Simon Gunn in *Social History*, 18, no. 3 (1993), pp. 405–08.

16 Morris, *Class, Sect and Party*, p. 331.

17 Linda Colley, *Britons: Forging the Nation 1707–1837* (1992), chapter 5 makes the connection between royal events and civic welfare, but her primary interest is in the development of national identity and she pays little attention to the crown's active support for voluntary associations.

18 Walter Arnstein, 'Queen Victoria and Religion', in *Religion in the Lives of English Women, 1760–1930*, ed. Gail Malmgreen (1986), p. 94.

19 Quoted in Pierre Crabites, *Victoria's Guardian Angel: A Study of Baron Stockmar* (1937), p. 147.

20 Baron E. von Stockmar, *Memoirs of Baron Stockmar*, 2 vols. (1972), vol. 2, pp. 97–8.

21 Rev. John Cumming, *Our Queen's Responsibilities and Rewards: A Sermon to Her Majesty, on her Coronation* (1838), pp. 10–13; see also *Darling Child: Private Correspondence of Queen Victoria and the German Crown Prin-*

cess, 1871–1878, ed. Roger Fulford (1976), p. 51.

22 *The Times*, 22 June 1838, p. 1; 25 June, p. 3; 26 June, p. 1; 28 June, p. 5; 29 June, pp. 2–7; July 6, pp. 5–6.

23 John Poland, *Records of the Miller Hospital and Royal Kent Dispensary* (1893), pp. 62–73.

24 RA PP Vic, Patronage, Index to Patronage and Charities, 1838–1851.

25 Between 1837 and 1879 she contributed over £10,000 to 77 disaster funds, including 13 colliery explosions. See RA PP Vic, Donations Made by Her Majesty the Queen to Sufferers by Fires, Explosions, Shipwrecks.

26 RA PP Vic, Civil List I/18, Privy Purse Accounts Balance Sheet, 1837–1871. The figures included £48,527 to individuals, £89,051 to institutions and £139,861 to annual charities, bringing the total to £277,439. The sovereign had no control over Class IV of the Civil List: royal bounty, alms and special services. The First Lord of the Treasury or his wife distributed the £13,200 set aside for Class IV. See William M. Kuhn, 'Queen Victoria's Civil List: What did she Do with It?', *The Historical Journal* 36, no. 3 (1993), p. 650.

27 RA PP Vic, Annual Charities List, 1882–1892.

28 She spent £11,000 a year on pensions to retired servants by the end of her reign. See Kuhn, 'Queen Victoria's Civil List: What did she Do with it?', p. 649.

29 The Neild bequest consisted of about £233,000 in cash and gilt-edged securities, together with a number of estates in Kent and Buckinghamshire and three town houses. The amount of the Neild bequest has been a subject of some confusion, for example in Philip Hall, *Royal Fortune: Tax, Money and the Monarchy* (1992), pp. 12–13. There is also confusion over what happened to the bequest. It was not spent on Balmoral, as is often said, but on the Frogmore Mausoleum, on the Paris visit of 1855, on annuities to Neild's servants, and on

trousseaux. A large share of it, £100,000, was settled on Princess Helena. Information from the Royal Archives. See also RA Add N3/266.

30 Kuhn, 'Queen Victoria's Civil List', pp. 653–8. I have excluded monies for household salaries, i.e., Class II of the Civil List, from my estimate.

31 F.M.L. Thompson, *English Landed Society in the Nineteenth Century* (1971), p. 210. Further work on the charitable contributions of landed society would be very helpful.

32 *Statistics of Middle-Class Expenditure*, British Library of Political and Economic Science, Pamphlet HD6/D267 (1896?), table IX. See also F.K. Prochaska, 'Philanthropy', in *The Cambridge Social History of Britain, 1750–1950*, 3 vols. (1990), vol. 3, p. 358.

33 Stockmar, *Memoirs of Baron Stockmar*, vol. 1, p. 366.

34 Bagehot first published this view of Prince Albert in the *Economist*, 21 December 1861. It reappeared in his *Biographical Studies*, ed. Richard Holt Hutton (1881), p. 323.

35 Quoted in *The Royal Encyclopedia*, eds. Ronald Allison and Sarah Riddell (1991), p. 10.

36 Quoted in Edwin Hodder, *The Life and Work of the Seventh Earl of Shaftesbury* (1892), p. 395.

37 *Ibid.*, p. 12.

38 Crabites, *Victoria's Guardian Angel: A Study of Baron Stockmar*, p. 148.

39 G.M. Young, *Victorian England: Portrait of an Age* (Galaxy edn, 1964), p. 79.

40 RA M51/75.

41 Young, *Victorian England: Portrait of an Age*, p. 79.

42 F.H. Myers, *Personal Recollections of Leopold, Duke of Albany*, p. 8, Myers Papers, 28/64, Trinity College, Cambridge. See also Jehanne Wake, *Princess Louise: Queen Victoria's Unconventional Daughter* (1988), p. 361.

43 *The Principal Speeches and Addresses of His Royal Highness the Prince Consort* (1862), pp. 81–2.

44 *Ibid.*, p. 176.

45 RA PP Vic, Patronage, Index to Patronage and Charities.

46 RA PP Vic, Prince Albert's Accounts.

47 Young, *Victorian England: Portrait of an Age*, p. 79.

48 Daphne Bennet, *King without a Crown: Albert, Prince Consort of England 1819–1861* (1977), pp. 154–5.

49 Jealousy of London remained common throughout the nineteenth century. See, for example, Henry Matthews, Home Secretary, to Sir H. Ponsonby, 1 January 1887, putting forward Birmingham's claims to a royal visit in the Queen's Jubilee year. RA L.11/1.

50 RA Add. C12/22.

51 He also contributed £50 to the recently opened Queen's Hospital, which he served as President. See Griffith, *History of the Free-Schools, Colleges, Hospitals and Asylums of Birmingham*, p. 202.

52 Quoted in Theodore Martin, *The Life of the Prince Consort*, 5 vols. (1875–80), vol. 1, p. 194.

53 *Ibid.*, p. 332.

54 Hermione Hobhouse, *Prince Albert: His Life and Work* (1983), pp. 58–61.

55 Martin, *The Life of the Prince Consort*, vol. 1, p. 336. For a discussion of the preparations for the Prince's visit see *The Builder*, 25 July 1846, p. 353.

56 Martin, *The Life of the Prince Consort*, vol. 1, p. 335.

57 *Ibid.*, p. 336.

58 *Ibid.*, p. 335.

59 RA Y204.

60 Martin, *The Life of the Prince Consort*, vol. 4, p. 12.

61 RA C56/12.

62 RA C56/47 and 47a.

63 Bennet, *King without a Crown*, p. 101; Elizabeth Longford, *Victoria R.I.* (1964), p. 197.

64 Quoted in Hodder, *The Life and Work of the Seventh Earl of Shaftesbury*, p. 395.

65 RA C56/56.

66 This episode is discussed in Robert Rhodes James, *Albert, Prince Consort: A Biography* (1983), pp. 190–1.

67 *The Principal Speeches and Addresses of His Royal Highness the Prince Consort* (1862), pp. 88–9.

68 *The Principal Speeches and Addresses of His Royal Highness the Prince Consort*, p. 89.

69 One is reminded of the similarities between Prince Albert and Robert Peel in reading Walter Bagehot's essay on Peel in his *Biographical Studies*.

70 The link between the business mentality and philanthropy is brought out in Harrison, *Peaceable Kingdom*, pp. 229–30.

71 Quoted in Geoffrey. B.A.M. Finlayson, *The Seventh Earl of Shaftesbury 1801–1885* (1981), p. 273.

72 Quoted in Roger Fulford, *The Prince Consort* (1949), p. 144; Giles St Aubyn, *Queen Victoria: A Portrait* (1991), p. 225.

73 RA C56/100.

74 RA C56/101.

75 *The Principal Speeches and Addresses of His Royal Highness the Prince Consort*, p. 135.

76 RA C59/1, 3, 10.

77 20 May 1849; RA C59/10.

78 19 May 1849; RA C59/11.

79 Hobhouse, *Prince Albert: His Life and Work*, p. 57.

80 Quoted in Martin, *The Life of His Royal Highness the Prince Consort*, vol. 2, p. 213.

81 *Ibid.*, vol. 2, pp. 401–2.

82 Quoted *ibid.*, vol. 4, p. 246.

83 Quoted in Hobhouse, *Prince Albert: His Life and Work*, pp. 59–61.

84 *Ibid.*, p. 61.

85 RA PP Vic, Annual Charities List 1853–1881.

86 *Letters of the Prince Consort, 1831–1861*, ed. Dr Kurt Jagow (1938), p. 154.

87 RA PP Vic, Prince Albert's Accounts.

88 RA C59/45. Colonel C. Grey to Henry Wood, 19 June 1850.

89 RA Information Sheet: The Prince Consort's Windsor Association.

90 *The Principal Speeches and Addresses of His Royal Highness The Prince Consort*, p. 175.

91 See John Nelson Tarn, *Five Per Cent Philanthropy: An Account of Housing in Urban Areas between 1840 and 1914* (1973), p. 20. For more detail on Prince Albert's role in the Great

Exhibition see Derek Hudson and Kenneth W. Luckhurst, *The Royal Society of Arts 1754–1954* (1954); Bennett, *King without a Crown*, pp. 198–211; Hobhouse, *Prince Albert: His Life and Work*, chapter 7.

92 Longford, *Victoria R.I.*, p. 395.

93 *Queen Victoria's Highland Journals*, ed. David Duff (1980), pp. 83–4.

94 Arthur H. Beavan, *Popular Royalty* (1897), pp. 24–5, 74–5.

95 See Prochaska, *Woman and Philanthropy in Nineteenth-Century England*, introduction.

96 William Ruskin, *Sesame and Lillies* (1865), pp. 146–7.

97 For an interesting discussion of this issue, see Dorothy Thompson, *Queen Victoria: Gender and Power* (1990).

98 Agnes Weston, *My Life among the Blue-Jackets* (1912), pp. 213–17. On Mary Carpenter, see RA B23/63; RA Queen Victoria's Journal, 13 March 1868.

99 Bevan, *Popular Monarchy*, p. 76.

100 *The Panmure Papers: Being a Selection from the Correspondence of Fox Maule, Second Baron Panmure, afterwards Eleventh Earl of Dalhousie*, eds. Sir George Douglas Bart and Sir George Dalhousie Ramsay, 2 vols. (1908), vol. 1, pp. 54, 75.

101 Quoted in Cecil Woodham-Smith, *Florence Nightingale, 1820–1910* (1950), p. 196.

102 RA F2/52, 54. 'List of sick and wounded NCO's and Privates from the Crimea . . . who have received Presents from . . . the Queen', 27 March 1855; 'List of Invalids returned from the Crimea who are to be seen by [Her] Majesty', 2 April 1855.

103 Quoted in Longford, *Victoria R.I.*, p. 249.

104 G.W.E. Russell, *Collections and Recollections* (1898), p. 305.

105 Woodham-Smith, *Florence Nightingale*, p. 264.

106 *Further Letters of Queen Victoria*, ed. Hector Bolitho (1938), p. 76; Woodham-Smith, *Queen Victoria*, p. 374.

107 Quoted in Woodham-Smith, *Queen Victoria*, p. 374.

108 For a discussion of the campaign, see Woodham-Smith, *Florence Nightingale*, chapter 12. See also *The Panmure Papers*, eds. Bart and Ramsay, vol. 2.

109 In the 1840s the royal family nominated scores of children for places at, for example, Christ's Hospital and Charterhouse. See RA PP Vic, Her Majesty's and His Royal Highness Prince Albert's Patronage Book, 1842.

110 RA M21/89 and further information from the Royal Archives.

111 RA HH1/24.

112 RA PP Vic Ledger, 1867–70.

113 RA HH1/24.

114 *Ibid.*

115 In 1859 she agreed to patronize its bazaar. Public Record Office HO 45 OS8064/1; see also *Annual Report of the Committee of the Leeds Mechanics' Institution and Literary Society for 1859* (1859).

116 RA PP Vic 2/108/11752; 2/109/11862.

117 See *Burdett's Hospitals and Charities* (1890, etc.).

118 Quoted in Lindsay Granshaw, ' "Fame and Fortune by Means of Bricks and Mortar": The Medical Profession and Specialist Hospitals in Britain, 1800–1948', in *The Hospital in History*, eds. Lindsay Granshaw and Roy Porter (1989), p. 207.

119 Arnold Sorsby, *Royal Eye Hospital, 1857–1957* (1957), pp. 3, 15–16.

120 David Owen, *English Philanthropy, 1660–1960* (1964) p. 92.

121 See *Burdett's Hospitals and Charities* (1890 etc.).

122 Elisabeth Darby and Nicola Smith, *The Cult of the Prince Consort* (1984), pp. 93–6.

123 See David Cannadine, 'The Context, Performance and Meaning of Ritual: The British Monarchy and the "Invention of Tradition" c. 1820–1977', in *The Invention of Tradition*, eds. Eric Hobsbawm and Terence Ranger (1983), p. 120. It may be misleading to use the availability of commemorative royal pottery as a guide to the monarchy's popularity. In the nineteenth century, British

monarchs were usually willing to permit their likenesses to be used on medals struck for charitable purposes, but they tended to be less happy with large-scale commercial exploitation, which lowered the tone of monarchy. See Darby and Smith, *The Cult of the Prince Consort* (New Haven), pp. 93–6.

124 Darby and Smith, *The Cult of the Prince Consort*, p. 88. See also *Burdett's Hospitals and Charities*, passim.

125 *The Builder*, 3 May 1862, p. 318. For several years after Prince Albert's death, *The Builder* rans articles on the many memorials to Prince Albert.

126 *The Times*, 3 February 1842, p. 3; 5 February 1845, p. 2; 2 February 1849, p. 2. The Queen delivered most of her speeches to Parliament until the death of Prince Albert, when she became more reluctant to do so.

127 *Ibid.*, 1 February 1850, p. 2.

128 John Stuart Mill, *Principles of Political Economy* (Penguin edn, 1970), pp. 312–13.

129 For a fascinating discussion of evangelicalism and the 'democratic revolution', see Bernard Semmel, *The Methodist Revolution* (New York, 1973); see also Gertrude Himmelfarb, *Victorian Minds* (New York, 1970), p. 283.

130 Quoted in Longford, *Victoria R.I.,* p. 352.

131 *Ibid.*, pp. 351–2.

Chapter 4

1 *The Times*, 9 January 1885, p. 9.

2 *Forty-Second Annual Report of the Charity Commissioners* (1895), p. 17.

3 Arthur Ponsonby, *Henry Ponsonby, Queen Victoria's Private Secretary: His Life from his Letters* (1942), p. 307.

4 Walter Bagehot, *The English Constitution* (1963), pp. 85, 100.

5 Walter Bagehot, *Physics and Politics* (1872), pp. 188–9.

6 Philip Howard, *The British Monarchy in the Twentieth Century* (1977), p. 80.

7 Sidney Lee, *Queen Victoria: A Biography* (1902), p. 546.

8 RA Vic. Add. Q8/3; Q8/40.

9 Mary Drew, *Catherine Gladstone* (1919), p. 96; see also RA F38/59.

10 RA Add. K/17.

11 Edwin A. Pratt, *Catherine Gladstone* (1898), pp. 116–17.

12 See, for example, RA M55/5 and Add Q1/69: Staffordshire colliery accident, 1866; B19/74: Hartley colliery accident, 1862.

13 RA N27/87.

14 RA PP Vic. 1876/20979, 1870/7030, 1875/19173; Queen Victoria's Journal, 13 March 1868.

15 Ponsonby, *Henry Ponsonby, Queen Victoria's Private Secretary*, p. 375.

16 *Darling Child: Private Correspondence of Queen Victoria and the German Crown Princess, 1871–1878*, ed. Roger Fulford (1976), p. 51.

17 *Further Letters of Queen Victoria*, ed. Hector Bolitho (1938), p. 155.

18 *The Times*, 22 June 1871, p. 12; E.M. McInness, *St Thomas' Hospital* (1963), p. 113.

19 *The Times*, 22 June 1871, p. 12.

20 *Punch*, 23 September 1865, p. 215.

21 *The Times*, 9 November 1871, p. 9.

22 Quoted in Giles St Aubyn, *Queen Victoria: A Portrait* (1991), p. 386.

23 *The Collected Works of Walter Bagehot*, ed. St John Stevas, 15 vols. (1974–86), vol. 5, p. 431. See also David Cannadine, 'The Context, Performance and Meaning of Ritual: The British Monarchy and the "Invention of Tradition", c. 1820–1977.' in *The Invention of Tradition*, eds. Eric Hobsbawm and Terence Ranger (1984), p. 119.

24 Elizabeth Longford, *Victoria R.I.* (1964), p. 379.

25 For a stimulating discussion of the 'Royalty Crisis', see Tom Nairn, *The Enchanted Glass: Britain and its Monarchy* (1990), pp. 325–31.

26 *The Collected Works of Walter Bagehot*, vol. 5, p. 432. See also Cannadine, 'The Context, Performance and Meaning of Ritual', p. 119.

27 Philip Guedalla, *The Queen and Mr. Gladstone*, 2 vols. (1933), vol. 1, p. 363.

28 Longford, *Victoria R.I.*, p. 388.
29 Ponsonby, *Henry Ponsonby, Queen Victoria's Private Secretary*, p. 71.
30 *The Letters of Queen Victoria*, ed. George Earle Buckle, 2nd series, 2 vols. (1926), vol. 2, p. 159.
31 Nairn, *The Enchanted Glass*, pp. 330–32.
32 Noble Frankland, *Witness of a Century: The Life and Times of Prince Arthur Duke of Connaught, 1850–1942* (1993), p. 51.
33 See Philip Magnus, *King Edward the Seventh* (1964), chapter 5.
34 Guedalla, *The Queen and Mr. Gladstone*, vol. 1, p. 321.
35 Ponsonby, *Henry Ponsonby, Queen Victoria's Private Secretary*, p. 100.
36 Guedalla, *The Queen and Mr. Gladstone*, vol. 1, p. 352. Lord Granville wrote to Gladstone some years later that 'the Prince of Wales is thoroughly though unintentionally indiscreet—and he is especially abusive of our foreign policy'. See Agatha Ramm, *The Political Correspondence of Mr. Gladstone and Lord Granville 1876–1886*, 2 vols. (1962), vol. 2, p. 370.
37 Guedalla, *The Queen and Mr. Gladstone*, vol. 1, pp. 320–21, 352.
38 Magnus, *King Edward the Seventh*, p. 116.
39 Ponsonby, *Henry Ponsonby, Queen Victoria's Private Secretary*, p. 103.
40 *Ibid.*, p. 109.
41 Guedalla, *The Queen and Mr. Gladstone*, vol. 1, pp. 375–7.
42 *Ibid.*, p. 352.
43 Philip Magnus, *Gladstone: A Biography* (1954), p. 427.
44 RA PP Vic, Patronage, Index to Patronage.
45 Henry C. Burdett, *Prince, Princess and People. An Account of the Public Life and Work of their Royal Highnesses the Prince and Princess of Wales, 1863–1889* (1889), pp. 352–4.
46 *Ibid.*, p. 346.
47 Magnus, *King Edward the Seventh*, p. 79.
48 RA T5/43, quoted in Magnus, *King Edward the Seventh*, pp. 112–13.
49 Guedalla, *The Queen and Mr. Gladstone*, vol. 1, p. 363.
50 RA Queen Victoria's Journal, 7 March 1876.
51 *Ibid*; see also the Diary of Life at Court of Eliza Jane Lady Waterpark, British Library, Add. MSS. 60750, f. 45.
52 Diary of Life at Court of Eliza Jane Lady Waterpark, BL, Add. MSS. 60750, f. 45; see also *The London Hospital Illustrated: 250 Years* (1990), pp. 16, 62. In the late nineteenth century, a man in Ross believed he only needed to get within touching distance of the Queen to be cured of his scrofula. Sheila MacDonald, 'Old-World Survivals in Ross-Shire', *Folklore* 14 (1903), p. 372.
53 James Pope-Hennessy, *Queen Mary 1867–1953* (1959), pp. 55–6.
54 Quoted in Paul Emden, *Behind the Throne* (1934), p. 68.
55 F.W.H. Myers, *Personal Recollections of Leopold, Duke of Albany*, Myers Papers 28/64, Trinity College, Cambridge.
56 *The Training of a Sovereign: An Abridged Selection from 'The Girlhood of Queen Victoria', Being Her Majesty's Diaries between the Years 1832 and 1840*, ed. Viscount Esher (1914), p. v.
57 Myers, *Personal Recollections of Leopold, Duke of Albany*, p. 4.
58 David Duff, *The Life Story of H.R.H. Princess Louise Duchess of Argyll* (1940), pp. 299–300; see also Frank Hardie, *The Political Influence of the Monarchy, 1868–1952* (1970), p. 5.
59 Quoted in Gillian Darnley, *Octavia Hill* (1990), p. 161.
60 Daphne Bennett, *Vicky: Princess Royal of England and German Empress* (1971), pp. 174–7, 315.
61 See David Duff, *Hessian Tapestry* (1967).
62 Darnley, *Octavia Hill*, p. 163.
63 Arthur H. Beavan, *Popular Royalty* (1897), p. 188.
64 John van der Kiste, *Queen Victoria's Children* (1986), pp. 67, 77, 154.
65 BL, Add. MSS. 45750, ff. 9–93, 98, 101–2.
66 Quoted in Anne Summers, *Angels into Citizens* (1988), p. 238.
67 See the well-researched biography by

Jehanne Wake, *Princess Louise: Queen Victoria's Unconventional Daughter* (1988).

68 Constance Battersea, *Reminiscences* (1922), pp. 434–5.

69 Darnley, *Octavia Hill*, p. 303.

70 RA Add. A 17/1964.

71 William Thomson Hill, *Octavia Hill* (1956), pp. 130–32.

72 M.E. Sara, *The Life and Times of H.R.H. Princess Beatrice* (1945), p. 63.

73 Kenneth Rose, *Kings, Queens and Courtiers* (1985), p. 32.

74 *The Times*, 28 October 1897, p. 10.

75 M. Vivian Hughes, *A London Girl of the Eighties* (1936), p. 62.

76 *The Times*, 28 October 1897, p. 10; C. Kinloch Cooke, *A Memoir of Her Royal Highness Princess Mary Adelaide Duchess of Teck*, 2 vols. (1900), passim.

77 Van der Kiste, *Queen Victoria's Children*, p. 60.

78 BL, Add. MSS., 63145.

79 Burdett, *Prince, Princess and People*, pp. 50–51. An account of a typical bazaar opening by the Prince and Princess of Wales can be found in William Finney, *Descriptive Sketch of the Recent Visit of the Prince and Princess of Wales to the Potteries* (1897), p. 22.

80 *The Countess of Huntingdon's New Magazine*, November 1851, p. 252.

81 Sir George Ashton, *His Royal Highness the Duke of Connaught and Strathearn* (1929), pp. 22–3, 144, 293–4, 331 and passim. Noble Frankland's more recent *Witness of a Century: The Life and Times of Prince Arthur Duke of Connaught, 1850–1942* covers Connaught's entire career but concentrates on his military role.

82 Brian McKinlay, *The First Royal Tour, 1867–1868* (1970), passim.

83 Myers, *Personal Recollections of Leopold, Duke of Albany*, pp. 8–11.

84 *Talks with the People by Men of Mark: H.R.H. Prince Leopold, K.G., Duke of Albany*, ed. Charles Bullock ([1882]), p. 57.

85 *Life and Speeches of His Royal Highness Prince Leopold, (Duke of Albany)*, (1884), p. 35.

86 *Ibid.*, p. 23.

87 *Ibid.*, p. 42.

88 Quoted in Magnus, *King Edward the Seventh*, p. 80.

89 Burdett, *Prince, Princess and People*, pp. 380–81.

90 *Ibid.*

91 *Ibid.*

92 The connection between hospital provision in the Empire and the Jubilees of 1887 and 1897 would repay careful study.

93 *Hansard's Parliamentary Debates*, 3rd series, vol. 284, pp. 1693–94.

94 David Owen, *English Philanthropy, 1660–1960*, (1964), p. 386.

95 Parliamentary Papers, Reports from Commissioners . . . 1884–85: First Report of Her Majesty's Commissioners for Inquiring into the Housing of the Working Classes, C. 4402, p. 594.

96 RA PP Edward VII, Patronage: Annual Charities and Donations to Institutions.

97 Magnus, *King Edward the Seventh*, pp. 241–2. On a socialist's reaction to the Prince's performance on the Royal Commission, see Raymond Postgate, *The Life of George Lansbury* (1951), p. 65.

98 F.K. Prochaska, *Philanthropy and the Hospitals of London: The King's Fund, 1897–1990* (1992), p. 16.

99 Burdett, *Prince, Princess and People*, pp. 306–13, passim; see also RA Edward VII, Patronage: King Edward when Prince of Wales.

100 *Hospital*, 14 May 1910, p. 193.

101 Burdett, *Prince, Princess and People*, p. 306.

102 *Ibid.*, pp. 348–51.

103 Georgina Battiscombe, *Queen Alexandra* (1969), p. 258.

104 Sir Frederick Treves, *The Elephant Man and Other Reminiscences* (1923), pp. 24–6; E.W. Morris, *The London Hospital* (1910), p. 230.

105 BL, Add. MSS., 46270, f. 392.

106 BL, Add. MSS., 45985, ff. 121–3.

107 RA Vic. Add. A21/205.

108 Burdett to Miss Knollys, 18 July 1905, Gwyer MSS, now in the Royal National Pension Fund for Nurses. See also Battiscombe, *Queen*

Alexandra, pp. 236–8.

109　See *Burdett's Hospitals and Charities 1926*, pp. 459–61.

110　Quoted in Summers, *Angels into Citizens*, p. 241.

111　*Ibid*. See also Battiscome, *Queen Alexandra*, pp. 232–6.

112　Myers, *Personal Recollections of Leopold, Duke of Albany*, p. 9.

113　Greater London Record Office, A/FWA/C/261/1.

114　Rev. Archer Gurney, *Loyalty and Church and State: A Sermon Preached . . . on the occasion of the National Thanksgiving for the Recovery of H.R.H. the Prince of Wales* (1872), p. 6.

115　*Ibid.*, p. 7.

116　See Gertrude Himmelfarb, *Poverty and Compassion: The Moral Imagination of the Victorians* (New York, 1991), pp. 205–6.

117　On Esher, see James Lees-Milne, *The Enigmatic Edwardian: The Life of Reginald, 2nd Viscount Esher* (1986) and Peter Fraser, *Lord Esher: A Political Biography* (1973). There is no biography of Burdett, but several helpful obituaries appeared in the *Hospital* in May 1920. See also Christopher Maggs, *A Century of Change: The Story of The Royal National Pension Fund for Nurses* (1987), pp. 13–16; Prochaska, *Philanthropy and the Hospitals of London*; Geoffrey Rivett, *The Development of the London Hospital System, 1823–1982* (1986), pp. 373–4.

118　Maggs, *A Century of Change*, p. 16.

119　Burdett, *Prince, Princess and People*, p. 8.

120　*Ibid.*, pp. 43–4.

121　See Burdett's papers (the Gwyer Papers) which have been deposited at the Royal National Pension Fund for Nurses and the Burdett material at the Bodleian Library, Oxford.

122　Memorandum titled 'Hospital Sunday Fund—A Record Year', Gwyer Papers, n.d., now in the Royal National Pension Fund for Nurses.

123　See *Souvenir of the Reception by Her Majesty Queen Alexandra of the Pension Fund Nurses at Marlborough House* ([1902]).

124　Maggs, *A Century of Change*, pp. 41–60, 131–5; *Hospital*, 13 June 1896, p. 182.

125　*Hospital*, 13 June 1896, p. 182.

126　H.C. Cameron, *Mr Guy's Hospital* (1954), pp. 260–1.

127　Burdett Memorandum, dated 1896, Gwyer Papers, now in the Royal National Pension Fund for Nurses.

128　*Hospital*, 20 June 1896, p. 196.

129　*Ibid*. For further details see Prochaska, *Philanthropy and the Hospitals of London*, pp. 17–18.

130　Burdett Memorandum, dated 1896, Gwyer Papers.

131　Cannadine, 'The Context, Performance and Meaning of Ritual', pp. 133–4.

132　See Lawrence Stone, 'History and Post-Modernism', *Past & Present* 135 (May 1992), pp. 189–94.

133　Cannadine, 'The Context, Performance and Meaning of Ritual', pp. 133.

134　RA W38/6

135　*The Times* throughout 1887 is an excellent source for a study of Jubilee projects. There are also many institutional histories that discuss individual appeals. See, for example, Peter Finch, *Voluntary Hospitals of Southend-on-Sea, 1887–1948* (1948), p. 1. *Burdett's Hospitals and Charities* is a good source on hospital building.

136　*The Times*, 16 March 1887, p. 12.

137　Sara, *The Life and Times of H.R.H. Princess Beatrice*, p. 74.

138　*The Times*, 7 January 1888, p. 9; see also, RA Add. J/254.

139　RA Add. J/160, 161, 254.

140　Magnus, *King Edward the Seventh*, pp. 199–200.

141　Cannadine, 'The Context, Performance and Meaning of Ritual', pp. 135–6.

142　Viscount Esher, 'The Voluntary Principle', *The Influence of King Edward* (1915), p. 114.

143　*Punch*, 22 May 1897, p. 241.

144　*Hospital*, 12 July 1919, p. 379.

145　See Elizabeth Hammerton and David Cannadine, 'Conflict and Consensus on a Ceremonial Occasion: The Diamond Jubilee in Cambridge in

1897', *Historical Journal* no. 24, 1 (1981), pp. 111–46.

146 W.E. Hume, *The Infirmary Newcastle Upon Tyne: A Brief Sketch, 1751–1951* ([1951]), p. 52; *Borough of Lewes: Record of Proceedings in Connection with the Celebration and Commemoration of the Long Reign of Sixty Years of Her Majesty Queen Victoria, 1897* (1897); see also *Burdett's Hospitals and Charities*, passim, and *The Times* throughout 1897.

147 Emden, *Behind the Throne*, p. 207.

148 RA 0.1/55,56; *Burdett's Hospitals and Charities, 1898*, vol. 1, p. 873. In 1900 the Queen gave an additional £1,000 to Indian famine relief. See *Report of the Central Executive Committee, Indian Famine Charitable Relief Fund, 1900* (Calcutta, 1901), p. 43.

149 Using the Retail Price Index figures provided by the Bank of England, it would have required £70 million in 1987 to buy the same amount of goods as could have been bought for £2 million in 1897. Between them, Band Aid and Live Aid raised £70 million worldwide. See Charlotte Gray, *Bob Geldof* (1987).

150 RA 01/50.

151 RA 08/29.

152 RA P11/69. See also *The Letters of Queen Victoria*, ed. George Earle Buckle, 3rd series, 3 vols. (1932), vol. 3, p. 582.

153 RA PP3/2/328.

154 RA P5/135; P8/69.

155 C.J. Montague, *Sixty Years in Waifdom; or, The Ragged School Movement in English History* (1904), p. 8.

Chapter 5

1 Geoffrey Finlayson, *Citizen, State, and Social Welfare in Britain, 1830–1990* (1994), pp. 106–7, 112; José Harris, *Private Lives, Public Spirit: Britain 1870–1914* (Penguin edn, 1994), p. 17.

2 Royal Commission on the Aged Poor, Parliamentary Papers, 1895, vol. 14, p. 222.

3 *Westminster Review*, 135 (1891), p. 373.

4 David Owen, *English Philanthropy, 1660–1960* (1964), p. 525.

5 Brian Abel-Smith, *The Hospitals, 1800–1948* (1964), p. 153.

6 Gwendoline M. Ayers, *England's First State Hospitals and the Metropolitan Asylums Board, 1867–1930* (1971), p. 98

7 *Hospital*, 22 July 1911, p. 417; 22 March 1913, pp. 679–82; 2 August 1913, p. 533.

8 See Harris, *Private Lives. Public Spirit*, p. 16.

9 Finlayson, *Citizen, State, and Social Welfare in Britain*, chapter 2; see also George Behlmer, *Child Abuse and Moral Reform in England, 1870–1908* (Stanford, 1982), p. 217.

10 Sidney Webb, 'Social Movements', in *The Cambridge Modern History*, eds. A.W. Ward, G.W. Prothero, and Stanley Leathes, 13 vols. (1902–11), vol. 12, p. 765. See also Harris, *Private Lives, Public Spirit*, p. 61.

11 Owen, *English Philanthropy, 1660–1960*, pp. 517–21. For a detailed discussion of the tensions between philanthropists and socialists on the Royal Commission see A.M. McBriar, *An Edwardan Mixed Doubles: The Bosanquets versus the Webbs: A Study of British Social Policy 1890–1929* (1987).

12 *The Diary of Beatrice Webb*, eds. Norman and Jeanne Mackenzie, 4 vols. (1982–85), vol. 2, p. 108.

13 *The Training of a Sovereign: An Abridged Selection from 'The Girlhood of Queen Victoria', Being Her Majesty's Diaries between the Years 1832 and 1840*, ed. Viscount Esher (1914), pp. vi–vii.

14 Philip Magnus, *King Edward the Seventh* (1964), p. 405. See also Kenneth O. Morgan, *Keir Hardie, Radical and Socialist* (1975), pp. 71–3.

15 British Library, Add. MSS. 41207, f. 22. See also RA R27/13.

16 *Ibid.*, ff. 152–3. See also RA27/114.

17 *Ibid.*, Add. MSS. 41208, f. 119.

18 RA W41/15. Esher to Knollys, 27 December 1907.

19 RA W41/11. Esher to Knollys, 1 December 1907.

20 Peter Fraser, *Lord Esher: A Political*

Biography (1973), p. 81.

21 G.R. Searle, *Corruption in British Politics. 1895–1930* (1987), p. 24; Magnus, *King Edward the Seventh*, p. 389.

22 Sir Charles Petrie, *Monarchy in the Twentieth Century* (1952), p. 217.

23 For a stimulating discussion of the plutocrats, see David Cannadine, *The Decline and Fall of the British Aristocracy* (1990), Chapter 8.

24 Anthony Allfrey, *Edward VII and his Jewish Court* (1991), p. 102.

25 RA W41/50. Esher to Knollys, 14 June 1908.

26 *Ibid.*

27 Cannadine, *The Decline and Fall of the British Aristocracy,* pp. 299–300. On the honours system see Ivan de La Bere, *The Queen's Orders of Chivalry* (1961); Michael De-la-Noy, *The Honours System* (1985); John Walker, *The Queen has been Pleased: The British Honours System at Work* (1986); *The Royal Encyclopedia*, eds. Ronald Allison and Sarah Riddell (1991); Hugo Vickers, *Royal Orders* (1994).

28 Oliver Warner, *The Life-boat Service: A History of the Royal National Lifeboat Institution, 1824–1974* (1974), p. 10.

29 F.G. Fairholme and W. Paine, *A Century of Work for Animals* (New York, 1924), p. 94.

30 Christopher Maggs, *A Century of Change: The Story of the Royal National Pension Fund for Nurses* (1987), p. 133.

31 The records of the League of Mercy were passed to the Public Record Office after it was wound up in 1947, and they are now included in the Ministry of Health files, MH/11/1–59. Further material on the institution is contained in the archives of the King's Fund, the Royal Archives, Windsor, and the Burdett Papers in the Bodleian Library, Oxford.

32 In 1933 the Garter King of Arms took the view that it was a decoration and not an order and that the word 'order' was a misnomer. See E.F. Grove to A.F. Flatow, 18 July 1962, RA PP GVI 184.

33 RA GV 26296/150a.

34 The money was used to build the King Edward VII Hospital Midhurst. See S.E. Large, *King Edward VII Hospital, Midhurst, 1901–1986: The King's Sanatorium.* (1986), p. 1.

35 Alec Waugh, *The Lipton Story* (1951), pp. 80–88. For further information on Lipton see the *Dictionary of Business Biography*, ed. David Jeremy, 5 vols. (1984–86).

36 Quoted in Cannadine, *The Decline and Fall of the British Aristocracy*, p. 299.

37 Searle, *Corruption in British Politics, 1895–1930*, p. 90.

38 BL. Add. MSS. 52513, ff. 62–3.

39 *The Royal Encyclopedia*, eds. Allison and Riddell, p. 193.

40 BL, Add. MSS. 52513, f. 66.

41 *Ibid.,* ff. 98–9. The man in question was Sir Henry Fowler, a former President of the Board of Trade and Chancellor of the Duchy of Lancaster. He was made a viscount in April 1908.

42 See Joan Austoker, *A History of the Imperial Cancer Research Fund, 1902–1986* (1988).

43 *Daily Telegraph*, 8 May 1889.

44 *Burdett's Hospitals and Charities, 1902*, p. 62.

45 *Imperialism and Popular Culture*, ed. John Mackenzie (1986), p. 4.

46 Quoted in Brian Harrison, 'For Church, Queen and Family: The Girls' Friendly Society, 1874–1920', *Past & Present* 61 (November 1973), p. 126.

47 John Cannon, 'The Modern British Monarchy: A Study in Adaptation', Stenton Lecture, University of Reading (1987), p. 13; *Darling Child: Private Correspondence of Queen Victoria and the German Crown Princess, 1871–1878*, ed. Roger Fulford (1976), p. 51.

48 Viscount Esher, 'The Voluntary Principle', *The Influence of King Edward* (1915), p. 117.

49 *Ibid.*, pp. 114–17.

50 *Ibid.*, p. 116.

51 This was very much Esher's view. See James Lees-Milne, *The Enigmatic Edwardian: The Life of Reginald, 2nd Viscount Esher* (1986), p. 310.

52 Viscount Esher, *To-day and Tomorrow and Other Essays* (1910), p. 227.

53 RA GV Q/724/113.

54 See the illustration of Edward VII in the *Illustrated London News*, 1 August 1903.

55 See, for example, BL, Add. MSS. 45985, ff. 95–6.

56 Public Record Office, HO/144 contains the files of about 2,500 applicants for royal patronage beween 1879 and 1920. See also Arnold Sorsby, *Royal Eye Hospital, 1857–1957* (1957), p. 19.

57 C.J. Montague, *Sixty Years in Waifdom; or, The Ragged School Movement in English History* (1904), pp. 3–4.

58 RA PP Edward VII, Patronage: Annual Charities and Donations to Institutions.

59 RA Add. A21/219A.

60 On the King's savings from the Civil List see Phillip Hall, *Royal Fortune: Tax, Money and the Monarchy* (1992), p. 25.

61 Between 1886 and 1910, the King earned £269,495 from stud fees. Magnus, *King Edward the Seventh*, p. 254.

62 Owen, *English Philanthropy, 1660–1960*, p. 515.

63 *Ibid.*, p. 516.

64 Frances Dimond, 'The Queen and the Camera', in *Crown and Camera*, ed. Frances Dimond and Roger Taylor (1987), p. 75.

65 Sir Sydney Lee, *King Edward VII: A Biography*, 2 vols. (1925–27). vol. 1, p. 566.

66 Quoted Magnus, *King Edward the Seventh*, p. 397.

67 *Hospital*, 19 August 1911, pp. 521–3.

68 F.K. Prochaska, *Philanthropy and the Hospitals of London: The King's Fund, 1897–1992* (1992), pp. 116–17.

69 For the setting up of the Fund, see *ibid.*, chapter 1.

70 A signed copy of this letter is in the Greater London Record Office, A/KE/641.

71 *Hospital*, 12 July 1919, p. 380.

72 See the extensive correspondence between Burdett and Knollys in the Burdett Papers, Bodleian Library.

73 Knollys to Burdett, 14 November 1897, Burdett Papers, Bodleian Library.

74 For contributions, see the King's Fund annual reports.

75 Wernher's bequest was one-twelfth of the residue of his estate. For more information on the wealth of several of the Fund's principal benefactors, see W.D. Rubinstein, *Men of Property* (1981).

76 A useful guide to these connections can be found in the *Dictionary of Business Biography*, ed. Jeremy. See especially Pat Thane's excellent entry on Cassel.

77 Philip Ziegler, *The Sixth Great Power: Barings 1762–1929* (1988), p. 289.

78 For the Fund's early investments, see GLRO, A/KE/2/1; A/KE/27/1.

79 GLRO, A/KE/574.

80 These tags turn up among Burdett's Papers in the Gwyer MSS and in the Samuel Lewis Trust Papers. I am indebted to Dr G.D. Black for information on Samuel Lewis and his wife, Ada.

81 This illustration is included in Geoffrey Rivett, *The Development of the London Hospital System, 1823–1982* (1986), p. 147.

82 GLRO A/KE/289/594; 292/366; *Hospital*, 5 June 1897, pp. 166–7.

83 *The Times*, 12 March 1898, p. 10.

84 *Daily News*, 27 February 1899.

85 *Hospital*, 13 February 1897, p. 335.

86 *Ibid.*

87 Charles Loch to Dr Robert Lee, 20 June 1899, GLRO, A/FWA/C/D261/1.

88 GLRO, A/FWA/C/261/1.

89 RA Add. A4/89; A4/101.

90 Burdett to King George V, 18 June 1915, RA GV 26296/208.

91 For details of the League's organization, see Rev. P.H. Ditchfield (ed.), *The Book of the League of Mercy* (1907). See also *Hospital*, 9 October 1909, p. 48.

92 PRO MH/11/53; MH/11/57. The League's annual contributions to the King's Fund can be found in the Fund's annual reports.

93 Magnus, *King Edward the Seventh*, p. 279.

94 For details of the appeal, see GLRO A/KE/299; A/KE/750/1–36.

95 See Tim Heald, *By Appointment: 150 Years of the Royal Warrant and its Holders* (1989).

96 RA W38/26. Esher to Knollys, 26 September 1901.

97 *Burdett's Hospitals and Charities, 1902*, p. 62.

98 *Ibid.*

99 Rev. H.G. Warner to Burdett, 31 May 1910, Gwyer MSS.

100 Sir Donald Mackenzie Wallace, *The Web of Empire* (1902), pp. 370–72.

101 Knollys to Burdett, 25 September 1902, Gwyer MSS.

102 For more financial details of the Coronation Appeal, see the Fund's annual reports.

103 RA GV C274/1.

104 Frank Long, *King Edward's Hospital Fund for London: The Story of its Foundation and Achievements, 1897–1942* (1942), p. 25.

105 RA GV C273/3; C273/16–17.

106 King's Fund, *Tenth Annual Report*, p. 8.

107 Bigge to J. Danvers Power, 18 October 1906, GLRO, A/KE/573/17. The Lewis estate was not wound up until 1949.

108 For information on George V's patronages before becoming King, see RA GV, HRH the Duke of York: Charitable Institutions.

109 GLRO, A/KE/27/2/179.

110 There are 270 items in the Royal Archives dealing with the Fund's constitution and its Act of Incorporation. See RA GV C1578.

111 RA GV C273/60.

112 GLRO, A/KE/572/17.

113 GLRO, A/KE/574.

114 *Ibid.*

115 *Parliamentary Debates*, 4th series., vol. 172 (1907), p. 448.

116 A.G.L. Ives to W. Hyde, 14 December 1939, King's Fund Archives, Nuffield Provincial Hospitals Trust file.

117 *Parliamentary Debates*, 4th series, vol. 172 (1907), pp. 457–8.

118 BL, Add. MSS. 41208, ff. 188–91.

119 See Prochaska, *Philanthropy and the Hospitals of London*, p. 68.

120 *Ibid.*, chapters 3 and 4.

121 For information on the finances of the Fund and its yearly distribution to the hospitals, see the annual reports.

122 See the manuscript Travel Diaries (Japan) of Sidney and Beatrice Webb, in the British Library of Political and Economic Science, London School of Economics.

123 *The Diary of Beatrice Webb*, eds. Norman and Jeanne Mackenzie, vol. 3, p. 139.

Chapter 6

1 See Harold Nicolson, *Diaries and Letters, 1945–1962*, ed. Nigel Nicolson (1971), pp. 133, 162.

2 Harold Nicolson, *King George the Fifth: His Life and Reign* (1967 edn.), pp. 217, 671. See also John Gore, *King George V: A Personal Memoir* (1941); and Kenneth Rose, *King George V* (1983), p. 224.

3 Kenneth O. Morgan, *Keir Hardie, Radical and Socialist* (1975), pp. 71, 263. See also *Parliamentary Debates*, 4th series, vol. 26 (1894), pp. 462–3.

4 Quoted in Raymond Postgate, *The Life of George Lansbury* (1951), p. 251; see also Tom Nairn, *The Enchanted Glass: Britain and its Monarchy* (1990), p. 341; Colin Cooke, *The Life of Richard Stafford Cripps* (1957), p. 162.

5 Herbert Morrison, *Herbert Morrison: An Autobiography* (1960), p. 129.

6 Ben Pimlott, *Hugh Dalton* (1985), p. 416.

7 George V to Queen Mary, 23 August 1911, RA GV CC4/74.

8 Edgar Wilson, *The Myth of British Monarchy* (1989), p. 45; Caroline Benn, *Keir Hardie* (1992), p. 322.

9 Nicolson, *King George the Fifth*, p. 220.

10 RA GV CC47/288.

11 RA PP GV A/1119. He repeated the advice in a letter to Charlotte Knollys the following day.

12 Philip Magnus, *King Edward the Seventh* (1964), p. 397.

13 *The Times*, 11 June 1909, p. 9.

14 Quoted in James Pope-Hennessy,

Queen Mary, 1867–1953 (1959), p. 469.

15 RA GV Q724/6.

16 Pope-Hennessy, *Queen Mary*, p. 470.

17 *The Times*, 15 June 1912, p. 10.

18 *Ibid., 28* June 1912, p. 8.

19 Quoted in Pope-Hennessy, *Queen Mary*, p. 470.

20 See *The Times*, 10 July 1912, p. 8.

21 RA GV CC26/22.

22 Quoted in Nicolson, *King George the Fifth*, p. 266; see also Pope-Hennessy, *Queen Mary*, pp. 471–2.

23 Robert Smillie, *My Life for Labour* (1924), pp. 196–9.

24 *Journals and Letters of Reginald Viscount Esher*, 4 vols. (1934–38), vol. 3, p. 84.

25 Nicolson, *Diaries and Letters, 1945–1962*, p. 162.

26 For an introduction to some of these war funds, see Diana Condell, 'A Gift for Christmas: The Story of Princess Mary's Gift Fund, 1914', *Imperial War Museum Review* 4 (1989), p. 77.

27 Geoffrey Finlayson, *Citizen, State, and Social Welfare in Britain, 1830–1990* (1994), p. 220.

28 RA PP GV, Abstract of Privy Purse Accounts 1915; Donations to Charities Connected with the War, 1914–1915. The first figure includes £2,000 for Royal Maundy distribution.

29 Nicolson, *King George the Fifth*, p. 330.

30 Pope-Hennessy, *Queen Mary*, p. 505.

31 Nicolson, *King George the Fifth*, p. 336.

32 Quoted in Pope-Hennessy, *Queen Mary*, p. 498.

33 Nicolson, *King George the Fifth*, p. 336.

34 Rose, *King George V*, p. 257

35 A.J.P. Taylor, *English History, 1914–1945* (1965), p. 175.

36 See the list of recipients published in *The Times*, 25 August 1917, p. 8; on Appleton, see Alice Prochaska, *History of the General Federation of Trade Unions, 1899–1980* (1982).

37 John Walker, *The Queen has been Pleased: The British Honours System at Work* (1986), pp. 13–14.

38 David Cannadine, *The Decline and Fall of the British Aristocracy* (1990), p. 301.

39 Rose, *King George V*, p. 258. Walker, *The Queen has been Pleased*, p. 12 puts the figure at 25,000 by the end of 1919.

40 RA GV CC26/93.

41 Pope-Hennessy, *Queen Mary*, p. 490.

42 RA GV CC44/215.

43 Quoted in Pope-Hennessy, *Queen Mary*, p. 490.

44 RA PP GV, Donations to Charities Connected with the War; Edward VIII, Patronage as Prince of Wales.

45 RA EPOW 1247; Pope-Hennessy, *Queen Mary*, p. 491.

46 *Final Report of the Administrtion of the National Relief Fund*, Cmd. 1272 (HMSO, 1921), p. 3.

47 RA EPOW 1247.

48 RA GV CC49/28.

49 Quoted in Pope-Hennessy, *Queen Mary*, p. 494.

50 *Thatched with Gold: The Memoirs of Mabell, Countess of Airlie*, ed. Jennifer Ellis (1962), p. 131.

51 Sir George Aston, *His Royal Highness the Duke of Connaught and Strathearn: A Life and Intimate Study* (1929), p. 294. On the Princess of Teck's war work see *For my Grandchildren: Some Reminiscences of Her Royal Highness Princess Alice, Countess of Athlone* (1966), pp. 156–61.

52 RA Add. A21/228/195.

53 Condell, 'A Gift for Christmas: The Story of Princess Mary's Gift Fund, 1914', pp. 69–78.

54 David Marquand, *Ramsay MacDonald*, (1977), p. 226.

55 Nicolson, *King George the Fifth*, pp. 402–3.

56 RA GV Q724/110.

57 *Thatched with Gold*, ed. Ellis, p. 141–2.

58 *Ibid.* According to Nicolson, *King George the Fifth*, p. 427, the King 'derived no impression of the shadows of vanity and suspicion that marred the splendour of Woodrow Wilson's mind and heart'. As Lady Airlie suggests, this was not so. The courtiers who took against Wilson would not have left the King in a

state of innocence about the President's 'shadows'. Esher feared that 'Great Britain would become an appanage of the U.S.A.', and in particular he resented Wilson's gross impertinence in lecturing the English about their behaviour to Ireland. RA GV Q724/101.

59 RA GV Q724/109.
60 RA GV Q724/110.
61 Viscount Esher, *The Influence of King Edward and Essays on Other Subjects*, (1915), pp. 105–6.
62 RA GV Q724/110.
63 RA O 1106/65/4. The letter is quoted in Nicolson, *King George the Fifth*, p. 403.
64 RA GV Q724/110.
65 RA GV Q724/111.
66 Quoted in Nicolson, *King George the Fifth*, p. 426.
67 RA GV Q724/113.
68 See George V's letter to Stamfordham in January 1920, quoted in Nicolson, *King George the Fifth*, p. 443.
69 *Ibid.*, p. 444.
70 RA GV P476/60.
71 *Thatched with Gold*, ed. Ellis, p. 170; Rose, *King George V*, p. 224.
72 RA GV K1740/1.
73 RA GV K1740/4.
74 RA GV K1740/5.
75 For a stimulating discussion of this trend, see Bruce P. Lenman, *The Eclipse of Parliament: Appearance and Reality in British Politics since 1914* (1992).
76 J. Ramsay MacDonald, *Socialism and Government*, 2 vols. (1910), vol. 2, p. 41. See also John Cannon and Ralph Griffiths, *The Oxford Illustrated History of the British Monarchy* (1988), p. 598.
77 Quoted in Rose, *King George V*, p. 227.
78 *Ibid.*, pp. 227–8.
79 James Lees Milne, *The Enigmatic Edwardian: The Life of Reginald, 2nd Viscount Esher* (1986), p. 332.
80 Sarah Bradford, *George VI* (1991), p. 103.
81 RA GV O1266/8–11.
82 José Harris, 'Society and the State in Twentieth-Century Britain', in *The Cambridge Social History of Britain*, ed.

F.M.L. Thompson, 3 vols. (1990), vol. 3, p. 84.
83 Pope-Hennessy, *Queen Mary*, p. 514.
84 Quoted in Philip Ziegler, *King Edward VIII* (1990), p. 108.
85 Quoted in Pope-Hennessy, *Queen Mary*, p. 515.
86 Ziegler, *King Edward VIII*, p. 111. The Prince was highly conscious of the need to work the industrial areas. See, for example, his letter to Alan Lascelles in 1922, cited, *In Royal Service. The Letters and Journals of Sir Alan Lascelles, 1920–36*, ed. Duff Hart-Davis (1989), p. 15.
87 Henry Hector Bolitho, *A Century of British Monarchy* (1951), p. 206.
88 *A King's Story. The Memoirs of the Duke of Windsor* (New York, 1951), p. 217.
89 Quoted in Ziegler, *King Edward VIII*, p. 114.
90 Bradford, *George VI*, p. 104.
91 *The Royal Encyclopedia*, eds. Ronald Allison and Sarah Riddell (1991), p. 220.
92 According to Hyde, Queen Mary played a part in the extension of the Society's work, *Industrial Welfare and Personnel Management*, vol. 30, no. 321, (1948), p. 173. There is a good discussion of the Duke of York's industrial work in Hector Bolitho, *George VI* (1937), chapter 7.
93 *Ibid.*
94 Bradford, *George VI*, p. 104.
95 Robert R. Hyde, *The Camp Book: Being some Account of the Duke of York's Experiment* (1930), p. 11.
96 Bradford, *George VI*, p. 108.
97 *The Times*, 19 April 1923, p. 9. See also Dorothy Laird, *Queen Elizabeth the Queen Mother and her Support to the Throne during Four Reigns* (1966), p. 45.
98 Laird, *Queen Elizabeth the Queen Mother*, p. 78. For a more recent biography of the Queen Mother, see Penelope Mortimer, *Queen Elizabeth: A Life of the Queen Mother* (1986).
99 *First Annual Report of the London Playing Fields Committee* (1891), p. 14.
100 *Give us a Place to Play: The National Playing Fields Association* (1925), p. 4.

101 RA EPOW 981.
102 Denis Judd, *Prince Philip* (1980), pp. 172–3; *The Royal Encyclopedia*, eds. Allison and Riddell, p. 350.
103 Bolitho, *George VI*, p. 135–6. *The Official Index to The Times* is a good starting point for a study of the public engagements of the royal family in the interwar years.
104 RA GVI 1627.
105 RA GV CC47/672.
106 Francis Watson, *Dawson of Penn* (1951), p. 130. On the Dawson Report see F.K. Prochaska, *Philanthropy and the Hospitals of London: The King's Fund, 1897–1990* (1992), pp. 90–92.
107 RA GV 30383.
108 *Ibid.*
109 Prochaska, *Philanthropy and the Hospitals of London*, p. 93.
110 RA EPOW/34, 5 April 1932.
111 This letter, illustrated here on page 199, was reproduced in large numbers and circulated by the King's Fund and the other charities active in the hospital appeal.
112 Prochaska, *Philanthropy and the Hospitals of London*, 99–100.
113 'The Final Report of the Hospitals of London Combined Appeal', *King's Fund: Twenty-Sixth Annual Report*, pp. 44–53.
114 *Ibid.*, p. 53.
115 *King's Fund: Twenty-Eighth Annual Report*, p. 17.
116 *A King's Story: The Memoirs of the Duke of Windsor*, pp. 215–16.
117 Ziegler, *King Edward VIII*, p. 108.
118 Interview with A.G.L. Ives, a former Secretary of the King's Fund, in February 1988.
119 *A King's Story: The Memoirs of the Duke of Windsor*, pp. 214–15.
120 RA EPOW: Patronage as Prince of Wales.
121 William Henry MacMenemey, *A History of the Worcester Royal Infirmary* (1947), pp. 318–19; *Wealth Well-Given: The Enterprise and Benevolence of Lord Nuffield*, ed. F. John Minns (Dover, NH, 1994), p. 129.
122 RA EPOW 2904A.
123 Ziegler, *King Edward VIII*, p. 219.
124 RA EPOW 1935.
125 *Ibid.*
126 *The Times*, 28 January 1932, p. 12.
127 *Ibid.*
128 Margaret Brasnett, *Voluntary Social Action: A History of the National Council of Social Service 1919–1969* (1969), pp. 70–71.
129 In January 1933 the Prince made a further appeal, in a broadcast, the first of a series of 'S.O.S.' talks on unemployment. See *The Times*, 7 January 1933, p. 10.
130 Bolitho, *A Century of British Monarchy*, p. 202.
131 *A King's Story: The Memoirs of the Duke of Windsor*, p. 248; see also Ziegler, *King Edward VIII*, p. 216.
132 RA EPOW 1935. From a newspaper cutting titled 'A Churlish Decision'.
133 Brasnett, *Voluntary Social Action*, pp. 69–71.
134 Richard Crossman, 'The Role of the Volunteer in the Modern Social Service', in *Traditions of Social Policy*, ed. A.H. Halsey (1976), p. 265.
135 General William Booth, *In Darkest England and the Way Out* (1890), pp. 79–80.
136 Nicolson, *King George the Fifth*, p. 172. See also Nairn, *The Enchanted Glass*, pp. 340–41.
137 'The Apple Cart', *Prefaces by Bernard Shaw*, (1938), p. 326.
138 Will Thorne, *My Life's Battles* (1925), p. 213. See also Ross M. Martin, *TUC: The Growth of a Pressure Group 1868–1976* (1980), p. 147.
139 John Hodge, *Workman's Cottage to Windsor Castle* ([1931]), pp. 190–91.
140 Philip Viscount Snowden, *An Autobiography*, 2 vols. (1934), vol. 2, pp. 829–30.
141 *The Diary of Beatrice Webb*, eds Norman and Jeanne MacKenzie, 4 vols. (1982–85), vol. 4, p. 193.
142 In the 1931 crisis, the King took advice from the three party leaders, but, according to Clive Wigram, he found the Liberal leader, Sir Herbert Samuel, the most persuasive. Samuel told the King, in Nicolson's words: 'in view of the fact that the necessary economies would prove most unpalatable to the working class, it would

be to the general interest if they could be imposed by a Labour Government. . . . The best alternative would be a National Government composed of members of the three parties. It would be preferable that Mr MacDonald should remain Prime Minister.' (p. 592). Nicolson is at pains to argue that George V's role in the crisis was constitutionally correct. He does not observe that the episode had effects on the Labour Party that would bring quiet satisfaction to the Palace, but then Nicolson often pulls his punches.

143 *TUC Report* (1935), p. 426.
144 Quoted in Marquand, *Ramsay MacDonald*, pp. 774–75.
145 Quoted in Nicolson, *King George the Fifth*, p. 669.
146 *Ibid.*, p. 669.
147 RA GV P633/324.
148 *The Collected Essays, Journals and Letters of George Orwell*, eds. Sonia Orwell and Ian Angus, 4 vols. (Penguin edn, 1970), vol. 3, p. 33.
149 *King's Fund: Thirty-Third Annual Report*, p. 48.
150 *The Times*, 25 April 1935, p. 10.
151 Greater London Record Office, AK/E/40/5 f. 27.
152 RA PP GV Silver Jubilee 24,000/B9a, B18; *The Times*, 22 April 1935, p. 12.
153 *The Times*, 7 May 1935, p. 16
154 See for example, *ibid.*, 22 April 1935, p. 12.
155 RA EPOW 2904A.
156 David Owen, *English Philanthropy, 1660–1960* (1964), p. 565.
157 *Punch*, 10 April and 15 May, 1935. A King George Jubilee (Berlin) Trust was set up to benefit needy British citizens in Berlin, *The Times*, 7 May 1935, p. 15.
158 Brian Robinson, *Silver Pennies and Linen Towels: The Story of the Royal Maundy* (1992), p. 50.
159 *The Times*, 27 December 1932, p. 10.
160 *Ibid.*, 27 June 1936, p. 11.
161 Only about 200 of Edward VIII's organizations were specifically charitable, but many of the remaining institutions had a charitable dimen-

sion. See RA PP Patronage Edward VIII; RA PP GVI 1/14.
162 Ziegler, *King Edward VIII*, p. 288.
163 The phrase 'something must be done' is usually attributed to the King, but according to the Welsh newspapers, for example the headline in the *South Wales Argus*, 19 November 1936, he actually said 'something will be done'. *The Times*, 19 November 1936, p. 16, reported the King as saying 'some kind of employment must be found'. For details of the organization and reception of the King's tour to south Wales in November 1936, see the recently released file in the Public Record Office, MH 58/309.

Chapter 7

1 Sarah Bradford, *George VI* (1991), p. 271.
2 *Ibid.*, p. 356.
3 On George VI's posthumous reputation, see Leonard M. Harris, *Long to Reign over Us? The Status of the Royal Family in the Sixties* (1966), pp. 130–32.
4 RA PP GVI 104.
5 RA PP GVI 529.
6 The letter is now on display in the Fund's offices.
7 RA PP GVI 525.
8 For the complete list of George VI's patronages, most of which did not receive annual contributions, see RA PP GVI 1/14a. George VI contributed to 278 institutions in 1943. A few of his charitable payments, amounting to just over £700, came out of Class III of the Civil List. RA PP GVI, Annual Suscriptions to Charities. The Home Office correspondence is in RA PP GVI 1/5. See also RA PP GVI 1/20.
9 For a list of his patronages see Noble Frankland, *Prince Henry, Duke of Gloucester* (1980), pp. 243–4.
10 See *The Memoirs of Princess Alice, Duchess of Gloucester* (1983), p. 115–16.
11 James Wentworth Day, *H.R.H. Princess Marina, Duchess of Kent* (1969), p.

185.

12 Dorothy Laird, *Queen Elizabeth the Queen Mother* (1966), pp. 165–6.

13 Harold Nicolson, *Diaries and Letters, 1945–1962*, ed. Nigel Nicolson (1971), p. 327.

14 See *The Times*, 28 December 1937, p. 12.

15 Laird, *Queen Elizabeth the Queen Mother*, p. 128.

16 *The Diary of Beatrice Webb*, eds. Norman and Jeanne Mackenzie, 4 vols. (1982–85), vol. 4, p. 435.

17 RA GVI PS 1627.

18 See *The Official Index to The Times* for 1937.

19 Greater London Record Office, A/KE/589.

20 Interviews with A.G.L. Ives, former Secretary of the King's Fund, 28 May and 23 July 1982.

21 See Geoffrey Finlayson, *Citizen, State, and Social Welfare in Britain 1830–1900* (1994), pp. 254–5; Paul Addison, *The Road to 1945* (1977), p. 49. See also Ben Pimlott, *Labour and the Left in the 1930s* (1977).

22 Douglas Jay, *The Socialist Case* (1937), p. 317, quoted in Peter Hennessy, *Never Again: Britain 1945–1951* (Vintage edn, 1993), p. 132.

23 Bertrand Russell, *The Scientific Outlook* (1931), p. 211.

24 G. A. Campbell, *The Civil Service in Britain* (1965), pp. 56, 69.

25 Moses Abramowitz and Vera F. Eliasberg, *The Growth of Public Employment in Great Britain* (Princeton, 1957), p. 43. Of the 700,000 public servants, 464,700 were in civilian agencies and the rest were non-industrial defence staff.

26 *Shaftesbury Magazine*, 97 (June 1945), p. 11.

27 See, for example, Theo Aronson, *The Royal Family at War* (1993); and Bradford, *George VI*, chapter 10.

28 See James Pope-Hennesy, *Queen Mary, 1867–1953* (1959), chapter 8.

29 Public Record Office, Prem 8/1270.

30 RA GVI PS 07449/83.

31 *King's Fund: Forty-Fifth Annual Report*, p. 16. See also GLRO, A/KE/324, and George C. Curnock, *Hospitals under Fire* (1941).

32 Marion Yass, *This is your War: Home Front Propaganda in the Second World War* (1983), p. 58.

33 Bradford, *George VI*, p. 427; see also Sir John W. Wheeler-Bennett, *King George VI: His Life and Reign* (1958), p. 467.

34 See *The London Hospital Illustrated: 250 Years* (1990), passim.

35 Quoted in Bradford, *George VI*, p. 430.

36 PRO INF 1/670. 37.

37 See *The Cottal's Saturday Night and the Queen's Broadcast* (n.d.).

38 Bradford, *George VI*, pp. 434–5; Laird, *Queen Elizabeth the Queen Mother*, p. 209; *The Memoirs of the Rt. Hon. the Earl of Woolton* (1959), p. 224.

39 See *The Royal Encyclopedia*, eds. Ronald Allison and Sarah Riddell (1991), pp. 224–5.

40 A.J.P. Taylor, *English History, 1914–1945* (1965), p. 455.

41 RA GVI PS 1627. Hyde to Hardinge, 5 August 1940.

42 *Ibid.*, and Hyde to Hardinge, 20 June 1940.

43 RA PP GVI 3892.

44 *Ibid.* Dawson to Alexander, 26 February 1942.

45 *Ibid.* Alexander to Dawson, 29 February 1942.

46 *Ibid.*, 12 December 1944, p. 2.

47 *Ibid.*, 19 July 1944, p. 2.

48 *Ibid.*, 24 May 1944, p. 7; Dermot Morrah, *Princess Elizabeth, Duchess of Edinburgh* (1950), p. 74.

49 See the minutes of the Medical Sub-Committee of the King's Fund, 6 August 1942, GLRO, A/KE/19.

50 Marion Crawford, *The Little Princesses* (New York, 1950), p. 226.

51 *In Royal Service: The Letters and Journals of Sir Alan Lascelles, 1920–36*, ed. Duff Hart-Davis (1989).

52 RA PP GVI 3892.

53 *The Diaries of Sir Henry Channon*, ed. Robert Rhodes James (1967), p. 463.

54 Quoted in Laird, *Queen Elizabeth the Queen Mother*, p. 239.

55 Aronson, *The Royal Family at War*, pp. 146, 218.

56 Wheeler-Bennett, *King George VI:*

His Life and Reign, pp. 650, 653.

57 Ibid., pp. 676–7.

58 Bruce P. Lenman, for example, in *The Eclipse of Parliament* (1992), p. 183, calls the NHS a 'not very Socialist achievement'.

59 *The Diary of Hugh Gaitskell, 1945–1956*, ed. Philip M. Williams (1983), p. 244. See Bradford, *George VI*, p. 511.

60 See *The Hospitals Year-Book, 1941* (1941), passim.

61 Wheeler-Bennett, *King George VI: His Life and Reign*, p. 652.

62 *The Diaries of Sir Henry Channon*, p. 463.

63 John Campbell, *Nye Bevan and the Mirage of British Socialism* (1987), p. 64.

64 Aneurin Bevan, *In Place of Fear* (1952), p. 79.

65 PRO, MH/80/29.

66 F.K. Prochaska, *Philanthropy and the Hospitals of London: The King's Fund, 1897–1990* (1992), pp. 151, 154–5.

67 Quoted in John E. Pater, *The Making of the National Health Service* (1981), p. 122.

68 PRO, MH/77/76–77.

69 *The Memoirs of the Rt. Hon. the Earl of Woolton*, p. 327.

70 PRO, MH/80/24. See also MH/77/76.

71 RA PP GVI 3892/2. For a visit of the King and Queen and Princess Margaret to the Royal Northern Infirmary, Inverness, in June 1948, see *The Royal Northern Infirmary, Inverness: The Further History of a Scottish Voluntary Hospital* (1950), pp. 110–11.

72 *The Times*, 19 March 1948, p. 4.

73 *Ibid.*, 8 May 1948, p. 3.

74 *Ibid.*, 7 May 1948, p. 3.

75 *Ibid.*, 19 June 1948, p. 7; 30 June, p. 7.

76 *Ibid.*, 5 July 1948, p. 5.

77 William Henry MacMenemey, *A History of the Worcester Royal Infirmary* (1947), p. viii. In 1956, the official historian of the Royal National Hospital in North London, patronized by the Duke of Gloucester, continued to have a decided reserve about government control. He con-

cluded on what was for him was a happier note: 'The tradition of voluntary service . . . stands unshaken today'. Eric C.O. Jewsbury, *The Royal Northern Hospital, 1856–1956: The Story of a Hundred Years' Work in North London* (1956), p. 141.

78 RA PP GVI 3892. H.A. Strutt to Alexander, 22 January 1947.

79 *Ibid.*

80 *Ibid.* Alexander to Strutt, 28 January 1947.

81 RA PP GVI 3892/2. Alexander to Gwynedd Lloyd, 15 March 1948; Alexander to Lord Courtauld-Thomson, 11 March 1948.

82 There were nearly 200 'disclaimed hospitals', several of them with royal patronage that remained outside the National Health Service. For a list of these institutions, see *The Times*, 1 April 1948, p. 2.

83 RA PP GVI 3892. Strutt to Alexander, 14 July 1948. See also RA PP GVI 3892/2.

84 *The Royal London Homoeopathic Hospital: Report of the Hospital Management Committee for the Period 5th July 1948 to 31st March 1950*, p. 8.

85 See, for example, *The Official Index to The Times* for 1949 and 1950.

86 *The London Hospital Illustrated: 250 Years*, p. 152.

87 Dermot Morrah, *The Royal Family* (1950), p. 121.

88 Campbell, *Nye Bevan and the Mirage of British Socialism*, p. 180.

89 HMC (48)25A. See also *The Times*, 8 January 1949, p. 4. A copy of this newspaper article is in RA PP GVI 7437.

90 King's Fund, Lord Wigram to Pooley, 3 February 1949, in the file entitled 'National Council of Social Service'.

91 Ferdinand Mount, *The British Constitution Now: Recovery or Decline?* (1992), p. 168.

92 See the interesting debate in the House of Lords in 1949, *Parliamentary Debates*, 5th series (Lords), vol. 163, pp. 75–135. See also Finlayson, *Citizen, State, and Social Welfare in Britain, 1830–1990*, pp. 281, 297.

93 Quoted in Asa Briggs and Anne

Macartney, *Toynbee Hall: The First Hundred Years* (1984), pp. 35–6.

94 Quoted in Hennessy, *Never Again: Britain 1945–1951*, p. 123.

95 Richard Crossman, *Planning for Freedom* (1965), p. 58.

96 *Ibid.*, p. 21.

97 King's Fund, Ives to John Trevelyan, 13 June 1950, in the file entitled 'Social Service Enquiry (Trevelyan)'.

98 Malcolm Muggeridge, *Things Past*, ed. Ian Hunter (1978), p. 111.

99 Quoted in E.R. Norman, *Church and Society in England, 1770–1970* (1976), p. 377. See also Hennessy, *Never Again: Britain 1945–1951*, p. 437.

100 José Harris, 'Society and the State in Twentieth-Century Britain', in *The Cambridge Social History of Britain*, ed. F.M.L. Thompson, 3 vols. (1990), vol. 3, p. 63. For a fascinating contemporary discussion of the changing relationship of the individual to the state, see Robert Nisbet, *The Quest for Community* (1952).

101 *Parliamentary Debates*, 5th series (Lords), vol. 163, pp. 89, 105.

102 William Beveridge, *Voluntary Action* (1948), pp. 10, 318.

103 *Parliamentary Debates*, 5th series (Lords), vol. 163, pp. 95–6.

104 *Ibid.*

105 A.F.C. Bourdillon (ed.), *Voluntary Social Services: Their Place in the Modern State* (1945), p. 15.

106 David Owen, *English Philanthropy, 1660–1960* (1964), pp. 532, 573.

107 *Save the Children Fund. Annual Report: The Thirty-Second Year* (1951), p. 4.

108 *The Times*, 27 December 1946, p. 4.

109 *Ibid.*, 27 December 1950, p. 4.

110 RA GVI PS 1627. Hyde to Lascelles, 28 January 1952.

111 *Ibid.*

112 RA PP GVI 4775.

113 Christopher Warwick, *Princess Margaret* (1983), pp. 40–41.

114 See the Annual Reports of the Save the Children Fund.

115 *Save the Children Fund. Annual Report. The Thirty-Fourth Year* (1953), p. 1.

116 *The Times*, 22 June 1949, p. 2.

117 *Ibid.*, 14 December 1950, p. 3.

Chapter 8

1 F.K. Prochaska, *Philanthropy and the Hospitals of London: The King's Fund, 1897–1990* (1992), pp. 175–6.

2 King's Fund, Ives to John Trevelyan, 13 June 1950, in the file entitled 'Social Service Enquiry (Trevelyan)'.

3 *Daily Telegraph*, 1 June 1962.

4 Joan Austoker, *A History of the Imperial Cancer Research Fund, 1902–1986* (1988), pp. 205–6, 317–18.

5 King's Fund, Management Committee Papers, 3716 (1965).

6 Richard Crossman, 'The Role of the Volunteer in the Modern Social Service', in *Traditions of Social Policy*, ed. A.H. Halsey (1976), p. 283.

7 *Ibid.*, p. 279.

8 Dermot Morrah, *The Work of the Queen* (1958), p. 43.

9 The best personal portrait of the Queen remains Elizabeth Longford's *Elizabeth R* (1983). For a detailed chronicle of the reign, see Charles Higham and Roy Moseley, *Elizabeth and Philip: The Untold Story* (1991).

10 See Brian Masters, *Dreams about H.M. The Queen and Other Members of the Royal Family* (1972).

11 *Voices out of the Air: The Royal Christmas Broadcasts 1932–1981*, introduced by Tom Fleming (1981), p. 103. For other speeches delivered by the Queen, including several with charitable themes, see *Speeches and Replies to Addresses by Her Majesty Queen Elizabeth II, January 1961–December 1973* (n.d.).

12 *Voices out of the Air: The Royal Christmas Broadcasts 1932–1981*, p. 105.

13 Morrah, *The Work of the Queen*, p. 109.

14 On the 'many representations' made to the Queen Mother see Elizabeth Longford, *The Queen Mother* (1981), pp. 144–5.

15 In discussions with the author, several charitable accountants have put the value of one royal fundraising event a year at 10 per cent or so

of the annual revenue of their institutions.

16 Christopher Warwick, *Princess Margaret* (1983), p. 67.

17 *Ibid.*, p. 68.

18 H.R.H. The Duke of Edinburgh, *A Question of Balance* (1982), p. 8. For a list of Prince Philip's patronages as of January 1991, see Denis Judd, *Prince Philip: A Biography* (1991), pp. 332–72.

19 When Prince Philip took over the presidency of the National Playing Fields Association in 1949 it was in a mess. Basil Boothroyd, *Philip: An Informal Biography* (1971), p. 168. In his first year in office he took part in fourteen events. *The Royal Encyclopedia*, eds. Ronald Allison and Sarah Riddell (1991), p. 350.

20 Judd, *Prince Philip: A Biography*, pp. 83, 316.

21 David Wainwright, *Youth in Action: The Duke of Edinburgh's Award Scheme, 1956–1966* (1966), pp. 133–5.

22 *The Wit of Prince Philip*, compiled by Peter Butler (1965), p. 46.

23 Wainwright, *Youth in Action*, p. 14 and passim; John Parker, *Prince Philip: A Critical Biography* (1990), p. 213.

24 Leonard M. Harris, *Long to Reign over us? The Status of the Royal Family in the Sixties* (1966), pp. 72–3.

25 *Ibid.*

26 Walter Bagehot, *The English Constitution*, introduced by R.H.S. Crossman (1961), p. 86.

27 Harris, *Long to Reign over us? The Status of the Royal Family in the Sixties*, pp. 37–8, 43, 78.

28 On the level of republicanism, see Philip Ziegler, *Crown and People* (1978), p. 127.

29 Harold Wilson, *The Labour Government 1964–1970: A Personal Record* (1971), p. 296.

30 Andrew Duncan, *The Reality of Monarchy* (1970), pp. 193–8.

31 See Jonathan Dimbleby, *The Prince of Wales. A Biography* (1994), passim.

32 Finlayson, *Citizen, State, and Social Welfare in Britain, 1830–1990* (1994), p. 352.

33 *Ibid.*, p. 353.

34 *Ibid.*, p. 355.

35 *Ibid.*, p. 369; *Guardian*, 11 April 1990, p. 21; *The Times*, 3 May 1988.

36 In 1986 alone the Charity Commissioners registered just under 4,000 institutions. See *Report of the Charity Commissioners for England and Wales for the Year 1986*, p. 8.

37 See *Selected Speeches, 1948–1955 by His Royal Highness Prince Philip Duke of Edinburgh* (1957).

38 *Prince Philip Speaks*, ed. Richard Ollard (1960), pp. 105–9.

39 H.R.H. The Duke of Edinburgh, *A Question of Balance*, pp. 34–5.

40 *Ibid.*, pp. 88–9, 124; see also the Duke of Edinburgh's Arnold Goodman Lecture 'Charity or Public Benefit', 9 June 1994.

41 *A Question of Balance*, pp. 24–5

42 Quoted in the thoughtful book by Maria Brenton, *The Voluntary Sector in British Social Services* (1985), pp. 143–4.

43 Finlayson, *Citizen, State, and Social Welfare in Britain, 1830–1990*, p. 375.

44 For a brilliant discussion of Mrs. Thatcher and Victorian values, see Raphael Samuel, 'Mrs. Thatcher's Return to Victorian Values', in *Victorian Values*, ed. T.C. Smout (1992), pp. 9–29. For a Conservative critique of Thatcherism for failing to emphasize personal responsibility see David G. Green, *Reinventing Civil Society: The Rediscovery of Welfare without Politics* (1993).

45 For definitions of civil society see Ernest Gellner, *Conditions of Liberty: Civil Society and its Rivals* (1994), p. 5; *Independent on Sunday*, 13 November 1994, p. 43.

46 *For my Grandchildren: Some Reminiscences of Her Royal Highness Princess Alice, Countess of Athlone* (1966), p. 7.

47 For an abbreviated list of royal patronages, see articles on individuals in the *Royal Encyclopedia*, eds. Allison and Riddell, and *Royal Patrons*, compiled by the Charities Aid Foundation (1988).

48 *The Times*, 22 September 1986, p. 11.

49 For a discussion of her work for the Save the Children Fund and a description of a year in her public life, see Paul James, *Anne: The Working Princess* (1987).

50 Dimbleby, *The Prince of Wales: A Biography*, p. 402.

51 See *Observer Magazine*, 11 December 1994, p. 20.

52 *Directory of Grant-Making Trusts 1995* (1995), p. 882. This work includes information on other royal trusts. The Princess Anne's Charities, for example, distributed £76,475 in grants in 1993.

53 Dimbleby, *The Prince of Wales: A Biography*, p. 385.

54 See *ibid.*, chapter 19. There is also information on the charitable work of the Prince of Wales in Anthony Holden, *Charles: A Biography* (1988).

55 Dimbleby, *The Prince of Wales: A Biography*, p. 327.

56 *Ibid.*, p. 556.

57 *Ibid.*, p. 226.

58 *A King's Story: The Memoirs of the Duke of Windsor* (New York, 1951), pp. 215–16.

59 *The Principal Speeches and Addresses of His Royal Highness the Prince Consort* (1862), pp. 89–90.

60 See the Speech by H.R.H. the Prince of Wales at the Conference to launch 'Volunteers', St James's Palace, 25 April 1990. I would like to thank the office of the Prince of Wales for a copy of this address.

61 Dimbleby, *The Prince of Wales: A Biography*, pp. 377–80.

62 *Ibid.*, pp. 379, 493.

63 *Ibid.*, p. 379.

64 See Peter Mandler's critique of the National Trust in *The Times*, 17 November 1994, p. 39.

65 *Speeches and Replies to Addresses by Her Majesty Queen Elizabeth II January 1961–December 1973*, p. 15.

66 I would like to thank Professor Leslie Rees, Dean of St Bartholomew's Hospital Medical College for this information. Technically, the Queen is not the Patron of St Bartholomew's, but she has taken an active interest in its activities over the years.

67 Ferdinand Mount, *The British Constitution Now: Recovery or Decline?* (1992), p. 108; *Independent*, 21 July 1993, p. 1; information from the King's Fund.

68 Mount, *The British Constitution Now: Recovery or Decline?*, p. 110.

69 *Independent*, 3 November 1994, p. 9. On Tony Blair's philosophy more generally, see the *Independent*, 18 January 1995, p. 19.

70 *Daily Telegraph*, 17 October 1994, p. 2.

71 *Independent*, 11 April 1987.

72 *Guardian*, 22 April 1987.

73 J.L. Stocks, *The Philanthropist in a Changing World* (1953), p. 22.

74 On duty, see David Selbourne, *The Principle of Duty: An Essay on the Foundations of the Civic Order* (1994). On self-help, see *Building Social Capital* (Institute of Public Policy Research, 1995). For an excellent introduction to shifting public perceptions of social policy see José Harris, 'Society and the State in Twentieth-Century Britain', in *The Cambridge Social History of Britain*, ed. F.M.L. Thompson, 3 vols. (1990), vol. 3, pp. 63–117.

75 For a right-wing analysis of the role of government in social policy see Green, *Reinventing Civil Society: The Rediscovery of Welfare without Politics*. For a Fabian analysis that is positive about the role of voluntary work, see *Social Justice: Strategies for National Renewal. The Report of the Commission on Social Justice* (1994).

76 Dimbleby, *The Prince of Wales: A Biography*, p. 380.

77 *The Spectator*, 7 January 1995, p. 16.

78 A.J.P. Taylor, *English History, 1914–1945* (1965), p. 175.

79 'New Republic', *Guardian*, 9 January 1995, p. 10.

80 I would like to thank the Press Office at Buckingham Palace for permission to look at the current patronage books of the royal family.

81 *The Times*, 4 October 1983, p. 4; *Guardian*, 15 December 1994, p. 9.

82 *Directory of Grant-Making Trusts, 1995*, p. 558.

83 The figures are drawn from the *The*

*Privy Purse Charitable Trust: Trustees'
Report and Accounts, 31 March 1994.*
Formerly, the charity was called The
January 1987 Charitable Trust.

84 *Ibid.* The administration expenses
comprise under 3 per cent of the
sums distributed.

85 See the patronage books at Buckingham Palace.

86 *The Times*, 26 December 1991, p.
19.

87 *Ibid.*

88 *Ibid.*

89 On this and other relevant matters,
see Gellner, *Conditions of Liberty:
Civil Society and its Rivals.*

90 Quoted in Brian Harrison, *Peaceable
Kingdom: Stability and Change in Modern Britain* (1982), p. 258.

91 For a discussion of the constitutional
role of the crown, see the forthcoming book by Vernon Bogdanor, *The
Monarchy and the Constitution,* to be
published by Oxford University
Press.

92 The Conference on the monarchy
hosted by Charter 88 and *The Times*
at the Queen Elizabeth Conference
Centre in May 1993 brought republicans and monarchists together on
the same platform. The discussion of
royal patronage was inconsequential.
See *Power and the Throne*, ed.
Anthony Barnett (1994).

Index

References to illustrations are in **bold**